OTTOMAN REFORM
IN SYRIA
AND PALESTINE
1840–1861

OTTOMAN REFORM IN SYRIA AND PALESTINE 1840–1861

The Impact of the Tanzimat on Politics and Society

BY

MOSHE MA'OZ

OXFORD
AT THE CLARENDON PRESS
1968

Oxford University Press, Ely House, London W. 1
GLASGOW NEW YORK TORONTO MELBOURNE WELLINGTON
CAPE TOWN SALISBURY IBADAN NAIROBI LUSAKA ADDIS ABABA
BOMBAY CALCUTTA MADRAS KARACHI LAHORE DACCA
KUALA LUMPUR HONG KONG TOKYO

PRINTED IN GREAT BRITAIN

FOR MY MOTHER

PREFACE

A NUMBER of scholarly works published in recent years have greatly contributed to the study of the Tanzimat period—that critical era of attempted reform and modernization in the nineteenth-century Ottoman Empire.[1] Yet these works deal mainly with the heart of the Empire—Turkey—and with the Balkans, while the Arab provinces have largely been neglected. The aim of the present study, consequently, is to fill this gap to a certain extent by reconstructing the evolution of the Tanzimat reforms in the Syrian provinces during the years 1840–61, and tracing their impact on government and administration, on social and economic developments, and on the position of the non-Muslim subjects.

The study opens with the year 1840, at which time the Syrian provinces were reconquered from the Egyptians and the Tanzimat reforms first introduced in them; it closes with the death of Sultan Abdülmecid in 1861, a year which both marked the end of the first stage in Ottoman Tanzimat and—following the events of 1860 in Damascus (and Lebanon)—the conclusion of an era in Syrian history. This era of transition, with some of its roots in the short period of Egyptian rule during the 1830s, was unique in the modern history of the area. It brought about an end to centuries of confusion and backwardness and opened a new age of stability and modernization. During these years local forces were destroyed, regional autonomies undermined, and a solid foundation of Ottoman direct rule was established. The old struggle for power in the Syrian cities was deprived of its violent nature and concentrated in the newly established local councils—the *meclis*es—institutions which provided the basis for self-rule and municipal life in the area. The years of the early Tanzimat also put an end to the long period of tyranny and oppression by the Turkish Pashas and introduced a milder and more liberal public atmosphere. During this era,

1 See the works by Bernard Lewis, Roderic Davison, Şerif Mardin, and Robert Devereux cited in the bibliography.

moreover, although grave outbreaks of religio-political hostilities took place, the seeds of political equality and of patriotic conceptions were for the first time sown in Syrian society.

The scope of this work covers the provinces of Aleppo, Damascus, and Sidon—commonly known as Syria and Palestine; it excludes the district of Mount Lebanon which, in many respects, underwent a separate development and thus deserves special attention. These provinces, which were of great importance to the Ottoman Empire due to their religious and commercial centres and strategic position, were inhabited by a very heterogeneous population. According to some estimates it amounted in the 1850s to more than a million and a half persons. The majority—over a million —were Muslims. These were mostly Sunni-Arabs; but among them there were also substantial numbers of non-Sunni Arabs —ʻAlawis, Druzes, and Mutawalis, and non-Arab Sunnis—Kurds and Turkomans. The second big religious group was the Christian population, which numbered about half a million (including some 200,000 Maronites in Lebanon) and consisted of Greek Catholics, Greek Orthodox, Armenians, and other small communities. The number of Jews in Syria and Palestine was only about 25,000.

The present study is divided into five parts. Part one contains a brief survey of the development of reform in the Ottoman Empire from the rise to power of Sultan Mahmud II in 1808, to the death of Sultan Abdülmecid in 1861; it also deals with the state of affairs in Syria and Palestine during the reign of Mahmud II, including the term of the Egyptian occupation. In part two an attempt is made to analyse some aspects of the new Ottoman administrative policy in the Syrian provinces and to examine the instruments with which this policy was carried out. Part three contains a description of the struggle for power between the Ottoman authorities on the one hand, and urban leaders, mountain chiefs and Bedouin tribes on the other. Part four seeks to consider the extent to which the social and economic reforms of the Tanzimat were carried out in the Syrian provinces and the strength of their impact on various spheres of life. Finally, part five analyses the state of Syrian non-Muslims in the light of the Tanzimat pledges to them; it also endeavours to examine the new attitudes of Muslims towards

Christians and Jews which emerged under the impact of the Ottoman reforms.

This work is based on a variety of sources, both published and unpublished. They include, firstly, both orders and firmans from the central government in Istanbul to the Turkish Pashas in Syria, and reports from the local authorities to the *Porte*. Secondly, use has been made of the available Arabic sources—manuscripts, records, and other contemporary material—among them testimonials from both Muslim and Christian quarters. The Jewish point of view is derived from a number of contemporary Hebrew documents and travellers' accounts. No less valuable and, in fact, indispensable have been the European consular reports, notably the detailed and informative dispatches of the British consuls. Other unpublished materials from English sources include missionary records and some private papers. Among the published sources in European languages, of considerable use have been the memoirs of European consuls and some contemporary observers.

I would like to express here my deep gratitude to persons and institutions who have helped me with preparing this study, which originally was written as a D.Phil. thesis submitted to Oxford University. My greatest debt is to Professor Albert Hourani, who has unfailingly directed me in all the stages of my work and whose great scholarship and sense of history have been a constant guide to my research. I owe a special debt to Professor David Ayalon, who introduced me to the study of Arab history and paved the way for my present research. I am deeply grateful also to St. Antony's College, Oxford, which in every way made it possible for me to prepare my thesis. I should like to thank as well Miss Elizabeth Monroe, Professor Uriel Heyd, Professor Peter Holt, and Dr. Shimon Shamir for their careful reading of my manuscript and for their many useful suggestions; and Professor Stanford Shaw for helping me to locate Ottoman archival materials.

The staffs of many libraries have been very helpful, particularly those of the Başvekâlet Arşivi in Istanbul, the National Library in Sofia, and the Muslim Shari'a Court in Jaffa. The Faculty of Humanities, Tel-Aviv University, and the General Federation of Labour in Israel, provided me with financial assistance during various stages of my research. The Editorial Board of the BSOAS were kind enough to allow me to reprint sections of an article which I had published in their journal. I also wish to thank Mrs. Hillary Bullard, Dr. Derek Hopwood, and Mr. Brian Knapheis for their painstaking help in various ways. To my wife, Rivka, who has devotedly encouraged and helped me throughout my work, I owe more than I could properly express in words.

M. MA'OZ

Department of Middle
Eastern History
Tel-Aviv University
November 1967

CONTENTS

PART I

Introduction: the background to the Tanzimat in Syria and Palestine

PART II

Aspects of Government and Administration

PART V

The State of the Christians and Jews and the Muslims' attitudes towards them

LIST OF ILLUSTRATIONS

NOTES ON TRANSCRIPTIONS AND NAMES

1. Turkish has been transcribed according to official Turkish orthography. It should be noted that the Turkish 'ç' is pronounced as 'ch' in English; 'c' as 'j'; 'ş' as 'sh'.

2. Arabic has been transcribed according to the system used by the *Encyclopaedia of Islam*—with some minor modifications:

(i) 'j' has been used in place of 'dj',
(ii) 'q' has been used in place of 'ḳ',
(iii) the digraph 'ay' has been used in place of 'ai'.

3. Hebrew has been transcribed according to the rules issued by the Academy of the Hebrew language—with the following changes:

ו *v*   כ kh   צ tz   שׁ sh

4. Well-known place names and Islamic terms have been rendered according to their accepted English spelling.

5. Ottoman religious and administrative terms have all been treated as Turkish words, except for those which have an anglicized form.

6. Proper names are spelt according to Arabic and Turkish pronunciation respectively.

ABBREVIATIONS

A.E.	Archives des Affaires Étrangères, France
BSOAS	*Bulletin of the School of Oriental and African Studies*
Cevdet.D.	Başvekâlet Arşivi, Istanbul, Cevdet, Dahiliye
Cevdet.Z.	,, ,, ,, Cevdet, Zaptiye
CM	Church Missionary Society, London
EI[1], *EI*[2]	*Encyclopaedia of Islam*, 1st and 2nd editions
F.O.	Foreign Office, Public Record Office, London
IA	*Islam Ansiklopedisi*
Irade D.	Başvekâlet Arşivi, Istanbul, Iradeler, Dahiliye
Irade H.	,, ,, ,, Iradeler, Hariciye
Irade M.M.	,, ,, ,, Iradeler, Meclis-i Mahsus
Irade M.V.	,, ,, ,, Iradeler, Meclis-i Valâ
MEJ	*Middle East Journal*
Mühimme	Başvekâlet Arşivi, Istanbul, Mühimme Defteri
PEF	*Palestine Exploration Fund*
ZDMG	*Zeitschrift der deutschen morgenländischen Gesellschaft*

The abbreviations of Muslim months are:

M	Muharrem	Saf.	Safer	RA	Rebiyülevvel
R	Rebiyülâhir	CA	Cemaziyelevvel	C	Cemaziyelâhir
B	Recep	Ş	Şaban	N	Ramazan
L	Şevval	ZA	Zilkade	Z	Zilhicce

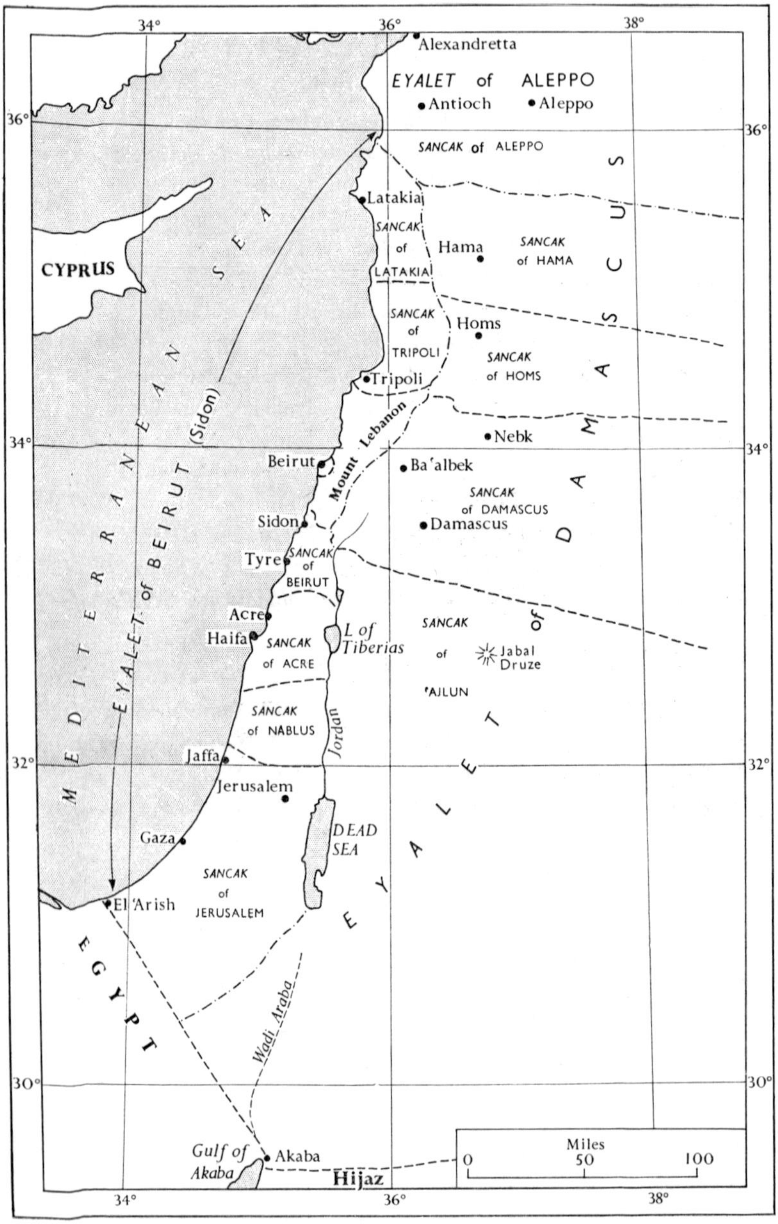

Alexandretta
EYALET of ALEPPO
Antioch
Aleppo
SANCAK of ALEPPO
Latakia
SANCAK of LATAKIA
Hama
SANCAK of HAMA
CYPRUS
SANCAK of TRIPOLI
Homs
SANCAK of HOMS
Tripoli
MEDITERRANEAN SEA
(Sidon)
Mount Lebanon
Nebk
EYALET of BEIRUT
Beirut
Ba'albek
SANCAK of DAMASCUS
Damascus
Sidon
Tyre
SANCAK of BEIRUT
EYALET of DAMASCUS
Acre
Haifa
SANCAK of ACRE
L of Tiberias
SANCAK of 'AJLUN
Jabal Druze
SANCAK of NABLUS
Jordan
Jaffa
Jerusalem
Gaza
DEAD SEA
SANCAK of JERUSALEM
El 'Arish
EGYPT
Wadi Araba
Gulf of Akaba
Akaba
Hijaz
Miles
0
50
100
34°
36°
38°
30°
32°

played, in fact, a predominant role in neutralizing the various reformist programmes of the eighteenth century, particularly the serious and comprehensive military reforms of Selim III at the end of that century.

Sultan Selim III (1789–1807), who was deeply influenced by France, was the first Ottoman monarch to introduce large-scale changes in the army. In 1792 and 1793 he promulgated a whole series of new instructions and regulations, known as the *Nizam-i Cedid*, which provided mainly for the raising of new troops, who were organized, trained, and equipped with French help.[1] The Janissaries, however, did not delay their resistance: encouraged by popular dissatisfaction and actively helped and guided by the leading 'Ulema of Istanbul,[2] they revolted in 1805 and induced the Sultan to abolish the *Nizam-i Cedid*. At the request of the Janissaries, Selim was deposed in May 1807, by virtue of a fetwa from the Chief Mufti, and the new army was at once dissolved.[3] A year later, during the reign of Sultan Mustafa IV, the Janissary corps was also able to crush a counter-revolution headed by Bayraktar Mustafa, an Ottoman high official, who desired to revive Selim's reforms.

B. *Mahmud II: the turning-point*

The failure of both Selim and Mustafa led the next Sultan, Mahmud II (1808–39), to avoid the fatal mistake of his predecessors; it convinced him that the old order, especially the Janissary army, must be abolished before a new order could be established. Not until 1826 did Mahmud succeed in crushing the Janissaries, who for the last time tried to resist the re-creation of a new army. This event, known as *Vak'a-i Hayriye* (The Auspicious Incident), was a turning point in Ottoman reform. In the first place, the opposition to change in Turkey was at last deprived of its chief instrument of resistance. It is true that there still remained another powerful conservative body, the 'Ulema, whom Mahmud, being aware of their spiritual influence, was careful not to antagonize

[1] Lewis, op. cit., pp. 58–59. On Selim's reforms see also F. E. Bailey, *British Policy and the Turkish Reform Movement* (Cambridge, Mass., 1942), pp. 26–29.

[2] U. Heyd, 'The Ottoman 'Ulemā and Westernization in the Time of Selim III and Mahmud II', in U. Heyd (ed.), *Studies in Islamic History and Civilization* (Jerusalem, 1961), p. 69.

[3] Lewis, op. cit., pp. 70–71.

PART I

Introduction: The Background to the Tanzimat in Syria and Palestine

---

I

THE PRE-TANZIMAT PERIOD AND THE ERA OF MAHMUD II

A. *Early reforms*

THE first attempts to introduce reforms into the Ottoman Empire were made at the beginning of the eighteenth century and were mainly concerned with the army. The need for such reform was felt as a result of the successive and decisiv defeats suffered by the Turkish army at the hands of its Europe rivals since the Ottoman retreat from Vienna in 1683. With bitter realization of Western military superiority, the Turks b to adopt European weapons, training, and techniques; and time to time during the eighteenth century army instructo imported from the West, technical schools established, and soldiers trained in the methods of European warfare.[1] these changes, although sporadic and superficial, e considerable opposition in Turkey almost from the The opposition was led by the Janissary corps, the Ottoman army, because the new military measures undermine their special position in the state.[2]

[1] For a detailed account of those early military reforms *The Emergence of Modern Turkey* (London, 1961), pp. *The Genesis of Young Ottoman Thought* (Princeton, 19 Roderic H. Davison, *Reform in the Ottoman Empire* 1963), pp. 21–22.

[2] Mardin, pp. 138–9. See also M. A. Ubicini, *L* 1856), i. 7.

directly.[1] None the less, by a series of administrative measures, he was able to deprive them of their financial and administrative autonomy, and thus to weaken, to a great extent, their political power.[2]

In the second place, unlike the early phase of reform which was concerned mainly with the army, the new phase consisted also of a programme of change in almost every field of life, particularly in the system of government and administration of the provinces, and also in areas such as education, clothing, taxation, and, to some extent, the state of the non-Muslim subjects.[3] Mahmud's first goals were to restore the authority of the central government in the virtually autonomous provinces of the Empire, and to re-establish his hegemony over the machinery of administration. To accomplish these ends, as well as to defend the Empire against its external enemies, the primary requirement was a strong and modern army. Thus the Sultan set up a new force, known as *Asakir-i Mansure-i Muhammediye* (The Victorious Muhammadan Soldiers). For the training and instructing of these troops, Prussian and British instructors were imported and a whole set of military and non-military schools were established.[4]

Another instrument which was needed, to carry out the policy of centralization and to transform the Empire into a modern state, was an efficient and reliable civil service. The Sultan therefore tried to improve the conditions and status of government employees by granting them regular salaries and by abolishing certain institutions and usages, which formerly had made their lives and property insecure.[5] And although the efforts to raise the standards of the civil officials and to make them both proficient and honest were not entirely successful,[6] Mahmud managed to establish, nevertheless, a modern government administration along Western lines.[7] Similarly, the newly created army, in spite of its serious defects, succeeded in curbing the rebellious provincial Pashas and in eliminating the powerful feudal chiefs in most parts of the

[1] Heyd, *The 'Ulemā*, p. 77.

[2] Lewis, op. cit., pp. 91–92, 95–96.

[3] Bailey, p. 150; Davison, *Reform*, p. 31; Ed. Engelhardt, *La Turqie et la Tanzimat* (Paris, 1882–4), i. 33; Lewis, op. cit., pp. 82–85, 98–101; Ubicini, ii. 110–11.

[4] Details in Lewis, op. cit., pp. 82–83.

[5] Ibid., p. 88; Mardin, pp. 150–1; H. Temperley, *England and the Near East, the Crimea* (London, 1936), p. 31.

[6] Davison, op. cit., p. 34; Temperley, pp. 27–28; Ubicini, ii. 439.

[7] Lewis, op. cit., pp. 88–97; Mardin, pp. 147–8, 150–4.

Empire,[1] though not in Syria and Palestine. In these areas Mahmud's reforms were hardly felt, and the new Turkish army was neither able completely to control the local rulers up to 1831, nor to overcome the Egyptian army which occupied these provinces from 1831 to 1840.

C. *Syria and Palestine up to 1831*

Almost from the beginning of its rule in Syria and Palestine in the sixteenth century, the scope of Turkish government in these lands was limited essentially to matters concerned with the preservation of Ottoman supremacy, the collection of revenue, the performance of the Ḥajj to Mecca, and the maintenance of the *status quo*.[2] All other matters, particularly in the social and economic spheres, were left to the subjects to deal with, through their own autonomous institutions. The government aims themselves were usually achieved by a loose control and by keeping a balance of power among the various forces in the provinces. Regarding governors who grew too strong or manifested their disobedience, the *Porte* made efforts to play off other Pashas against them in order to cause their downfall.[3] If unsuccessful, the *Porte* acted in accordance with the old Turkish proverb *Kesemediğin eli öp* (the hand you cannot cut off—kiss). It flattered and honoured those whom it could not ruin, and waited for a favourable opportunity to regain its authority.[4]

The decay of the central government since the seventeenth century weakened its control over the Syrian provinces and gave rise to strong local rulers, either Ottoman governors or native leaders, who were able to establish themselves more firmly than ever before. Thus local dynasts, like the ʿAẓms, Ḍāhir al-ʿUmar, and Aḥmad al-Jazzār, established themselves in the course of the eighteenth century as autonomous rulers in various parts of Syria

[1] See Davison, *Reform*, pp. 26–27; Bailey, pp. 36–37.

[2] H. A. R. Gibb and H. Bowen, *Islamic Society and the West*, vol. i; *Islamic Society in the Eighteenth Century* (London, 1950), i. 200; U. Heyd, *Ottoman Documents on Palestine 1552–1615* (Oxford, 1960), p. 43. See also J. L. Burckhardt, *Travels in Syria and Holy Land* (London, 1822), p. 648; J. L. Porter, *Five Years in Damascus* (London, 1855), i. 132.

[3] Examples in Ibrāhīm al-ʿAwra, *Ta'rīkh wilāyat Sulaymān Bāshā al-ʿādil* (Sidon, 1936), pp. 225–6; Yūsuf al-Dibs, *Ta'rīkh Sūriyya* (Beirut, 1893–1905), viii. 629, 636, 639; Porter, op. cit. i. 133.

[4] Gibb and Bowen, i. 231–2; Burckhardt, pp. 169, 648.

and Palestine.[1] They were able to maintain their provinces in tolerable order, to keep the Bedouin tribes off the centres of the inhabited areas, and thus to attract communal loyalties in a population that had lost faith in the power of the central government.[2] At the same time, however, large parts of the countryside were subjected to violent tribes, who caused destruction in agriculture and commerce, and were sometimes able to levy duties upon a number of small towns.[3] In the mountains autonomous life had continued to develop, particularly in Houran and Mount Lebanon.[4]

This state of affairs continued in Syria and Palestine in the first part of the nineteenth century under the great reformer Sultan Mahmud II. While many provinces in Rumelia and Anatolia (and later in Iraq and Kurdistan too) were brought under the control of the central government,[5] most Syrian districts were ruled by rebellious or autonomous governors, and by virtually independent Bedouin chieftains and mountain chiefs. For instance, ʿAbdullāh Paşa, the *vali* of Sidon (1818–31), followed the path of al-Jazzār and openly disobeyed the Ottoman government, as the historian-monographer al-Bayṭār describes it: '. . . *tajāwaza fi'l-aḥkām al-ḥudūd wa-ashhara al-ʿiṣyān ʿalā al-dawla dhāt al-shawka wa'l-ṣawla, āmilan bi'l-istiqlāl*' ['he exceeded the (divinely, ordained) limits in his judgements and manifested disobedience against the government, the possession of powers and authority, hoping to become independent'].[6] The *Porte*, it is true, ordered

1 Gibb and Bowen, i. 219 ff., 232–4. For a study on Ḍāhir al-ʿUmar, see U. Heyd, *Ḍāhir al-ʿUmar shallīṭ ha-Galīl ba-me'ah ha-yod-ḥet* (Jerusalem, 1942). On the ʿAẓms, see S. Shamir, *The ʿAẓm wālīs of Syria, 1724–1785* (unpublished Ph.D. thesis, Princeton, 1960); see also L. H. Bodman, *Political Factions in Aleppo, 1760–1826* (University of North Carolina, 1963), p. 5.

2 Cf. A. H. Hourani, 'The Changing Face of the Fertile Crescent in the Eighteenth Century', in *A Vision of History* (Beirut, 1961), pp. 40–41.

3 Gibb and Bowen, i. 233–4; Bodman, p. 5.

4 Shamir, op. cit., pp. 245–7; W. R. Polk, *The Opening of South Lebanon 1788–1840* (Cambridge, Mass., 1963), pp. 10 ff.

5 Davison, op. cit., p. 26; S. H. Longrigg, *Four Centuries of Modern Iraq* (Oxford, 1925), pp. 282–8.

6 ʿAbd al-Razzāq al-Bayṭār, *Ḥilyat al-bashar fī ta'rīkh al-qarn al-thālith ʿashar* (Damascus, 1961–3), ii. 949. Cf. the following undated firman (presumably from the mid-nineteenth century) which starts: 'In the past, certain *vali*s of Sidon assumed the permission to themselves to commit deeds against the Supreme will. . . .' Sofia, Bulgarian Archives, N.B. V.K./OR, No. 285/10.

For similar comments on the relations between ʿAbdullāh and the Sultan, see Asad Rustum, *Bashīr bayna al-Sultān wa'l-ʿazīz* (Beirut, 1950), p. 36; E. B. B. Barker, *Syria and Egypt Under the Last five Sultans of Turkey* (London, 1876), ii. 23.

ʿAbdullāh's dismissal after he tried to extend his rule over the *paşalık* of Damascus;[1] the *vali*s of Damascus and Aleppo were sent to enforce the order upon him, but, unable to overcome his stronghold in Acre, the Ottomans eventually pardoned ʿAbdullāh and recognized him as the *vali* of Sidon.[2]

Similarly, the government of Mahmud II was also unable to exercise its control over the mountainous areas of Syria and Palestine which were ruled by semi-independent local chiefs. Apart from Mount Lebanon,[3] there existed four such major areas—two in Syria and two in Palestine. Those in Syria were held by two heterodox Islamic minority groups, the Druzes and the ʿAlawis (or Nusayris). The former established their autonomous life in Mount Houran, or Jabal Druze,[4] while the latter concentrated in Jabal Ansariyya, or the mountains of Latakia.[5] The autonomous hilly areas in Palestine were inhabited by Sunni Muslims. They were: Jabal Nablus, which was ruled by powerful families, virtually independent of the Turkish Pashas,[6] and the mountains around Jerusalem where a number of local chiefs were able to acquire a certain degree of autonomy.[7]

Even in the cities and towns where Ottoman officials and troops resided the real power did not always lie with the *Porte*'s representatives. A fierce struggle for power took place in a number of

[1] In 1831, ʿAbdullāh in fact succeeded in cutting the districts of Nablus and Jerusalem from the *paşalık* of Damascus. S. N. Spyridon (ed.), *Annals of Palestine 1821–1841* (Jerusalem, 1938), p. 55. Iḥsān al-Nimr, *Ta'rīkh Jabal Nāblus wa'l-Balqā'* (Damascus, 1938), p. 239.

[2] Al-Dibs, viii. 637–41; Asʿad Manṣūr, *Ta'rīkh al-Nāṣira* (Egypt, 1924), p. 60. It seems that ʿAbdullāh did not content himself with his title as *vali* of Sidon. In an order he sent to the authorities of Tiberias and Nazareth he signed his name as follows: *ʿAbdullāh wālī Ṣaydā wā-Miṣr wa'l-ʿArīsh wa-Ghazza . . .*, ibid., p. 296; also ʿĀrif al-ʿĀrif, *Ta'rīkh Ghazza* (Jerusalem, 1943), p. 185.

[3] On the position of the autonomous prince of Lebanon, Amir Bashīr Shihāb II (1788–1840), see Ṭannūs al-Shidyāq, *Akhbār al-aʿyān fī Jabal Lubnān* (Beirut, 1859), pp. 358–9, 371, 382; Burckhardt, pp. 10–11, 194; al-Dibs, viii. 628, 638–9; see also Anṭūn Ḍāhir al-ʿAqīqī, p. 9, *Thawra wa-fitna fī Lubnān* (Beirut, 1938), p. 53. For a study on the politics of Mount Lebanon, see Polk, pp. 10 ff.

[4] See, for example, Burckhardt, pp. 291, 305, 308; K. Baedeker, *Palestine and Syria, Handbook for travellers* (Leipzig, 1876), p. 412.

[5] See F. Walpole, *The Ansayrii and the Assassins* (London, 1851), iii. 353; Burckhardt, p. 141.

[6] See Qusṭanṭīn al-Bāshā (ed.), *Mudhakkirāt ta'rīkhīyya* (Lebanon, n.d.), p. 100; al-Nimr, pp. 161, 171–5, 184, 219, 235–6, 243–5; E. T. Rogers, *Notices of the Modern Samaritans* (London, 1855), p. 17.

[7] See, for example, Spyridon, pp. 30–39; Baedeker, p. 139.

towns between various forces of which the Turkish Pasha was only one.[1] In Aleppo, for example, the real power lay with the Janissaries and the *eşraf* (the lineal descendants of the Prophet; in Arab. *ashrāf*) who fought each other for authority. From time to time the Ottoman *vali*, allying himself with one or other faction, was able to rule the city for a short period, but before long the rival groups would manage to unite and to overcome the authority of the Pasha and even to expel him from the city.[2] In 1813, for instance, a certain Jalāl al-Dīn Paşa was able to restore the *Porte*'s authority in Aleppo; in 1814 the Aleppines revolted against his successor, Muḥammad Paşa, and deprived him of his power.[3] After years of tension, popular rebellion, inspired by the local notables, broke out again in 1819 as a result of heavy taxation, and was only suppressed after the arrival of reinforcements.[4] A similar revolt, based on the same motives and probably led by the Janissaries, occurred in Damascus in 1831; as a result the *vali* was killed, the army expelled, and government buildings burnt down.[5] In Tripoli too a constant struggle existed between the Janissaries and the *eşraf*, frequently ending in the expulsion of the governor.[6] In Jerusalem in 1808–9 and again in 1825 local forces succeeded in expelling the Turkish authorities,[7] and similar incidents occurred in certain other places on the northern border of Syria, as well as in Gaza near the Egyptian border.[8]

These popular uprisings against the Turkish authorities did not, however, indicate a challenge to the ultimate authority of the Sultan and the Empire. The widespread discontent in the Syrian towns, normally fomented and guided by local notables, was

[1] See Gibb and Bowen, i. 218–21; Shamir, *The ʿAẓm*, pp. 220 ff.; Bodman, pp. 103 ff.; Ṣalāḥ al-Dīn al-Munajjid, *Wulāt Dimashq fī al-ʿahd al-ʿUthmānī* (Damascus, 1949), p. 70.

[2] Examples in Burckhardt, pp. 649–55. The author indicates that the Turkish *valis* usually 'occupied the Serai more like state prisoners than governors', p. 653. See also Bodman, pp. 66–67, 112, 122–3. On the background of the *eşraf* of Aleppo, see Bodman, pp. 79–102.

[3] Barker, i. 78–80, 138–9.

[4] Ibid. i. 302; [Anon.], *Rambles in the Desert of Syria* (London, 1864), p. 45; Yūsuf Qarā'lī (ed.), *Ahamm ḥawādith Ḥalab* (Egypt, n.d.), pp. 37–43, 45–58.

[5] Al-Bāshā, pp. 33–34; Jamīl al-Shāṭṭī, *Rawḍ al-bashar fī aʿyān Dimashq fī al-qarn al-thālith ʿashar* (Damascus, 1946), pp. 119–20.

[6] Burckhardt, pp. 169–70; A. Y. Kayat, *A Voice from Lebanon* (London, 1847), p. 69; Bodman, pp. 66–67.

[7] Al-ʿAwra, p. 88; Spyridon, pp. 32–38.

[8] Burckhardt, pp. 124–5, 132, 138; al-ʿĀrif, p. 185; see also al-Nimr, p. 21.

usually directed against the extortion and oppression of the individual Turkish governors.[1] These Pashas, who possessed extensive powers within their provinces,[2] would often use their authority to tyrannize and bereave the population. For one thing, they would frequently execute many people, among them innocent persons, without a trial, in order to prevent an alleged insurrection or to render the populace submissive.[3] Secondly, and more often, the *vali* would extort large sums of money from the population either through the *mültezims* (tax-farmers) or by imposing unjust taxes (*avanias*).[4] The Pashas were not only unsalaried by the government, but they were themselves quite uncertain of their future prospect—they might be recalled and executed or their property confiscated—and they therefore were apt to 'treat their provinces as mere transient possessions and take care to make no improvement for the benefit of their successors; on the contrary, they hasten to exhaust them of the produce, and to reap in one day, if possible, the fruit of many years'.[5]

The inevitable consequence of this state of affairs was the impoverishment and depopulation of both the towns and the countryside.[6] Even the few just governors, such as the ʿAẓm Pashas in Syria in the eighteenth century,[7] and Sulaymān Paşa in Palestine at the beginning of the nineteenth century, were unable to stop this process of destruction.

But apart from the oppressive Pashas, the local inhabitants themselves contributed in no small measure to their misfortunes, by their own rivalries and feuds. In the towns serious contests took place, as we have already seen, between various local factions. In the countryside frequent hostilities occurred between rival villages and clans: in Jabal Ansariyya, for example, Nusayri clans

[1] Al-Bāshā, pp. 2–4; Barker, i. 302–3; Qarā'lı, *Ḥalab*, p. 40; cf. Gibb and Bowen, i. 232.

[2] Al-ʿAwra, p. 263; Bailey, p. 13; Bodman, pp. 20–21, 27–28; Engelhardt, ii. 106; Shamir, *The ʿAẓm*, p. 226; Temperley, p. 236.

[3] Bodman, pp. 21, 112.

[4] Al-ʿAwra, pp. 16, 57; [Anon.], *Ḥasr al-lithām ʿan nakabāt al-Shām* (Egypt, 1890), pp. 27–28; Bodman, pp. 40, 112; Burckhardt, pp. 6, 10–11, 13, 169, 194, 299–300; Gibb and Bowen, i. 269–70; Muḥammad Salīm al-Jundī, *Ta'rīkh Maʿarrat al-Nuʿmān* (Damascus, 1923), i. 197–8; al-Munajjid, pp. 4–5.

[5] C. F. Volney, *Travels to Syria and Egypt* (London, 1787), ii. 380.

[6] Al-ʿAwra, p. 57; Burckhardt, pp. 5, 10–11, 31, 147, 341 n.

[7] Bodman, pp. 103–4; Hourani, *The Fertile Crescent*, p. 40; Shamir, op. cit., pp. 254–5.

fought each other or were engaged in warfare with other sects in the neighbourhood.[1] In a number of areas in Palestine (as well as in Lebanon) the population was divided into the ancient factions of Qays and Yaman, and families and villages of the rival parties were engaged in a 'perpetual civil war' in the districts of Nablus, Jerusalem, and Hebron, involving on each side corresponding factions of Bedouin.[2]

The latter indeed not only took part in the bloody peasant warfare, but in fact were themselves the chief cause of the destruction of the countryside and the subsequent ruin of agriculture and commerce. These powerful nomads infested the Syrian provinces, pillaged caravans and travellers along the roads, ravaged large pieces of cultivated land, and even dared to raid villages that were situated on the outskirts of big towns. In some places the Bedouin spared villages and 'protected' the peasants if they paid a regular protection-fee.[3] Even Turkish *vali*s in Damascus paid an annual tribute (*sürre*) to certain Bedouin tribes, which controlled the pilgrims' route, for the passage of the Ḥajj caravans to Mecca.[4] This tribute which in practice, however, did not always safeguard the caravans[5] was, perhaps, characteristic of the Ottoman policy towards this most turbulent element; it was, on the whole, conciliatory and infirm, and thus could not deter the Bedouin from laying waste the countryside.[6]

Moreover, the Turkish règime not only failed to maintain order and security in the country; it was also responsible for the widespread failure to protect and develop the Syrian economy. Utilities

[1] See, for example, Burckhardt, pp. 141, 152–3.

[2] J. Finn, *Stirring Times* (London, 1878), i. 226 ff.; R. A. S. Macalister and E. W. G. Masterman, 'Occasional Papers on the modern inhabitants of Palestine', *Palestine Exploration Fund*, 1905, pp. 343–56, 1906, pp. 33–50, 114 ff.; al-Nimr, pp. 130–4; Volney, ii. 323–6. On the Qays–Yaman rivalry in the Lebanon, see al-'Aqīqī, p. 23; al-Shidyāq, pp. 136–7.

[3] Burckhardt, pp. 213, 264–5, 299, 301 ff., 343, 352 ff., 403, 433, 655; al-Nimr, p. 21.

[4] Burckhardt, pp. 242, 660; Volney, ii. 251, 273.

[5] Burckhardt, pp. 244–5; al-Munajjid, pp. 7, 52, 57, 60. Note, for instance, the famous attack on the 1757 caravan.

[6] Burckhardt, pp. 56–57, 264–5, 364; al-Munajjid, pp. 53–54. Note, for example, Ibrāhīm Paşa's remark in a letter he sent to his father, after he had occupied Palestine and Syria: '*annahu lam yabqa sukkān fī qurā al-Shām min jawr al-'arab wa-ẓulm al-wuzarā' al-sābiqin*' ('there remained no inhabitants in the villages of Syria because of the Bedouin usurpation and the oppression of the former vezirs'). See Asad Rustum, *al-Maḥfūẓāt al-malikiyya al-Miṣriyya* (Beirut, 1840–2), iii. 165, No. 4766.

and public works were neglected, heavy taxation and confiscations took place, and sudden devaluations of the Ottoman currency occasionally occurred.[1] Nor was this all. Legal redress hardly existed because of the venality and corruption in the courts, and because the execution of the court decrees depended upon the good will of the very administration against which they were directed.[2]

The victims of this harmful system were all the Ottoman subjects in Syria and Palestine, Muslim and non-Muslim alike. But the latter suffered a great deal more since they were in addition regarded as second-class citizens both by the government and by the Muslim public. By law they had to wear distinctive dress, and to pay a poll-tax (*cizye*), and their evidence was invalid in the courts. Christians and Jews were denied permits to build or repair places of worship and were prohibited from performing ceremonies such as the ringing of church bells and the carrying of crosses in public. In addition they were not allowed to ride horses in the towns, nor to walk in certain places within them, and were also exposed to many other indignities.[3] In many places throughout Syria and Palestine non-Muslims were often subjected to oppression, extortion, and violence by both the local authorities and the Muslim population.[4]

It is true that a number of attempts were made by Sultan Mahmud II to reform some of the above abuses, and particularly to subdue the local forces in both the cities and the mountains to Ottoman direct rule. But these attempts were foiled by the powerful local opposition to change.[5] Yet apart from this opposition, there were other factors which prevented Mahmud II from establishing centralized rule and introducing reforms in Syria and

[1] Burckhardt, p. 21; Gibb and Bowen, i. 208, 270–1, ii. 57–58; Kayat, p. 59; Lewis, *Emergence*, pp. 29, 108–9.

[2] Gibb and Bowen, i. 208; *Ḥasr al-lithām*, p. 31; Shamir, *The 'Aẓm*, pp. 241–2. Cf. Ubicini, i. 183–4.

[3] Al-'Awra, p. 197; Barker, i. 306; Bodman, pp. 45, 98; Burckhardt, p. 308; Gibb and Bowen, ii. 208, 251; *Ḥasr al-lithām*, pp. 36–39, 43–44; Kayat, pp. 52–53; A. Ya'ari (ed.), 'Massa' David de-beyt Hillel (1824)', in *Massa'ot Eretz-Israel* (Tel Aviv, 1946), p. 619. Cf. R. H. Davison, 'Turkish Attitudes concerning Christian-Muslim Equality in the Nineteenth Century', *American Historical Review*, lix. 844–5.

[4] Examples in al-'Awra, pp. 90, 109; Burckhardt, pp. 160, 180, 315; *Ḥasr al-lithām*, pp. 40, 42. For a detailed survey on the state of the non-Muslim subjects, see below, Chap. XIV.

[5] Al-Bāshā, p. 100; Bodman, pp. 128 ff.; al-Nimr, pp. 219, 235–6; Rogers, p. 17.

Palestine. It was not until 1826 that the Sultan raised the new army which enabled him to restore his authority in a number of semi-independent provinces; and between 1826 and 1831 Mahmud could not possibly have spared the large military force necessary for action in Syria.[1] The long Greek war was a great drain on Turkish military resources and the battle of Navarino in 1827 saw the virtual destruction of the Ottoman fleet. Even more crippling was the Russian-Turkish war of 1828–9, during which the Sultan was again forced to seek military help from Muḥammad ʿAlī of Egypt.[2] Hardly did the Turkish army recover from this war when it was employed to quell another rebellion in the Balkans and to restore Ottoman rule in Baghdad.[3] And when in 1831 it seemed as if the Syrian provinces might have been the next target for Mahmud's reformist policy, there came the vigorous Egyptian invasion which made such a campaign impossible. Thus Syria and Palestine became completely isolated from Ottoman rule and reform up to 1840.

[1] See Sulaymān Abū ʿIzz al-Dīn, *Ibrāhīm Bāshā fī Sūriyya* (Beirut, 1929), p. 34.

[2] Rustum, *Maḥfūẓāt*, i. 109, Nos. 264 and 265; p. 110, No. 270.

[3] Ibid., pp. 122–3, Nos. 312 and 317; ʿAbd al-Raḥmān al-Rāfiʿī, *ʿAṣr Muḥammad ʿAlī* (Cairo, 1918), p. 191; Longrigg, pp. 263 ff.

II

REFORM IN SYRIA AND PALESTINE UNDER IBRĀHĪM PAŞA

IT was, in fact, under Egyptian rule that for the first time reforms were introduced into Syria and Palestine. The Egyptian occupation, which lasted from 1831 to 1840,[1] put an end to a long period of confusion and backwardness, and opened a new era in Syrian history. Bold measures which were carried out by Ibrāhīm Paşa brought about a profound change in almost every aspect of the old life, and in certain respects paved the way for the later Ottoman reforms of the Tanzimat.

A. *Government and administration*

After a short transitional period during which local rule remained temporarily in the hands of the old order,[2] the first administrative measures were adopted: the former division of the country into *paşalık*s was abolished and Syria and Palestine were put under a *hükümdar* (a civil Governor-General), the Egyptian Sharīf Paşa, who resided in Damascus and was represented in each district town by a *mütesellim* (civil governor), usually a local Arab.[3] Ibrāhīm Paşa, whose official title was that of *serasker* (C.-in-C. of the army), had in fact a ruling hand in both military and civil affairs of the country.[4] For indeed, the Egyptian army, which in terms of those days was enormous in relation to the size of the

[1] For the motives, factors, and pretexts which led to the invasion, see: Rustum, *Maḥfūẓāt*, i. 123–4, No. 317; p. 145, No. 385; p. 163, No. 425; p. 164, No. 429; ii. 48, No. 1388; p. 52, No. 1415; p. 102, No. 1763; p. 149, No. 2078; p. 211, No. 2430; al-Rāfiʿī, pp. 188–92; ʿAbd al-Raḥmān Zakī, *al-Taʾrīkh al-ḥarbi li-ʿaṣr Muḥammad ʿAlī* (Egypt, 1950), pp. 377, 379, 381; Abū ʿIzz al-Dīn, pp. 33–34.

[2] Rustum, op. cit. i. 128–9, No. 342; p. 283, No. 820; Polk, p. 112.

[3] See, for example, al-Bāshā, pp. 69, 99, 176; Kayat, p. 264; Rustum, op. cit. i. 278, No. 280. For a detailed study on the Egyptian administration in Syria see Itzhak Hofman, *Muḥammad ʿAlī in Syria* (unpublished Ph.D. thesis, Jerusalem, 1963), pp. 34 ff.

[4] See, for example, Rustum, op. cit. iii. 417–18, No. 5496. This situation was a source of friction between Ibrāhīm and Sharīf; see ibid. 68, No. 4350; iv. 205–6, No. 6000.

population,[1] played a predominant role in the new Syrian administration. Only with the help of this military force was the new régime able to shift the old balance of power in favour of the

*Estimations of the Egyptian military forces in Syria and Palestine between 1831 and 1840**

Period		*Numbers*
1831–2		25,000–30,000†
1833–4	A.	30,000‡
	B.	50,000§
	C.	85,000‖
1836	A.	40,000
	B.	45,000
	C.	60,000**
1839–40	A.	60,000††
	B.	70,000–80,000‡‡
	C.	85,000§§
	D.	90,000‖‖

* Some of the figures included also irregular troops which apparently were as efficient as the regular army; F.O. 78/580, Werry to Aberdeen, No. 12, Aleppo, 31 Dec. 1841. Note that the total number of the Egyptian military force in 1833 was some 100,000 troops, see below, n. §.

† Al-Rāfiʿī, p. 193; Zakī, p. 39.

‡ F.O. 78/243, Farren to Palmerston, No. 38, Damascus, 3 Oct. (should be Nov.) 1834.

§ G. Douin, *La Mission du Baron de Boislecomte* . . . (Cairo, n.d.), p. 113.

‖ Al-Rāfiʿī, pp. 415–18.

** Respective estimations by Consuls Farren, Moore, and Campbell, in F.O. 78/283, Campbell's report, No. 3, 31 July 1836.

†† A letter from Damascus of 27 Feb. 1841, in Wood's Papers, St. Antony's College, Oxford.

‡‡ C. Napier, *The War in Syria* (London, 1842), i. xxxiv, ii. 283.

§§ A. Jochmus, *The Syrian War and the Decline of the Ottoman Empire* (Berlin, 1883), pp. 5–6.

‖‖ Polk, p. 169.

government and to carry out reforms which altered the social structure of the country.

But it was not without a powerful local resistance that these changes were implemented. Thus, for example, in the Ansariyya

[1] Walpole, i. 41; also al-Bāshā, pp. 58, 61. For figures on the Egyptian army in Syria see Table above.

mountains the Egyptians established control only after quelling two successive uprisings.[1] Similarly in Palestine a peasants' revolt, under the leadership of Nablus notables, as a reaction to conscription, broke out in 1834 and was bloodily suppressed.[2] At the same time, however, Ibrāhīm failed to break the power of the warlike Druzes; in 1837 the Houran Druzes revolted and defeated several Egyptian military expeditions which were sent against their stronghold of Leja.[3]

Another difficult barrier to overcome was the powerful Bedouin tribes which showed resistance to the new régime right from the beginning.[4] And although the Egyptians succeeded in curbing most of the local nomad tribes and even managed to disarm and collect taxes from certain clans,[5] they were, nevertheless, unable to keep in permanent check the Bedouin east of Jordan and the Negeb, who from time to time disturbed peace and order.[6]

B. *Destruction of urban leadership; social and economic reforms*

In the towns the Egyptian régime effected a radical change by undermining the position of the local leadership and by establishing its officials as the sole authority. Regular conscription and disarmament served to drain the military strength of local big families and urban organizations,[7] while the secularization of the judicial system deprived the ʿUlema of their influential position. The Muslim court (*mahkeme*), now under strict inspection, was allowed to deal only with matters of personal status, property holdings, and the like, while criminal cases were turned over to the

[1] Walpole, iii. 353; al-Dibs, viii. 650; ʿAbdullāh Ḥabīb Nawfal', 'Makhṭūṭat Nawfal Nawfal al-Ṭarābulsi', *al-Kulliyya*, xi. 170.

[2] For details on the peasants' revolt in central Palestine, see Spyridon, pp. 74–76; Abū ʿIzz al-Dīn, pp. 171–2; Rustum, *Maḥfūẓāt*, ii. 399, No. 3438.

[3] Al-Dibs, pp. 650–1; Mīkhā'īl Mishāqa, *Muntakhabāt min al-jawāb ʿalā iqtirāḥ al-aḥbāb* (Beirut, 1955), pp. 123–8; Nawfal, op. cit., p. 182; al-Bāshā, pp. 120–41, 167–8.

[4] See Rustum, *Maḥfūẓāt*, i. 300, No. 923; p. 302, No. 931; p. 303, No. 941; p. 309, No. 980; Abū ʿIzz al-Dīn, pp. 169–73; Manṣūr, pp. 72–73.

[5] Rustum, op. cit. i. 295, No. 890; p. 302, No. 931; p. 303, No. 941; ii. 96, No. 1726; p. 116, No. 1864; iv. 222–3, No. 6028; p. 255, No. 6088; *P.E.F.* (1906), pp. 39, 133.

[6] Abū ʿIzz al-Dīn, p. 189; Rustum, op. cit. i. 238, No. 671; ii. 104, No. 1778; F.O. 78/243, Farren to Palmerston, No. 10, Damascus, 6 June 1834.

[7] Cf. al-ʿĀrif, p. 214; al-Jundī, p. 197; Rustum, op. cit. ii. 347, No. 3433; *Rambles*, p. 45.

müteselim, and administrative and commercial issues to the newly created local council (*meclis*).[1]

In view of all this it is not surprising that the urban notables took an active part in the rebellions which broke out in many towns throughout Palestine and Syria, either in connexion with the peasants' revolt[2] or in other uprisings.[3] All these insurrections were crushed with an iron hand by the Egyptians and their ringleaders ('Ulema and other notables) executed or imprisoned.[4]

Strong antagonism to the Egyptian régime was felt not only by the former ruling class, which was the principal victim of the new order; it was also shared by the great majority of the Syrian population which seemingly might have possessed substantial motives for favouring the new government. Indeed, under the rule of Ibrāhīm Paşa, the Syrian population enjoyed for the first time considerable security of life and property, greater justice and opportunity for legal redress, and a more equable system of taxation.[5] The public security which was established in the countryside and along the roads made it possible for agriculture and commerce to flourish,[6]

1 For details on the formation and the work of the *meclis* (*majlis* in Arab.) under the Egyptians, see: al-Bāshā, p. 56; Abū 'Izz al-Dīn, pp. 135–8; Hofman, pp. 57 ff.; Kayat, p. 264; Rustum, *Maḥfūẓāt*, ii. 358, No. 3204; idem, *Bashīr*, p. 103. See also, F.O. 78/283, Report on Syria encl. in Campbell to Palmerston, No. 29, Alexandria, 23 Aug. 1836; H. Guys, *Esquisse de l'état politique et commercial de la Syrie* (Paris, 1862), p. 48; Mishāqa, *Muntakhabāt*, p. 120.

2 The peasants' revolt in central Palestine was followed by rebellions in cities such as Jerusalem (Spyridon, pp. 78–80, 106–7); Hebron (al-Bāshā, pp. 100–1; Abū 'Izz al-Dīn, p. 172; al-Rāfi'ī, p. 304); Safed (Rustum, *Maḥfūẓāt*, ii. 411, No. 3501; G. Kresel (ed.), *Qorot ha-'itīm* [*including a manuscript of Menahem Mendel of Kaminitz*] (Jerusalem, 1950), pp. 36 ff.); Tiberias (F.O. 78/243, Farren to Palmerston, No. 13, Damascus, 25 June 1834); Tripoli and some neighbouring towns (Rustum, op. cit. ii. 432, No. 3596; pp. 365–6, No. 3163). Damascus was on the eve of rebellion; F.O. 78/283, Farren to Palmerston, No. 14, 26 June 1834. For a detailed study on the 1834 revolt see, M. Abir, *Ha-mered neged ha-shilton ha-Mitzri be-eretz Israel bi-shnat 1834 ve-rig 'o*, (unpublished M.A. thesis, The Hebrew University, Jerusalem, 1961).

3 On the revolt in Tripoli in 1833, see al-Dibs, viii. 650; Nawfal, *al-Kulliyya*, xi. 130. On Gaza, see al-'Ārif, p. 214. On a plot by the 'Ulema of Jerusalem to revolt in 1832, see Rustum, op. cit. i. 189–90, No. 499. On a Druze plan in 1837 to collaborate with the people of Damascus in revolt against the Egyptians, see al-Bāshā, p. 26.

4 Ibid., see in particular al-Bāshā, pp. 86, 118, 127; Manṣūr, p. 72; Rustum, op. cit. ii. 489, No. 3868; *P.E.F.* (1906), p. 33; Spyridon, pp. 93, 97.

5 Barker, ii. 204; R. Edwards, *La Syrie 1840–1862* (Paris, 1862), p. 11.

6 See, for example, al-Bāshā, pp. 95–96; K. M. Bazili, *Syria i Palestina pod turetzkim pravitel'stvom* (St. Petersburg, 1875), i. 192; Nu'mān al-Qasāṭilī, *Kitāb al-rawḍa al-ghanna fī Dimashq al-fayḥā'* (Beirut, 1879), p. 90; E. Robinson, *Later Biblical researches in Palestine* (London, 1856), ii. 377–8.

and the authorities themselves did much to promote economic development. In the field of agriculture Egyptian experts introduced new methods and crops, marshes were drained, deserted lands were recultivated, and peasants were given tools, seeds, loans, and sometimes even tax reductions.[1] Similarly local trade was encouraged not only as a result of greater stability, but also because of the army's need for supplies.[2] In industry too some development took place as new factories (mainly for military purposes) were set up, natural resources exploited, and apprentices sent to Egypt to acquire new professions.[3]

But all these improvements were not valued by most of the people, not only because certain monopolies were imposed on some branches of agriculture and commerce,[4] but also, and more important, because of the number of changes which the new régime tried to effect in the way of life of the Syrian population. The two main causes of popular unrest were firstly the general conscription of young Muslims, which led, as already noted, to a series of uprisings throughout the country,[5] and secondly the levying of a personal tax, called *ferde*.[6] The new tax was theoretically a progressive income-tax; it was levied on every male from the age of twelve, and ranged from 15 to 500 piastres according to wealth.[7] In fact the *ferde* turned out to be a great burden on the population, probably because it was not collected in accordance with the original assessments.[8] In addition there was the humiliation

[1] Rustum, *Maḥfūẓāt*, ii. 264, No. 2696; p. 287, No. 2811; p. 326, No. 3015.

[2] See al-Bāshā, p. 58; *Birjīs Barīs*, ii (1860), No. 29; al-Qasāṭilī, p. 90; Rustum, *Bashīr*, p. 101; F.O. 78/243, Farren to Palmerston, Damascus, 7 Feb. 1843.

[3] Rustum, *Maḥfūẓāt*, iii. 123, No. 4581; p. 148, No. 4689; pp. 229–30, No. 4964; Barker, ii. 209; Guys, *Esquisse*, p. 170; J. L. Farley, *Two Years in Syria* (London, 1858), p. 26; cf. Polk, pp. 118–19, 168. See also Hofman, pp. 218 ff.

[4] Rustum, op. cit. ii. 285, No. 2801; p. 296, No. 2853; p. 357, No. 3195; Polk, pp. 167–8, 170–1.

[5] On the popular opposition to conscription, see al-Bāshā, p. 103; Barker, ii. 204–6; R. R. Madden, *The Turkish Empire* (London, 1862), ii. 48; Mishāqa, *Muntakhabāt*, p. 122; Būlus Qarā'lī (ed.), *Futūḥāt Ibrāhīm Bāshā* (Ḥarīṣa, 1937), pp. 43–44; Rustum, op. cit. ii. 402, No. 3457.

[6] Al-Bāshā, pp. 77, 197, 213; Philippe and Farid Khāzin, *al-Muḥarrarāt al-siyāsiyya* (Jūniya, 1910–11), i. 8–9, 86; Mishāqa, op. cit., p. 122.

[7] Al-Bāshā, p. 90; al-'Aqīqī, pp. 26, 49; al-Jundī, p. 12; Madden, ii. 46.

[8] Muḥammad 'Alī in a letter to Ibrāhīm stressed, for example, that the *ferde* which was levied in Syria was burdensome (*bāhiẓa*), and suggested that it be put on the same level as in Egypt. Rustum, op. cit. ii. 344, No. 3126. See also Mishāqa, op. cit., p. 121; F.O. 78/243, Farren to Palmerston, No. 8, Damascus, 29 May 1834.

caused to the Muslims, who regarded the tax as a poll-tax (*cizye*) only to be levied on Christians and Jews.[1] But even taxes other than the *ferde* which were neither new nor in excess of the former rates[2] aroused great opposition, since the Egyptian taxation system was on the whole more permanent, general, and systematic than that of the Turks; it was based on a direct collection by soldiers and left less room for evasion.[3] Add to this the system of ill-paid forced labour of men and animals,[4] and the great measure of cruelty and tyranny exercised by the Egyptian authorities,[5] and the main motives for the Syrians' hostility to Ibrāhīm's régime clearly emerge.

C. *The state of the Christian subjects*

As if all these factors were not enough to incite vigorous opposition to the Egyptian rule, there were further aspects of the new order which filled the cup of Muslim resentment to overflowing. For one thing, Muslim religious feelings were severely aroused when Egyptian troops marched through the cities playing musical instruments like Europeans, or when Muslim places of worship were used as barracks.[6] Another innovation, which deeply irritated the Muslims, was the setting up of European consulates for the first time in Damascus and Jerusalem,[7] and the permitting of missionary activities in the country.[8] But the main blow to Muslim feelings and pride was the equal status granted to the Christian subjects. Indeed under Egyptian rule Christians (and, to a lesser extent, Jews also) enjoyed full equality and complete security of life, property, and honour.[9] They were no longer subjected to oppression and extortion by Muslim notables, nor to

[1] Al-Bāshā, pp. 90–91; Mishāqa, *Muntakhabāt*, p. 181.

[2] See Rustum, *Maḥfūẓāt*, iii. 186–8, No. 4851.

[3] Madden, ii. 47. Compare Polk, p. 159; Baedeker, p. 71; F.O. 78/455, Rose to Palmerston, No. 30, Beirut, 3 May 1841; Kayat, p. 264.

[4] F.O. 78/243, Campbell's Report, 31 July 1836, answers to questions Nos. 17, 18; Abū ʿIzz al-Dīn, pp. 159–60; Rustum, *Maḥfūẓāt*, ii. 364–5, No. 3245; Polk, pp. 142, 157–8, 168.

[5] Al-Bāshā, pp. 86, 127, 184–5; al-Shāṭṭī, p. 12; Baedeker, p. 71; Barker, ii. 205–6; Bazili, i. 178.

[6] Spyridon, p. 64; al-Bayṭār, i. 25; al-Shāṭṭī, p. 12; al-Bāshā, p. 87.

[7] Ibid., p. 93; Porter, *Damascus*, i. 134; Rustum, op. cit. ii. 330, No. 3041.

[8] A. Tibawi, *British Interests in Palestine, 1800–1901* (London, 1961), pp. 13, 16.

[9] Mishāqa, *Muntakhabāt*, p. 139; *Ḥasr al-lithām*, p. 45; Kayat, p. 88; Rustum, *Bashīr*, p. 100; F.O. 78/283, Campbell's Report, op. cit., answers to questions, Nos. 15, 16.

assaults and attacks by Muslim mobs.[1] Non-Muslim communities were permitted to build and repair their places of worship without limit,[2] while their representatives took part in the work of the *meclis* alongside Muslim deputies.[3] Moreover, the new rights of the Syrian Christians sometimes exceeded even those of the Muslims: they were, for example, exempted from conscription[4] and became also relatively richer and more acceptable to the public administration.[5]

This profound change in their status filled the Syrian Christians with joy, self-confidence, and even insolence; and they were not slow to exercise, if not to flaunt, their new liberties and privileges in the face of the Muslims, for example, by carrying crosses in public processions. Such behaviour and the fact that Christian soldiers from Lebanon were employed to quell Nusayri and Druze uprisings and occasionally also marched through the streets of Damascus,[6] all seriously affected Muslim sensitivities and prestige: 'the Mussulmans . . . deeply deplored the loss of that sort of superiority which they all and individually exercised over and against the other sects.'[7] Muslims were likewise reported to have said to each other: '*yā akhī, al-dawla ṣārat dawlat Naṣāra, khalaṣat dawlat al-Islām*' ('O my brother, the state has become a Christians' state, the Islamic state has ended').[8] This statement no doubt reflected the deep concern of the Muslim majority in Syria not merely about the loss of their supremacy over the Christians but also about the change in the character of their state. Hence their bitter resentment not only of the Christians but mainly of the Egyptian régime.[9]

[1] Abū 'Izz al-Dīn, p. 76; al-Bāshā, p. 84; Bazili, p. 138; Kayat, p. 88; Qarā'lī, *Futūḥāt*, p. 15; Rustum, *Maḥfūẓāt*, ii. 117, No. 1871; Spyridon, p. 57.

[2] Finn, i. 135; Rustum, op. cit. ii. 325–6, No. 3011; p. 336, No. 3077; iii. 126, No. 4596; p. 215, No. 4926.

[3] Rustum, *Bashīr*, p. 103; al-Bāshā, p. 56.

[4] Except for a few cases, when Christians were recruited as a punishment for taking part in the 1834 revolt; they were, however, released afterwards. Rustum, *Maḥfūẓāt*, ii. 481, No. 3824.

[5] Al-Bāshā, pp. 79–80; *Ḥasr al-lithām*, p. 67; Polk, pp. 132, 135, 175; Walpole, i. 225.

[6] See al-Bāshā, pp. 57, 67, 68, 80, 82–83, 87, 131; Nawfal, *al-Kulliyya*, xi. 130 ff., 170 ff.; Rustum, op. cit. iii. 339, No. 5312; compare A. Hourani, *Arabic Thought in the Liberal Age* (London, 1962), p. 60.

[7] F.O. 78/283, Campbell's Report, p. 242, encl. in Campbell to Palmerston, No. 29, Alexandria, 23 Aug. 1836.

[8] Al-Bāshā, p. 77. See also Nawfal, op. cit. xi. 273.

[9] F.O. 78/495, Rose to Canning, No. 36, Beirut, 29 May 1842; Bazili, ii. 2–3;

To sum up, Egyptian rule, which at the beginning had been well received by certain elements of the leadership and the people,[1] became most unpopular within a few years. The entire Muslim population of Syria turned against Ibrāhīm, essentially because of his measures concerning centralization, conscription, taxation, and equality for non-Muslims, which affected all classes of this society. Ibrāhīm Paşa was indeed able to check the intense local opposition by ruling the Syrians with a rod of iron.[2] But when he withdrew in 1840, there took place throughout the country a total reaction against regular rule and order and against the Christians, which made it extremely difficult for the returning Ottomans to resume their authority and introduce reform. Yet the Egyptian rule in Syria and Palestine had certainly a long-term impact on the local society. It provided the Syrians with a new experience of security and of a regular system of government after a long period of chaos and oppression. It possibly also 'had sown the seeds of political equality in the mind of the Syrians'[3] by giving the Muslims a taste of equality with the non-Muslims. In addition, under the Egyptians, Syria and Palestine were widely opened for the first time to European activity and influence, after a long period of traditional isolated life. In short, the major significance of the Egyptian rule lies in the opening of a new era in the history of Syria, and in preparing the ground for the coming reforms of the Tanzimat.

In this respect the reforms of Muḥammad ʿAlī in Syria were more advanced than the reforms of Mahmud II in the other provinces of the Empire. The most important work of both reformers was the destruction of an old order and the creation of the beginning of a new one, which anticipated the future main lines of the

al-Bāshā, pp. 57, 59, 68, 77, 79–80, 83, 85, 104, 125, 131, 134; Qarā'lī, *Futūḥāt*, p. 41. Manṣūr claims that one of the motives for the 1834 rebellion was the Muslim hatred of Christians; see pp. 71–72. According to Campbell, this motive 'had more deep roots than all other just motives of complaint'. See Campbell's Report, op. cit., p. 242.

[1] Rustum, *Maḥfūẓāt*, i. 123, No. 316; p. 164, No. 429; al-Bayṭār, pp. 26–27; F.O. 78/215, Farren to Palmerston, Beirut, 7 Aug. 1832; F.O. 78/243, Farren to Palmerston, Damascus, 29 May 1834; Spyridon, p. 64; Bazili, p. 178. Even the population of South Anatolia welcomed the Egyptian army. Rustum, op. cit. ii. 149, No. 2078; C. MacFarlane, *Turkey and its Destiny* (London, 1850), i. 302.

[2] Ibrāhīm, for example, was reported to have said: 'I am the only man to manage the Arabs. I could and did cut their heads, which the Turks never will do.' F.O. 78/431, No. 70, 21 Feb. 1841, in Temperley, p. 29.

[3] Barker, ii. 315; see also Walpole, i. 225–6; Edwards, p. 8.

Tanzimat. But whereas the central problems of Islamic society—its legal basis and the place of the non-Muslim subjects within it—were not challenged at all by Mahmud II,[1] Muḥammad ʿAlī dealt with them indirectly by means of administrative measures.[2] It was only under Sultan Abdülmecid that legal changes were introduced into the Ottoman Empire—including Syria and Palestine—together with other reforms in government and administration and in the welfare of the subjects.

[1] Lewis, *Emergence*, p. 101.

[2] Ibrāhīm, for instance, did not change the legal status of the Christians and Jews who continued to pay the *cizye* (poll-tax) under his rule. See Mishāqa, *Muntakhabāt*, p. 121; Polk, p. 135.

III

THE REFORMS OF THE TANZIMAT AND THE STRUGGLE FOR CHANGE WITHIN THE *PORTE* (1839–61)

A. *The era of the Hatt-ı Şerif*

THE first great reforming edict of the Tanzimat era, the *Hatt-ı Hümayun*, or *Hatt-ı Şerif*, of Gülhane[1] (the Imperial, or noble Rescript of the Rose chamber), was promulgated on 3 November 1839, a short time after Abdülmecid succeeded his father, Mahmud II, as Sultan of the Ottoman Empire. The decree was issued mainly as a result of a great endeavours and a sincere desire on the part of its architect, Mustafa Reşid Paşa, to preserve the Empire and to improve the conditions of its inhabitants.[2] The timing of the proclamation was calculated to gain the support of the European powers against the rebellious Pasha of Egypt, Muḥammad ʿAlī, who threatened the integrity of the Empire.[3]

The reforms of the Gülhane decree can be divided roughly into three groups, a division which may also be applied to the reforms of the entire Tanzimat period. Firstly the decree dealt with administration and government; secondly with the welfare of the Ottoman subjects; and thirdly with the status of the non-Muslim citizens and with the legal basis of the Empire. After a short prologue, which attributed the decline of the Empire to the failure to preserve the Holy Law, the *hat* suggested the introduction of 'new laws' (or 'new rules': *kavanin-i cedide*),[4] in order to give the

[1] For text, see *Düstur* (Istanbul, 1871–1928), i. 4–7. A modern Turkish transliteration in Enver Ziya Karal, *Osmanlı Tarihi* (Ankara, 1947), v. 263–6. English translation in J. C. Hurewitz, *Diplomacy in the Near and Middle East* (Princeton, 1956), i. 113–16.

[2] Bailey, pp. 186, 192; Lewis, op. cit., pp. 103–4.

[3] Cf. Ahmed Cevdet, *Tezakir* (Ankara, 1953), i. 7; Davison, *Reform*, p. 38; Lewis, op. cit., p. 105; Temperley, pp. 160, 170. For other comments on the motives behind the Gülhane decree, see Bailey, pp. 181, 186, 228; Ṣāṭiʿ al-Ḥuṣrī, *al-Bilād al-ʿArabiyya wa'l-dawla al-ʿUthmāniyya* (Beirut, 1960), p. 91.

[4] *Kavanin*, pl. of *kanun*. Note that although in the theory of the Muslim jurists there was no law other than the Holy Law, Ottoman Sultans used nevertheless to issue *kanun*s to complement or correct the *Şeriat* and this practice was

Ottoman Empire the benefit of a good administration. It went on to elaborate the new laws: there were to be guarantees to ensure the Ottoman subjects security of life, honour, and fortune, a regular system of assessing and levying taxes to replace the tax-farming, and a regular system for the levying of troops and establishing their terms of service. In addition, other provisions were made regarding the various branches of administration, including the payment of fixed salaries to government officials and the elimination of bribery. As for financial management, the Gülhane edict recommended the promulgation of special laws to fix and limit army and other expenditures.

Reform of the administration and government, however, was not the crux of this *hat*, although it apparently was the chief concern of Mustafa Reşid Paşa. Instead, the *hat* appeared in a way more like a charter of rights for the Ottoman subjects, since both in general and specific terms it dealt largely with the improvement of their conditions of life. The leitmotive which recurred quite clearly throughout the Gülhane decree was the guarantee to secure life, honour, and property:[1] 'nothing in the world is more precious than life and honour'—stressed the *hat* and promised a number of steps towards the well-being of the citizens. It criticized the ruinous system of *iltizam* and monopolies and undertook to fix and regulate the taxes levied on the inhabitants. It also assured the free possession and use of private property without interference, and guaranteed the legal rights of innocent heirs against arbitrary confiscation. The decree also pledged fair and public trial to persons accused of crimes.

But the most remarkable point of this Imperial Rescript was contained in a brief passage which, for the first time in Ottoman history, officially promised equality before the law for Muslims and non-Muslims alike. The passage reads as follows: 'The Muslim and other peoples (*ahali-i islam ve milel-i saire*) who are among the subjects of our imperial sultanate, shall be the object of our imperial favours without exception.' This proclamation, which

tolerated by the Muslim jurists. More about the *kanun*, see *EI*[1]. A study on the Ottoman *kanun* is now in preparation by Prof. Uriel Heyd.

[1] According to Reşid the Gülhane edict 'only intended to introduce a complete security of the life, property, and honour of the individuals and regulate the internal and military expenditures of the Porte'; Nicholas Milev, 'Réchid Pacha et la Réforme Ottomane', *Zeitschrift für Osteuropäische Geschichte* (1912), ii. 388. Cf. Engelhardt, i. 36.

indicated a radical break with Islamic tradition, reflected perhaps the most acute problem of Ottoman reform. In including this issue in the Gülhane decree, Reşid and his colleagues truly aimed at changing the state from an Islamic sultanate to one in which all its subjects, irrespective of their religion, would be equal members of the same political community. But the cautious words used for the equality pledge as well as the tribute the *hat* gives to the *Şeriat* suggest that Reşid was aware of the conservative Muslim reaction to such innovations and wished to avoid an open challenge to Islamic law.[1] Yet the measures which followed the Gülhane decree indicated more obvious violations of the *Şeriat*. The Penal Code (*Kanun-i Ceraim*) of May 1840, though generally in accordance with the Holy Law, involved two significant changes: one was the affirmation of equality of all Ottoman subjects before the regulations of this code, and the other was the fact that a legislative body was created to prepare and promulgate this legal code.[2]

The Penal Code, which was followed by new codes in 1851 and 1858,[3] provided legal guarantees for the promises made by the *Hatt-ı Şerif* regarding the subjects' rights, and laid down penalties for deeds of corruption in the civil service. More reforms along the lines set up by the 1839 *hat* were introduced in the course of the 1840s and the early 1850s, in the areas of administration, finance, education, and the judicial system.[4] Among these measures the most radical was the commercial code of 1850. The enactment of this code, which had been delayed since 1841 because of the 'Ulema's opposition, was the first formal recognition in Turkey of

[1] At the same time, however, Reşid regarded it as politic to make the equality promise to the Great Powers in somewhat clearer words in order to gain their goodwill. Hence the two versions of the clause dealing with the equality issue: whereas the official text in French speaks of 'subjects of whatever religion or sect they may be', the Turkish text speaks of 'The Muslim and other people . . .'. This version appears also in the Arabic text sent to the Syrian provinces while still under the Egyptian rule; it refers also to *Ahl al-Islām wa-sā'ir al-milal*, see Jaffa *Sijill* of the Muslim Sharī'a Court, No. 13, firman of Evahir N 1255 registered on Gurre M 1256. Cf. Davison, *Reform*, p. 40.

[2] Cf. Lewis, *Emergence*, pp. 107–8.

[3] For text of the revised Penal Code, see *Düstur*, i. 527 ff.; Ahmed Lûtfi, *Mirat-i Adalet* (Istanbul, A.H. 1304), pp. 128–46; English translation and analysis in J. A. S. Bucknill and H. A. S. Utidjian, *The Imperial Ottoman Penal Code* (London and Nicosia, 1913). For more comments on the code, see Engelhardt, i. 40; Ubicini, i. 163–5.

[4] For a brief enumeration of the various reforms, see Lewis, op. cit., pp. 108 ff.; Mardin, p. 163. A more detailed survey on the measures introduced in each area will be made in the relevant chapters below.

a system of law and of judicature independent of the 'Ulema and the *Şeriat.*[1]

Indeed it was not without an acute struggle against the conservative elements that the Ottoman reformers were able to issue and introduce the measures of the Tanzimat, which were unpopular with large sections of the population. Compared with the reformist party, which consisted of a small élite group of senior officials, the conservative opposition party was both more numerous and more strongly represented in the high ranks of the 'Ulema and the civil service.[2] While the reformers were assisted in their endeavours by the English and French emissaries, the reactionaries were indirectly helped by Russia and Austria who were hostile to the Tanzimat for their own reasons.[3]

As for the Sultan Abdülmecid, his position in this struggle for the future of the Empire did not always prove to be useful to the cause of reform. The new Sultan was, admittedly, in favour of change and willing to continue his father's work.[4] But being inexperienced and irresolute, he was easily influenced by both liberals and conservatives, and often at the mercy of his advisors.[5] Despite the increasingly autocratic rule of the Sultan during the Tanzimat period, facilitated by the abolition of former checks on his power, Abdülmecid, unlike Mahmud, was basically incapable of leading the reform movement. It was only intermittently and with the aid of the British and French ambassadors,[6] that Reşid and his disciples, Fuad and Âli, were able to secure the Sultan's attention and carry out the reforms they sincerely believed to be necessary.

When the young Sultan succeeded his father in 1839, the

[1] Lewis, *Emergence*, pp. 108, 112; for text, see *Düstur*, i. 375 ff.

[2] Engelhardt, i. 158; Melek Hanum, *Thirty Years in the Harem* (London, 1871), p. 44 [French edition, Mme Kibrizli Mehmet Pacha, *Trente ane dans les Harems d'Orient* (Paris, 1892), p. 35]. A certain number of 'Ulema co-operated, however, with the reform movement. Examples in Engelhardt, i. 42; Heyd, *The 'Ulemā*, pp. 63–64, 82–84; Temperley, pp. 161, 227.

[3] Engelhardt, i. 85; Melek Hanum, p. 165.

[4] Engelhardt, i. 36; Madden, ii. 390. For specific examples see *Irade D.*, No. 31308, 11 N 1277; *Takvim-i Vekayi*, No. 274, 11 Ş 1260; F.O. 78/620, Rose to Aberdeen, No. 55, Beirut, 7 Oct. 1845.

[5] Engelhardt, i. 35; MacFarlane, ii. 230; Bailey, p. 180; S. Lane Poole, *Turkey* (London, 1922), pp. 347, 349; cf. Mardin, pp. 108, n., 111.

[6] Engelhardt, i. 85; MacFarlane, ii. 246; E. Poujade, *Le Liban et la Syrie 1845–1860* (Paris, 1867), p. 40; F.O. 78/517, Canning to Aberdeen, No. 48, 2 Mar. 1843 in Bailey, p. 212.

reforming party was already in power and increasing both in number and influence owing to Mahmud's active backing.[1] The defeat of the Turkish army by Ibrāhīm Paşa at Nezib, and Turkey's need to demonstrate to Europe her liberal intentions in order to secure support against Egypt, served further to strengthen Reşid's position and contributed towards initiating the *hat* of Gülhane in November 1839, as already mentioned. But the reform movement was not allowed to carry on with its programme of change for long. Many of its measures, especially those regarding non-Muslim equality, were unpopular;[2] some caused losses in the state's revenue, while the collapse of Ibrāhīm's power in Syria removed one of the most important motives for the adoption by the Empire of a liberal policy.[3] Consequently, at the beginning of 1841, following his attempt to enact the Commercial Code, which aroused the 'Ulema's strong resistance, Reşid was dismissed by the Sultan from the post of Grand Vezir.

The reactionaries, headed by Izzet Paşa as Grand Vezir, assumed the reins of government and refrained from carrying out the major innovations of the Gülhane.[4] But even under their rule, the process of reform did not stop completely. This was partly due to the Sultan's intervention and partly to the new ministers themselves. In 1842 the Sultan reconstituted the Council of Justice—the chief organ of the Tanzimat—and nominated more moderate conservatives, Rıza and Rauf, to the posts of Grand Vezir and Head of the Council respectively. In addition, he urged the *Porte* to improve the conditions of his subjects and to carry on with reforms in the government and the army.[5] The conservative ministers, who proved to be better administrators than the liberals,[6] were, in fact, themselves eager to carry out this policy and during their term of office all branches of the administration were systematically revised;[7] in 1843 the army was successfully

[1] J. L. Farley, *Turkey* (London, 1866), p. 11.

[2] Engelhardt, i. 44. Reşid's opponents did not hesitate to call him *gavur* (giaour), ibid., i. 39. See also Cevdet, *Tezakir*, i. 8.

[3] Engelhardt, i. 37–39, 42–45; Temperley, pp. 163–6.

[4] Engelhardt, i. 50; Temperley, pp. 165–6; C. White, *Three Years in Constantinople* (London, 1845), i. 111–12.

[5] *Takvim-i Vekayi*, No. 274, 11 Ş 1260; Bailey, p. 208; Engelhardt, i. 74, 76.

[6] MacFarlane, i. 515; Poujade, p. 41. Compare also Temperley, p. 158.

[7] Ubicini, i. 27; Ali Haydar Midhat, *The Life of Midhat Pasha* (London, 1903), p. 22.

reorganized on Western lines and turned into an able and reliable fighting force.[1] Yet, with regard to the other objectives of the reform, such as provincial administration, taxation, and, particularly, the status of the non-Muslims, the anti-reform government turned the clock back and revived the old institutions and customs.[2]

In 1845, a new phase of reform began when Reşid Paşa returned to the Ministry of Foreign Affairs with the assistance of the British ambassador in Istanbul, Stratford Canning.[3] In the following year, Reşid was appointed to the Grand Vezirate, an office which he was to hold on six different occasions until 1858.[4] During the next seven years Reşid was able to introduce many of the Tanzimat reforms, though not without several interruptions: he was periodically unseated by the conservatives for short terms, mainly owing to the influence of the Sultan's mother, and while Canning was absent from the Turkish capital.[5] Moreover, his prestige had begun to diminish during the years 1848–50, as a result of the financial difficulties, unrest in some European provinces, and an obvious Russian threat which faced the Empire. For most of these setbacks he was held responsible,[6] and in 1852 Reşid was again dismissed from the Grand Vezirate, his new system of provincial administration was abrogated, and the whole movement of reform came to a standstill.[7] During the years 1852 and 1853, popular resentment to change in general and to Christian equality in particular gained momentum as a result of Russia's claims over the Holy Places in Palestine and her demands to protect the Greek Orthodox subjects in Turkey; this led to the outbreak of the Crimean War, and to a further setback in the reform.

[1] Engelhardt, i. 71, 82, 115, 120; MacFarlane, i. 515; Temperley, pp. 166–8. See also below, para. on the army, pp. 44 ff.

[2] F.O. 78/476, Canning to Aberdeen, No. 67, 27 March 1842, cited in Bailey, p. 209; also ibid., p. 213; Temperley, pp. 225–7.

[3] Lane-Poole, pp. 348–50; MacFarlane, ii. 246; Temperley, p. 230. Compare also Engelhardt, i. 79.

[4] For the list of the Grand Vezirs and their terms of office during the reign of Abdülmecid, see Karal, v. 260–1; Midhat Sertoğlu, *Resimli Osmanlı Tarihi Ansiklopedisi* (Istanbul, 1958), p. 277.

[5] Bailey, p. 217; MacFarlane, ii. 246; Temperley, p. 231.

[6] Engelhardt, i. 86–87, 99; MacFarlane, ii. 249–50, 679–80; Temperley, p. 241.

[7] Lewis, *Emergence*, p. 103. On Reşid's dismissal, see *Irade D.*, No. 15212, 4 RA 1258.

B. *The era of the* Hatt-ı Hümayun

Paradoxically, however, this very issue of Christian equality constituted the crux of the new phase of reform, which began in the course of the Crimean War. Once more the Ottomans were in urgent need of winning the goodwill and support of the Western Powers against the formidable Russian enemy. And now, once again, the Turkish government tried to prove its sincerity to Europe by issuing a new charter of rights which was concerned essentially with the status of Turkey's Christian subjects. The new reform edict, the *Hatt-ı Hümayun* (The Imperial Rescript), was promulgated by Abdülmecid in February 1856, as part of the preliminaries of the treaty of Paris.[1] Bearing clear signs of foreign dictation,[2] the *hat* reaffirmed the principles of the Gülhane edict, and went so far as to declare in both specific and categorical terms the equal rights of 'the Christian communities and other non-Muslim subjects'.[3] It was also concerned with the well-being of all Ottoman citizens, as it suggested reforms in taxation and in the prison system and promised to encourage agriculture and commerce. With regard to matters of government and administration, the *Hatt-ı Hümayun* provided for popular representation in provincial councils as well as in the State's High Council, and outlined the manner in which these bodies were to function. As well as a strict observance of annual budgets, it also called for a number of other economic and financial measures and urged the payment of regular salaries to public officials. Finally, the decree promised to introduce further legal reforms and improve the administration of justice.

It is indeed true that the five years that followed the 1856 edict and ended with the death of Sultan Abdülmecid in 1861, witnessed further steps in legal reform: a land code and a new penal code were issued in 1858; a reorganization of the new legal

[1] It was issued in Evail C 1272 (8–17 Feb. 1856). For text, see *Düstur*, i. 7–14. A modern Turkish transliteration in Karal, v. 266–72; Eng. trans. in Hurewitz, i. 149–53. The edict was known in Turkey as *Islahat Fermanı* (Reform Edict).

[2] On the English and French intervention and pressure, see Cevdet, *Tezakir*, i. 26 ff.; see also Engelhardt, ii. 268, 271; F.O. 78/1298, Brant to Clarendon, London, 14 Feb. 1857. For a detailed analysis of the 1856 *hat*, see Davison, *Reform*, pp. 52 ff.; Karal, vi. 1–7; Cevdet, op. cit. i. 67 ff.; Engelhardt, i. 139 ff.

[3] For a detailed study on these rights, see below, the chapter on the state of the non-Muslims.

administration was effected in 1860; and further commercial and maritime codes were promulgated in 1861.[1]

At the same time, however, except for a few financial and other measures,[2] little was done during the years 1856–61 to improve the administrative structure of the Empire, and the conditions of its population.[3] This was partly due to the general unsettled state of the Ottoman provinces, which undermined the introduction of reforms, but mainly it was because of the growing financial crisis in Turkey which seriously damaged the instruments which were to effect the change. The financial crisis which resulted from the heavy expenditure on the Crimean War, the Sultan's extravagance, and the corruption in the administration,[4] left the Ottoman treasury empty, the army and civil service unpaid, and paralysed the country's economy.[5] Consequently the government was forced to obtain large loans which by 1860 made the Ottoman public debt reach its limits and which eventually led Turkey to bankruptcy.[6]

More disastrous were the attempts to put into practice the major promise of the 1856 *hat* on equal rights for the Christians; they were met with strong opposition from the conservatives and even some liberal elements, and provoked disturbances and uprisings throughout the Empire. For one thing, it was perhaps an irony of fate that Reşid Paşa, for long the leader of the reformers, took steps in his last years to denounce the promises of the new edict. Although he was twice again Grand Vezir for short periods before his death in 1858, Reşid had no part either in the preparation, enactment, or introduction of the *Hatt-ı Hümayun*. These tasks, together with the leadership of the reform movement, had passed into the hands of his former disciples and present rivals, Âli and Fuad. Reşid now sharply criticized the latter for going too

[1] For references to these reforms, consult Lewis, *Emergence*, p. 116 and n.

[2] *Birjīs Barīs*, i. No. 12, 23 Nov. 1859; No. 16, 18 Jan. 1860; F.O. 78/1637, Redcliffe to Russell, No. 104, Constantinople, 21 Feb. 1860.

[3] Engelhardt, i. 155, 161 ff.; F.O. 78/1637, Papers relating to the administrative and financial reform in Turkey, 1858–61, No. 1, Malmesbury to Redcliffe, 9 Aug. 1858.

[4] MacFarlane, ii. 247–8; Madden, ii. 545–7, ii. 390; Melek Hanum, p. 46.

[5] Engelhardt, i. 156, 165; ii. 45–46, 313; F.O. 78/1219, Moore to Clarendon, No. 31, Beirut, 7 July 1856.

[6] Engelhardt, ii. 314; Madden, i. 540–1. For a study on the Ottoman public debt, see D. C. Blaisdell, *European Financial Control of the Ottoman Empire* (N.Y., 1929).

far in granting political privileges to Christians, while giving way to foreign pressure and intervention.[1]

The reaction of the conservative elements of Turkey to these concessions was obviously much more intense, and in many places throughout the Empire there occurred violent outbursts of Muslims against Christians and Europeans.[2] In Maraş the reading of the *Hatt-ı Hümayun* provoked a Muslim attack on the English consular agent, a local Christian, in which he and his family were killed.[3] This was followed by the murder of the English and French consuls in Jidda in 1858 by a Muslim mob.[4] Even the Ottoman reformists were not spared during this vehement wave of protest. In 1859 a conspiracy against the Sultan and the reformers, known as the Kuleli Affair, was discovered in Istanbul; it was led by senior army officers and 'Ulema who were strongly opposed to Westernization and to Christian equality.[5] But Muslim resistance to Christian equality continued in other parts of the Empire, reaching its climax in 1860 with the massacres of thousands of Christians in Damascus.

Hardly did the reform movement recover from this setback when on 20 June 1861 the Sultan Abdülmecid died and was succeeded by his brother, Abdülaziz, a capricious and obstinate man, who was not in favour of reform. At this point there came to an end the first stage of the Ottoman Tanzimat.

[1] Cevdet, *Tezakir*, i. 76 ff.; Engelhardt, i. 141, 271.

[2] On the reaction of the Muslims, see Cevdet, op. cit., pp. 68 ff. See also Davison, *Reform*, p. 104; Engelhardt, i. 140.

[3] Cevdet, op. cit., p. 89; F.O. 78/1220, Letter from Maraş, encl. in Barker to Clarendon, No. 8, Aleppo, 21 Apr. 1856.

[4] Cevdet, op. cit. ii. 51; al-Bayṭār, ii. 1035.

[5] *Birjīs Barīs*, i. No. 8, 29 Sept. 1859; No. 9, 13 Oct. 1859; Engelhardt, i. 157–8. See also Davison, op. cit., pp. 100–3; Mardin, p. 18; for a study on the Kuleli Incident, see Uluğ Iğdemir, *Kuleli Vakası Hakkında bir Araştırma* (Ankara, 1937).

PART II

Aspects of Government and Administration

IV

THE *PORTE*'S ADMINISTRATIVE POLICY IN SYRIA AND PALESTINE

> 'It is regarded necessary and important to lay down and establish henceforth a number of new laws for the purpose of administering well our supreme state and protected provinces.'
>
> (From the Gülhane decree of 1839)

THE primary objective of Reşid in his programme of change, though not emphasized in the Gülhane edict, was to transform the Ottoman Empire into a modern centralized state and to re-establish a firm control over its semi-autonomous and virtually independent provinces.[1] In this policy of centralization, which the conservative party in Istanbul did not oppose in principle, Syria and Palestine held, possibly, a high priority owing to their vital importance to the Ottomans. It was, to begin with, a matter of great prestige to the Sultan and his Islamic state to possess Syria, with its traditional pilgrimage route to Mecca, and Palestine, with its Holy Places to Islam in Jerusalem.[2] Indeed, one of the major annual tasks undertaken by the *Porte* for centuries was the organization and conduct of the great Ḥajj caravan, whose starting and terminal points alike were in Damascus.[3] This caravan, which con-

[1] Compare Davison, *Reform*, p. 32; Engelhardt, ii. 283; Hourani, *Arabic Thought*, p. 44; Young, i. 29.

[2] Many Muslim pilgrims used, for example, to visit the Holy Places in Jerusalem after their return from Mecca; see Heyd, *Documents*, p. 39; al-ʿAwra, pp. 266–7.

[3] It involved great administrative, military, and financial activities not only

sisted of thousands of pilgrims, from outside as well as within the Ottoman Empire, was significant from a commercial point of view too.[1] Syria of course had further commercial importance because of the centres of international trade in Aleppo and, to a certain degree, Damascus.[2]

In addition the Ottomans' desire to strengthen their grip on Syria and other Asian provinces became more apparent during the nineteenth century as their power declined in Europe.[3] There was also the need to safeguard further the southern borders of Palestine lest another Egyptian attempt were made to threaten the integrity of the Empire.[4] Related to this was, presumably, the Ottoman ambition to recover their damaged prestige over the loss of Syria and Palestine to the Egyptians: for as we know, Sultan Mahmud II, who had initiated the policy of centralization, in spite of all efforts, failed to restore Ottoman rule in these provinces.

It is therefore not surprising that the very first major action undertaken by the new Sultan Abdülmecid, after he came to the throne, was directed towards recovering the Syrian provinces from the rebellious Pasha of Egypt. Involved in this move was, as already noted, the proclamation of the *Hatt-ı Şerif* with the aim of securing the Western Powers' military help in this operation.

A. *Administrative division*

One of the major features of the new Ottoman administrative policy in Syria and Palestine was paradoxically the revival, although with some changes, of the old system of division into *paşalık*s, which in the past had in fact encouraged decentralization.[5] Syria was divided again into basically the same three

in Damascus, but also in other Asian provinces and in Istanbul. Examples in *Mühimme*, No. 254, pp. 125–6, 129–36; No. 255, pp. 11–16, 91–96; No. 257, pp. 125–30, 193–9; No. 258, pp. 14–19.

[1] See, for instance, F.O. 78/959, Wood to Clarendon, No. 42, Damascus, 25 July 1853; F.O. 78/1586, Wrench to Russell, No. 9, Damascus, 16 May 1861.

[2] See, for example, D. Segur, *La Syrie et les Bedouins sous l'administration Turque* (Paris, 1855), pp. 9–10.

[3] Cf. F.O. 78/801, Wood to Canning, No. 20, encl. in Wood to Palmerston, No. 23, Damascus, 25 Sept. 1849.

[4] Cf. F.O. 195/194, Rose to Bankhead, No. 6, Beirut, 7 Feb. 1842; A. E. Jérusalem I, from Lantivy, No. 72, 10 July 1844.

[5] The first Ottoman reorganization of Syria was into three *eyalets*: Aleppo, Damascus, and Tripoli. Later on a fourth *eyalet* of Sidon was formed; Heyd.

provinces (*eyalet*s or *paşalık*s) of Aleppo (Halep), Damascus (Şam), and Sidon (Sayda), while the former fourth unsteady *paşalık* of Tripoli (Trablusşam) was absorbed in Sidon.[1] The sub-division was also roughly similar to that in the pre-Egyptian system; each *eyalet* was divided into several *sancak*s (or *liva*s), the *sancak* into *kaza*s and the latter into *nahiye*s. At the head of each *eyalet* was a *vali*; the *sancak* was governed by a *kaymakam*, the *kaza* by a *müdir*, and the *nahiye* by a *muhtar*.[2]

In the various *eyalet*s several changes were made in the districts within their jurisdiction. The *eyalet* of Aleppo remained the same as before except for two alterations which turned out to be burdensome for both the local merchants and the provincial government. Alexandretta, the natural port of the commercial city of Aleppo, was separated from the *paşalık* and put under the jurisdiction of the *vali* of Adana, while the turbulent non-Arab district of Urfa was annexed to Aleppo.[3] The *eyalet* of Damascus kept its traditional districts of Homs, Hama, and the area east of the Jordan, but the western and south-western borders were considerably changed; the rich areas of al-Biqāʿ were cut off from Mount Lebanon and placed under Damascus,[4] while the Palestinian districts of Nablus, Jerusalem, and Gaza, which officially belonged under Damascus in the pre-Egyptian period and for a short time also in the year 1840–1, were transferred to the *eyalet* of Sidon.[5] The *paşalık* of

Documents, p. 58; Gibb and Bowen, i. 222. From time to time there took place changes in this division when certain Pashas were strong enough to annex a neighbouring district.

[1] *Irade D.*, No. 2117/7, C 1257. *Ceride-i Havadis* No. 102, Selh B 1258; *Takvim-i Vekayi*, No. 245, Gurre L 1258. In the pre-Egyptian period it was often the case that Tripoli was absorbed into one of its bordering provinces, Sidon or Damascus; see examples in Gibb and Bowen, i. 224; Burckhardt, pp. 170–1, 648; Jibrāʾīl Saʿāda, *Muḥāfaẓat al-Laddaqiyya* (Damascus, 1961), p. 28. Cf. map at end.

[2] For a detailed administrative division of the Syrian provinces in the Tanzimat period, see *Salname* 1266, pp. 84–87; Ubicini, i. 44–46; Edwards, p. 5. See also Guys, *Esquisse*, p. 27. Compare with the division in the pre-Tanzimat period; Burckhardt, p. 648; Ubicini, i. 40–41.

[3] F. A. Neale, *Eight Years in Syria* (London, 1851), ii. 153–4; *Irade D.*, No. 3254, 28 B 1258; *Ceride-i Havadis*, No. 102, Selh B 1258; *Takvim-i Vekayi*, No. 245, Gurre L 1258. For a detailed sub-division of Aleppo, see F. Taoutel, (ed.), *Wathāʾiq taʾrīkhiyya ʿan Ḥalab* (Aleppo, 1958–62), ii. 88.

[4] F.O. 78/1118, Wood to Redcliffe, No. 12, encl. in Wood to Clarendon, No. 13, Damascus, 1 Mar. 1855; C. W. M. Van de Velde, *Narrative of a Journey through Syria and Palestine* (London, 1854), i. 133.

[5] With regard to the pre-Egyptian period, see: B. Lewis, 'Studies in the Ottoman Archives', *BSOAS* 16 (1954), p. 472. On the year 1840–1 see, *Mühimme*

Sidon with its new capital in Beirut,[1] included most of Lebanon and Palestine and was now larger than it had ever been.[2] Indeed, this *paşalık* became almost as important as the *paşalık* of Damascus, while Beirut, which in the early forties was virtually the headquarters of the government of the whole of Syria, turned out to be the second chief city in Syria after Damascus. Within the *eyalet* of Sidon, however, there were two areas with special status. Firstly, Mount Lebanon was divided in 1841 into two districts, governed by Druze and Maronite *kaymakams* respectively, both of whom enjoyed a certain degree of autonomy.[3] Secondly, the *sancak* of Jerusalem with its tributary *sancaks* of Nablus and Gaza formed together a separate district (normally called *mutasarrıflık*) within the *eyalet* of Sidon.[4] It was governed by a *mutasarrıf*, usually a Pasha of one or two horse-tails (*mirmiran* or *ferik*)[5] who intermittently was subject directly to the *Porte* or to the *vali* of Sidon.[6] During the year 1854, Jerusalem became officially an *eyalet* and was governed by a Pasha of three *tuğs* (*müşir*), who was independent of Sidon and responsible only to Istanbul.[7] Henceforth

No. 254, p. 88, Evahir N 1256; ditto, pp. 120–1, Evail CA 1257; F.O. 78/447, Werry to Palmerston, No. 6, Damascus, 22 Mar. 1841.

[1] Beirut replaced Acre as the central town of the *paşalıck* in 1841; see al-Shidyāq, ii. 249. On the importance of Acre before the Tanzimat, see al-ʿAwra, p. 308.

[2] This was, in a way, an official confirmation of what had happened several times in the past, when the *vali* of Sidon occupied these areas or at least exerted a considerable influence over them; it was especially the case with al-Jazzār and ʿAbdullāh.

[3] Yūsuf Khaṭār Abū Shaqrā', *al-ḥarakāt fī Lubnān 'ilā 'ahd al-mutaṣarrifiyya* (Beirut, 1952), pp. 46, 64.

[4] *Cevdet D.*, No. 4996, CA 1265; Bazili, ii. 3; Edwards, p. 5; Finn, i. 159; Spyridon, p. 17 n.

[5] These were military ranks granted also to civil governors; see Ahmed Lûtfi, *Tarih-i Lûtfi* (Istanbul, 1290–1328), vii. 64. With regard to the Pashas' ranks in Jerusalem, see ibid. vii. 71, 93; *Irade D.*, No. 6318, 22 R 1262. One of Jerusalem's first governors, Tayyar Paşa, was even raised from *ferik* to *müşir*, *Irade D.*, No. 2327/1, 20 N 1257.

[6] Khalīl Sarkīs, *Ta'rīkh 'urshalīm* (Beirut, 1874), p. 192. Tayyar Paşa, for instance, received orders directly from the *Porte* at the same level as the Pashas of Aleppo and Damascus; he was usually referred to as the Governor of the *sancaks* of Jerusalem and Gaza (*Mühimme*, No. 254, pp. 120–1, Evail CA 1257), but also as *ferik* of the *eyalet* of Jerusalem (*Irade D.*, No. 2327/1, 20 N 1257). But when Edhem Paşa was nominated to this *mutasarrıflık*, he was categorically ordered by the *Porte* to obey the orders of the *vali* of Sidon; *Cevdet D.*, No. 4996 CA 1265.

[7] F.O. 78/1022, Kayat to Clarendon, No. 2, Jaffa, 20 Mar. 1854; *Mühimme*, No. 259, pp. 17–18, Evahir Saf. 1271; *Salname* 1271, p. 72.

Jerusalem continued to enjoy a considerable degree of autonomy within the *eyalet* of Sidon.[1]

Similarly, a few more *sancak*s in Syria enjoyed at times a somewhat special status within their *eyalet*s owing, possibly, to their strategic position. Such were, for example, the *sancak* of Acre in Sidon and those of al-Raqqa and Dayr al-Zūr in Aleppo, whose governors received at times direct orders from the *Porte*.[2] On the whole the governors of the *sancak*s, the *kaymakam*s, though responsible to their respective *vali*s, were appointed or dismissed by virtue of an order from the *Porte*.[3]

B. *Restrictions on the* vali*'s authority*

From this system of administrative division it is apparent that the *Porte*'s aims were to centralize in Istanbul its rule over the Syrian provinces, to keep a balance of power among the various governors of these provinces, and to limit the *vali*'s authority. This again was not new in Ottoman politics; it was rather a revival of the old ruling idea in the *Porte*, reinforced by long experience of distrust, fear of treachery, or of unregulated ambition on the part of its officials. But whereas in the past this policy could not prevent the rise of virtually independent Pashas in Syria, it now became effective to such a degree that it made the *vali* almost powerless. Indeed, the Governor-General of the *eyalet* emerged as the major victim of this new policy of centralization, not only because he did not possess full authority over the sub-governors in his province, but for factors of more weight. To begin with, the *vali* was appointed to his post usually for only one year, and sometimes for a shorter period. This practice which was neither new nor exclusive in Syria[4] prevailed, with a few exceptions, throughout the Tanzi-

[1] See, for example, F.O. 78/1217, Finn to Clarendon, No. 35, Jerusalem, 31 May 1855; F.O. 78/1383, Finn to Malmesbury, No. 26, Jerusalem, 9 Oct. 1858.

[2] Acre was governed by a junior Pasha, usually called *muhafiz*, but sometimes also *mutasarrıf*; Lûtfi, *Tarih*, vii. 6, 93; *Mühimme*, No. 257, p. 224, Evahir Ş 1266; *Ceride-i Havadis*, No. 27, 22 CA 1277. On the separate status of Dayr al-Zūr, see *Irade M.V.*, No. 13688, 23 R 1271. On al-Raqqa, see *Mühimme*, No. 255, p. 19, year 1258; No. 257, p. 244, Evahir Ş 1266.

[3] See for example *Irade M.V.*, No. 9073, 21 Z 1268; *Ceride-i Havadis*, No. 27, 22 CA 1277; compare with the position of the *sancak* before the Tanzimat, Lewis, *BSOAS*, p. 471; Ubicini, i. 40–41.

[4] On this policy in eighteenth-century Syria, see Gibb and Bowen, i. 201; S. Shamir, 'As'ad Pasha al-'Aẓm and Ottoman rule in Damascus (1743–1758)', *BSOAS*, xxvi, pt. I, p. 2. Cf. Davison, *Reform*, pp. 168–9.

mat era and contributed to the undermining of Turkish authority in the country.[1] Even more crucial to the position of *vali* were the checks exercised on him by other high officials in his *paşalık* who were independent of him. In the first place, the Pasha was often unable to perform his tasks, mainly military in nature, since he had no control over the regular military force stationed in his province. He was normally allowed to employ only irregular cavalry which were generally corrupt and inefficient; the regular troops (*Nizam*), under the command of the local military officer, received their orders from the *serasker*, the Commander-in-Chief in Damascus.[2]

Another official who counterbalanced the Pasha's authority was the *defterdar*, who was in charge of collecting the revenue and defraying the expenditure, and was responsible directly to the Minister of Finance in Istanbul. As in the past, the *defterdar* accumulated in his hands a great deal of power owing to his functions, his independent administrative machine, and his relatively long term of office.[3] He had, for example, the power to fix the salaries of junior civil servants, to limit the number of irregular troops in the *paşalık*, and to refuse to defray the expenses of military expeditions or other operations.[4]

A further check on the *vali*'s authority came from yet another creation of the new administrative system: this was the provincial council (*meclis*) which was set up nominally to assist the Governor-General.[5] In fact, as will be seen, the *meclis*, by virtue of its extensive powers granted by the *Porte*, and its local preponderance,

[1] On the frequent change of Pashas in Damascus, see F.O. 78/872, Wood to Canning, No. 8, encl. in Wood to Palmerston, No. 13, Damascus, 28 Apr. 1851; al-Munajjid, p. 91. As regards Aleppo, see A.E. Alep, i, from Guys, No. 1, 31 Mar. 1843; Taoutel, ii. 52, 85, 87. As regards Jerusalem, see Bazili, ii. 5; Finn, i. 160; ii. 162–3. Note, however, that in the *eyalet* of Sidon things were different: Vamık Paşa, for instance, served as the *vali* of Beirut for about eight years between 1848 and 1856; see *Salname* 1264 and onwards.

[2] See, for example, Bazili, ii. 13; Finn, i. 165, 257; F.O. 78/1297, Barker to Redcliffe, No. 3, encl. in Barker to Clarendon, No. 3, Aleppo, 10 Feb. 1857. Compare Engelhardt, i. 107; MacFarlane, i. 163. See also below, the para. on the *serasker*. Compare with the situation before the Tanzimat; Gibb and Bowen, i. 201–2.

[3] On the powerful position of the *defterdar* in eighteenth-century Syria, see Gibb and Bowen, i. 201; Shamir, *The 'Azm*, pp. 227–8; on the early history of the post of *defterdar*, see Heyd, *Documents*, p. 42.

[4] F.O. 78/579, Wood to Aberdeen, No. 11, Damascus, 1 Apr. 1844; F.O. 78/618, Rose to Aberdeen, No. 32, Beirut, 13 May 1845; A. A. Paton, *The Modern Syrians* (London, 1844), p. 204.

[5] Engelhardt, i. 107; ii. 283; Ubicini, i. 45–46.

actively interfered with the administrative affairs of the province and frequently obstructed the process of the Tanzimat.[1]

Finally, the legal powers of the Pasha with regard to the keeping of public order were also restricted, as he was not permitted to use capital punishment or flogging against criminals.[2] As a result of all these checks and restrictions, the *vali* was often unable to perform his tasks: public order was undermined, the machinery of government was damaged, and reform was occasionally impeded.

By 1852 the *Porte* realized the evils of this prematurely centralized administration, and decided to remove them by extending the powers of the *vali* and making him once more the effective authority in his province. A firman of 28 November 1852 placed under the *vali*'s immediate control every branch of administration —including the military and financial officers, as well as the provincial council. The *vali* was now entitled to call out the regular forces, to inspect the financial accounts, and to nominate or remove members of the *meclis*. In addition, the firman empowered the *vali* to appoint and dismiss any subordinate civil official within his jurisdiction, including *kaymakams* and *müdirs*. At the same time the Pasha's legal powers were extended to enable him to maintain public order: he was authorized to punish all minor crimes without reference to Istanbul and to carry out capital punishment after the sentence had been confirmed by the *Porte*.[3] Thus theoretically the *vali*'s powers at the end of 1852 were almost as extensive as those of the Pasha in the past who, in those days, was the authoritative ruler of his province.[4] But in fact the firman of 1852 brought about little essential change in the position of the *vali vis-à-vis* his principal rivals, or in the degree of his authority in the *paşalık*.

The *defterdar*, it is true, no longer constituted a check on the *vali*'s authority. His post was amalgamated in 1852 with that of the president of the provincial council, and the new functionary,

[1] See below, the chapter on the *meclis*, pp. 87 ff.

[2] Engelhardt, i. 109; ii. 285–6; F.O. 78/963, Finn to Clarendon, No. 8, Jerusalem, 26 Apr. 1853.

[3] Text in *Mühimme*, No. 258, pp. 198–201; Jaffa *Sijill*, No. 18, 9 R 1269; see also F.O. 78/963, Finn to Rose, Jerusalem, 3 Dec. 1852, encl. in Finn to Malmesbury, No. 2, 3 Feb. 1853. Cf. Engelhardt, i. 109–10; ii. 286; Karal, vi. 31–32; Lûtfi, *Mirat*, p. 155.

[4] On the *vali* and his wide authority before the Tanzimat, see Bailey, pp. 13–16; Bodman, pp. 20–21, 27–28; Gibb and Bowen, i. 201; Engelhardt, i. 105; ii. 284; Temperley, p. 286.

whose rank was of second or third grade, did not appear to be a threat to the *vali*.[1] Furthermore, in 1860 the office of *defterdar* was suspended for motives of economy and replaced with that of a *muhasebeci* (chief accountant);[2] the *defterdar* was reappointed, however, a few months later but at a decreased salary and with reduced rank.[3] Yet at the same time, the *vali* continued to be restricted to a certain degree in his military authority by the *serasker*, and more so in his administrative powers—by the *meclis*.

At this point it should be noted that the measure of authority the *vali* could exercise in his *paşalık* depended, both before and after 1852, mainly on his personality and the degree of support he possessed in Istanbul. A resolute and energetic Pasha with a strong backing in the *Porte* was in a position to counterbalance his opponents, to make them co-operate with him, or even to overshadow them. For example, the prominent *vali* of Aleppo, Asad Paşa, effected as early as 1842 the dismissal of a reluctant *defterdar*, assumed his functions, and later replaced him with a *mal müdir-i* (a lower financial officer) who remained in that office until 1852.[4] Similarly, a bold and influential Pasha could force the military commander to obey his orders and dominate the regular troops;[5] he was, likewise, in a position to restrain the members of the *meclis* and imprison resistant elements.[6] Indeed, a certain number of *vali*s of this calibre served in the Syrian *paşalık*s in the course of the period 1840–61, and contributed in no small measure to the establishment of direct Turkish rule and the carrying out of some reforms in the country. But the number of such able governors was limited; and although some of them were allowed to stay in their posts for more than the usual term,[7] others were recalled to Istanbul or posted elsewhere after a relatively short period in

[1] See *Salname*, years 1269–76. See also A.E. Damas, iv, from Outrey, No. 26, 12 Feb. 1857.

[2] See F.O. 78/1519, Moore to Bulwer, No. 3, encl. in Moore to Russell, No. 1, Beirut, 18 Jan. 1860. Compare *Salname* 1277, pp. 79–80.

[3] F.O. 78/1519, Moore to Bulwer, Beirut, 2 Apr. 1860, encl. in Moore to Russell, No. 6, 7 Apr. 1860; F.O. 78/1537, Brant to Bulwer, Damascus, 8 Apr. 1860, encl. in Brant to Russell, No. 6, 21 Apr. 1860.

[4] *Irade D.*, no. 2543, 17 RA 1258; *Takvim-i Vekayi*, No. 242, 6 CA 1258; *Salname* 1263–1269.

[5] See, for example, F.O. 78/1383, Finn to Malmesbury, No. 20, Jerusalem, 28 Sept. 1858.

[6] See below, p. 96.

[7] See, for example, F.O. 78/1454, Finn to Malmesbury, No. 21, Jerusalem, 11 Nov. 1859. Note also the example of Vamık Paşa cited above, p. 35, n.1.

office.[1] Consequently it was not infrequently that certain improvements achieved by an able *vali* were nullified when his successor was an incapable or even an ordinary person; for, as will be seen later, the mediocre Pasha who usually served in Syria found it still very difficult to cope with the powerful *meclis* or with an authoritative *serasker*.

In conclusion, this system of checks which the *Porte* exercised in the provinces (particularly up to 1852) no doubt had its merits: the Syrian *vali* of the early Tanzimat was completely subservient and obedient to Istanbul,[2] and was no longer able to become a defiant and independent autocrat such as ʿAbdullāh Paşa had been only a short time previously. But at the same time the status and authority of the provincial Pasha was greatly diminished and, in the eyes of a populace accustomed to being governed by quite other means, he occasionally appeared as 'merely a cipher'.

C. *The office of* serasker

Whereas the position of the Ottoman provincial *vali* was on the wane in the course of the Tanzimat, there emerged instead in the Syrian provinces during that period a new position, that of *serasker*; it concentrated in one pair of hands some of the major powers that the *vali* lacked, and constituted another outstanding feature of the *Porte*'s new policy of centralization.

The title of *serasker* was an old one in Ottoman history and was given to army officers for the purpose of carrying out an *ad hoc* military operation.[3] Mahmud II revived this title when he reconstructed his new army and applied it to the officer who combined the functions of Commander-in-Chief and Minister of War.[4] During the Egyptian occupation of Syria the title *serasker* was adopted by Ibrāhīm Paşa, who was the Commander-in-Chief of the army and the supreme Egyptian authority in the country.[5] It appears that the post of *serasker* in the Syrian provinces during

[1] Compare F.O. 78/705, Finn to Palmerston, No. 13, Jerusalem, 13 July 1847.

[2] See examples in *Irade D.*, No. 14661, 24 Z 1267; F.O. 78/448, Werry to Ponsonby, Aleppo, 2 Aug. 1841; F.O. 78/910, Wood to Malmesbury, No. 21, Damascus, 30 June 1852; F.O. 78/1448, Finn to Russell, No. 42, Jerusalem, 16 Nov. 1859; Manṣūr, p. 69. Compare Guys, *Esquisse*, p. 45.

[3] See, for example, Shamir, *The ʿAẓm*, p. 248; Bodman, pp. 104, 111.

[4] Lewis, *Emergence*, p. 79; Sertoğlu, p. 291.

[5] See above, p. 12.

the period 1840–61 was basically that of Commander-in-Chief, but also embodied wide administrative powers. It started as an *ad hoc* task, developed into a somewhat similar office to that which had existed in the Egyptian period, and later became connected with the post of *vali* of Damascus.

To begin with, Syria and Palestine of the early 1840s were regarded by the *Porte* as provinces that required special treatment. The primary tasks in 1840 were to reconquer this area and to establish a new administration; and it was to accomplish these ends that the first *serasker*, Izzet Paşa, was appointed as Commander-in-Chief of the army and what was also described as Governor of Syria; he was thus engaged in both military operations and administrative organization.[1] At the beginning of 1841, being promoted to the Grand Vezirate, Izzet Paşa was succeeded by a new *serasker*, Zakariyya Paşa,[2] who was replaced a few months later by the *vali* of Sidon, Selim Paşa.[3] The latter, holding now both posts of *serasker* and *vali*, was also engaged, like his predecessors, in administrative and military activities.[4] However, the outbreak of the civil war in Lebanon and the general disorderly state of affairs in the whole area, led the *Porte* to discharge Selim Paşa and to nominate at the end of 1841 its Minister of War, Mustafa Nuri Paşa as *serasker* in Syria.[5] This official set about restoring order in the Lebanon and at the same time inspected matters of government in all the provinces while giving directions to their *valis*.[6] At this time it was suggested at the *Porte* (according to Consul Wood) that Mustafa or another Minister should be nominated as 'Inspector or Governor-General' of Syria, but this idea was not put into effect.[7] Instead, Mustafa Paşa was relieved

[1] Barker, ii. 312; Khāzin, i. 87; Napier, i. 109; Spyridon, p. 138; F.O. 195/171, Wood to Ponsonby, No. 19, Beirut, 28 Oct. 1840. See also Great Britain, *Parliamentary Papers, Accounts and Papers*, LX (1843), ii, No. 42, from Wood, Damascus, 30 Sept. 1841.

[2] Lûtfi, *Tarih*, vii. 6; F.O. 195/170, Werry to Ponsonby, Aleppo, 16 Mar. 1841.

[3] F.O. 78/447, Wood to Palmerston, No. 2, Beirut, 2 Aug. 1841; *Mühimme*, No. 254, pp. 103–4, Evail Saf. 1257.

[4] A.E. Damas, i, from Munton, No. 11, 13 Mar. 1841; *Accounts and Papers*, LX (1843), ii, No. 5, from Rose, Beirut, 22 May 1841; F.O. 78/444, Young to Ponsonby, No. 14, Jerusalem, 28 June 1841.

[5] Lûtfi, op. cit. vii. 34, 38; *Accounts and Papers*, LX (1843), i, No. 31, from Bankhead, Pera, 31 Dec. 1841.

[6] Lûtfi, op. cit. vii. 46; F.O. 78/498, Wood to Aberdeen, No. 20, Damascus, 23 Feb. 1842; F.O. 78/495, Rose to Aberdeen, No. 53, Beirut, 25 July 1842.

[7] F.O. 78/498, Wood to Aberdeen, No. 9, Damascus, 5 Jan. 1842.

of his post of *serasker* in September 1842 and was replaced by Asad Paşa, the newly appointed *vali* of Sidon who held the joint office of *serasker* and *vali*.[1] Asad remained in office for some two years and his dismissal in 1844 marked the end of the first phase in the office of *serasker* of Syria in which the office was filled *ad hoc* by a special delegate from the Porte or by the *vali* of Sidon, and was administered from Beirut. Henceforward the *serasker* was in fact the Commander-in-Chief of the Turkish army in the region, whose headquarters were in Damascus.

The first officer of this kind was Namık Paşa, who, following the general reorganization of the Ottoman army in 1843, was appointed in April 1844 as *serasker* or Commander-in-Chief of the Army of Arabistan.[2] This appointment was preceded by a preliminary survey in the country by Lieut.-Colonel Hasan Paşa who was reported to have drafted a plan whereby the Syrian provinces should be placed under a military Governor-General.[3] Indeed, the functions of Namık Paşa were numerous and ranged over most aspects of government and administration: he had to maintain peace and order in the country and keep the Bedouin in check;[4] he was engaged in the collection of taxes in various parts of the country,[5] and was even directed by the *Porte* 'to strengthen the action of the authorities against the powerful and influential corps of Effendis and Ulemas'.[6] In other words, the *serasker* was ordered to tackle the major problems of the land and to provide the provincial governors with the military sanction for the execution of their tasks. In this way the *Porte* presumably hoped to accomplish the following aims: to introduce the new order in the country, to restrict the *vali*'s authority, and at the same time, bearing in mind the distance of Syria from the capital and the lack of fast communications, to add a local focus of centralization.

This policy could have been and, in fact, occasionally was, considerably successful, had there been full co-operation between the

[1] *Irade D.*, No. 2837, 15 CA 1258; Lûtfi, *Tarih*, vii. 56; F.O. 78/497, Werry to Aberdeen, No. 1, Aleppo, 1 Oct. 1842.

[2] Ahmed Cevdet, *Tarih-i Cevdet* (Istanbul, A.H. 1301–9), xii. 223; *Ceride-i Havadis*, No. 158, 17 Z 1259.

[3] A.E. Damas, i, No. 6, 30 Nov. 1843; see also F.O. 78/538, Wood to Aberdeen, No. 39, Damascus, 6 Nov. 1843.

[4] See, for example, Namık's report to the *Porte* in *Irade H.*, No. 2295, 13 N 1263; see also F.O. 195/207, Werry to Canning, No. 19, Aleppo, 24 Aug. 1844.

[5] *Irade D.*, No. 8417/1, 15 ZA 1263.

[6] F.O. 78/579, Wood to Aberdeen, No. 15, Damascus, 8 May 1844.

serasker and the *vali*, or had the Commander-in-Chief possessed complete authority over all the provincial Pashas. But for one thing the Syrian *vali*s were not officially subordinate to the *serasker*, although on the occasion of the appointment of a new *serasker*, Kıbrıslı Paşa, in 1851–2, they were 'enjoined to consult him and take his opinion on matters of administration'.[1] Each *vali* was officially the Governor-General of his *eyalet* and was, in fact, responsible before the Porte for its administration. Secondly, not every provincial Pasha was willing to depend on the Commander-in-Chief for permission to employ regular troops, particularly if the *vali* had the same military rank as the *serasker* (the rank of *müşir*), or the highest administrative rank of *vezir*.[2] On the other hand, the *serasker* could exploit his indispensable military powers in order to establish himself as the chief authority in the country while interfering with the internal affairs of each *eyalet*. This was in fact what was done by both Namık Paşa during his long term in office (1844–9) and Mehmed Kıbrıslı Paşa during his brief period as *serasker* (1851–2). (But Emin Paşa who occupied this post in the interim apparently refrained from this practice.) Each of these officials took advantage of his prominent position and established himself as virtually the military and civil governor of all Syrian provinces,[3] and this despite the governors of these *paşalık*s who struggled to remain independent of the *serasker*. The interference of both Namık and Kıbrıslı was felt particularly strongly and frequently in the *eyalet* of Damascus and occasionally resulted in the removal of the local *vali*;[4] this was partly due to the authority the *serasker* apparently had over the Pasha of Damascus,[5] and partly because the city was the headquarters of both functionaries.

At the beginning of 1853, after Kıbrıslı Paşa was recalled to the capital, the *Porte* decided to amalgamate the office of Commander-in-Chief with that of the *vali* of Damascus.[6] This change, which

[1] F.O. 195/368, Wood to Canning, No. 2, Damascus, 21 Feb. 1852.

[2] Cf. *Salname* 1263 and onwards.

[3] F.O. 78/761, Wood to Canning, No. 29, encl. in Wood to Palmerston, No. 30, Damascus, 25 Nov. 1848. See also, A.E. Jérusalem, ii, from Jorelle, No. 18, 14 Oct. 1846; F.O. 78/871, Werry to Canning, No. 46, encl. in Werry to Palmerston, No. 20, Aleppo, 10 Dec. 1851.

[4] See F.O. 78/761, Wood to Palmerston, No. 22, Damascus, 28 Aug. 1848; F.O. 78/910, Wood to Malmesbury, No. 20, Damascus, 29 June 1852.

[5] F.O. 78/761, Wood to Palmerston, No. 20, Damascus, July 1848. See, for example, F.O. 78/622, Wood to Aberdeen, No. 38, Damascus, 10 Nov. 1845.

[6] *Irade D.*, No. 1916, 8 Ş 1270.

was probably related to the recent extension of the powers of the *vali* in 1852, marked a decline in the position of *serasker* in Syria, and his influence over the general administration of the Syrian provinces was now hardly felt outside the *eyalet* of Damascus. Yet it was not without some confusion and apparent indecision that this change was finally achieved. To begin with, not until 1854 were the posts of Commander-in-Chief and the *vali* of Damascus combined, while in other Ottoman provinces a similar reorganization had been already carried out in 1852.[1] For when Kıbrıslı left his post in 1853, he was succeeded by a new *serasker*, a certain Vasıf Paşa, whereas the *vali* of Damascus, Aşkar Paşa, remained in his office and showed great opposition to the new official.[2] Only in October 1854, after both Aşkar and Vasıf had been recalled to the capital, and for economic reasons related possibly to the Crimean War, Ârif Paşa was nominated as a joint *müşir* of the Army of Arabistan and the *vali* of Damascus.[3] However, before long the new office was split once again—in April 1855—into the separate posts of *serasker* and *vali*: Ârif Paşa was held responsible for certain disorders in the *paşalık*, and was dismissed, and in his place Vamık Paşa, the *vali* of Sidon, was appointed *vali* of Damascus. The post of *serasker* then remained vacant for more than a year, while the president of the military council in Damascus, Izzet Paşa, acted as *serasker*, and placed himself under the orders of the new *vali* of Damascus.[4] Afterwards, from October 1856 and for some two years, the office of *serasker* was filled by Kerim Paşa and İsmail Paşa successively.[5] At the beginning of 1859 the *Porte* decided again to unite the posts of Commander-in-Chief and *vali* of Damascus in the hands of Ahmed Izzet Paşa, who had successfully held the post of *vali* of Damascus for about a year in 1856–7 and the office of *serasker* since the end of 1859.[6] The joint office was divided again in July 1860 following

[1] Namık Paşa, for instance, who in 1849 had been nominated C.-in-C. of the army of Iraq and Hijaz, was appointed in 1852 as a joint C.-in-C. and *vali* of Baghdad; Cevdet, *Tarih*, xii. 223; *Irade D.*, No. 15015, 21 RA 1268.

[2] F.O. 195/390, Moore to Redcliffe, No. 3, Beirut, 3 May 1853; F.O. 78/959, Wood to Redcliffe, No. 48, encl. in Wood to Clarendon, No. 56, Damascus, 11 Oct. 1853.

[3] *Mühimme*, No. 259, p. 12, Evahir CA 1270.

[4] A.E. Damas, iii, from de Barrère, No. 22, 15 Apr. 1855.

[5] *Salname*, 1273, p. 56; 1274, p. 63.

[6] *Mühimme*, No. 259, pp. 101–2, Evahir M 1273; ibid., p. 222, Evasit R 1274; *Irade D.*, No. 27668, 24 R 1275; al-Bayṭār, i. 260.

Ahmed Paşa's execution for his part in the massacre of the Christians in Damascus.[1]

At this stage, Fuad Paşa, the Foreign Minister, arrived in Syria and assumed the supreme authority over the country. And when he left for Istanbul in December 1861, Syria continued still to be under special administration as a report of that month points out: 'The Seriasker Halim Pasha has been entrusted with the temporary government of the country and has been invested with the same functions with which Fuad Pasha had himself been charged including the power of administering capital punishment.'[2] But this was apparently not for long. The 1860 events in Syria forced the *Porte* to adopt a more definite approach to the problem of provincial administration. This approach, which was later to be crystallized in the Law of Vilayets of 1864, produced at the beginning of 1861 a new plan, according to which Damascus, Beirut, and Aleppo were to retain separate headquarters and each was to be equally dependent on Istanbul while the military commander was to remain independent of all centres.[3]

[1] *Salname* 1276, 1277. Note a suggestion by the *serasker* in Istanbul in June 1860 to re-divide this office in Syria and to appoint new officials for the separate posts of *vali* and C.-in-C. *Irade D.*, No. 30264, 13 ZA 1276.

[2] F.O. 78/1586, Rogers to Bulwer, No. 49, encl. in Rogers to Russell, No. 29, Damascus, 2 Dec. 1861.

[3] See F.O. 78/1628 (1), Dufferin to Bulwer, No. 119, Beirut, 12 Feb. 1861; on the impact of the 1860 events on Fuad Paşa's observation with regard to the provincial administration and in the later Law of Vilayets, see Karal, vi. 31; compare Davison, *Reform*, pp. 108, 142.

V

INSTRUMENTS OF GOVERNMENT AND ADMINISTRATION

In the last chapter an attempt was made to study the main lines of the Tanzimat administrative policy in Syria and Palestine, and to analyse the respective positions of *vali* and *serasker* within the new provincial system. In this chapter we shall try to examine some of the instruments which were employed by the Ottoman authorities to carry out the new order; for, as will be seen, the shape of government and the fate of reform in the Syrian provinces were determined in no small measure by the nature and quality of the army and of other instruments of government and administration.

A. *The Army*

'Asker Padişah'ın elidir.'
['The army is the (right) arm of the Sultan']
(Fuad Paşa)[1]

The role which the Turkish regular army played in governing the Syrian provinces and in carrying out the Tanzimat reforms in them during the period 1840–61 was predominant and unequalled as compared to other organs. In a country like Syria, with a totally armed population, warlike mountaineers and powerful nomad tribes, the establishment of a stable government and a regular administration was impossible without strong military support. In the face of intense local desire for autonomy and popular opposition to change, extensive use of the army was also necessary to impose upon Syria and Palestine various measures, particularly those concerning direct rule—conscription and taxation. Furthermore, the regular army had also to perform from time to time the functions of a police force owing to the ineffectiveness of the local police organization—the irregular troops. Thus for example, the *Nizam* was often employed to maintain order in both

[1] From Fuad Paşa's speech before the Turkish army in Damascus after the massacre of 1860, in Cevdet, *Tezakir*, ii. 110.

the towns and the countryside,[1] and to collect revenue and tax-arrears in certain disorderly areas.[2] In addition, there was the special annual task of escorting the Ḥajj caravan which occupied so many regular and irregular soldiers that their numbers sometimes exceeded those of the pilgrims themselves.[3] All these tasks were carried out in addition to the ordinary military functions of defending Syria's eastern borders against seasonal Bedouin intrusions and protecting the southern borders against a possible Egyptian threat.[4]

Hence it emerges that the measure of tranquillity and order established in Syria and the extent of change introduced depended largely on the size and quality of the regular troops stationed in these provinces. When, for instance, the *Nizam* was deployed in this area in considerable numbers, and was well organized and wisely employed, the country was usually quiet and the government could carry out its functions and reforms fairly regularly. Sometimes even the mere presence of an able military force or its public display served as a check on the local turbulent elements.[5] But when, conversely, the detachments of the *Nizam* in the area were inadequate or disorganized, the country fell into confusion and anarchy; local chiefs threw off government control, Bedouin tribes ravaged the countryside, peasants' factions fought each other, and there was chaos everywhere.

Such was the case at the restoration of the Ottoman rule in Syria in 1840 and for the subsequent four years. Although the size of the Turkish *Nizam* in the area during these years was between 15,000 and 20,000 men,[6] it was not sufficient to establish a new

[1] *Cevdet Z.*, No. 1582, Eylûl 1264; F.O. 195/226, Wood to Canning, No. 12, Damascus, 2 Sep. 1846; F.O. 78/1118, Werry to Clarendon, No. 13, Aleppo, 22 May 1855.

[2] *Irade D.*, No. 6661, from 20, 25, 27 ZA 1262; *Irade M.V.*, No. 6103, 16 RA 1267; F.O. 78/1603, Skene to Bulwer, encl. in Skene to Russell, No. 25, Aleppo, 1 Apr. 1861.

[3] F.O. 78/498, Wood to Aberdeen, No. 8, Damascus, 5 Jan. 1842; F.O. 78/1586, Wrench to Bulwer, No. 15, encl. in Wrench to Russell, No. 9, Damascus, 16 May 1861; *Mühimme*, No. 255, p. 174, 9 RA 1259.

[4] F.O. 195/194, Rose to Bankhead, No. 6, Beirut, 7 Feb. 1842; A.E. Jérusalem, i, from Lantivy, No. 72, 10 July 1844.

[5] For example, see F.O. 78/621, Werry to Aberdeen, Aleppo, 3 July 1845; F.O. 195/210, Young to Rose, No. 3, encl. in Young to Canning, private, No. 4, Jerusalem, 17 Feb. 1845; Finn, i. 405–6, 472–3.

[6] *Irade D.*, No. 1867, 27 Saf. 1257; F.O. 195/171, Moore to Ponsonby, No. 1, Beirut, 1 Feb. 1841; F.O. 78/498, Wood to Aberdeen, No. 29, Damascus, 29 Mar. 1842; Bazili, ii. 7.

regular administration and to maintain order among a population which heartily opposed the new régime.[1] Moreover, the size of this army was frequently reduced when some of its units, which were stationed in Syria only temporarily, were recalled to their original *ordu* (army or camp).[2] They were usually replaced by second-grade and undisciplined soldiers: *başıbozuk*s (irregulars), *sipahi*s (feudal cavalry), *redif* (reserves), and the most turbulent Albanian troops.[3] A further handicap was that the soldiers as a whole—*Nizam* and irregulars alike—were ill-paid[4] and depended to a great extent on the local population for their food supply[5]—factors which were likely to undermine their loyalty and discipline. The Turkish regular army in that period suffered also from serious defects in its training, command, and organization which made its military capacity doubtful.[6] All these factors were fundamental reasons for the general disorganized situation which prevailed in the country between 1840 and 1844. It was only the military reorganization of 1843, which in Syria took place in 1844–5, that turned the *Nizam* into a more efficient force, and helped to place the country under firmer Turkish control.

As already mentioned, the first big reorganization of the Ottoman army along modern lines took place in 1826, after the destruction of the old Janissary corps by Sultan Mahmud II.[7] This was undoubtedly a very significant point in the history of the Empire; the old professional but disintegrating army which served the reactionaries' cause and was beyond the Sultan's control was re-

[1] A.E. Jérusalem, i, from Lantivy, No. 56, 22 Apr. 1844; F.O. 78/448, Werry to Palmerston, Aleppo, 15 Feb. 1841; F.O. 78/539, Moore to Bidwell, No. 5, Beirut, 6 Mar. 1843; F.O. 78/581, Young to Aberdeen, No. 37, Jerusalem, 23 Oct. 1844; *Irade D.*, No. 2931, 7 R 1258.

[2] Ibid., No. 3067, 17 CA 1258; ibid., No. 4168, 13 M 1260; ibid., No. 1579, 16 Ş 1262.

[3] F.O. 195/207, Werry to Canning, No. 1, Aleppo, 14 Jan. 1843; *Irade D.*, No. 2580/6, 27 C 1257; *Takvim-i Vekayi*, No. 244, 29 C 1258; Lûtfi, *Tarih*, vii. 31.

[4] *Irade D.*, No. 1218, 21 N 1256; F.O. 78/498, Wood to Aberdeen, Damascus, 29 Mar. 1842; A.E. Jérusalem, i, from Lantivy, No. 67, 27 June 1844.

[5] F.O. 195/170, Werry to Ponsonby, No. 3, Damascus, 5 Mar. 1841; ibid., Young to Ponsonby, No. 19, Jerusalem, 30 July 1841.

[6] Cf. F.O. 195/171, Captain Wilbraham's Report on Turkish Army and Navy, Constantinople, 8 June 1841; Napier, i. 47; *Irade D.*, No. 1218, 21 N 1256; *Accounts and Papers*, LX (1843), i, No. 7, Ponsonby to Palmerston, encl. No. 3, from Wood, Therapia, 23 May 1841.

[7] On this reorganization and on early attempts to reform the army, see above, pp. 2–3.

placed by new troops raised by popular conscription and committed to the Sultan and his reform movement. However, despite Mahmud's great efforts to build up his new force, the army was largely deficient and in fact suffered some decisive defeats on the battlefield: it was badly defeated by the Russians in 1828–9 and by the Egyptian army in 1831–2 and in 1839. One of the reasons for this was that recruitment methods were arbitrary and unjust, as the new conscripts had to serve in the army a much longer period than the official term of twelve years.[1] The actual fighting force was in addition relatively small—40,000 out of 300,000 troops —and the soldiers were ill-disciplined, ill-trained, and ill-paid. There was also an acute shortage of intelligent and able officers, tactics were inadequate, and military organization defective.[2]

Sultan Abdülmecid, who succeeded Mahmud II, was also concerned about the army and in his *Hatt-ı Şerif* of Gülhane he suggested remedies for some of the army's defects. The *hat* criticized mainly the unjust conscription system as harmful and ruinous, and laid down the principle of regular recruitment limited from four to five years only. But despite this pledge, conscription in Turkey continued to be, for some time still, irregular and arbitrary;[3] and the army, although increasing in size,[4] was yet unable to occupy Syria and Palestine without the help of the British and other European forces.[5]

The comprehensive reorganization of September 1843 carried out by the conservative cabinet put an end to many shortcomings in the *Nizam* and turned it into a more able and reliable force. (Thus, for example the Turkish army in its next confrontation against the Russians in the Crimean War, made a far better stand than in 1828–9.)[6] The firman of reorganization at last fixed the duration of the military service to five years in the regular troops

[1] Lûtfi, *Tarih*, vii. 74; Engelhardt, i. 71; al-Ḥuṣrī, p. 251.

[2] Marmount de Raguse, in *Foreign Quarterly Review*, No. 24, London, 1840, pp. 395 ff., quoted in Bailey, p. 15. See also Bailey, pp. 140–1; Temperley, pp. 29–31, 55.

[3] Ibid.; Lûtfi, op. cit., p. 74; F.O. 78/761, Wood to Palmerston, No. 15, Damascus, 4 May 1848.

[4] See J. H. Skene, *The Three Eras of Ottoman History* (London, n.d.), pp. 61–63, in Urquhart's papers, Balliol College, Oxford, iii, No. 26; Temperley, p. 167; 'Tanzimat ve Ordu', in *Tanzimat*, i (Turkey, Ministry of Education, Istanbul, 1940), p. 130.

[5] For detailed accounts of the Syrian war, see A. Jochmus; C. Napier; W. P. Hunter, *Narrative of the Late Expedition to Syria* (London, 1848).

[6] Temperley, pp. 167–8; Engelhardt, i. 115 ff., ii. 242; Farley, *Turkey*, p. 29.

(*Nizam*) and seven more years in the reserves (*redif*). The former were to consist of 150,000 men and the latter of 90,000. The army was divided into five *ordu*es—two stationed in Istanbul, one in Rumelia, and one in Anatolia; the fifth was the Army of Arabistan with its headquarters in Damascus.[1] (A sixth *ordu*, that of Iraq and Hijaz, was formed in 1848 with its centre in Baghdad.)[2]

According to the 1843 decree, the *ordu* of Arabistan was to consist of 25,000 men (19,000 infantry, 4,000 regular cavalry, and 2,000 artillerymen equipped with seventy-two guns) under the command of *müşir* Namık Paşa.[3] After a preliminary survey at the end of 1843, Namık Paşa arrived in Syria in April 1844, and a few months later the Syrian army had almost reached its recommended strength.[4] Owing, however, to the shortage of regular soldiers, a certain part of the *ordu* consisted of *redif* troops who were raised in the Anatolian and Iraqi provinces adjacent to Aleppo and were incorporated into the *Nizam*. This measure, which had been started in September 1843 and continued by Namık Paşa until 1845, was accompanied by the dissolution of the undisciplined Albanians and some *sipahi*s. All these steps, taken mainly in northern Syria, involved the withdrawal of most of the regular troops from southern Syria, and their concentration in Aleppo where Namık Paşa established his headquarters.[5] The result was that complete tranquillity prevailed in the *eyalet* of Aleppo, whereas Palestine was thrown into a state of disorder.[6]

Only in September 1845 did Namık Paşa transfer his headquarters to Damascus, where a military council of the *ordu* was formed; at the same time Turkish soldiers were deployed in key positions throughout Syria and Palestine, leaving about half the

[1] On the firman of reorganization and its provisions, see *Takvim-i Vekayi*, No. 259, 21 N 1259; *Ceride-i Havadis*, No. 147, 28 Ş 1259; Cevdet, *Tezakir*, i. 9; Lûtfi, *Tarih*, vii. 77; *Tanzimat*, p. 132.

[2] Cevdet, op. cit., p. 10; Engelhardt, i. 90.

[3] F.O. 78/577, Rose to Canning, No. 21, encl. in Rose to Aberdeen, No. 20, Beirut, 10 May 1844.

[4] *Ceride-i Havadis*, No. 177, 2 RA 1260; 'Return of regiments forming the army of Arabia under the Seraskier Namik Pasha,' encl. in F.O. 78/622, Wood to Aberdeen, No. 31, Damascus, 8 Sept. 1845. Consul Wood indicates, however, that the regiments were incomplete.

[5] F.O. 78/576, Rose to Aberdeen, No. 13, Beirut, 12 Apr. 1844; F.O. 78/621, Werry to Aberdeen, No. 12, Aleppo, 3 July 1845.

[6] F.O. 78/581, Young to Aberdeen, No. 37, Jerusalem, 23 Oct. 1844; F.O. 78/578, Reports from British officers, encl. No. 2 in Rose to Aberdeen, No. 49, Beirut, 7 Nov. 1844.

army in Damascus within Namık's reach.[1] Hence, until 1852, the Turkish military, encouraged by the reformist cabinet in Istanbul, played a decisive role in pacifying the Syrian provinces and in carrying out various measures there. Troops were employed successfully to impose direct rule, to collect taxes, and to levy conscription throughout the country.[2]

Nevertheless, despite great efforts, the army was unable to overcome during this period the two most powerful and insubordinate elements of Syria—the Bedouin tribes of the desert and east of the Jordan, and the Druzes of Houran.[3] This was partly because these warriors were equal to the Turkish soldiers in their fighting capacity and partly because of the natural protection they derived from their respective strongholds in the desert and Jabal Druze. It was also due to some shortcomings in both the quality and quantity of the Turkish army in Syria: although considerable improvement took place in the *Nizam* after its reorganization, it still suffered from defects in its command, training, equipment and maintenance.[4] A further weakness of the Turkish military establishment and one which recurred throughout the entire period 1840–61, was the acute shortage of financial resources; it caused military expeditions to be countermanded[5] and provided acts of indiscipline, desertion, and mutiny among ill-paid troops.[6] Chronic financial difficulty was also one of the reasons for the inadequacy of troops in Syria during the entire period under review. The size of the Army of Arabistan during this period never reached the originally assigned number of 25,000; even at its largest in 1845 the *Nizam* consisted of barely 20,000 troops.[7]

[1] For a detailed scheme of the Turkish troops in Syria in 1845 consult 'Return of regiments', above, p. 48, n. 4. See also F.O. 78/620, Rose to Aberdeen, No. 52, Beirut, 12 Sept. 1845; *Salname*, 1263.

[2] See, for example, *Irade D.*, No. 6661, 27 ZA 1262; ibid., No. 8020, 27 N 1263; Melek Hanum, pp. 86–89; see also below, p. 78.

[3] See below, the respective chapters on the Bedouin and the Druzes.

[4] F.O. 78/712, Rose to Palmerston, No. 2, Beirut, 9 Jan. 1847; Melek Hanum, pp. 89–90. Compare also *Irade D.*, No. 13527, 2 Saf. 1267; Finn, i. 218.

[5] *Birjīs Barīs*, i, No. 9, 13 Oct. 1859; A.E. Damas, i, No. 13, 6 Mar. 1844; F.O. 78/579, Wood to Aberdeen, No. 15, Damascus, 8 May 1844.

[6] Engelhardt, i. 101; Walpole, iii. 224; F.O. 78/871, Werry to Canning, No. 38, encl. in Werry to Palmerston, No. 15, Aleppo, 29 Sept. 1851. Compare also, *Irade D.*, No. 5774, dated 1261.

[7] According to *Irade D.*, No. 12649, 17 B 1266, the figures are 20–22,000. The English Consul-General gives, however, the number of 17,000; F.O. 78/620, Rose to Aberdeen, No. 52, Beirut, 12 Sept. 1845.

This force, which was only about a quarter of the size of the Egyptian army in Syria during 1839–40, was also employed outside the Syrian provinces: military expeditions were sent from time to time to curb rebellions in Iraq, or to reinforce garrisons in Hijaz,[1] provinces which until 1848 were placed within the jurisdiction of the fifth *ordu*—the Syrian army. Furthermore, in view of the general shortage of troops in the Nizam, regular soldiers were withdrawn from Syria whenever an emergency arose in other parts of the Empire,[2] and the vacuum usually remained unfilled for some time after a crisis was over, despite calls for reinforcements on the part of Syrian military authorities.[3] In this manner the Turkish army in Syria fell to 15,000 troops in 1848 and after a further withdrawal in 1849 it stood at only 12,000 in 1850.[4]

In that year the *Porte* decided to increase the size of the *ordu* of Arabistan by means of conscription among the Syrian inhabitants, who until that time had been virtually exempt from it.[5]

The compulsory recruitment of 1850 provoked, however, a popular rebellion in Aleppo, which was followed by similar uprisings in other parts of the country, notably at the Leja in 1852. But when reinforcements arrived, most rebellions were put down and conscription was carried out in the whole area except for the Houran.[6] Yet, although part of the fresh Syrian conscripts were employed in Syria itself,[7] the military force in the country remained still relatively small and hardly fit to maintain order.[8] In September 1852 *serasker* Kıbrıslı Paşa asked for reinforcements of more 'Turkish troops', which he indeed received with an additional financial allocation.[9] This considerable improvement in the military situation for a while helped maintain tranquillity and order; it was, however, lost in the second half of 1853, when the greater

[1] F.O. 78/715, Werry to Palmerston, No. 10, Aleppo, 29 Apr. 1847; F.O. 78/1118, Werry to Clarendon, No. 2, Aleppo, 30 Jan. 1855.

[2] Compare A. Lyall, *The Life of the Marquis of Dufferin and Ava* (London, 1905), p. 107. See, for example, A.E. Alep, i, from Guys, No. 13, 3 Nov. 1844.

[3] F.O. 78/761, Wood to Palmerston, No. 15, Damascus, 4 May 1848.

[4] *Irade D.*, No. 12649, 17 B 1266; F.O. 195/331, Moore to Canning, No. 23, Beirut, 25 Apr. 1849; A.E. Damas, ii, 2 Jan. 1850.

[5] See below, pp. 81–82.

[6] See below, pp. 125.

[7] F.O. 78/910, Werry to Granville, No. 2, Aleppo, 29 Jan. 1852.

[8] 14,000 troops according to F.O. 78/872, Wood to Canning, No. 23, encl. in Wood to Palmerston, No. 29, Damascus, 26 Aug. 1851; see also F.O. 78/910, Werry to Granville, No. 2, Aleppo, 29 Jan. 1852; Finn, i. 165, 258.

[9] Letter from Kıbrıslı Paşa in *Irade D.*, No. 16001/1, 20 ZA 1268.

part of the *Nizam* in Syria, numbering about 17,000 in all, was withdrawn and dispatched to the Crimean battlefield.[1] By the beginning of 1854 only a few regular regiments remained in the country; most Turkish officers were recalled and the whole military establishment greatly diminished.[2]

The numerous and serious functions of the *Nizam* were now transferred to several thousand irregular troops, *redif* and Albanian soldiers,[3] who, being unreliable or ineffective, could not prevent a great many parts of Syria from falling into confusion and anarchy during the years 1854–5.[4]

At the end of the Crimean War regular troops began to return gradually to Syria, replacing part of the *başıbozuk*s and restoring law and order in a number of areas.[5] But their numbers were again very limited and subject to frequent reductions as a result of the successive uprisings in the Balkan provinces at that period. During 1858 the military force in Syria, which by then amounted to only about 8,000 troops, was further diminished to such a degree that it was impossible for it to control the country and maintain peace.[6] This made the *Porte* send new reinforcements to Syria at the end of 1858, but most of these were recalled to the capital in May–June 1859, and in order to fill this vacuum a new irregular force called *avniye* (auxiliaries) was organized in place of the old *başıbozuk*s with the aim of helping the *Nizam* to perform its duties in the country.[7] The new unit was, however, neither adequate nor

[1] For return of the military force in Syria and Palestine in September 1853, see F.O. 78/958, Calvert to Redcliffe, No. 30, encl. in Calvert to Clarendon, No. 23, Damascus, 19 Sept. 1853; cf. *Irade D.*, No. 17199, 6 L 1269; *Ceride-i Havadis*, No. 651, 21 M 1270.

[2] Compare *Takvim-i Vekayi*, No. 269, 3 R 1270; *Salname* 1270, pp. 90, 92; ibid., 1271, pp. 100, 102.

[3] F.O. 78/962, Finn to Clarendon, No. 9, Jerusalem, 19 July 1853; F.O. 78/1033, Werry to Nolan, 13 May, encl. in Werry to Clarendon, No. 8, Aleppo, 23 May 1854; *Ceride-i Havadis*, No. 695, 11 L 1270.

[4] See *Irade D.*, No. 17218, 11 Ş 1269; A.E. Jérusalem, ii, from Botta, No. 64, 12 Oct. 1853; F.O. 78/1033, Werry to Redcliffe, No. 17, encl. in Werry to Clarendon, No. 10, Aleppo, 13 June 1854.

[5] *Irade D.*, No. 26417, 9 Ş 1274; F.O. 78/1220, Barker to Redcliffe, No. 20, encl. in Barker to Clarendon, No. 10, Aleppo, 3 June 1856; A.E. Jérusalem, v, from de Barrère, No. 19, 28 Aug. 1856.

[6] *Irade M.M.*, No. 385/8, 12 B 1273; *Irade M.V.*, No. 16795, 23 RA 1274; F.O. 78/1383, Finn to Malmesbury, No. 25, Jerusalem, 9 Oct. 1858; F.O. 78/1389, Skene to Alison, No. 20, encl. in Skene to Malmesbury, No. 33, 7 Aug. 1858.

[7] F.O. 78/1454, Brant to Bulwer, No. 22, encl. in Brant to Malmesbury, Damascus, 20 June 1859; F.O. 78/1452, Skene to Bulwer, encl. in Skene to

effective enough to stop the deterioration of the state of affairs in Syria.

The situation indeed went from bad to worse when in May 1860 more regular troops were evacuated by an order from Istanbul,[1] a step that served further to deepen the concern that the local Turkish authorities had already felt.[2] It is true that in view of the *serasker*'s growing opposition to the withdrawal of soldiers and his constant demands for reinforcements, the *Porte* stopped the evacuation of more troops, and in June 1860 dispatched some 2,000 soldiers to Syria.[3] But those steps were taken too late and were inadequate; the total regular force in Syria and Palestine even then did not exceed 7,000 troops, a figure which represented less than one-third of the number put forward in the original plan of 1843, or about a tenth of the Egyptian army which had effectively ruled the country in the 1830s. In fact, that was the smallest military force the Turks had deployed in Syria since its restoration to their hands, excluding the period of the Crimean War. Moreover, segments of that army were untrained, ill-paid, and ill-fed,[4] and a certain number of the troops were local Syrian recruits who were undisciplined and maltreated by their officers.[5] Nevertheless, with only 1,000 troops the Pasha of Jerusalem was able to maintain order and to subject some mountainous areas to direct rule in the course of that critical period of 1858–60.[6] Similarly the military authorities of Aleppo, being both energetic and decisive, managed

Malmesbury, No. 42, Aleppo, 30 June 1859; *Irade M.V.*, No. 17600, Gurre Saf. 1275.

[1] F.O. 78/1519, Moore to Bulwer, No. 17, encl. in Moore to Russell, No. 9, Beirut, 24 May 1860; F.O. 78/1538, Skene to Bulwer, No. 14, encl. in Skene to Russell, No. 26, Aleppo, 12 May 1860.

[2] F.O. 78/1454, Brant to Bulwer, No. 22, encl. in Brant to Malmesbury, Damascus, 20 June 1859; F.O. 78/1452, Skene to Bulwer, separate, encl. in Skene to Malmesbury, No. 42, Aleppo, 30 June 1859; F.O. 78/1538, Skene to Bulwer, No. 14, encl. in Skene to Russell, No. 26, Aleppo, 12 May 1860.

[3] *Irade M.M.*, No. 864/2, 19 Saf. 1276; *Irade D.*, No. 30429, 22 Z 1276; F.O. 78/1519, Moore to Bulwer, No. 17, 12 May 1860.

[4] F.O. 78/1383, Finn to Malmesbury, No. 35, Jerusalem, 23 Dec. 1858; F.O. 78/1521, Finn to Dufferin, 14 Nov. 1860, encl. in Finn to Russell, No. 46, Jerusalem, 23 Nov. 1860; A.E. Damas, vi, from Outrey, No. 114, 23 Mar. 1861; CM/063d. No. 513a, from Sanreczki, Jerusalem, June 1860–Jan. 1861.

[5] Ibid., F.O. and CM. dispatches; also, F.O. 78/1520, Brant to Bulwer, encl. in Brant to Russell, No. 10, Damascus, 28 July 1860.

[6] A.E. Jérusalem, vi, from de Barrère, No. 9, 20 July 1858; F.O. 78/1383, Finn to Malmesbury, No. 35, Jerusalem, 23 Oct. 1858; F.O. 78/1521, Finn to Russell, No. 1, Jerusalem, 4 Jan. 1860.

to keep the *paşalik* in tolerable order with barely 2,000 regular soldiers.[1] Furthermore, the Turkish authorities in both Aleppo and Jerusalem took precautions in June–July 1860 against Muslim agitators and firmly employed their garrisons to preserve peace and to avoid calamity.[2]

In Lebanon and Damascus, however, events followed a different course: their respective governors, Hurşid and Ahmed, bitterly complained, on the eve of the massacres, that their military forces were insufficient.[3] This claim was not entirely groundless: according to the English Consul-General Moore, the regular army in both these *eyalet*s numbered, on the outbreak of the 1860 events, some 4,000 regular soldiers. Of this number 1,500 *Nizam* troops (and the same amount of irregulars) were stationed in the *paşalık* of Damascus, but the garrison in the city of Damascus comprised only one battalion of infantry, whereas the main portion of the army was stationed in the neighbourhood of Houran to protect the area against the Bedouin tribes.[4] The rest of the regular force was distributed in Lebanon in units of 200 to 600 soldiers in the areas where the disturbances took place, while under Hurşid's immediate command there were only 750 *Nizam* and 1,000 undisciplined irregulars.[5]

The sparse deployment of the army on the eve of the outbreaks in Lebanon and Damascus, presumably failed to deter, and even encouraged the rioters in both areas to launch their attack on the Christians. Moreover, once the disturbances broke out, both Hurşid and Ahmed refrained from employing their troops, however limited they were, to stop the assault at the start, as had been done by Pashas in other parts of the country. That omission no doubt

[1] F.O. 78/1452, Skene to Bulwer, separate, encl. in Skene to Malmesbury, No. 42, Aleppo, 30 June 1859; F.O. 78/1538, Skene to Bulwer, No. 14, encl. in Skene to Russell, No. 26, Aleppo, 26 May 1860.

[2] F.O. 78/1557, Skene to Bulwer, No. 21, encl. in Skene to Russell, No. 36, Aleppo, 28 June 1860; F.O. 78/1521, Finn to Bulwer, No. 23, encl. in Finn to Russell, No. 14, Jerusalem, 19 June 1860.

[3] See letter of Hurşid Paşa, the *vali* of Beirut, to the Grand Vezir, of 13 ZA 1276, in F.O. 78/1557, Bulwer to Russell, No. 366, Therapia, 2 July 1860. As for the *vali* of Damascus, see above, p. 52, n. 2.

[4] F.O. 78/1557, Brant to Bulwer, separate, 30 June 1860, encl. in Brant to Russell, No. 7, 2 July 1860. But according to the Austrian consul in Damascus, 5,000 troops both regulars and irregulars were stationed in the city; see Madden, ii. 327.

[5] F.O. 78/1519, Moore to Russell, No. 29, Beirut, 6 Aug. 1860; Madden, ii. 290–2.

ruled out the only chance of avoiding the massacres,[1] for a handful of soldiers who did make some attempts to drive back the attacking mob in Damascus were able to halt the slaughter for a while.[2] But on the whole the military force in both Lebanon and Damascus, which was 'mostly composed of natives of the province',[3] remained either passive during the events, or lent a hand in one way or another to the Druze and Muslim rioters.[4]

The conduct of these troops and their officers was certainly a 'bloodstain on the honour of the Ottoman army' and it constituted a source of deep disappointment for the liberal elements within the *Porte*.[5] However, the *Porte* itself was not completely exempt from responsibility for these massacres in view of its dangerous practice of depleting the *Nizam* in the Syrian provinces during the critical years of 1858–60, and of employing among the troops Syrian Muslim soldiers.

Yet what the *Porte* ignored and failed to see before the massacres it tried to amend afterwards. Immediately following the events in Damascus more than 20,000 troops, mostly well-equipped and well-trained, arrived in Syria bringing the total military force in the country to about 30,000.[6] At that stage the Ottoman authorities seemed determined to support their rule and introduce reforms into Syria by a big army and through tighter military control. As Faud Paşa declared before leaving the country in June 1861: 'Since the control of all places has been completed by a sufficient

[1] Cf. F.O. 78/1520, Brant to Russell, No. 8, Damascus, 16 July 1860. See also M. Mishāqa, *al-Jawāb ʿalā iqtirāḥ al-aḥbāb* (MS. 956. 9, A.U.B.), pp. 352–3.

[2] Ibid.; F.O. 78/1586, 'Translation of a Testimonial signed by the leading Christians in Damascus in favour of Colonel Saleh Zeki Bey, received 3 June 1861', in F.O. 78/1586, Moore to Bulwer, No. 24, encl. in Moore to Russell, No. 6, Beirut, 7 June 1861. See also *Irade M.V.*, No. 19910/3, 7 C 1277.

[3] F.O. 78/1520, Brant to Bulwer, 18 July, encl. in Brant to Russell, No. 10, 28 July 1860. Compare above, p. 52, n. 5, and *Irade D.*, No. 25812, 16 R 1274.

[4] With regard to Lebanon, see Lyall, p. 108; Khazin, ii. 132, 136–7; *Ḥasr al-lithām*, pp. 211 ff.; F.O. 78/1519, Moore to Russell, No. 25, Beirut, 28 July 1860; A.E. Damas, vi, No. 86, 19 June 1860; see also 'Sentences of Hurshid and Tahir Pashas' in F.O. 78/1627, Dufferin reports. As for Damascus, see, for instance, F.O. 78/1157, Brant to Moore, 10 June 1860, encl. in Moore to Russell, No. 20, Beirut, 13 July 1860; A.E. Damas, vi, No. 88, 17 July 1860; Edwards, p. 178; see also below, a chapter on the 1860 events in Damascus.

[5] Cevdet, *Tezakir*, ii. 110–11; Khāzin, ii. 172; Farley, *Turkey*, p. 37.

[6] *Irade D.*, No. 30745, Gurre RA 1277; al-Bayṭār, i. 267; Edwards, p. 370; F.O. 78/1586, Rogers to Bulwer, No. 39, encl. in Rogers to Russell, No. 25, Damascus, 9 Sept. 1861.

military power, it is apparent that henceforth the peace of the kingdom shall not be disturbed.'[1]

B. *The Irregular Troops*

'Eski hamam eski tas.' ['old bath—old bowl'][2]
(A Turkish proverb)

Unlike the regular army which was the chief instrument of government and reform in Syria, the irregular forces, operating in the country during the period 1840–61, proved to be one of the major obstacles to stability and change. For though the Ottomans managed to replace the old Janissary corps by a modern and generally reliable army, they failed to abolish other military organizations, which had been in the past, along with the Janissaries, the forces supporting local groups and interests and creating grave disturbances and bloodshed.[3] A number of these forces were in fact re-established in Syria during the Tanzimat era, nominally to help the *vali* who, having no control over the *Nizam*, needed such assistance in order to administer his *paşalık* properly. But, owing to their composition and the way in which they were organized and behaved, such assistance was, as in the past, more of a liability than an asset.

The irregular troops, generally called *zaptiye* (gendarmerie), and composed of cavalrymen (*süvari*) and infantry (*piyade*), were employed as a police force and as auxiliaries of the *Nizam* in both the towns and the countryside in numbers which did not exceed 2,000 men in each *eyalet*.[4] Those posted in the cities were called *tüfekci*s (riflemen) and acted as municipal police; their duties were to maintain order, guard city gates and public buildings, imprison and punish criminals, and also to carry messages among government

[1] F.O. 78/1605, 'Translation of a public Arabic printed notice', in Kayat to Russell, No. 11, Jaffa, 19 June 1861; *Irade D.*, No. 31753/3, 13 Z 1277.

[2] 'There has been no change, all is as it was before, or: you must not expect anything new in an old . . . institution.' See P. Wittek, *Turkish* (London, 1956), p. 19, n. 5.

[3] On the military organizations in Syria in the eighteenth century and their role in political life, see Gibb and Bowen, i. 192 ff., 218 ff.; Shamir, *The 'Azm*, pp. 223 ff.; Bodman, pp. 23–24.

[4] See *Cevdet Z.*, No. 1509, year 1259; *Irade M.V.*, No. 15122, 11 CA 1272. In 1850 the total number of the irregular troops in all Syrian provinces amounted to 5,000 men. See A.E. Damas, ii, No. 3, 25 Feb. 1850.

departments.[1] However, not in every city and town did this police force in fact fulfil its tasks satisfactorily. In cities like Aleppo and Beirut the police forces were usually well organized and were able to maintain security and order over long periods of time.[2] But in Damascus and Jerusalem, where the police was generally corrupt and inefficient, there was a considerable amount of violence.[3] In Damascus, for example, some of the *tufekci başıs* (Heads of Police), being Turkish, were unfamiliar with the local conditions; and others were themselves involved in various illegal activities. One chief of police in Damascus was implicated in a murder while another in Jerusalem was known to be the head of the local burglars.[4]

The troops that were employed in the countryside were usually called *başıbozuks* (empty heads) or sometimes by the old name *deli* (mad).[5] Their major duties were to collect taxes in the villages, garrison forts and guard-houses, escort caravans such as the Ḥajj, and generally protect the countryside from Bedouin ravages.[6] But the manner in which these troops performed their tasks was generally harmful to the population and disadvantageous to the authorities. This was partly because of the undisciplined character of the *başıbozuk* force but mainly because of its irregular methods of recruitment, management, and maintenance.

The ordinary type of *başıbozuk*, usually a man from the dregs of society, was neither recruited directly by the government nor

[1] See examples in *Cevdet Z.*, No. 2897, year 1265; ibid., No. 3747, 15 B 1267; Finn, i. 349.

[2] See *Irade M.V.*, No. 17203/5, 16 L 1274; ibid., No. 17507/3, 29 Z 1275; F.O. 195/207, Werry to Canning, No. 2, Aleppo, 14 Feb. 1846; F.O. 195/302, Werry to Canning, No. 1, Aleppo, 2 Feb. 1850; Farley, *Syria*, p. 50. See also Taoutel, iii. 154–5, 158, 169.

[3] See F.O. 78/447, Wood to Aberdeen, No. 33, Damascus, 20 Nov. 1841; F.O. 195/210, Young to Canning, No. 4, Jerusalem, 30 Jan. 1844; F.O. 78/782, Wood to Palmerston, No. 5, Damascus, 22 Jan. 1851; see also F.O. 78/1588, Finn to Russell, No. 7, Jerusalem, 1 Mar. 1861; compare MacFarlane, i. 28, 81; Midhat, pp. 181–2.

[4] Finn, i. 356; see also *Irade M.V.*, No. 7787, 4 RA 1268; F.O. 78/872, Wood to Palmerston, No. 5, Damascus, 22 Jan. 1851; see also *Cevdet D.*, No. 5600, R 1274.

[5] F.O. 195/292, Finn to Canning, No. 11, Jerusalem, 12 Apr. 1849; Finn, i. 350. The old term *deli* (see Gibb and Bowen, i. 218), although abolished by Mahmud II, was used in Syria for some time during the 1840s; A.E. Alep, i, from Guys, No. 70, 16 Nov. 1841; Melek Hanum, pp. 64–65.

[6] *Cevdet Z.*, No. 3747, 15 B 1261; *Irade M.V.*, No. 3560, 20 Saf. 1265; *Irade D.*, No. 2117/3, 29 CA 1257; Taoutel, iii. 139; *Rambles*, pp. 64, 295; Walpole, i. 185.

employed under the command of a Turkish officer. He was, instead, hired by the leader of a group of mercenaries, known as *sergerde*, *ağa*, or *delibaşı*,[1] normally a military adventurer who offered his services to the government and received in payment a certain sum out of which he then paid his troops and covered all other expenses. But since he had to buy his nomination from the authorities, usually by means of bribery,[2] the *ağa* would in fact reduce the number of his troops considerably in order to recover his expenses by means of his pay list.[3]

The soldiers themselves were under-paid and ill-fed; and since they had to supply their own arms and equipment, they were also ill-dressed and badly armed.[4] Consequently, while carrying out their functions in the villages, the *başıbozuk*s would force the peasants to feed them and their animals and occasionally used to rob and assault their unprotected hosts.[5] But when confronted with armed brigands or powerful Bedouin, the irregular troops either were often defeated or preferred to withdraw.[6] In some cases the *başıbozuk*s would make Bedouin tribes their secret allies so that both parties could sack the villages in co-operation.[7] Moreover, not only were these irregular troops ineffective and oppressive, but they would occasionally also revolt against the Turkish authorities themselves on grounds of ill-payment.[8]

Another type of irregular force was one whose members were drawn from the warriors of semi-nomadic tribes or local minority groups. Such groups included Bedouin and Turkoman nomads,

[1] For the use of *sergerde*, see, for example, *Cevdet Z.*, No. 2897, year 1265. On the title of *ağa*, see EI². The old title of *delibaşı* was often used in the Tanzimat period; see, for example, *Irade M.V.*, No. 14648/54, 27 Z 1271; *Rambles*, pp. 64–65. [2] See, for example, *Irade M.V.*, No. 14648/54, 27 Z 1271.

[3] Finn, i. 167, 395, 399; *Rambles*, p. 65; F.O. 78/1389, Skene to Bulwer, No. 31, encl. in Skene to Malmesbury, No. 42, Aleppo, 18 Sept. 1858.

[4] An irregular soldier was paid about 70 Kuruş a month. *Cevdet Z.*, No. 1603, Tişrin II, 1277; see also Finn, i. 167–70.

[5] Ibid.; F.O. 78/959, Wood to Clarendon, No. 43, Damascus, 4 Aug. 1853; F.O. 78/1118, Barker to Redcliffe, No. 12, encl. in Barker to Clarendon, No. 7, Aleppo, 27 Mar. 1855.

[6] *Rambles*, p. 64; F.O. 78/959, Wood to Redcliffe, No. 40, encl. in Wood to Clarendon, No. 43, Damascus, 4 Aug. 1853; F.O. 78/1383, Finn to Malmesbury, No. 20, Jerusalem, 28 Sept. 1858; F.O. 78/1452, Skene to Bulwer, No. 42, encl. in Skene to Russell, No. 77, Aleppo, 26 Nov. 1859.

[7] F.O. 78/1586, Rogers to Bulwer, No. 37, encl. in Rogers to Russell, No. 24, Damascus, 26 Aug. 1861.

[8] F.O. 195/194, Rose to Canning, No. 25, Beirut, 21 Mar. 1842; F.O. 78/1032, Finn to Clarendon, No. 2, Jerusalem, 8 Feb. 1854.

Druze and Mutawali mountaineers, as well as Kurds and North Africans from Syrian towns and villages.[1] These forces were usually employed under their own chiefs in their respective areas to protect the roads and to check Bedouin raids across the desert border. They were on the whole quite effective in performing their duties,[2] but most of them became so powerful in the course of the service that they often constituted a serious threat to the authority of the government. Thus, for example, when certain Kurdish irregular officers were discharged from the service, they became highwaymen and thus forced the authorities to reappoint them in order to restore order.[3] Similar positions were attained by Druze and Mutawali chiefs, like Shiblī al-ʿAryān of Jabal Druze and certain Ḥarfush Amirs from Baʿalbek, who served at times as heads of irregular troops comprised of their own followers.[4] Such appointments would, of course, encourage the autonomous tendencies of these mountain people and occasionally give them an advantage *vis-à-vis* the authorities.[5] In addition, the fact that these irregular bodies were made up of various minority groups sometimes promoted intercommunal feuds on religious or sectional grounds. In this manner, frequent hostilities prevailed between Kurdish and Druze mercenaries or between Druze and Mutawali warriors, which involved also their respective communities.[6] Likewise feuds broke out from time to time between Bedouin irregulars and Kurdish or Druze troops.[7] At the same time, both Druze and Kurdish mercenaries would often use their position to oppress local non-Muslim inhabitants.[8]

[1] See, for example, *Cevdet Z.*, No. 2703, Kanun II, 1277. On Bedouin bodies of irregular troops, see below, the chapter on the Bedouin, pp. 130 ff.

[2] See F.O. 78/447, Werry to Ponsonby, No. 5, Aleppo, 6 May 1841; F.O. 78/536, Rose to Aberdeen, No. 42, Beirut, 6 May 1843.

[3] F.O. 78/1586, Rogers to Bulwer, No. 44, encl. in Rogers to Russell, No. 27, Damascus, 18 Nov. 1861; see also F.O. 78/579, Wood to Aberdeen, No. 19, Damascus, 6 June 1844.

[4] F.O. 78/1028, Wood to Clarendon, No. 13, Damascus, 27 Feb. 1854; F.O. 78/447, Werry to Palmerston, No. 8, Damascus, 17 Apr. 1841; F.O. 78/456, Rose to Palmerston, No. 72, Gazir, 23 July 1841.

[5] See below, the relevant sections on the government in Anti-Lebanon and Jabal Druze, pp. 111–13, 123–8.

[6] F.O. 78/959, Wood to Rose, encl. in Wood to Malmesbury, Damascus, 15 Jan. 1853; F.O. 78/1028, Wood to Redcliffe, No. 13, encl. in Wood to Clarendon, No. 22, Damascus, 13 Apr. 1854.

[7] *Irade M.M.*, No. 398/20, 6 Ş 1273; Manṣūr, p. 74.

[8] F.O. 78/447, Wood to Aberdeen, No. 3, Damascus, 3 Nov. 1841; F.O. 78/959. Wood to Clarendon, No. 38, Damascus, 16 July 1853.

Finally, the most violent and turbulent irregulars, although excellent soldiers, were the Albanian mercenaries. When they were brought to Syria in the early 1840s, these troops committed grave outrages against the local population and occasionally rebelled against the authorities.[1] Their misbehaviour reached such a degree that it provoked a counter-attack from the oppressed population of Aleppo in 1841, and led the government to dissolve the corps in 1844–5.[2] But when the Crimean War broke out and the *Nizam* withdrew, the Albanian troops returned to Syria and renewed their violence.[3]

Indeed, the Turkish authorities in Syria made many efforts to reduce the number of all irregular troops in their pay, or to reform them. But the frequent depletion of the *Nizam*, particularly during the Crimean War, forced the government to increase again the number of irregulars;[4] and the series of reorganizations which were carried out among the *başıbozuk*s proved a failure. Thus, for example, up to 1857 the number of irregular troops in Syria was twice reduced, in 1843 and 1856,[5] and twice plans for a general reorganization were carried through, in 1845 and 1853–4,[6] but without noticeable improvement. Between 1857 and 1859 further measures were introduced and a new force was set up under the fresh name *avniye* (auxiliaries), which was largely composed of local Arabs—peasants, townsmen, and Bedouin.[7] To avoid corruption, these soldiers were to receive their salaries directly from the treasury rather than through their officers. The officers themselves were changed, given new uniforms and new military titles, and were placed under the command of the regular army.[8]

[1] See *Irade D.*, No. 1638, 7 M 1257; *Cevdet D.*, No. 15294, 21 B 1259; F.O. 78/498, Wood to Aberdeen, No. 29, Damascus, 29 Mar. 1842.

[2] Kāmil al-Ghazzī, *Nahr al-dhahab fī ta'rīkh Ḥalab* (Aleppo, A.H. 1342–5), ii. 364–5.

[3] F.O. 78/959, Wood to Redcliffe, No. 40, encl. in Wood to Clarendon, No. 43, Damascus, 4 Aug. 1853.

[4] See, for example, F.O. 78/1033, Werry to Redcliffe, No. 17, encl. in Werry to Clarendon, No. 10, Aleppo, 13 June 1854.

[5] F.O. 195/207, Werry to Canning, No. 4, Aleppo, 11 Mar. 1843; F.O. 78/1220, Barker to Redcliffe, No. 40, encl. in Barker to Clarendon, No. 16, Aleppo, 10 Dec. 1856.

[6] F.O. 195/207, Werry to Canning, No. 9, Aleppo, 12 Apr. 1845; *Irade M.V.*, No. 9481/2, Selh Saf. 1269; F.O. 78/959, Wood to Clarendon, No. 43, Damascus, 4 Aug. 1853; Jaffa *Sijill*, No. 18, 12 CA 1271; Finn, i. 166–7.

[7] Compare *Cevdet Z.*, No. 2703, Kanun II, 1277.

[8] F.O. 78/1297, Barker to Redcliffe, No. 8, encl. in Barker to Clarendon,

The new *avniye*, however, soon proved to be no better than the old *başıbozuks*. The actual size of the force was much smaller than had been designed and its soldiers were again unreliable, corrupt, and oppressive.[1] Moreover, the fact that many of the *avniye*'s recruits were local Muslim Arabs, was highly significant in view of the Muslim–Christian tension during that period: in the course of the 1860 events, the new irregular force was, indeed, one of the chief participants in the massacre of Christians in both Lebanon and Damascus.[2]

Here again the Ottoman authorities hurried to repair a mistake which they had overlooked or ignored before: in the early 1860s the *avniye* was revised again and placed within the framework of the *Nizam*, and subjected to military discipline.[3]

C. *The civil service*

> 'The servants of the state should be superior to the mass of the people in ability and competence. But if there is no recompense . . . only mediocrities (will) carry on the business of the state . . .' (Cevdet Paşa)[4]
>
> 'Balık Baştan Kokar.' ['Fish begins to stink at the head']
> (A Turkish proverb)

The transformation of the Ottoman Empire during the reform era from a quasi-feudal into a modern centralized state, substantially increased the need for a well-trained and highly reliable civil service in the provinces to carry out the vast administrative

No. 5, Aleppo, 28 Apr. 1857; *Cevdet Z.*, No. 2636, 23 M 1275; *Irade M.V.*, No. 17600/1, Gurre Saf. 1275; compare MacFarlane, ii. 327.

[1] F.O. 78/1389, Skene to Bulwer, No. 31, encl. in Skene to Malmesbury, No. 42, Aleppo, 18 Sept. 1858; F.O. 78/1454, Brant to Bulwer, No. 22, encl. in Brant to Malmesbury, Damascus, 20 June 1859.

[2] F.O. 78/1519, Moore to Russell, No. 25, Beirut, 28 July 1860; ibid., 'copy of a letter from a Turkish Muslim in Damascus', in Moore to Russell, No. 27, Beirut, 4 Aug. 1860; F.O. 78/1625, Revd. Robson's report, in Dufferin to Russell, No. 9, Beirut, 23 Sept. 1860; compare also: 'Extraits du dossier de la procédure des personnes qui ont commis de crimes pendant les événements de Damas 1860', in F.O. 78/1628.

[3] *Irade D.*, 1277, No. 30683, 18 Saf. 1277; F.O. 78/1586, Rogers to Bulwer, No. 37, encl. in Rogers to Russell, No. 24, Damascus, 26 Aug. 1861; Manṣūr, p. 78.

[4] TOEM No. 43 (A.H. 1333), p. 103, cited in Lewis, *Emergence*, p. 383.

changes. Similarly, while the presence of an adequate armed force was required as a sanction behind the provincial government, the maintenance of the Ottoman authority and the day-to-day management of the *eyalet* depended almost entirely upon able and competent officials. Moreover, the introduction of the unpopular and controversial reforms of the Tanzimat was impossible without the assistance of a solid cadre of enlightened functionaries, entirely devoted to the cause of reform. In short, the civil service, which was assigned to lay the foundation of the new order in the Ottoman provinces, required three groups of qualities, namely, honesty and integrity, intelligence and efficiency, devotion and enlightenment. The creation of such a service was, however, an appallingly difficult task for the reform movement, since the Ottoman officialdom of the pre-reform era was known to possess quite the opposite qualities: the corruption, inefficiency, and cynicism of the old unsalaried civil service had taken such root that these vices had ceased to be regarded as immoral and had become rather second nature.[1]

Mahmud II, the first Sultan to tackle the problem of the civil service (*mülkiye*), made a considerable effort to raise the standards of his officials with regard both to their proficiency and honesty. He granted them regular salaries, abolished the office of confiscation and escheat, and set up a system of secular schools to train public servants.[2]

Under the rule of Sultan Abdülmecid, attempts to root out corruption and to raise efficiency were continued by a series of decrees and laws. The Sultan's first reform edict, the *Hatt-ı Şerif*, strongly denounced bribery, describing it as contradictory to the Holy Law and as one of the major causes of the Empire's destruction. To combat it the *hat* stated that any public servant who broke the law should be punished, regardless of rank; it urged also that the salaries of all Ottoman officials should be regulated. Legal regulations following the *hat* confirmed these declarations, and in December 1839 the Ottoman government decreed that, from March 1840, public officials were to be paid fixed salaries and to be promoted only according to merit.[3] Likewise

[1] Compare Gibb and Bowen, i. 207; Davison, *Reform*, pp. 34–35.

[2] See above, p. 3.

[3] F.O. 78/360, Ponsonby to Palmerston, No. 346, 31 Dec. 1839, in Bailey, p. 198; MacFarlane, ii. 41–42.

the Penal Code of May 1840 dealt in a rather elaborate way with offences and misuse of powers by public servants making them liable to heavy punishment.[1]

But in actuality all these decrees and laws remained dead letters; the authorities continued to pay their civil servants irregular salaries, and the latter did not cease to be corrupt. Indeed, seventeen years after the promulgation of the Gülhane edict, the *Hatt-ı Hümayun* of 1856 demanded again that 'there should begin a regular payment of the salaries which have been allocated to each official'; and a year earlier, at the beginning of 1855, a special criminal code was issued to deal with the corruption in the civil service.[2] Nor were the *mülkiye* schools more successful in carrying out the role originally laid down for them: there continued to be throughout the Empire a serious shortage of trained and honest officials.[3]

All these shortcomings and defects affected, of course, government administration in Syria too, but here there was an additional problem. In other Ottoman provinces the basis of the new public service had been already laid down by Mahmud II in the 1820s; in Syria there were no such foundations, and in 1840, after the Ottoman restoration, it was necessary to make an entirely new start. The Turkish authorities, although at that stage helped to some extent by previous Egyptian experience in various areas of administration,[4] did not employ the officials of the former régime. Most of these withdrew with Ibrāhīm and the remainder, or some at least, were discharged by the new rulers.[5] To replace them, a considerable number of senior officials were imported into Syria from

[1] See paras. 95–111, 152–3 of the Penal Code in Bucknill and Utidjian, pp. 74–86, 112–13.

[2] See, '*mani irtikâba dair ceza kanunnamesi*' (Istanbul, 10 CA 1271).

[3] Lewis, *Emergence*, pp. 368, 381; Davison, *Reform*, p. 140; Engelhardt, i. 80.

[4] One field, for instance, was the system of levying the *ferde*; see letter from Namık Paşa, *serasker* of Syria, to his government in *Irade M.V.*, No. 1201, Selh M 1261; A.E. Alep, i, from Guys, No. 68, 16 Oct. 1841; F.O. 195/207, Werry to Canning, No. 2, Aleppo, 21 May 1842. Another field was the organization of the *meclis*; see below, p. 91. According to al-Bāshā, the Ottoman government decided on its return to Syria to follow the example of the Egyptian reforms, and was assisted by Egyptian experts for this purpose; see al-Bāshā, p. 216. On the general impact of the Egyptian reform movement on Turkey, see Mardin, pp. 191–2.

[5] See, for example, Jaffa *Sijill*, No. 13, 27 Ş 1256; see also F.O. 78/447, Werry to Ponsonby, No. 1, encl. in Werry to Palmerston, No. 1, Damascus, 21 Jan. 1841.

Istanbul and other centres in the Empire,[1] and substantial efforts were made to provide a regular payment of salaries to local officials in accordance with the recent decrees.[2] But the faults of the newly established administrative machinery soon appeared. For one thing, not only was there a big gap between the salaries of the senior and the junior officials, but whereas the former received their pay fairly regularly, the latter continued to be paid in a most haphazard way.[3] This made a large number of public servants more than ever prone to accept bribes and misuse their powers (or prefer to resign from government service);[4] and among governors of *sancak*s and *kaza*s such dishonesty was very common, and led to frequent changes of *kaymakam*s and *müdir*s.[5] At the same time the enormous wages paid to the *vali*s and other senior officials, while constituting a big drain on the treasury, in no way reduced their corruption.[6] On the contrary, it seems that corruption now became more extreme than during the pre-reform era, because the Pasha no longer feared arbitrary execution and confiscation of his property.[7] Nor was this the limit; corruption and venality were not confined to the level of provincial governors, but reached also the ministerial one, and in this respect there was almost no difference between reformist and conservative ministers and liberal and traditional *vali*s.[8]

Mustafa Reşid Paşa and a few prominent officials of both parties formed perhaps an exception. Reşid, being personally concerned with the low moral standards of the civil servants, used every method to bring about the penetration of the new principles of public service into the *mülkiye*.[9] On the one hand, he harshly

[1] *Mühimme*, No. 254, p. 88, Evahir N 1256, *Ceride-i Havadis*, No. 27, 4 Ş 1257; *Irade D.*, No. 1402, 16 ZA 1256.

[2] Ibid., No. 1832, 9 R 1257; *Irade M.V.*, No. 1388, 2 M 1262; F.O. 78/499, Wood to Aberdeen, No. 56, Damascus, 20 July 1842.

[3] *Irade M.V.*, No. 17321/16 and 21, 14 ZA and Gurre Z 1274.

[4] Ibid., No. 12830, 10 Ş 1270; ibid., No. 14706, 14 M 1272; cf. F.O. 78/392, Ponsonby to Palmerston, No. 96, 3 Mar. 1840 in Bailey, p. 198.

[5] *Irade M.V.*, No. 17321/16 and 21, 14 ZA and Gurre Z 1274; ibid., No. 19508/6, 14 ZA 1277; F.O. 78/622, Wood to Canning, No. 13, encl. in Wood to Aberdeen, No. 21, Damascus, 24 June 1845.

[6] Barker, ii. 309–11; MacFarlane, i. 106; ii. 42; Urquhart, ii. 367. On the scale of salaries see Ubicini, i. 292; F.O. 78/499, Wood to Aberdeen, No. 56, Damascus, 20 July 1852.

[7] Cf. F.O. 78/437, Moore to Redcliffe, No. 48, Beirut, 2 Sept. 1854; see also Lewis, *Emergence*, p. 102.

[8] Ibid.; MacFarlane, ii. 44–45, 137–9.

[9] Engelhardt, i. 29, 39, 42; Temperley claims, however, that Reşid was personally corrupt; p. 158.

punished functionaries who were involved in corruption;[1] on the other hand, he privately appealed to his followers' sense of responsibility to the common cause of reform and urged them not to accept bribes. Thus, when in 1844 Kıbrıslı Paşa was nominated by the conservative cabinet to a governorship in Palestine, his protector Reşid, who was then in disfavour, summoned him and he begged: 'Vous allez en Arabie n'acceptez, je vous en prie, jamais de présent'.[2] Indeed, Kıbrıslı did not accept presents and acted with great integrity and competence during his two terms of office in Palestine and Syria.[3] (But his wife received the presents which he rejected, and she also engaged in the commercial activities not permitted to public servants, with Kıbrıslı's tacit approval.)[4]

Apart from Kıbrıslı Paşa (who became Grand Vezir in 1853), two or three other Pashas who served in Syria in the course of the 1840s were apparently just and honest, and there were two or three other senior officials of this sort in the 1850s.[5] But these, as well as perhaps a small number of others, were by no means representative and certainly could not dispel the general atmosphere of rapacity that prevailed and the increased use of *bahşiş* (tip, bribe).

The provincial Pasha, it is true, no longer needed to buy his appointment from Istanbul as in the past, but he did sometimes have to bribe certain officials in the *Porte* in order to secure or maintain his nomination.[6] In return the Pasha would accept bribes and presents from subordinate officials or local individuals who wished to gain his goodwill or to be nominated for a certain government post.[7] The junior civil servants, who were ill-paid

[1] Farley, *Turkey*, p. 24; Engelhardt, i. 29; Temperley, p. 239.

[2] Kibrizli, p. 55 (Melek Hanum, p. 67).

[3] Melek Hanum, p. 68; Finn, i. 453; A.E. Jérusalem, ii, from Jorelle, No. 29, 14 Mar. 1847; F.O. 195/302, Werry to Canning, No. 20, Aleppo, 10 May 1851. But according to another source Kıbrıslı was held responsible (by Midhat Paşa who was sent to Syria in 1851 as inspector) for some irregularities in the *paşalık*s of Aleppo and Damascus; see Midhat, p. 32.

[4] Melek Hanum, pp. 68, 71–75, 84.

[5] For instance Safveti Paşa, the *vali* of Damascus in 1846–8, who belonged to the conservative group; A.E. Damas, ii, from Borbie, No. 13, 23 May 1848; F.O. 195/226, Wood to Canning, No. 12, Damascus, 2 Sept. 1846; see also, F.O. 78/959, Wood to Redcliffe, No. 48, encl. in Wood to Clarendon, No. 56, Damascus, 11 Oct. 1853; Finn, ii. 453–4.

[6] Barker, ii. 309; MacFarlane, ii. 42.

[7] *Irade M.V.*, No. 14648/54, 27 Z 1271; F.O. 78/447, Wood to Aberdeen, No. 30, Damascus, 4 Nov. 1844; F.O. 78/1296, Kayat to Clarendon, separate, Jaffa, 3 July 1857.

and who had sometimes to bribe their superiors, exploited every possibility of extorting money from the population. Thus almost the whole administration of the province—from the Governor-General, lieutenant governors, *defterdar*s, military officers, to tax-collectors, chiefs of irregular troops, and many others—was engaged in corruption in one way or another.[1]

The central government was of course aware of this degree of corruption in the Syrian provinces and constantly tried to check it; it kept dispatching to the Syrian *vali*s strong firmans against bribery, venality, and embezzlement.[2] In 1841 and 1850, for example, all public servants throughout Syria were obliged to take a solemn oath on their respective sacred books never to accept bribes or gifts or to show any partiality in the performance of their duties.[3] But decrees and ceremonies were useless; and the central government therefore set up a system of inspection which operated in several different ways. Firstly, the *Porte* would occasionally send officials to examine the state of affairs in Syria the conduct of governmental functionaries in the various *paşalık*s.[4] Secondly, there was a fairly frequent flow of functionaries sent by their respective ministries in Istanbul to check specific matters such as accounts, or the position of the army.[5] Thirdly, some of these functionaries received secret instructions to investigate matters outside their official missions;[6] and fourthly, special commissions were set up from time to time—as in 1845—to survey

[1] For a few selected evidences, see *Ceride-i Havadis*, No. 107, 4 N 1258; *Mühimme*, No. 256, p. 47, Evahir Ş 1261; *Irade M.M.*, No. 412/50, 9 Z 1273; *Irade M.V.*, No. 16751/8, 6 R 1274; F.O. 78/444, Young to Palmerston, No. 28, Jaffa, 19 Sept. 1841; F.O. 78/872, Wood to Palmerston, No. 6, Damascus, 29 Jan. 1851; F.O. 78/1217, Barker to Redcliffe, No. 8, encl. in Barker to Clarendon, No. 5, Aleppo, 28 Apr. 1857; Bazili, ii. 5; Finn, i. 453; Paton, p. 206.

[2] *Irade D.*, No. 2117/4, 29 CA 1257; *Irade H.*, No. 468/4, 3 Nisan 1258; *Mühimme*, No. 250, p. 47, Evahir Ş 1261; F.O. 195/207, Werry to Canning, No. 4, Aleppo, 4 Apr. 1846.

[3] Al-Bāshā, p. 245; F.O. 78/836, Moore to Palmerston, No. 12, Beirut, 28 Feb. 1850; F.O. 78/837, Wood to Palmerston, No. 3, Damascus, 6 Mar. 1850.

[4] *Irade M.M.*, No. 813, 19 N 1276; F.O. 78/538, Wood to Aberdeen, No. 39, Damascus, 6 Nov. 1843.

[5] *Irade D.*, No. 24204, 22 CA 1273; F.O. 78/714, Timoni to Palmerston, No. 13, Damascus, 30 June 1857; F.O. 78/538, Wood to Aberdeen, No. 39, Damascus, 6 Nov. 1843.

[6] See examples in F.O. 78/447, Wood to Bidwell, No. 38, Damascus, 2 Dec. 1841; F.O. 78/1217, Finn to Clarendon, No. 4, Jerusalem, 19 Jan. 1856; *Ceride-i Havadis*, No. 102, Selh B 1258.

the general situation in the provinces and the introduction of reforms, or to inquire into certain mishaps which had taken place.[1] The *meclis*es and local inhabitants in their turn would send reports and petitions to Istanbul and some foreign consuls would notify the *Porte* of various matters, either on their own initiative or at the *Porte*'s request.[2] Thus it would appear that quite a tight system of check and countercheck was in operation; and according to the findings of this inspection, a considerable number of officials of various ranks and posts were indeed dismissed or punished.[3] But at the same time a great many functionaries, particularly of high rank, who were involved in embezzlement and other offences remained unpunished. Being either backed by their inspectors or supported by their protectors in Istanbul they were, if discovered, normally transferred to other posts, sometimes even without returning their illegal gains;[4] and although removed, these corrupt Pashas bequeathed to their successors contempt, loss of influence, and lack of respect on the part of the population.

A further defect in the Ottoman official was lack of all sense of duty, responsibility, and discipline in service to the government,[5] nor were his professional standards very high. In many instances he was ignorant of the local language, habits, and conditions, making it difficult for him to become acquainted with the needs of the population or independently to master the local affairs.[6] The methods of administrative work continued also to follow along

[1] See firman of 7 R 1261 in *Takvim-i Vekayi*, No. 285, 5 R 1261; see also F.O. 78/910, Wood to Malmesbury, No. 40, Damascus, 27 Dec. 1852; Engelhardt, i. 76; MacFarlane, ii. 46.

[2] Cf. Wood's papers, 'Copie d'une Lettre à son excellence Rifat Pasha. . .', Therapia, 23 Apr. 1841. See also F.O. 78/1302, Moore to Clarendon, No. 34, Beirut, Aug. 1854; *Irade M.V.*, No. 16685/2, 13 RA 1274.

[3] *Takvim-i Vekayi*, No. 271, 6 C 1260; *Irade M.V.*, No. 3920, 13 R 1265; *Irade M.M.*, No. 412/50, 9 Z 1273; F.O. 78/836, Wood to Canning, No. 6, encl. in Wood to Palmerston, No. 5, Damascus, 30 Mar. 1850.

[4] F.O. 78/497, Werry to Bidwell, separate, Aleppo, 31 Dec. 1842; F.O. 78/622, Wood to Canning, No. 13, encl. in Wood to Aberdeen, No. 21, Damascus, 24 June 1845; F.O. 78/1297, Skene to Clarendon, No. 15, Aleppo, 11 Aug. 1857; F.O. 78/1521, Finn to Russell, No. 1, Jerusalem, 4 Jan. 1860; cf. MacFarlane, ii. 44–45.

[5] F.O. 78/448, Werry to Bidwell, No. 13, Aleppo, 17 June 1841; F.O. 78/1116, Moore to Redcliffe, No. 22, encl. in Moore to Clarendon, No. 34, Beirut, 14 May 1855; Finn, i. 160, 278–9; ii. 306.

[6] F.O. 78/622, Wood to Canning, No. 13, encl. in Wood to Aberdeen, No. 21, Damascus, 31 May 1845; F.O. 78/1626, Dufferin to Bulwer, No. 40, Beirut, 3 Nov. 1860; Finn, i. 162–4; cf. *al-Jinān* (1871), No. 23, p. 79; Engelhardt, i. 80; MacFarlane, i. 189–90; ii. 144, 153, 166.

the old inefficient lines: for example, the Pasha who was frequently transferred from one post to another would take with him his official papers and his assistants.[1] Here again, all this does not mean that Syria and Palestine were completely devoid of qualified and efficient officials, particularly in the high ranks of administration; in fact the Syrian *paşalık*s occasionally did enjoy the service of some able Pashas who gave these provinces the benefit of good administration.[2] The most distinguished among them were senior officials who filled, in various stages of their careers, ministerial posts in the *Porte*. Three of these, for instance, Izzet, Kıbrıslı, and Fuad, were promoted from their respective Syrian assignments to the Grand Vezirate in 1841, 1853, and 1861 respectively. Three others—Mustafa Nuri, Said, and Kâmil—came to Syria in 1842, 1849, and 1857, after each of them had been holding the office of Minister of War. Three more Pashas—Necib, Safveti, and Mahmud—served as *vali*s of Damascus in 1841–2, 1846–8, and 1855–6 after being previously Minister of Justice, Minister of Finance, and the Foreign Minister respectively.[3]

These series of nominations indicate, of course, the *Porte*'s sincere intentions with regard to the efficient administration of the Syrian provinces, but at the same time it should be noted that some of these officials were sent to Syria during periods of emergency when a vigorous 'troubleshooter' had to be appointed to carry out drastic measures in the country. Thus, for example, after Syria was restored to the *Porte* in 1840–1 and needed to be reorganized, a number of prominent Ottoman officials, including Izzet and Mustafa, were sent there, as already noted. Likewise, when in 1850 a strong man was required to put down the Aleppo revolt and to impose conscription in all Syrian *paşalık*s, Kıbrıslı Paşa was first nominated governor of Aleppo and a year later

[1] Bazili, ii. 13; Finn, i. 161; cf. MacFarlane, ii. 153–4; Davison, *Reform*, p. 138.

[2] *Cevdet D.*, No. 14011, 26 Saf. 1264; *Irade M.V.*, No. 18653/5, 11 CA 1276; F.O. 78/959, Wood to Redcliffe, No. 48, encl. in Wood to Clarendon, No. 56, Damascus, 11 Oct. 1853; F.O. 78/1219, Moore to Clarendon, No. 54, Beirut, 6 Nov. 1856; A.E. Jérusalem, ii, from Jorelle, No. 33, 9 June 1847.

[3] On Necib, see A.E. Damas, i, from Munton, No. 9, 27 Mar. 1841. On Safveti Paşa see Cevdet, *Tezakir*, i. 10; F.O. 78/660A, Wood to Aberdeen, No. 10, Damascus, 10 Apr. 1846. On Mahmud see F.O. 78/1385, Moore to Malmesbury, No. 19, Beirut, 29 Apr. 1858. On Kıbrıslı's career see Cevdet, op. cit., i. 24–26; Melek Hanum, pp. 64 ff., 234 ff.; see also Davison, *Reform*, pp. 103–4. For the careers of Ottoman senior officials, consult Mehmed Süreyya, *Sicill-i Osmani* (Istanbul, A.H. 1308–15).

appointed *serasker* of Syria. Again, after the massacres of 1860, Fuad Paşa was sent to Syria to restore order and peace and to punish the culprits. But in ordinary times the Syrian provinces were governed by mediocrities of the kind mentioned above, owing mainly to the limited number of qualified and able senior officials at the *Porte*'s disposal.

Another category among the prominent officials sent to Syria were politically influential rivals whose nominations to that distant and turbulent country aimed at removing them from the capital and damaging their prestige.[1] As things were, many of these officials belonged, in effect, to the anti-reform group, being removed by the liberal cabinet which was in power during most of the period 1840–61. Among them there were Izzet Paşa who in 1841 became the Grand Vezir in a reactionary cabinet, and Necib Paşa who, according to the French consul, was reported to have taken part in a conservative plot to establish in Syria an anti-reformist centre.[2] Such officials were obviously not keen to introduce reform in their provinces, particularly as far as the rights of the non-Muslim subjects were concerned.[3] And although enlightened Pashas were indeed to be found among the high ranks of the Turkish officialdom in Syria, they needed to possess a remarkably strong will and a firm character to overcome the intense reactionary pressure exerted upon them. Such pressure came in the first place from local bodies like the *meclis* and the 'Ulema, some of which were reported to have been connected with the anti-reform party in Istanbul.[4] In the second place pressure was exercised on the liberal official also from conservative elements in Istanbul, as one Pasha expressed:

> What am I to do? I govern a province and the Grand Vizier sends me an order which is framed on the new ideas that we profess. The Sheik al-Islam complains against me because I do not act upon the old laws, which with him are still sacred. I say the two things are incompatible and I

[1] See Kibrizli, pp. 138, 141–2, 195 (Melek Hanum, pp. 164–5, 168–9); A.E. Damas, i, from Munton, No. 9, 27 Mar. 1842; compare Davison, *Reform*, p. 138; MacFarlane, ii. 164–6.

[2] A.E. Damas, i, from Munton, No. 9, 27 Mar. 1842.

[3] See below, pp. 221–3.

[4] See, for example, F.O. 195/302, Werry to Rose, No. 51, encl. in Werry to Canning, No. 12, Aleppo, 23 Nov. 1850; Khāzin, i. 201; Baedeker, p. 84; compare MacFarlane, ii. 62.

am told I must follow our own usages, but I must give them a new dress. I don't know what I am about.[1]

Under these circumstances it is not surprising that not all the well-intentioned Pashas (and they were not many) were able to carry out the new order in the country. Moreover, if this was the situation in Syrian centres where a considerable degree of the *Porte*'s control did exist, and where the foreign consuls' eyes were widely open to report on any slight maltreatment of Christians or on other miscarriages; in the small towns things were even worse. In these communities junior governors, either Muslim Ottomans of the lower grades or local Arabs, totally ignored the Tanzimat and very often endeavoured to impede progress and nullify the enlightened reforms of Istanbul.[2]

D. *Aspects of the financial administration*

'... a state certainly needs armies and other necessary services in order to preserve its lands; and this is done with money, and money is obtained from the taxes of the subjects. It is therefore very important to deal with it efficiently.'

[From the *Hatt-ı Şerif* of Gülhane]

It has already been indicated that one of the major handicaps to the Ottoman reform movement was the chronic financial difficulty which persisted in the Empire throughout the Tanzimat era and which finally resulted in the bankruptcy and collapse of the 1870s.[3] Syria and Palestine faced during the period 1840–61 the same difficulties which sprang from the permanent deficit in receipts over expenditures. The causes for this situation were to be found mainly in the mismanagement and inefficiency of the financial administration.

To start with, the Ottomans on their return to Syria not only

[1] Madden, ii. 408, quoting Sir H. Bulwer, the British Ambassador in Istanbul.

[2] Cf. *Irade M.V.*, No. 3920, 13 R 1265; F.O. 78/1294, Finn to Clarendon, No. 1, Jerusalem, 1 Jan. 1857 in A. M. Hyamson (ed.), *The British Consulate in Jerusalem* (London, 1939, 1942), i. 245–6; Finn, i. 187; Farley, *Turkey*, pp. 23–24; G. M. Wortabet, *Syria and the Syrians* (London, 1856), ii. 88–89, 135.

[3] See above, p. 28; also Madden, i. 555; MacFarlane, ii. 247–9; F. S. Rodkey, 'Ottoman Concern about western economic penetration in the Levant, 1849–1856', *Journal of Modern History*, 30, No. 4, pp. 348–9.

allowed the former sound economic establishment (already existing in part) to be wasted by venal mishandling, but also failed to use the Egyptian tax-registers for their own needs.[1] Another example can be seen in the way in which the Turks mismanaged the relevying of the much hated *ferde*. Not only had they promised to abolish this tax, and thus provoked wide popular resistance and tax-evasion by its reimposition,[2] but they failed to collect it efficiently and equitably.[3] As a result of all this, tax-arrears amounted over the years to prodigious sums—for example, in the province of Damascus alone, during the years 1841–6, these debts reached the equivalent of two years' tribute; and although subsequently reduced, they were always large especially in times of disorder.[4]

Another major source for the loss of revenue was to be found in the system of tax-farming (*iltizam*) which prevailed in the Syrian provinces throughout the period under survey although officially it had been abolished by successive Imperial firmans.[5] Indeed, the *iltizam*, which was the most widely used system of tax-collection, proved to be disadvantageous both to the treasury and the peasants, while the real gainers were a small group of extortionate tax-farmers (*mültezim*) and their protectors among the public officials. It is true that in a few areas, particularly in Aleppo, the *iltizam* was from time to time farmed out for its real value,[6] while in other places the villages themselves had the option to buy the privilege of collecting their own taxes;[7] and in such places these arrangements apparently served to increase the public revenue and sometimes also to lighten the peasants' burden. But in most areas, notably in the *eyalet*s of Damascus and Sidon, it was usually the case that a *mültezim* would farm the revenue of a certain district for a relatively small sum (although nominally the *iltizam*

[1] F.O. 78/538, Wood to Aberdeen, No. 24, Damascus, 20 July 1843; Bazili, ii. 5.

[2] Al-Jundī, p. 284; F.O. 78/444, Young to Ponsonby, No. 15, Jerusalem, 14 July 1841; F.O. 78/456, Rose to Palmerston, No. 71, Gazir, 23 July 1841.

[3] See below, pp. 183–4.

[4] See F.O. 78/660A, Wood to Canning, No. 4, encl. in Wood to Aberdeen, No. 8, Damascus, 21 Mar. 1846; see also *Irade D.*, No. 3848, 22 C 1259; *Irade M.V.*, No. 2571, 8 M 1264.

[5] See below, p. 81.

[6] N.B.V.K./OR, No. 285/17, Year 1263–4; F.O. 78/1297, Skene to Redcliffe, No. 24, encl. in Skene to Clarendon, No. 9, Aleppo, 15 July 1857.

[7] F.O. 195/207, Werry to Canning, No. 9, Aleppo, 12 Apr. 1845; F.O. 78/660A, Wood to Canning, No. 4, encl. in Wood to Aberdeen, No. 8, Damascus, 21 Mar. 1846.

was farmed out in a public auction). He would then squeeze from the peasants higher tax-rates than officially fixed, and would likewise draw himself the benefit of any rise in the prices of wheat (which was given in kind as part of the tax), thus depriving both the government and the villages of the legitimate profit.[1] Out of his illegal gains, the *mültezim* would bribe senior government officials and influential members of the *meclis*, who in return would grant him his *appalto* (tax-farming privilege) and ignore his extortive methods.[2] Consequently the provincial treasury itself would receive only a small part of the total amount of the revenue collected.[3] Indeed, the actual revenue which the Ottomans drew annually from Syria in the 1840s and 1850s was less than half the income which the Egyptians had managed to collect in the 1830s[4], although the Syrians did not pay lower taxes under the Turkish régime.[5]

Thus, whereas the Egyptians were able to recover from Syrian revenue a large part of their expenditure—including the maintenance of their huge army—Turkish expenditure in Syria was far in excess of revenue. The maintenance of the *Nizam* alone, whose size was considerably less than the Egyptian force, amounted to an average of 40,000 purses annually, a sum which already absorbed a major part of the total Syrian revenue.[6] The second big

[1] F.O. 78/499, Wood to Aberdeen, No. 56, Damascus, 20 July 1842; 'Memorandum sur l'état et l'administration de la Syrie', encl. in F.O. 78/872, Wood to Palmerston, No. 6, Damascus, 29 Jan. 1851; Walpole, i. 353.

[2] F.O. 78/538, Wood to Aberdeen, No. 30, Damascus, 30 Aug. 1843; F.O. 78/577, Rose to Canning, No. 29, encl. in Rose to Aberdeen, No. 20, Beirut, 10 May 1844; Poujade, p. 200.

[3] F.O. 78/499, Wood to Aberdeen, No. 44, Damascus, June 1842; F.O. 195/302, Werry to Canning, No. 4, Aleppo, 8 Sept. 1849; F.O. 78/1586, Rogers to Bulwer, Damascus, 20 May 1861; compare Engelhardt, ii. 314; Finn, i. 162–4, 284, 286.

[4] The Egyptians drew from the provinces of Damascus and Sidon about 14 m. piasters more than the Turks. They levied from all Syrian provinces including Adana, 163 m. piasters which was at least 2½ times more than the Turks drew. See and compare F.O. 78/499, Wood to Aberdeen, No. 73, Damascus, 5 Oct. 1842; Bazili, ii. 326–33; *Accounts and Papers*, LX (1843), Pt. i, No. 7, Ponsonby to Palmerston, encl. No. 3 from Wood, Therapia, 22 May 1841. 500 piasters = one purse = £4.25.

[5] F.O. 78/622, Wood to Canning, No. 13, encl. in Wood to Aberdeen, No. 21, Damascus, 24 June 1845.

[6] *Irade D.*, No. 3210/5, B 1258 (38,584 purses); ibid., No. 5654/3, 27 N 1261 (35,000 purses); Bazili, ii. 7, 335 (about 43,000 purses in the year 1847); F.O. 195/207, Werry to Canning, No. 23, Aleppo, 6 Sept. 1845 (about 40,000 purses).

item of the expenditure was the Ḥajj caravan which required about 10,000 purses yearly, twice as much as the Egyptians had spent.[1] And although these two big items of expenditure were partly covered by remittances from Istanbul and allocations from other non-Syrian provinces,[2] the main burden fell on the Syrian *eyalet*s.

An additional strain on the Syrian treasury was, as already indicated, the disproportionately big salaries paid to senior officials which, in 1841 for example, amounted to one quarter of the total revenue.[3] Measures which were taken from time to time to reduce the salaries of high functionaries, or to diminish the number of the civil servants, did not bring about an essential change.[4] Above all, the mismanagement in the financial administration and the frequent embezzlement of public money by corrupt officials, contributed appallingly to the increase in expenditure and with it the deficit of most Syrian provinces.[5] The province of Aleppo, however, formed an exception in this respect; owing partly to the more just collection system within it, partly to its relative stability, and partly to its commercial prosperity, its revenue was steadily increasing and could usually cover the expenditure. But in Damascus and Sidon the deficit was normally big: in Damascus, for example, it amounted in 1846 to 70,000 purses,[6] while in 1847 the total Syrian deficit was about 140,000 purses.[7]

[1] F.O. 78/1388, Brant to Bulwer, No. 63, encl. in Brant to Malmesbury, No. 17, Damascus, 29 Dec. 1858; Bazili, ii. 331; A.E. Damas, ii, from Segur, No. 20, 12 Aug. 1851.

[2] On the *Porte*'s assistance to the pilgrimage, see F.O. 78/498, Wood to Aberdeen, No. 8, Damascus, 5 Jan. 1842. The *paşalık* of Adana, for example, contributed each month 500 purses to cover the expenses of the Turkish army of Arabistan. See F.O. 195/207, Werry to Canning, No. 23, Aleppo, 6 Sept. 1845; compare Bazili, ii. 333. This was in addition to the aid from Istanbul; see ibid., ii. 329.

[3] *Accounts and Papers*, LX (1843), Pt. i, No. 7, Ponsonby to Palmerston, encl. No. 3 from Wood, Therapia, 22 May 1841; compare also Urquhart, ii. 367.

[4] See, for example, F.O. 78/498, Wood to Aberdeen, No. 20, Damascus, 23 Feb. 1842; F.O. 78/1537, Brant to Bulwer, No. 14, encl. in Brant to Russell, No. 13, Damascus, 1 June 1860.

[5] See, for example, F.O. 78/497, Werry to Bidwell, private, Aleppo, 31 Dec. 1842; Bazili, ii. 335; Midhat, pp. 32–33; Taoutel, ii. 92; *Rambles*, pp. 51 ff.

[6] F.O. 78/660A, Wood to Canning, No. 4, encl. in Wood to Aberdeen, No. 8, Damascus, 21 Mar. 1846. See also A.E. Damas, ii, from Segur, No. 5, 13 Feb. 1851.

[7] Bazili, ii. 7. In 1841 the total deficit was estimated at 68,000 purses; see *Accounts and Papers*, LX (1843), Pt. i, No. 7, Ponsonby to Palmerston, encl. No. 3 from Wood, Therapia, 22 May 1841.

The local authorities tried several methods of dealing with this chronic deficit, but often only succeeded in making matters worse. One such step was to take loans from rich merchants, both foreign and local, for high rates of interest.[1] Another measure occasionally adopted was for the government to impose compulsory loans on the wealthy classes of the population as well as on the minorities, who were not always keen to lend their money.[2] In return for these loans the authorities issued treasury bonds; but as these bonds were not discharged on their maturity, the sums required could not be obtained without promise of exorbitant rates of interest, sometimes as high as thirty per cent. per annum; the government debt would thus swell into many millions of piasters.[3] The local authorities would then apply to Istanbul for financial support, but the central treasury, being itself in constant distress, would reject the demand or cover only part of the deficit.[4] A further measure sometimes taken by the authorities to meet their financial difficulties was the devaluation of the Ottoman currency. This inflationary step seriously depressed economic activity for long periods and caused substantial losses to the local population, though for the treasury it provided only temporary relief.[5] The provincial treasury, being thus practically empty over the greater part of the time, was frequently unable to pay the salaries of the public officials or to defray other expenses. Instead, it would issue *havale*s (bills of exchange) which the holders, usually being unable to cash them for a long time, were compelled to discount privately at fifteen to forty per cent.[6] This would produce among the *havale* holders, who were mainly junior civil servants and soldiers, feelings of disloyalty and cynicism and would encourage corruption within the whole administration. Similarly the

[1] *Irade D.*, No. 1867/2, 2 RA 1257; F.O. 78/801, Wood to Palmerston, No. 19, Damascus, 28 July 1849; F.O. 78/1586, Rogers to Bulwer, No. 49, encl. in Rogers to Russell, No. 29, Damascus, 2 Dec. 1861; Barker, ii. 310; Finn, ii. 44.

[2] F.O. 78/622, Wood to Aberdeen, No. 2, Damascus, 9 Jan. 1845; F.O. 78/715, Werry to Palmerston, No. 10, Aleppo, 29 Apr. 1847; Finn, ii. 44; Taoutel, iii. 163, 166.

[3] See, for example, F.O. 78/1586, Rogers to Bulwer, Damascus, 20 Aug. 1861.

[4] F.O. 78/499, Wood to Aberdeen, No. 44, Damascus, 1 June 1842; F.O. 78/1388, 'Report on the state of the Pashalik of Damascus', encl. in Brant to Malmesbury, No. 32, Damascus, 17 June 1858; Barker, ii. 309–11.

[5] See below, pp. 170–1.

[6] F.O. 78/622, Wood to Canning, No. 13, encl. in Wood to Aberdeen, No. 21, Damascus, 24 June 1845; F.O. 78/1538, Skene to Bulwer, encl. in Skene to Russell, No. 47, Aleppo, 4 Aug. 1860.

acute shortage of financial resources frequently impaired the effectiveness of the *Nizam*, while contributing on the whole to the disruption of orderly administration and of the programme of reform.[1]

[1] See F.O. 78/449, Moore to Palmerston, No. 25, Beirut, 4 May 1841; F.O. 195/291, 'Memorandum sur l'administration et l'état de la Syrie', by Consul Wood, Pera, 30 Oct. 1850; F.O. 78/1586, Rogers to Bulwer, Damascus, 20 Aug. 1861; Finn, i. 164.

PART III

Ottoman Rule in Syria and Palestine
1840–61

VI

POLICY AND MEASURES OF DIRECT RULE

> 'Niẓām mā na'ṭī wa-farda mā naḥuṭṭ wa-silāḥ dā'iman yabqā ma'anā.' ['We shall not give recruits, nor shall we put up with the *ferde*, and we shall retain our arms for ever.'] (Conditions of Druze Lebanese rebels to Ibrāhīm Paṣa in 1840)[1]

> ''Askar mā na'ṭī, farda mā na'ṭī.' ['We shall neither give recruits nor the *ferde*.']
> (Rebels' slogan in the 1850 revolt of Aleppo)[2]

FROM what has been said in the previous chapters, it is apparent that the Ottoman establishment in the Syrian provinces during the period 1840–61 was deficient in many respects: the powers of the *vali*s were greatly restricted, the civil service and the irregular troops were ineffective and corrupt, and the country's finances were at a low ebb. The only effective instruments of government were, in fact, the regular army, when deployed in sufficient numbers, and a handful of able Ottoman Pashas—*serasker*s and *vali*s who occasionally served in the various provinces.

One of the major aims of this Turkish establishment was to impose direct rule in the country which had been long known for its centres of local autonomous life and for its heterogeneous population whose members were notorious for their rebellious

[1] Al-Bāshā, p. 213.

[2] Al-Ghazzī, ii. 375.

spirit and turbulent behaviour.[1] The Syrian hilly districts had been for ages inhabited by warlike people, who were ruled by their hereditary chiefs virtually independently of the Ottoman authorities. The Syrian desert, the area east of the Jordan, and the Negeb were the strongholds of vigorous Bedouin tribes who, over long periods, were able to dominate and ravage large parts of the Syrian countryside. Even in the Syrian towns powerful local notables, possessing great wealth and influence and controlling para-military organizations and armed mobs, had a long record of defiance against the Turkish authorities as well as of expulsion and killing of Ottoman Pashas.[2]

To impose a direct rule in such a country therefore required, apart from specific steps in each area, the adoption of certain comprehensive measures to undermine the basis of local autonomy. These were firstly, total conscription and disarmament of the population in order to deprive the local chiefs and leaders of their military strength; secondly, a system of direct taxation to replace the old quasi-feudal systems which had constituted the source of the notables' social and economic powers. Conscription and taxation were, furthermore, needed to supply men and money to the new army which was to put into practice the new system of reforms.

However, the history of Ottoman rule in Syria and Palestine had clearly reflected the Syrians' reluctant attitude to measures of this kind. Even Sultan Mahmud II, the great Ottoman reformer, who was the first Sultan to introduce regular recruitment and taxation to his Empire, failed to apply these innovations in the Syrian provinces.[3]

Only Ibrāhīm Paşa, the energetic Egyptian commander, succeeded, as already noted, in imposing on the Syrian population conscription, disarmament, and direct taxation, and thus managed to subject the country to his direct rule.[4]

But on the Egyptian withdrawal from Syria in 1840–1, a general reaction against Ibrāhīm's rule and reforms took place in the whole

[1] Cf. *Irade D.*, No. 1867/1, 27 Saf. 1257; F.O. 78/444, Young to Palmerston, No. 5, Jaffa, 25 Jan. 1841; al-Bāshā, p. 3; Heyd, *Documents*, p. 43; al-Jundī, p. 265; Kibrizli, p. 57; al-Shāṭṭī, p. 119.

[2] See above, pp. 6–7.

[3] F.O. 78/243, Farren to Palmerston, Damascus, 29 May 1833; al-Nimr, pp. 171–5, 183–4, 195–9; compare Lewis, *Emergence*, pp. 88–89; Bodman, p. 128.

[4] See above, pp. 14–15.

area: local chiefs and notables, both in the countryside and the towns, began to restore their autonomous positions; Bedouin tribes renewed their turbulent activities, and large portions of the population rearmed and ceased to pay taxes.[1] The Ottomans, anxious to gain the Syrians' support in driving out the Egyptians, even encouraged these reactionary tendencies by distributing among the population great quantities of arms and spreading promises about the exemption and reduction of taxes.[2] By so doing the Turkish government not only missed the opportunity provided by the former régime to carry on and complete the destruction of the local forces; it in fact helped to rebuild the power of the local elements and to promote their autonomous trends. This practice was continued during the first few years of the restored Ottoman rule in Syria when arms were not collected from the population nor were recruits raised nor taxes properly levied. At the same time, administrative matters were allowed, in many places, to follow more or less their own course without a firm attempt on behalf of the authorities to create a regular system of government.[3]

The reasons for this behaviour were not only the desire of the government to acquire popularity with the powerful leadership and make them co-operative in the introduction of the new order.[4] It was mainly the result of the weakness of the Turkish establishment in Syria during the early 1840s: the administrative machinery was inefficient, the financial resources inadequate, and the military forces insufficient and unorganized.[5]

This transitional period came to an end in the mid-1840s

[1] See, for example, F.O. 78/448, Werry to Ponsonby, Aleppo, 2 Aug. 1841; A.E. Damas, i, from Beaudin, No. 8, 11 July 1842; Jaffa *Sijill*, No. 13, 17 R 1258; see also Finn, i. 232 ff.

[2] Al-Bāshā, pp. 210–12; Kayat, p. 276; Lûtfi, *Tarih*, vi. 119; Napier, i. 76, 147; ii. 301–2; Rustum, *Maḥfūẓāt*, iv. 243, No. 6401; al-Shidyāq, i. 121; ii. 238–9; F.O. 195/171, encl. Nos. 4 and 6 in Wood to Ponsonby, No. 10, Beirut, 31 Oct. 1840; F.O. 78/444, Young to Palmerston, No. 5, Jaffa, 25 Jan. 1841. Consul Young estimates the number of arms distributed at 70,000.

[3] F.O. 78/449, Wood to Ponsonby, Beirut, 17 Feb. 1841; *Irade D.*, No. 2837, 15 CA 1258; A.E. Damas, i, from Munton, No. 2, 6 Jan. 1841; compare also Mishāqa, *Muntakhabāt*, p. 151; Spyridon, p. 138.

[4] F.O. 78/448, Werry to Palmerston, No. 6, Aleppo, 15 Feb. 1841; F.O. 195/196, Wood to Canning, No. 42, Damascus, 26 June 1842; A.E. Damas, i, No. 6, 30 Nov. 1843.

[5] *Irade D.*, No. 2837, 15 CA 1258; F.O. 78/448, Werry to Bidwell, No. 13, Aleppo, 17 June 1841; also see above, pp. 45–46.

following the reorganization of the Turkish army in Syria in 1844–5 and the nomination of its Commander-in-Chief as *serasker* of the area. The new government policy was bluntly expressed by Namık Paşa in a statement to certain disobedient sheikhs: 'Formerly the Turkish Government was weak in Syria and we could not compel you always to obey us, but now we are strong, and if you are insubordinate I will . . . throw you into the sea.'[1]

Indeed during subsequent years considerable efforts were made by the authorities to impose direct rule and carry out measures of taxation, conscription and disarmament. But although it now employed a more effective army and abler Pashas, the Turkish government was faced with great difficulties in applying its new measures. This was partly owing to certain shortcomings in government policy and partly owing to the power and unrivalled influence of the local leadership, which the government itself had helped to build during the early 1840s. Consequently, concessions had to be made and measures were carried out by halves.

A. *Direct taxation*

One of the major ways of achieving centralization and establishing direct rule in the Ottoman provinces was through the abolition of all forms of feudalism, both old and new, both military and fiscal, and replacing them by a direct system of tax-collection.

In 1831 Mahmud II was able to abolish finally the old system of *timar* (military fief) and *sipahi*s (feudal cavalry), which had been in decline for a long time, and thus to bring under central control large parts of the Empire.[2] But he failed to challenge the new kind of fiscal feudalism which had been replacing the *timar*, mainly through the system of tax-farming (*iltizam*). It was only under the reign of Abdülmecid that the *iltizam* was for the first time challenged: the *Hatt-ı Şerif* of Gülhane severely criticized this system and demanded its replacement by fixed and direct taxation. This reform, however, was not entirely accomplished during the era of Abdülmecid, and the system of *iltizam* continued to exist alongside the direct methods of tax-collection.

In Syria and Palestine reform in taxation was even more backward. It is true that on their return to the country the Ottomans tried to

[1] F.O. 78/712, Rose to Palmerston, No. 3, Beirut, 10 Jan. 1847.

[2] On the *timar* system, see *EI*[1]. See also Lewis, op. cit., pp. 89–90; Gibb and Bowen, i. 47 ff.

introduce a direct system of taxation. At first civilian tax-gatherers (*muhassıls*) were appointed to collect taxes directly from the population; but having met with great difficulties they were partly replaced at the end of 1841 by local military governors.[1] By 1842, however, the *iltizam* system which had been both officially abolished by the 1839 *hat* and virtually abrogated in Syria by Ibrāhīm Paşa, was revived in most parts of the country,[2] apparently because it was easier for the government and allegedly more profitable for the treasury. Henceforth, while some taxes continued to be collected directly either by *muhassıls* or by the military authorities,[3] the *iltizam* became the major system of tax-collection; alongside it there existed also other indirect systems including the old institution of *sipahis*. Consul Werry, for example, reported in 1845 that out of 500 villages situated in the vicinity of Aleppo, ten belonged to *sipahis*, fifty were *vakf*, sixty *malikâne*, and 300 villages, which were government-owned *miri*, were chiefly farmed out by *iltizam*.[4] As for the *malikâne* (life tenancy), whereas in Turkey this system was completely abolished by 1840,[5] in Syria it continued to prevail afterwards, mainly in the *paşalık* of Aleppo. In 1851 an attempt was made to abrogate the *malikâne* and compensate their holders, mainly influential *âyan* (notables) who resided in the city;[6] but as late as 1860 it still existed in some parts of Syria.[7]

The *vakf* (pious foundation), which constituted a stronghold for the 'Ulema, could not be controlled entirely, either in Turkey[8]

[1] F.O. 78/447, Wood to Aberdeen, No. 30, Damascus, 4 Nov. 1841. In other parts of the Empire this measure was carried out only in the beginning of 1842. See Engelhardt, i. 50; Lewis, op. cit., p. 380; Temperley, p. 166. On the *muhassıl* see Lûtfi, *Tarih*, vi. 68–69.

[2] F.O. 78/499, Wood to Aberdeen, No. 56, Damascus, 20 July 1842; *Irade D.*, No. 4835, 8 M 1261; *Irade M.V.*, No. 1823, 29 Ş 1263; N.B.V.K./OR, No. 285/17, year 1263–4; Finn, i. 281; Poujade, p. 200. Compare Ubicini, i. 281–2.

[3] F.O. 195/226, Wood to Canning, No. 13, Damascus, 31 May 1845; *Irade D.*, No. 8417, 15 Z 1263; *Irade M.V.*, No. 10638, 28 N 1269.

[4] 'Rural Syria in 1845' (a report by Consul Werry), *M.E.J.*, No. 16, p. 511.

[5] Ubicini, i. 296. For details on this system, see Gibb and Bowen, i. 255–9.

[6] F.O. 78/871, Werry to Palmerston, No. 1, Aleppo, 28 Feb. 1851; F.O. 78/872, Wood to Canning, No. 25, encl. in Wood to Palmerston, No. 31, Damascus, 27 Aug. 1851.

[7] F.O. 78/1389, General Report on Aleppo, encl. in Skene to Malmesbury, No. 25, Aleppo, 17 June 1858; F.O. 78/1538, Skene to Bulwer, No. 27, encl. in Skene to Russell, No. 47, Aleppo, 4 Aug. 1860.

[8] See Lewis, op. cit., pp. 91–92 and n.; MacFarlane, i. 106, 396; Ubicini, i, letter 12. See also Davison, *Reform*, pp. 256–60.

or in the Syrian provinces. In these provinces attempts at reform were made in the 1840s and in the early 1850s but without noticeable success.[1] It appears that the continued existence of the *vakf* was tolerated by the authorities in Syria not only because it was in the hands of the powerful ʿUlema, but also because part of its income was dedicated to pious foundations and particularly to the Ḥajj facilities.[2]

The latter issue seems also to provide the explanation why *timars* and *sipahis* were still existing in Syria while in Turkey they had been completely abolished by 1840.[3] Attempts to abolish the *timar* in the Syrian provinces were made by Sultan Mahmud II in 1826–7: according to a local Nablus historian a firman was received in that year ordering the conversion of the *timars* into *mukataas* (or *iltizams*), but this order was apparently only partly carried out;[4] for as already mentioned, this system still existed in some parts of Syria in the early 1840s.[5] In 1845 another Imperial firman ordered the final disbandment of the Syrian *sipahis*,[6] but as late as 1859, these troops continued to render their military service as police force and particularly as the Ḥajj escort.[7]

Yet whereas the *sipahi* system in Syria was of no great weight and hardly impeded the government policy of centralization, the system of *iltizam*, being widespread, was not only contradictory to the Tanzimat, but in fact interposed itself between the taxpayer and the treasury and thus undermined the Ottoman policy

[1] *Irade D.*, No. 3735, 17 R 1259; *Takvim-i Vekayi*, No. 288, 5 C 1261; F.O. 78/538, Wood to Aberdeen, No. 36, Damascus, 6 Oct. 1843.

[2] F.O. 78/1389, General Report on Aleppo, encl. in Skene to Malmesbury, No. 25, Aleppo, 17 June 1858; F.O. 78/1588, Finn to Dufferin, No. 8, encl. in Finn to Russell, No. 5, Jerusalem, 29 Jan. 1861.

[3] Bailey, p. 36; Lewis, op. cit., pp. 89–90, 131, 378, 442; Madden, i. 560. On the *sipahi* system before the Tanzimat, see Gibb and Bowen, i. 47 ff., 185 ff., 237 ff.; Ubicini, i. 256-8.

[4] Al-Nimr who reports this indicates that the families of Nablus followed the order and converted their *timars* into *mukataas*. See al-Nimr, p. 235. But in a report by Sharīf Paşa, the Egyptian Governor-General of Syria during the 1830s, the *timar* is mentioned as one of the major forms of land tenure. See Rustum, *Maḥfūẓāt*, iii. 186, No. 4851.

[5] See also *Takvim-i Vekayi*, No. 228, 28 CA 1257; *Irade D.*, No. 2110, 19 C 1257; F.O. 195/207, Werry to Canning, No. 1, Aleppo, 14 Jan. 1843; F.O. 78/579, Wood to Aberdeen, No. 34, Damascus, 6 Nov. 1844.

[6] F.O. 78/622, Wood to Aberdeen, No. 9, Damascus, 7 Mar. 1845.

[7] F.O. 78/713, Rose to Cowley, No. 53, encl. in Rose to Palmerston, No. 57, Broumana, 7 Oct. 1847; *Irade M.V.*, No. 10543, 10 Ş 1269; N.B.V.K./OR, No. 278/15; F.O. 78/1452, Skene to Bulwer, encl. in Skene to Malmesbury, No. 42, Aleppo, 30 June 1859; *Rambles*, p. 57.

of direct rule. It is true that in the course of the early 1850s further attempts were made to uproot this system: two firmans of 1850 and 1852 respectively ordered that the *iltizam* should be abolished or revised and be replaced by direct collection of taxes.[1] But these orders were again not carried out, and in 1856 even the authors of the *Hatt-ı Hümayun*, while denouncing once more the *iltizam*, realized the impossibility of replacing it all at once by a direct system of taxation. The *iltizam* system continued indeed to exist in the Syrian provinces throughout the whole Tanzimat era.[2]

B. *Conscription and disarmament*

Another chief measure of direct rule which was not fully implemented in the Syrian provinces during the period under survey was regular conscription. Opposition to this measure was expressed by the Syrian Muslim population right from the beginning of the restored Turkish rule. Consul Werry of Aleppo, while reporting in April 1841 on the local reaction to the Gülhane edict, points out: 'ce hatcherif a fait une sensation désagréable sur l'esprit des habitants en égard à ce qu'il y est dit au sujet de la conscription.'[3] Indeed, the Syrian Muslims as a whole refused to be enlisted in the army for fear that they would never return home, and the memory of the harsh conscription by Ibrāhīm Paşa further strengthened their opposition. The local chiefs of the mountains and the countryside were particularly reluctant to accept such a measure which was likely to drain their military force and thus undermine their autonomous position. Therefore, when during the years 1843–6 attempts were made to introduce a census in Syria as a preliminary step for conscription, and also to force recruitment in certain areas, the Syrians reacted with violent armed resistance.[4]

[1] For translation of substance of this firman dated 16 M 1267, see F.O. 78/872, Wood to Palmerston, No. 9, Damascus, 19 Mar. 1851; see also F.O. 78/910, Werry to Granville, No. 5, Aleppo, 10 Mar. 1852; *Irade M.V.*, No. 8480, 28 Ş 1268; compare 'Copie d'une lettre à Mehmed pacha' signed D. Urquhart, Pera, 24 Nov. 1850, in Urquhart papers, i, c. 10, 11.

[2] See for example F.O. 78/1521, Finn to Russell, No. 1, Jerusalem, 4 Jan. 1860; *al-Jinān*, xiv (1870) 423 ff.

[3] F.O. 78/448, Werry to Ponsonby, 12 Apr. 1841, encl. in Werry to Palmerston, No. 10, Aleppo, 16 Apr. 1841; see also A.E. Alep, i, from Guys, No. 67, 30 Sept. 1841; A.E. Damas, i, from Beaudin, No. 6, 30 Nov. 1843.

[4] *Irade M.V.*, No. 1620/6, 26 N 1262; *Cevdet D.*, No. 13253, 9 L 1260; F.O. 78/622, Wood to Aberdeen, No. 2, Damascus, 9 Jan. 1845; A.E. Jérusalem, ii, from Jorelle, No. 1, 15 Oct. 1845; Kibrizli, pp. 71–73.

The only recruits the Turks managed to raise at that time were a number of outlaws and some turbulent elements.[1]

The Turkish authorities for fear of general revolt decided then to suspend conscription for the meantime and to reintroduce this measure step by step only after careful preparations.[2] Firstly, the census was to be taken gradually in the course of the next three to four years, *sancak* after *sancak*; secondly, pains were taken to demonstrate to the Syrians that the term of military service was limited to five years only: public ceremonies were held from time to time throughout the country to mark the discharge of Turkish soldiers who had completed their service.[3] At the same time publicity was given to punishments inflicted on neighbouring chiefs who refused to provide recruits; and various criminals from Syrian towns continued to be seized for military service.[4] All this, however, did not appear to soften the Syrians' attitude: when in 1848, following a general conscription in the Empire in 1847, a census was again introduced in the Syrian provinces, thousands of people fled to the mountains or to the desert, while others armed themselves in order to resist this measure. The census, although finally carried out under heavy military supervision, failed fully to achieve its aims because of acts of evasion and opposition by the population.[5] General conscription based on this incomplete census began only in 1850, after a series of more preparatory steps and military precautions had been adopted. Imperial firmans published in both Turkish and Arabic stressed that the conscription was to be exercised through a ballot system in which merely one of eleven men aged between twenty and twenty-five would be called up; invalids, only sons, and those engaged in study were to be exempted altogether.[6]

[1] F.O. 195/207, Werry to Canning, No. 7, Aleppo, 22 Apr. 1843; ibid., No. 5, 15 Feb. 1845.

[2] *Irade M.V.*, No. 1620, 3 N 1262 and 15 RA 1262; compare also F.O. 195/207, Werry to Canning, No. 21, Aleppo, 18 Nov. 1843; A.E. Jérusalem, ii, from Jorelle, No. 5, 1 Mar. 1846.

[3] See, for example, A.E. Alep, i, from Guys, No. 44, 9 Oct. 1846; Taoutel, iii. 114.

[4] F.O. 78/622, Wood to Aberdeen, No. 30, Damascus, 8 Sept. 1845; A.E. Damas, ii, from Bourville, No. 10, 2 Mar. 1848.

[5] *Irade D.*, No. 9310, 27 C 1264; F.O. 195/291, Wood to Cowley, No. 9, Damascus, 23 Feb. 1848; A.E. Damas, ii, from Bourville, No. 10, 2 Mar. 1848; al-Ghazzī, i. 331–2; ii. 366; Manṣūr, p. 85; Porter, i. 138; al-Shidyāq, ii. 345; Taoutel, iii. 130; Walpole, i. 46 n.

[6] *Irade D.*, No. 12649, 17 B 1266; Jaffa *Sijill*, No. 18, Firman of Evahir

The authorities, in addition, appealed to local notables and 'Ulema to assist them in introducing this measure, indicating its vital importance for the state and pointing out the sanction obtained from the *Şeyh-ül-Islam* for this purpose.[1] At the same time, extensive military preparations were made to meet any possible resistance: reinforcements arrived in the country and troops paraded in public places.[2]

It is evident that the mild Turkish demands as well as their great military precautions made people more responsive to the recruitment in many places, particularly in the towns, where this measure was executed fairly easily.[3] But on the other hand, a considerable number of young urban dwellers evaded the ballot either by fleeing away or by maiming themselves.[4] In the city of Aleppo there occurred, furthermore, a popular revolt against the government mainly as a result of the approaching recruitment.[5] In many other areas, particularly in the mountains and in the nomadic areas, the conscription was likewise met with violent resistance. The inhabitants of all hilly districts, except those of the Palestinian mountains, rose in rebellion; so did the Turkoman and Bedouin nomads of the Syrian plains, who in some places formed alliances with the mountain peoples, as did the latter among themselves, in order to repel government forces.[6] All these uprisings, which lasted some two years and caused general confusion, were eventually crushed by the Turkish *Nizam* or concluded through

B 1266; F.O. 78/837, Calvert to Palmerston, No. 8, Damascus, 29 Apr. 1850; A.E. Damas, ii, No. 8, 29 June 1850; Urquhart, i. 192. The total number of soldiers required from the Syrian provinces, excluding the non-Arab districts, was only about 9,000.

1 *Irade D.*, No. 13183/6, 24 Z 1266; A.E. Alep, ii, from de Lesseps, No. 11, 28 Nov. 1850.

2 *Irade D.*, No. 12805, 27 N 1266; F.O. 78/837, Calvert to Palmerston, No. 8, Damascus, 29 Apr. 1850; Walpole, iii. 340.

3 *Irade D.*, No. 13158, 6 Z 1266; ibid, No. 14872, 14 Saf. 1268; F.O. 78/837, Calvert to Palmerston, No. 22, Damascus, 26 Sept. 1850; F.O. 195/302, Elias to Werry, No. 18, Latakia, 9 July 1852, encl. in Werry to Malmesbury, No. 12, Aleppo, 13 July 1852; A.E. Damas, ii, No. 18, 13 Nov. 1850.

4 A.E. Damas, ii, No. 8, 29 June 1850; F.O. 195/302, Werry to Canning, No. 14, Aleppo, 15 Mar. 1851; F.O. 78/874, Finn to Palmerston, No. 8, Jerusalem, 29 Nov. 1851; Finn, ii. 43, 334; Neale, ii. 126.

5 See below, pp. 103 ff.

6 F.O. 78/761, Wood to Palmerston, No. 14, Damascus, 8 Apr. 1848; F.O. 78/836, Rose to Palmerston, No. 47, Broumana, 14 Oct. 1850; F.O. 195/302, Werry to Canning, No. 22, Aleppo, 17 May 1851; A.E. Damas, ii, No. 14, 30 Oct. 1850.

peace negotiations.[1] The only area, apart from the Bedouin strongholds, where the Ottomans were by no means able to raise recruits, was Jabal Druze of Houran: neither heavy military offensives nor mediation could make the Druzes submit to conscription.[2]

From 1853 onwards compulsory recruitment ceased to be an issue between the government and the Syrian population, mainly because this measure was carried out on a rather small scale and gave sufficient scope for evasion. In certain places, such as Aleppo and Beirut, no fresh recruits, except for some reserves, were levied until 1861.[3] In such areas where conscription did take place, the men raised were either turbulent elements or members of the lower classes, who were chosen by the local notables instead of being drawn by ballot; sons of the rich and influential people managed to be exempted or to buy their discharge.[4] The next general conscription on a large scale followed the 1860 events in Lebanon and Damascus when thousands of young men were taken into the army as a punishment; several hundreds of them managed, however, to buy their exemption by paying heavy ransom money or bribing government officials.[5]

In conclusion, conscription in Syria and Palestine during the period under survey, despite its shortcomings, helped to a certain extent to weaken the military strength of the Syrian population and to advance Turkish direct rule in the area. This was particularly so as far as the Syrian towns were concerned: there the Ottomans managed to complete the destruction of the para-military organizations and to exert their unchallengeable military superiority. In the mountainous areas, however, conscription had less effect on the local elements, partly because it was not total and partly because it was not accompanied by a proper disarmament of the population.

[1] F.O. 195/219, Calvert to Canning, No. 25, Damascus, 20 Oct. 1850; F.O. 78/910, Werry to Granville, No. 3, Aleppo, 9 Feb. 1852; al-Shidyāq, i. 170–1, ii. 322; Robinson, p. 39.

[2] See below, pp. 125–8.

[3] F.O. 78/1538, Skene to Bulwer, No. 35, encl. in Skene to Russell, No. 66, Aleppo, 13 Nov. 1860; F.O. 78/1519, Moore to Bulwer, No. 65, 3 Sept., encl. in Moore to Russell, No. 39, Beirut, 7 Sept. 1860; Taoutel, ii. 86.

[4] F.O. 78/1298, Misk to Clarendon, No. 15, Damascus, 28 Sept. 1857; F.O. 78/1388, 'Report on the State of the Pashalik of Damascus', in Brant to Malmesbury, No. 32, Damascus, 17 June 1858.

[5] F.O. 78/1519, Moore to Russell, No. 40, Beirut, 8 Sept. 1860; F.O. 78/1520, Brant to Russell, No. 30, Damascus, 5 Oct. 1860; *Rambles*, pp. 263–4.

The failure of the Turks to disarm the Syrians was one of the greatest mistakes of their administration. By rearming the population on their return to the country in 1840, the Ottomans failed to take advantage of the enormous endeavours made by their predecessors, the Egyptians, to break the power of the Syrians, and thus impeded their own efforts to impose direct rule in the Syrian countryside.[1] After the Egyptian evacuation, the authorities refrained, in effect, from disarming the population for several years, contenting themselves with the publication of orders which prohibited the sale of arms.[2] Only from 1845 onwards were Turkish Pashas in Syria sporadically engaged in trying to disarm the population in their respective districts; but even then their efforts met with little success.[3] The arms they managed to collect represented, in fact, only a small proportion, and probably not the best one, of what the inhabitants really possessed. For the latter would hide their rifles and pistols whenever a search was made; they would, moreover, renew their dwindling arsenals with modern weapons smuggled by sea or through the Sinai desert.[4] These arms were used in the constant warfare between the various peasant factions or were directed against travellers and peaceful inhabitants throughout the country. Above all, they were employed by the Syrian population to resist Turkish direct rule and order, thus, in a sense, making the Turks pay for their miscalculation on their return to Syria in 1840, as Ibrāhīm Paşa was reported to have stated to a Turkish general: 'You with the assistance of the English have expelled me; you have again put arms into the hands of the mountaineers; it cost me nine years and ninety thousand men to disarm them. You will yet invite me back to govern them.'[5]

The Turks, obviously, did not invite Ibrāhīm back, but on the other hand, they were not able to accomplish themselves within twenty years what the Egyptians had achieved in a mere nine. With their limited military force which amounted on the average

[1] Compare Mishāqa, *Muntakhabāt*, pp. 138–9; J. Schwartz, *Tvu'ot ha-aretz* (Jerusalem, 5603), ii. 452.

[2] F.O. 78/444, Young to Ponsonby, No. 17, Jerusalem, 24 July 1841; F.O. 78/538, Wood to Aberdeen, No. 36, Damascus, 6 Oct. 1843.

[3] *Irade D.*, No. 30932/2, 14 R 1277; F.O. 78/705, Finn to Palmerston, No. 13, Jerusalem, 13 Mar. 1847; F.O. 78/1520, Wrench to Bulwer, No. 58, encl. in Wrench to Russell, No. 36, Damascus, 5 Nov. 1860.

[4] F.O. 78/1383, Finn to Malmesbury, No. 25, Jerusalem, 9 Oct. 1858; Finn, ii. 188–9; J. Murray, *A Handbook for Travellers in Syria and Palestine* (London, 1858), i. 185.

[5] Walpole, iii. 127.

to 15,000 men, the Ottomans could only effect half measures: the conscripts they were able to raise, the arms they managed to collect, and the taxes they could levy, represented only a small part of what the energetic Egyptians had been able to accomplish. Accordingly, the degree of direct rule exerted by Ibrāhīm Paşa in Syria within a few years could not be reached by the Turkish government during the whole of the period 1840–61.

VII

URBAN POLITICS: THE *MECLIS*

'. . . hádhihi al-awrāq al-wārida min al-Sulṭān
al-mushtamila 'alā awāmir lā tunāsib al-awān
fa'lqaynāhā fi'l-baṭṭāl
wa-lam na'mal bihā biḥāl
wa-lam nakhsha min ḥākim wa-lā kabīr
wa-la qāḍī wa-lā wazīr.'
['. . . These papers coming from the
Sultan and consisting of orders which did not suit the times,
we therefore threw them away unused and did not act upon
them at all; we did not fear a ruler nor a great one, neither a
judge nor a Vezir.']
(Sheikh 'Umar *efendi* al-Ghazzī of *meclis* Damascus)[1]

ONE of the major political and social results of the Ottoman régime in Syria and Palestine during the mid-nineteenth century was the transformation which it wrought upon the rule in the towns. The era of Turkish reform not only gave a new shape and a different content to the struggle for authority in the city between the Ottoman government and the local forces; it also contributed in no small measure to the crystallization and consolidation of the urban leadership of 'Ulema and *âyan*[2] by the establishment of local councils (*meclis*) in the towns which formed the main basis for the future municipal life and autonomy in the area. It has already been pointed out that during the pre-reform period the authority in the Syrian towns did not always rest with the Ottoman governor: a fierce and bloody struggle for power took place in many cities between various forces of which the Turkish Pasha was only one; and it was not infrequently that the local rival forces managed to unite and to nullify the *vali*'s authority, and even to expel him from the city.

A decisive shift in this balance of power in favour of the government occurred under the Egyptian occupation: the vigorous

[1] Statement by the Shāfi'ī mufti and a member of the provincial council of Damascus for more than twenty years without interruption; al-Bayṭār, ii. 1135.

[2] Note that the 'Ulema were part of the *âyan*, the landed aristocracy.

Egyptian Pasha Ibrāhīm was able to destroy the local forces and to establish his own delegate as the sole authority in each town. Conscription and disarmament drained the source of military strength, while strict government control undermined the position of the town notables. The secularization of the judicial administration, like other anti-clerical measures, severely damaged the prestige of the 'Ulema and served to deprive them of their political influence.[1]

But when the Ottomans resumed their government in Syria in 1840, the balance of power within the towns shifted again. Theoretically, according to the Tanzimat concepts, the Turkish authorities now possessed aims similar to those of the Egyptians with regard to the setting up of a centralized direct rule in the Syrian towns. In practice, however, they acted contrarily, weakening their governors' authority and promoting local self-rule. Not only did they refrain from carrying on the subjection of the old leadership on the same lines as the former régime; they also helped to restore a measure of power to the local elements. The traditional oligarchy of 'Ulema and *âyan* was again given a big share in local administration; upon their members were conferred fairly high administrative ranks as well as various imperial medals.[2]

The administration of justice and the management of the religious institutions (whose high prestige was revived) were again placed exclusively in the hands of the 'Ulema.[3] Although the Muslim court (*mahkeme*) was, as under the Egyptians, deprived of most of its functions, its senior functionaries were not greatly affected: they were usually appointed to administer the new secular judicial system. The chief 'Ulema in each town and city were furthermore nominated *ex officio* to the local councils which had both administrative and judicial powers. The opinion of these senior religious and learned men was again sought and highly valued by the Turkish government.[4] Their influence and pres-

[1] See above, pp. 14–15.

[2] *Takvim-i Vekayi*, No. 238, 3 M 1258; *Irade D.*, No. 6129, 11 R 1262; No. 17752, 6 Saf. 1270; *Irade M.V.*, No. 6498, 20 CA 1267; *Irade H.*, No. 1884, 11 R 1263; *Cevdet D.*, No. 2094, 2 Z 1266.

[3] *Irade D.*, No. 4597, 9 N 1260; *Cevdet D.*, No. 3351, 22 R 1260; al-Bayṭār, ii. 924; al-Shāṭṭī, pp. 37, 48, 54, 58, 100, 101–2, 104, 110, 118, 136, 208; 'Abdullāh Ḥabīb Nawfal, *Kitāb tarājim 'ulamā' Ṭarāblus al-fayḥā' wa-'udabā'ihā* (Tripoli, 1929), pp. 81, 122, 154–5, 258.

[4] See, for example, *Irade D.*, No. 13193, 29 Z 1266; F.O. 195/351, Moore to Canning, No. 10, Beirut, 26 May 1851; F.O. 78/1629, Dufferin to Russell, No. 26, Damascus, 19 Apr. 1861; al-Shāṭṭī, p. 352; al-Bayṭār, i. 349–50, ii. 748–9.

tige spread again beyond their cities into other towns, including Istanbul; prominent 'Ulema from the big Syrian cities would occasionally correspond with, or go to, the capital—some of them upon a special invitation from the Sultan and at his expense.[1]

At the same time other urban leading elements, members of the *âyan* (provincial notables comprised of big proprietors and land owners), were further improving their positions under the new régime by taking a direct share in government administration.[2] Some of the chief notables of the town were chosen as deputies to the *meclis*, while others held important posts in all branches of administration, as, for example, the governorships of provincial towns or sub-governorships of big cities.[3]

In view of the increasing powers of the city leaders, it is not surprising that the Turkish Pasha whose powers, as we know, were now weaker than before, was frequently unable to cope with these urban elements. However, the encounters between the Ottoman *vali* and the local forces in the town were no longer warlike and violent as in the past. Apart from some instances, notably Aleppo in 1850, they did not lead again to popular rebellions against the Turkish governor or armed hostilities among the urban para-military organizations. While the latter were in decline since the Egyptian occupation, Ottoman military supremacy in the towns became generally recognized and unchallenged. The struggle for power in the city was now conducted on more modern and sophisticated lines and was concentrated mainly in the local council—the *meclis*.

A. *The* meclis

The system of local councils set up by Reşid Paşa on a French model in the early 1840s was an important innovation in the Ottoman Empire—although the principle of consultative meetings was not uncommon either in the Empire or generally in Islam; so far as Syria and Palestine were concerned, the *meclis* system was hardly new at all. A similar system had prevailed in

[1] *Irade D.*, No. 11668, 6 ZA 1265; al-Bayṭār, i. 464–9, ii. 841; al-Shāṭṭī, pp. 209–10, 219, 234, 236; Taoutel, iii. 47.

[2] On the *âyan* and their position before the era of the Tanzimat see Gibb and Bowen, i. 198–9, 256 f., 303.

[3] *Irade M.V.*, No. 7796, 8 RA 1268; F.O. 195/210, Young to Canning, No. 3, Jerusalem, 23 Jan. 1844; F.O. 195/302, Werry to Canning, No. 12, Aleppo, 23 Nov. 1850; Nawfal, op. cit., pp. 108, 148–9; Finn, i. 232–3; Manṣūr, p. 300; al-Nimr, p. 303.

these provinces during the Egyptian régime, and a form of local council had existed there even before the Egyptian occupation. Before 1831 a provincial council (*divan*) operated in the chief Syrian cities under the *vali*. As well as senior officials—the *vali*, *mütesellim*, and *defterdar*—and the military commanders, the *divan* included also the leading 'Ulema—the kadi (who was sometimes a Turk), mufti, and *nakib-ul-eṣraf*—and some local *âyan*. In its extended form the council took in more members of the 'Ulema, and representatives of merchants, guilds, and mystical orders.[1] The *divan*, however, did not admit representatives of the non-Muslim communities although Jews and Christians sat occasionally on the council in the capacity of senior provincial officials.[2]

Though the *divan* consisted of leading figures in the city, it had little administrative or political significance. This was a consequence of its sporadic nature as well as of the deficiency of its official powers; the provincial council used to meet infrequently upon the *vali*'s call and under his presidency, merely to discuss problems of finance, trade, maintenance of order, and the like.[3] Its lack of power also resulted from the immaturity of the political consciousness possessed by the local urban leadership. Although they had great influence in their provinces as well as in Istanbul, the city notables would rarely act against a Pasha unless he constituted a threat to their private interests.[4]

An important change in the formation and nature of the local council occurred under Ibrāhīm's rule. When the Egyptians occupied Palestine and Syria, they replaced the *divan* by a comprehensive and regular system of local councils, which was also more representative. The *meclis* (or *divan*) which was set up in every city and town to assist the governor, included government officials, notables, merchants, and other representatives from all the communities, Muslim and non-Muslim alike.[5] Apart from its

[1] Al-'Awra, p. 73; Bodman, pp. 34–36; Hourani, *Arabic Thought*, pp. 31–32; Shamir, *The 'Aẓm*, pp. 219, 238; *Ḥasr al-lithām*, p. 31.

[2] See, for example, al-'Awra, pp. 72, 234.

[3] Bodman, p. 39; Shamir, op. cit., p. 219; *Ḥasr al-lithām*, op. cit., p. 31.

[4] Bodman, p. 36; Shamir, op. cit., pp. 219–20, 240; Barker, i. 145, 148; *Ḥasr al-lithām*, p. 26.

[5] For details on the formation and work of the *meclis*, see al-Bāshā, p. 56; Abū 'Izz al-Dīn, pp. 135–8; Kayat, p. 264; Rustum, *Maḥfūẓāt*, ii. 358, No. 3204; idem, *Bashīr*, p. 103; Guys, *Esquisse*, pp. 48 ff; Hofman, pp. 57 ff; The council was usually called in Arabic *majlis al-shūrā* (advisory council).

function of discussing matters of administration, finance, and local trade, the *meclis* sat also in the capacity of a court for civil cases.[1] Commercial disputes were at the same time settled by a separate commercial council, which was established in the chief Syrian cities and was composed of Muslim, Christian, and Jewish merchants nominated by the authorities.[2] But the Egyptian *meclis*, although investing its members with a variety of duties, did not give them enough scope to exercise their influence. The local members of the *meclis*, whose decisions were of an advisory nature, were kept subservient to the local governor, who presided over and firmly controlled the council. Appeals against the local council could be made to the provincial *meclis* and from there to the central council in Damascus—which was directed and closely supervised by the Egyptian heads of the Syrian administration.[3]

When the Egyptians withdrew from Syria in 1840, their *meclis* system continued to constitute the basis for the newly established council; it probably also had a certain effect on the new *meclis* system which was introduced in the whole Ottoman Empire.[4] Indeed the new *meclis* was also to consist of government officials and Muslim and non-Muslim religious leaders—all appointed by the authorities—and to include Muslim and non-Muslim deputies elected by their respective communities.[5] Like the Egyptian council, the Ottoman *meclis* was to deal with both the administrative and judicial affairs of the province or the district. Yet the Egyptian pattern was not followed immediately in the arrangements made for commercial disputes; at first the commercial suits were transferred from the jurisdiction of the *mahkeme* to

[1] F.O. 78/283, Campbell's report; Rustum, *Bashīr*, p. 103; idem, *Maḥfūẓāt*, ii. 68–69, No. 1535; p. 359, No. 3207; Abu 'Izz al-Dīn, pp. 135–8; Nawfal, *al-Kulliyya*, xi. 130.

[2] *Irade D.*, No. 1867, 27 Saf. 1257; F.O. 78/412, Werry to Palmerston, No. 7, Aleppo, 20 Feb. 1840.

[3] Ḥana Baḥrī acted as the president and inspector of this *meclis*. See Mishāqa, *Muntakhabāt*, p. 120. Sharīf Bey was in charge of the judicial matters; Rustum, *Maḥfūẓāt*, ii. 383, No. 3359. Even Ibrāhīm Paşa used, from time to time, to inspect the work of the Damascus *meclis*; Rustum, op. cit. iii. 417, No. 5496; Guys, *Esquisse*, p. 48.

[4] See Moshe Maoz, 'Syrian Urban Politics in the Tanzimat Period between 1840 and 1861', *BSOAS*, vol. 29, pt. II, pp. 282–3.

[5] *Maliyeden Müdevver*, No. 9061, dated 1257 (1841). See also *Takvim-i Vekayi*, No. 238, 3 M 1258 (Feb. 1842); order from Selim Paşa of 5 Eylul (Sept. 1841) in A.E. Alep, i, from Guys, No. 66, 10 Sept. 1841; Khazīn, i. 56–57.

that of the new local council.[1] But in the early 1850s, following the setting up in 1849 of commercial courts in Istanbul and other Ottoman cities,[2] a *meclis-i ticaret* (commercial council) was established in each of the cities of Beirut, Damascus, and Aleppo.[3]

But whereas the framework of the Ottoman *meclis* system was similar to the Egyptian one, its substance and the character it developed were completely different. To begin with, the new *meclis* in Syria was not representative, either in the sense in which it aimed to be, or as the Egyptian council had been; it resembled rather the pre-Egyptian *divan* in its composition. For the new *meclis* included hardly any deputies from either the lower classes, or the middle classes, such as merchants who, under the Egyptian régime, formed the backbone of the local *meclis*. As well as the lower and middle classes of the Muslim population, the non-Muslim communities also were not fairly represented in the *meclis*. Although Christian and Jewish deputies were admitted to the local councils, they were disproportionately out-numbered by the Muslim members and had no equal status there: they were usually abused by the majority, were not allowed to take an active part in the council's work, and sometimes were even forced to withdraw.[4]

Moreover, whereas the great majority of the Syrian population, Muslim and non-Muslim alike, was under-represented in the local councils, the upper class of Muslim religious leaders and notables were greatly over-represented, far beyond the official limits.[5] Indeed, apart from government officials, the council consisted mainly of the traditional leadership of ʻUlema and heads of prominent families (*âyan*): the kadi, mufti, and *nakib-ul-eşraf* who were appointed to the *meclis ex officio*, and great landowners or other large proprietors who nominally were elected.[6] In fact, the latter became members of the council by virtue of their local influence or by bribing certain persons either in Istanbul or in

[1] F.O. 195/170, 'Copy of Zeccharia Pacha's letter to the Musselim of Damascus' in Werry to Ponsonby, Damascus, 5 Mar. 1841; F.O. 78/800, Moore to Canning, No. 53, encl. in Moore to Palmerston, No. 41, Beirut, 31 Oct. 1849; Paton, p. 269.

[2] G. Young, *Corps de droit Ottoman* (Oxford, 1905–6), i. 225; Ubicini claims that the commercial councils were established in 1847, Ubicini, i. 173–4.

[3] See below, pp. 174–5.

[4] See below, pp. 198–9.

[5] For details, see Maoz, op. cit., pp. 283–5.

[6] See, for example, *Irade D.*, No. 1867, 27 Saf. 1257; *Irade M.V.*, No. 9481, 3 M 1269; *Cevdet Z.*, No. 2703 Kanun, II 1277.

Syria.[1] In this way, the oligarchical knot of 'Ulema and *âyan* who sat in the local council almost perpetually[2] used their official status to reinforce their political position and to further their private interests.

B. *Powers of the* meclis

Another major feature which characterized the Tanzimat *meclis* in the Syrian cities was the unprecedented amount of power which it was invested with by the *Porte*. Indeed the authority of the *meclis* rested in nearly all areas of administration, finance, and justice. It was authorized, for example, to assess and farm out taxes, keep the tax-registers, inspect the tax-collectors, and receive revenue from them. The local council was entitled to rate the customs duties and to supervise the production, marketing, and prices of agricultural produce; it examined and registered land transactions, managed public works, and controlled the entry of foreign visitors. The provincial *meclis*, in addition to the above functions, had also a hand in recruiting and employing irregular troops as part of its duty to help maintain peace and security, Members of the council would also occasionally be nominated to investigate various disorders or even to settle armed disputes. The *meclis* also had the power to confirm nominations of junior governors in the districts, and to fix rates of pensions and inspect the conduct of public officials. The provincial council supervised likewise the work of the district councils and was required to exercise a general supervision over the execution of the reforms in its province.[3] In short, all administrative and financial affairs were to pass through the *meclis*; and although it was nominally an advisory body, in effect almost no action could be taken in these fields without its consent which was given in the form of a *mazbata* (official rcport).[4]

[1] See, for example, F.O. 78/622, Wood to Canning, 31 May, encl. in Wood to Aberdeen, No. 21, Damascus, 24 June 1845; F.O. 78/1031, Moore to Clarendon, No. 43, Beirut, 28 Sept. 1854.

[2] See, for instance, F.O. 195/302, Werry to Canning, No. 1, Aleppo, 2 Feb. 1850; F.O. 78/1521, Finn to Bulwer, encl. in Finn to Russell, No. 21, Jerusalem, 19 July 1860. Compare also al-Bayṭār, ii. 1134.

[3] For detailed references on the functions of the *meclis* see Maoz, pp. 285–6, f.ns. 50–56.

[4] See, for example, *Irade D.*, No. 2580/27, C 1257; F.O. 195/170, Werry to Ponsonby, Aleppo, 2 Aug. 1841; F.O. 78/872, Wood to Canning, No. 12, encl. in Wood to Palmerston, No. 17, 29 May 1851; F.O. 78/1388, Brant to Alison,

Another vast area of public life which came under the control of the local council was the administration of justice. One of the very first orders given to the newly created councils in Syria was to assume the management of judicial affairs[1] leaving thus the Muslim court (*mahkeme*) to deal only with matters of personal status, property holdings, and the like.[2] The judicial powers of local councils in small towns were, apparently, very limited; as in the administrative field, they referred the major cases to the provincial *meclis*, which acted also as a court of appeal against their decisions. The provincial council would discuss the civil and judicial suits which came before it and would submit its findings in a *mazbata*; but its powers to inflict punishment were limited to certain categories. Major cases were to be referred to the Supreme Council of Justice in Istanbul for confirmation; in 1852, however, the *vali* was authorized to confirm and execute most verdicts of his *meclis*, within certain limits.[3]

All these functions of administration, finance, and justice were performed by the provincial council, called *meclis-i kebir* (grand council) or *meclis-i eyalet* (provincial council), which met two or three times a week. In district towns many of these functions were carried out on a lower level by the *meclis* of the *sancak* presided over by the *kaymakam*, and by the *meclis* of the *kaza* presided over by the *müdir*.[4] The various councils were assisted in the performance of their duties by the *muhtar*s of the town quarters and the sheikhs of the artisan guilds;[5] within the *meclis* itself, the councillors, who received regular salaries, were assisted by one or two clerks and a financial officer. The expansion of government administration and the introduction of new measures during the

No. 11, encl. in Brant to Clarendon, No. 11, Damascus, 24 Feb. 1858; A.E. Damas, iii, from de Barrère, No. 22, 15 Aug. 1855; Finn, ii. 407; Urquhart, ii. 161–4. Compare also Engelhardt, i. 108.

[1] *Maliyeden Müdevver*, No. 9061, dated 1257; A.E. Damas, i, from Munton, No. 11, 13 Mar. 1841; Khāzin, i. 55–57; Paton, p. 206; *Accounts and Papers*, LX (1843), pt. ii, no. 27, Wood to Palmerston, Beirut, 9 Sept. 1841.

[2] See, for example, Jaffa *Sijill*, No. 18, Gurre Saf. 1270; Ben Zvi Institute, Jerusalem, *Navon Collection*, two documents from Gurre B 1271 and 28 ZA respectively.

[3] Lûtfi, *Mirat*, pp. 131–2, 155; *Takvim-i Vekayi*, No. 238, 3 M 1258; Engelhardt, i. 83; Ubicini, i. 47–49, 170–1; Urquhart, ii. 217–22.

[4] See, for example, *Irade D.*, No. 7692/21, 5 R 1263; *Irade M.V.*, No. 16751/6, 27 Ş 1274; *Cevdet D.*, No. 5153, 14 ZA 1275; F.O. 78/1630, Dufferin to Russell, No. 113, Beirut, 10 May 1861.

[5] *I ade M.V.*, No. 4386, 8 ZA 1265.

Tanzimat period required the creation of new posts and the allocation of areas of responsibility amongst the council members. Thus, apart from the offices of *kâtib-i tahrirat* (registrar) and *kâtib-i mal* (financial officer), there appeared in the *meclis* during the 1840s new appointments like *nazır-ı nüfus* (census inspector), *müdir-i evkaf* (director of *vakf*s), and *müdir-i ziraat* (agricultural director).[1]

Despite these arrangements, it appears that some of the councils were unable to tackle all their numerous duties efficiently; the provincial *meclis* of Damascus, for example, was instructed in 1850 to manage its affairs in a more orderly way by dealing with its civil and financial affairs in separate sessions.[2] A further step in this direction was taken in 1854, when each provincial council was reshaped into two bodies, an administrative one called *meclis-i idare* (administrative council) and a judicial body named *meclis-i tahkik* (council of investigation), each limited to its own duties.[3] In some places these two councils were, in fact, two forms of the same body, which held its meetings under separate titles. In other cities the members of *meclis-i tahkik* headed by *memur-i tahkikat* were drawn from the provincial *meclis*, which continued to hold supreme authority in both judicial and administrative affairs.[4]

C. *The* meclis, *the Pasha, and the Tanzimat reforms*

Furnished with these enormous powers, the *meclis* was nominally set up to advise and assist the governor in carrying out his duties within the area under his jurisdiction. In fact, however, this institution constituted a further check on the Pasha's authority which was already restricted by other Turkish officials in his province. Unlike the governors in small towns, who presided over

[1] See, for example, *Irade D.*, No. 29302/15, Gurre Z 1275; *Cevdet Z.*, No. 2703, Kanun II. 1277; *Irade M.V.*, No. 14648, 27 Z 1271; *Takvim-ı Vekayı*, No. 238, 3 M 1258. The office of *müdir-i ziraat* was common especially in the small towns.

[2] *Irade M.V.*, No. 4571, 23 Saf. 1266.

[3] See *Irade M.V.*, No. 13697, 25 RA 1274; *Irade M.M.*, No. 412/16, 11 Ş 1273; al-Ghazzī, i. 337. In Lebanon the council of investigation was called *meclis-i muhakeme* (council of judgement); see Abū Shaqrā', pp. 66, 147.

[4] See F.O. 78/1450, Brant to Bulwer, No. 1, encl. in Brant to Malmesbury, No. 2, Damascus, 15 Jan. 1859; F.O. 78/1630, 'Memo. by Vice-Consul White on the Madjlisses in Syria', encl. in Dufferin to Russell, No. 113, Beirut, 10 May 1861; compare also *Irade M.V.*, No. 15697, 21 Z 1272; *Irade M.M.*, No. 412/4, 21 L 1273.

their local councils, the *vali* was not the official head of the *meclis-i eyalet*, though he usually took part in its work and the final executive authority rested with him. The president of this council was usually a senior Turkish official who was nominated directly from the Supreme Council in Istanbul, to which he and his *meclis* were responsible.[1] Not until 1852, when the Pasha's powers were extended, was the provincial council, now headed by the *defterdar*, put under the direct control of the *vali*.[2]

This, however, neither basically changed the inferior position of the *vali vis-à-vis* his *meclis*, nor made him the real master of the provincial council. The Pasha's authority was increased, it is true, but the wide powers of the *meclis* were not diminished, nor did a change take place in the composition of the council. As before 1852, the *vali* had to struggle constantly with the *meclis*; he could take no action unless it had been endorsed by a *mazbata* from his council. Only a small number of strong *vali*s were able to dominate their *meclis* and to force its members to sign the *mazbata* while dismissing or arresting the reluctant ones.[3] But as soon as an energetic governor was replaced, the unfavoured councillor would be restored and the old struggle revived.[4] The mediocre Pasha, who usually served in these provinces, depended on the *mazbata* and was unable to contend with the sitting members of the *meclis* whose superior information and useful contacts were indispensable.[5] He would often not dare to antagonize these notables for fear of their great influence in both Syria and Istanbul. If he did they would arouse local disorders and bring the public administration to a standstill; or they would use their influence in the

[1] *Irade M.V.*, No. 5220, 17 B 1266; Urquhart, ii. 160–4. Compare Gibb and Bowen, i. 202. The president of the provincial council in Beirut was, however, a local notable by name of ʿAbd al-Fattāḥ; see *Mühimme*, No. 257, pp. 116–17, Evasit R 1265; *Irade H.*, No. 2273/15, 23 Ş 1263.

[2] *Irade D.*, No. 5970, 21 Saf. 1267; F.O. 78/871, Werry to Canning, No. 9, encl. in Werry to F.O., No. 6, Aleppo, 10 Apr. 1852; compare Ubicini, i. 44–46.

[3] *Cevdet D.*, No. 5575, R 1274; *Irade M.V.*, No. 16700/12, 19 RA 1274; F.O. 78/660A, Wood to Wellesley, No. 16, encl. in Wood to Aberdeen, No. 17, Damascus, 7 Dec. 1846; F.O. 78/1219, Moore to Clarendon, No. 62, Beirut, 19 Dec. 1856; A.E. Jérusalem, iv, from Botta, No. 92, 7 July 1854; Finn, i. 473–4; Paton, p. 206; Taoutel, iii. 146.

[4] See, for example, F.O. 195/226, Wood to Canning, No. 9, Damascus, 8 July 1846.

[5] F.O. 195/302, Werry to Canning, No. 1, Aleppo, 2 Feb. 1850; compare F.O. 78/962, Finn to Redcliffe, No. 26, encl. in Finn to Clarendon, No. 13, Jerusalem, 12 Aug. 1853; F.O. 78/1538, Skene to Bulwer, No. 27, encl. in Skene to Russell, No. 47, Aleppo, 4 Aug. 1860.

Porte to have him replaced.[1] It sometimes happened that a Pasha would play off the council's factions against each other in order to dominate it; but it was no less frequently that the *meclis* would collaborate with other senior officials in the province to control the *vali*.[2] Many *vali*s therefore preferred to leave the management of local affairs to the council, though in the process they often became its tool.[3] Corrupt governors would choose to collaborate with the councillors to rule the province arbitrarily and rob both its inhabitants and the public treasury.[4] Similarly, it was sometimes the case that a Pasha would simply shelter behind the *mazbata* to avoid assuming responsibility; he would likewise refrain from performing his duty with the plea that he ought to consult first his *meclis*.[5] In short, the local councils of the Tanzimat era, in Engelhardt's words: '. . . étaient devenus un obstâcle au bien, tout en n'empêchant pas le mal'.[6] Even David Urquhart, who was an ardent supporter of the *meclis* system, admits: 'It will be seen that all power is taken out of the hands of the Pasha. The *Mejilis* is not his council. . . . It seems then that the point has been passed where a check was desirable over the Pasha, and that now the danger lies in the *Mejilis*.'[7]

In these circumstances, the application of the Ottoman Tanzimat

[1] See, for example, F.O. 78/872, Wood to Canning, No. 8, encl. in Wood to Palmerston, No. 13, Damascus, 28 Apr. 1851; A.E. Damas, ii, 6 Feb. 1853; F.O. 78/1220, Barker to Redcliffe, No. 35, encl. in Barker to Clarendon, No. 15, Aleppo, 24 Sept. 1856; Finn. i. 163, ii. 194–7.

[2] F.O. 78/761, Wood to Canning, No. 29, encl. in Wood to Palmerston, No. 30, Damascus, 25 Nov. 1848; F.O. 78/1630, Dufferin to Russell, No. 113, Beirut, 10 May 1861.

[3] F.O. 195/292, Finn to Canning, No. 13, Jerusalem, 21 Aug. 1850; F.O. 78/1452, Skene to Bulwer, separate, encl. in Skene to Malmesbury, No. 42, Aleppo, 30 June 1859; Taoutel, ii. 100.

[4] See, for instance, F.O. 195/194, Rose to Canning, No. 14, Beirut, 3 Mar. 1842; F.O. 78/801, Wood to Palmerston, No. 9, Damascus, 28 Apr. 1849; F.O. 78/1120, Finn to Redcliffe, No. 45, encl. in Finn to Clarendon, No. 49, Jerusalem, 19 Dec. 1855; F.O. 78/1389, Skene to Bulwer, No. 29, encl. in Skene to Malmesbury, No. 41, Aleppo, 4 Sept. 1858; Barker, i. 145; Finn, i. 397.

[5] F.O. 195/292, Finn to Canning, No. 8, Jerusalem, 1 Mar. 1849; F.O. 78/1388, Brant to Alison, No. 11, encl. in Brant to Clarendon, No. 11, Damascus, 24 Feb. 1858; A.E. Damas, iii, from de Barrère, No. 22, 25 Apr. 1855; Madden, i. 457–8, ii. 408.

[6] Engelhardt, i. 108. See also F.O. 78/1538, Skene to Bulwer, No. 27, encl. in Skene to Russell, No. 47, Aleppo, 4 Aug. 1860; A.E. Alep, i, from Guys, No. 41, 27 June 1846; *Rambles*, pp. 61 ff. On the *meclis*'s vices in other parts of the Empire, see Davison, *Reform*, pp. 48–49, 140–1; MacFarlane, i. 152, ii. 27, 28; Temperley, pp. 237–8.

[7] Urquhart, ii. 164.

in each area of life was largely determined by the results of the encounter between the various forces and interests which prevailed in the Syrian cities. As things were, there emerged in the course of that period a fairly steady co-operation in certain aspects between the urban leadership and local Turkish authorities on a basis of a mutual interest which at times was incompatible with the Tanzimat. The most conspicuous co-operation between the two sides was in the maintenance of law and order.

It is apparent that, the Syrian 'Ulema and *âyan* were themselves interested in the preservation of peace and stability in their cities since, having owed their public positions to the Ottoman régime, they ultimately threw in their lot with it. Therefore they were often willing to assist the government in maintaining order and in introducing even such unpopular measures as conscription and taxation.[1] For, many town notables no longer possessed any strong motive against conscription, since they now derived their power from sources other than military strength and were thus unable to challenge the Ottoman military supremacy. Moreover, in their capacity as members of the *meclis* and as rich proprietors, the notables managed to exempt their young relatives from recruitment, either by influence or by bribery.[2] The councillors also contrived to avoid the direct impact of taxation and even make it beneficial; firstly, they would divide among themselves and their relatives the *iltizam*s of the surrounding rural areas, out of which they would draw great profits at the expense of both the population and the public treasury. Secondly, they would levy, as we shall see later, the town's biggest tax—the *ferde* (personal tax)—in a manner that did not affect their own sectarian interest, but was prejudicial both to the lower classes and the non-Muslim communities.[3]

The deeds of oppression and injustice, especially those concerned with excessive taxation, meant, in effect, a rebuff to another major concept of the Tanzimat, the well-being of the population. Accordingly, they provoked from time to time popular outbursts of resentment and violence, not merely against the authori-

[1] *Irade D.*, No. 13183/6, 24 Z 1266; F.O. 195/207, Werry to Canning, No. 2, Aleppo, 27 Jan. 1844; also F.O. 195/292, Finn to Canning, No. 18, Jerusalem, 26 Nov. 1850. At the same time, however, some 'Ulema from Damascus took pains to incite the neighbouring population against recruitment; see F.O. 78/910, Wood to Malmesbury, No. 38, Damascus, 7 Dec. 1852.

[2] See above, p. 84.

[3] See below, p. 183.

ties, but particularly against the local notables themselves.[1] This phenomenon, although not completely new in Syrian life, represented in a sense a break with a tendency of the past, whereby the urban population, headed by their leaders, formed a solid block in order to resist measures of taxation and conscription imposed by the Egyptian, and sometimes also the Ottoman, authorities. The increasing gap between the Muslim masses and their traditional leadership can be attributed to the new conditions created in Syria during the Tanzimat period. In these circumstances the city notables, seeing no other possible way of avoiding the impact of these unpopular reforms, took to assisting the authorities in putting the main burden of these measures upon the masses. On the other hand, the local Turkish Pasha, unable to take these steps without the notables' help, was compelled, by way of compromise, to ignore their evasion and oppression.

This illicit co-operation between the authorities and the councillors was more remarkable, as we shall see later, with regard to the reform in the status of the non-Muslim subjects (*reaya*), another principle in the Ottoman Tanzimat. As a matter of fact, the 'Ulema and other urban conservative elements were the champions of *reaya* inequality, an issue over which they were deeply sensitive. They therefore used their official positions to subvert the rights granted to the non-Muslim population.[2] In this issue too the Muslim notables usually enjoyed the silent consent and sometimes even the secret support of many Turkish governors, who, on the whole, shared the Syrian Muslims' opposition to Christian equality.[3] This unofficial and ill-omened agreement was furthermore the source of many anti-Christian activities which occurred in the Syrian towns during the early Tanzimat period. The 1860 massacre of Damascus Christians in particular had some of its main roots in this tacit alliance; the chief 'Ulema took the lead in this bloodshed while the local Turkish Pasha remained passive.[4]

It is true that the *Porte* realized fairly soon the danger to its New Order which was latent within that form of local *meclis*. Accordingly, the central government made great efforts during the years 1840–61 to curb the *meclis* by reducing its numbers and by replacing its ruling clique of 'Ulema and *âyan* with

[1] See below, p. 185.
[2] See below, pp. 195 ff.
[3] See below, pp. 222 ff.
[4] See below, pp. 233 ff.

representatives from all classes and communities. But, lacking a proper policy and the necessary instruments, the *Porte* failed to accomplish these aims.

Already in the early 1840s an order was issued for a reduction of the number of councillors in both Damascus and Aleppo.[1] This step, taken for economic reasons, did not seem to be effective; and in 1844, the new *serasker* of Syria, Namık Paşa, was enjoined by Istanbul 'to strengthen the action of the authorities against the powerful and influential corps of Effendis and Ulemas'.[2] But this able Pasha appeased and flattered the town notables, as did, in fact, other prominent Turkish officials.[3] Five to six years later, a general reorganization of the provincial councils was carried out; at Beirut and Jerusalem in 1849, at Damascus in 1850, and at Aleppo in 1851. The number of Muslim notables was reduced again to the official figure, while Christian and Jewish deputies were granted a slightly larger representation. In most places, however, the old Muslim members were partly restored to the *meclis* and partly replaced by other Muslim notables; only in Aleppo (and in Jerusalem ten years later) were the *âyan* replaced by deputies from the lower classes[4]—but not for very long: the number of Muslim ʿUlema and effendis was increased again in this council during the 1850s.[5]

In 1856 the Ottoman reformers still felt a strong need for another general reorganization of the *meclis* system; their second great edict, the *Hatt-ı Hümayun*, declared:

In order to render fairness in the choice of the deputies in the provincial and district councils, from among the Muslim, Christian, and other subjects; and in order to ensure freedom of opinion . . . proceedings shall be taken . . . to control their . . . decisions . . . by reforming

[1] F.O. 78/499, Wood to Aberdeen, No. 20, Damascus, 23 Feb. 1842; *Irade M.V.*, No. 1036/1, 13 Z 1259.

[2] F.O. 78/579, Wood to Aberdeen, No. 15, Damascus, 8 May 1844.

[3] A.E. Damas, i, No. 15, 6 Mar. 1844; *Irade M.V.*, No. 967, 27 CA 1259; F.O. 195/351, Moore to Canning, No. 10, Beirut, 26 May 1851.

[4] See *Irade D.*, No. 11287, 12 Saf. 1265; *Irade M.V.*, No. 5220, 28 Ş 1266; *Cevdet D.*, No. 786, 16 RA 1267; A.E. Jérusalem, iii, No. 16, 10 Nov. 1849; F.O. 195/331, Moore to Canning, No. 26, Beirut, 31 May 1849; F.O. 78/837, Calvert to Palmerston, No. 10, Damascus, 30 May 1850; F.O. 78/871, Werry to Palmerston, No. 1, 28 Feb. 1851. A similar measure of replacing notables by shopkeepers took place in Jerusalem in 1860; see F.O. 78/1521, Finn to Bulwer, encl. in Finn to Russell, No. 21, Jerusalem, 19 July 1860.

[5] See *Irade M.V.*, No. 18868/7, 11 C 1276; *Cevdet Z.*, No. 2703, Kanun II 1277; *Cevdet D.*, No. 7367, 17 N 1273.

the regulations regarding the way these councils are formed and organized. . . .

It seems, however, that these recommendations were again not put into practice in Syria and Palestine before 1860–1 when another reconstruction was carried out in some provincial councils.[1]

D. *Aleppo: balance of power in a big city*

This was the broad pattern of urban politics in most Syrian cities during the period 1840–61; the local *meclis* emerged as the principal ruling institution and the major scene of the Tanzimat-inspired relations between the Turkish Pasha and the local leadership. It was, however, a gradual process which within that period reached various stages in different places. On the whole the small towns tended to lag behind the big cities since they were, generally, less open than the cities to the impact of the new era.[2] Placed in this category was also the big town of Aleppo, whose political history during that period might represent the process of transformation which the Tanzimat gave rise to in the Syrian town.

During the 1840s the internal politics of Aleppo were restored to a position somewhat similar to that of the pre-Egyptian period, chiefly because of the local para-military organizations which managed to survive the harsh Egyptian rule. It has already been noted that in the pre-reform period, real power in Aleppo lay with the Janissary and *eşraf* factions which violently fought each other for authority in the city. A Turkish Pasha was able to rule Aleppo only if he sided with one of the two local forces; but occasionally the rival groups would co-operate, nullify the *vali*'s power, or even expel him from the town. This struggle was usually accompanied by armed clashes between the various forces, resulting in destruction and loss of life in the city.[3]

Only Ibrāhīm, the energetic Egyptian Pasha, managed to subdue the local strife and to control the city. He was able to do this

[1] F.O. 78/1521, Finn to Bulwer, encl. in Finn to Russell, No. 21, Jerusalem, 19 July 1860; F.O. 78/1586, Wrench to Bulwer, No. 4, encl. in Wrench to Russell, No. 3, Damascus, 7 Feb. 1861.

[2] On the politics in the small town see Maoz, pp. 297–300.

[3] See above, pp. 6–7. In particular see Bodman, ch. V.

by appointing ʿAbdullāh Bey Babilsī, the veteran Janissaries' leader, as *mütesellim* (civil governor) of Aleppo.[1] When the Ottomans returned to Syria they reappointed ʿAbdullāh as *mütesellim* of the city and bestowed upon him great honours.[2] This was also the policy with regard to other big cities, where the authorities had to appoint local notables as sub-governors for a transitional period. But whereas in cities like Damascus and Jerusalem these notables were replaced by Turks as soon as the government had established itself strongly,[3] in Aleppo things were different. ʿAbdullāh, who commanded many thousands of armed followers from among the urban, rural, and tribal populations, was the only person capable of maintaining order in Aleppo, and in fact held most of the strings of its government.[4] At the same time, however, the Ottoman authorities backed the local rival faction, the *eşraf*, allowing their chief members to dominate the provincial *meclis* and nominating their leader, Yūsuf Bey Sharīf, as *kaymakam* (military governor) of Aleppo.[5] Thus, the Turkish government which apparently, was trying to play off the old rivals against each other, found itself completely powerless, while ʿAbdullāh and Yūsuf shared the authority. In the frame of their offices each faction managed to accumulate a great deal of wealth by holding the *iltizams* of the province and also by keeping to themselves large parts of the revenue.[6]

It was not until 1850 that the Turkish authorities dared to challenge openly these powerful bodies: Mustafa Zarif Paşa, the Ottoman *vali*, demanded from the leading members of both groups the payment of the long-standing *iltizam*-arrears, threatening them with imprisonment and confiscation of their property.[7] Moreover, ʿAbdullāh Bey, whose official powers had earlier been

[1] F.O. 78/539, Werry to Bidwell, private, Aleppo, 2 June 1843; Paton, p. 245.

[2] *Takvim-i Vekayi*, No. 238, 3 M 1258; *Irade D.*, No. 2860/5, 21 RA 1258; *Irade D.*, No. 13493/8, Selh Saf. 1267; Taoutel, iii. 26–28; Paton, p. 247.

[3] F.O. 78/444, Young to Ponsonby, No. 4, Jerusalem, 5 Mar. 1841; F.O. 195/210, Young to Canning, No. 3, 23 Jan. 1844; al-Bāshā, p. 240.

[4] F.O. 78/448, Werry to Ponsonby, Aleppo, 15 May 1848; F.O. 78/539, Werry to Rose, Aleppo, 1 May 1843, encl. in Rose to Aberdeen, No. 42, Beirut, 6 May 1843; Barker, ii. 289; Paton, p. 247.

[5] *Takvim-i Vekayi*, No. 238, 3 M 1258; *Irade D.*, No. 2053, 25 CA 1257; Taoutel, iii. 26–28; Paton, p. 248.

[6] Cf. a petition by inhabitants of the *paşalık* of Aleppo in *Irade D.*, No. 13493/8, Selh Saf. 1267; al-Ghazzī, ii. 371; F.O. 78/539, Werry to Bidwell, private, Aleppo, 2 June 1843; 'Rural Syria in 1845', *M.E.J.*, No. 16, p. 511.

[7] *Irade D.*, No. 13493/8, Selh Saf. 1267; al-Ghazzī, ii. 371.

reduced by the Ottomans,[1] was now removed from his office as *mütesellim* and was forbidden to farm any more *iltizam*s.[2] This bold action of the Turks, who seem to have underrated ʿAbdullāh's actual strength, constituted one of the major factors leading to the revolt of 1850 in Aleppo. The other factors were the imposition of conscription and the poll-tax—*ferde*—on the population.

After his dismissal, ʿAbdullāh approached Yūsuf, the leader of the *eşraf*, and urged him to co-operate in inciting a popular uprising against the Ottoman authorities by exploiting the approaching conscription and the recent levy of *ferde*. In ʿAbdullāh's view, the authorities, being unable to quell the revolt themselves, since their garrison was extremely small, would be forced to seek the help of ʿAbdullāh and Yūsuf and as a reward would also concede them the tax-arrears.[3] The *eşraf* agreed to help in carrying out the plot, although, apart from the tax-arrears issue, they did not share ʿAbdullāh's motives for the uprising. As great proprietors they would disagree with the popular demand represented by the veteran Janissaries to convert the *ferde* from a personal-tax to a property-levy.[4] As a body which was composed of a relatively small number of notables who derived their power from great wealth and by controlling local public institutions, the *eşraf* were not likely to be affected by conscription so much as ʿAbdullāh's group, which was based on mass military organization. Yet the *eşraf* and their followers possessed a rather substantial grievance which the Janissaries did not fully share: strong opposition to the concept of Christian equality which deeply affronted their sensitivities.[5] (It must be noted here that the anti-Christian feelings reached their climax in Aleppo on the eve of the 1850 revolt against the government, when the Greek Catholic patriarch had made a triumphant entry into the city at the head of a procession

[1] F.O. 78/539, Werry to Bidwell, Aleppo, 2 June 1843; F.O. 195/207, Werry to Canning, No. 4, Aleppo, 4 Apr. 1846.

[2] F.O. 195/302, Werry to Canning, No. 8, Aleppo, 26 Oct. 1850.

[3] Al-Ghazzī, ii. 372; see also Qarā'lī, *Ḥalab*, pp. 79–80. Compare Barker, ii. 290.

[4] Compare F.O. 195/207, Werry to Canning, No. 2, Aleppo, 14 Feb. 1846; F.O. 78/960, Werry to Rose, 29 Jan., encl. in Werry to F.O., No. 4, Aleppo, 3 Feb. 1853; Taoutel, iii. 109.

[5] See a petition by Muslim notables of Aleppo in *Irade D.*, No. 13268/6, Gurre M 1267; F.O. 78/836, Werry to Canning, No. 7, encl. in Rose to Palmerston, No. 49, Beirut, 5 Nov. 1850; CM/063 from Sandreczki, No. 349, Ayntāb, 5 Nov. 1850.

carrying crosses and other church ornaments.)[1] It seems doubtful, however, that the *eşraf* were prepared to risk their position in Aleppo over this issue. For, unlike ʿAbdullāh and his partisans, who had nothing to lose from an uprising and a good chance to regain their position, the *eşraf* had little to gain and much to lose by rising against the Turkish authorities. They had already established themselves strongly in local government by dominating the *meclis* as well as the judicial and religious systems, thus throwing in their lot with the Ottoman régime; an unsuccessful revolt against the Ottomans, therefore, would mean political suicide. Indeed, the experienced and cautious notables, who did not command a substantial military force, presumably did not share ʿAbdullāh's confidence in his local military superiority, which he apparently based on both his old and recent experiences with the Ottomans.[2] The *eşraf* were rather more inclined to believe in the ultimate military supremacy of the Turkish authorities, which would eventually suppress any local revolt.

All this, then, lay behind the ambivalent attitude of Yūsuf Bey Sharīf and the notables towards ʿAbdullāh's suggestion of revolt; they seemingly agreed to co-operate with the Janissaries, but at the same time continued to show their loyalty to the *vali*. If the rebellion were to fail, their great rival ʿAbdullāh would be once and for all destroyed;[3] if it were to be a success, the *eşraf* would achieve their limited aims.

In this context it should also be remembered that originally the conspirators intended to provoke a local insurrection on a small scale only; to threaten the Ottoman authorities rather than to overthrow them. But the uprising that broke out in mid-October 1850 took such a gigantic form that even ʿAbdullāh could hardly control it;[4] it also involved such calamities as the plotters them-

[1] F.O. 78/836, Rose to Canning, No. 48, Beirut, 31 Oct. 1850, encl. in Rose to Palmerston, No. 49, Beirut, 5 Nov. 1850. Compare also *Irade D.*, No. 13268/6, Gurre M 1267; al-Ghazzī, ii. 375.

[2] In 1841, for example, only the military intervention of ʿAbdullāh could save the *serasker*, Zakariyya Paşa, from a rebellion by the government *başibozuk*s wherefore 'The Government lost somewhat of its influence and power in the eyes of the inhabitants . . .', F.O. 78/448, Werry to Ponsonby, Aleppo, 15 May 1841.

[3] Compare Barker's suggestion claiming that the initiative for the plot did come from Yūsuf Bey who wanted in this way to ruin his rival ʿAbdullāh; Barker, ii. 290. See also F.O. 78/836, Werry to Canning, No. 43, Aleppo, 24 Oct., encl. in Rose to Palmerston, No. 49, Beirut, 5 Nov. 1850.

[4] Al-Ghazzī, ii. 373.

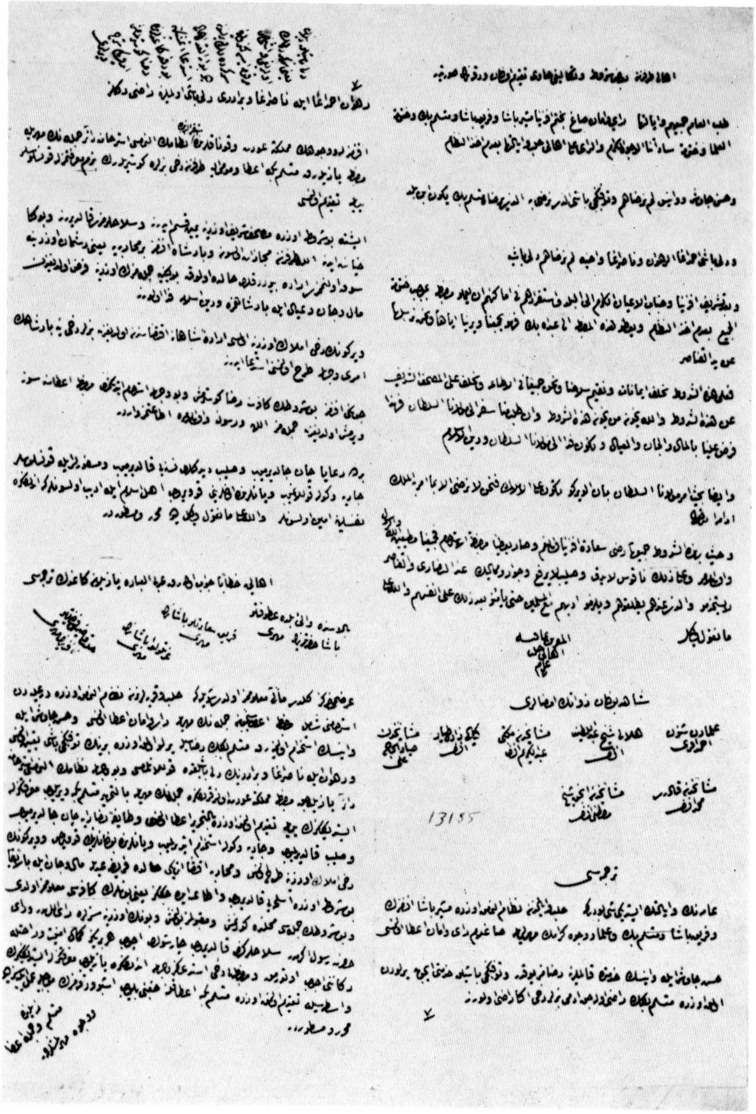

FIG. 2. Text of Aleppo rebels' conditions for laying down arms (in 1850)

selves could not possibly have foreseen. This was partly owing to the strong rumours about wide resistance to conscription around Damascus which augmented the size of the insurrection;[1] and partly because of the outburst of Muslim fanaticism fomented by the recent Christian provocation, and encouraged by a desire to loot, which turned the rebellion against the authorities into riots against the Christians of Aleppo as well. Finally, the city garrison was small and the behaviour of the *vali*, Mustafa Zarif Paşa, cowardly—he refrained from employing his troops to curb the disturbances—and this served also to aggravate the outbreak.

The tumult began when thousands of Muslims, mainly ʿAbdullāh's partisans, composed of the Aleppo mob and neighbouring nomad elements, invaded the city and attacked the *vali*'s residence. The latter hurriedly withdrew with his 500 regular soldiers and some members of the *meclis* to Shaykh Yabrak, a fortress on the outskirts of Aleppo. The insurgents, encouraged by this retreat and accompanied by fresh Aleppo crowds, turned then to the Christian quarter, attacking and massacring Christians, looting houses, and burning down churches and sacking them.[2]

Zarif Paşa, unable to master the events, appointed ʿAbdullāh Bey as *kaymakam* of Aleppo, while calling for reinforcements from Damascus and Istanbul. ʿAbdullāh managed to restore order but the city remained occupied by the rebels—ʿAbdullāh's followers. The *vali*, still in Shaykh Yabrak, entered, through ʿAbdullāh's mediation, into peace negotiations with the rebels, apparently in order to gain time. Their principal conditions for laying down arms were: abolition of conscription, renomination of a native of Aleppo (ʿAbdullāh) as the city *mütesellim*, and the turning of the *ferde* into a property-tax. An additional series of demands were that church bells must not be rung, neither must crosses be carried in processions, and that Muslim male and female servants were not to be employed in Christian houses.[3] Zarif Paşa

[1] F.O. 78/836, Werry to Canning, No. 7, Aleppo, 19 Oct., encl. in Rose to Palmerston, No. 49, Beirut, 5 Nov. 1850.

[2] For details of these events, see *Irade D.*, No. 13185, 14 Z 1266; ibid., No. 13493/8, Selh Saf. 1267; F.O. 195/302, Werry to Canning, No. 7, Aleppo, 19 Oct. 1850; A.E. Alep, ii, from de Lesseps, No. 9, 29 Oct. 1850; Barker, ii. 292 ff.; al-Ghazzī, ii. 372 ff.; Qarā'lī, *Ḥalab*, pp. 79 ff.; Neale, ii. 118 ff.; Taoutel, iii. 143.

[3] For full text of the rebels' conditions, see *Irade D.*, No. 13185/14, encl. in 26 Z 1266, in the facing page. Cf. F.O. 195/302, Werry to Canning, No. 8, Aleppo, 26 Oct. 1850; al-Ghazzī, ii. 376–7.

seemingly agreed to accomplish most of these demands, while preparing his offensive with the reinforcements he had meanwhile received from Damascus and Anatolia. At the beginning of November 1850, after Aleppo had been occupied by the rebels for about a fortnight, the *vali* made his first move to regain authority; he suddenly arrested ʿAbdullāh and appointed Yūsuf Bey Sharīf in his place. Consequently the population divided into two groups: one, the veteran Janissaries and their allies from among the peasants and Bedouin, all of whom continued their rebellion under the command of ʿAbdullāh's cousin; and the other, the *eşraf* and their followers, who now sided openly with the Turkish authorities.[1] After a few days of intense fighting, which involved a great loss of life (3,000 to 5,000 people), the Ottoman army was able to recapture the city. Hundreds of rebels were arrested and banished; among them was also ʿAbdullāh, who was poisoned on his way to exile. This was followed by the dismissal of the *vali*, Mustafa Zarif Paşa, and the nomination in his place of Mehmed Kıbrıslı Paşa, who was specially summoned from London where he filled the post of ambassador.[2]

Kıbrıslı, who arrived in Aleppo in December 1850 with more troops, took steps to complete the punishment of the culprits, impose conscription, and compensate the Christian inhabitants for their losses. Above all, the new *vali* adopted strong measures to procure the destruction of the local leadership and reorganize the local *meclis*. He banished also Yūsuf Bey, the chief mufti of Aleppo, and other notables, for the alleged part they had played in the revolt.[3] In addition, Kibrıslı Paşa reshaped the town council, excluding from it the *âyan* and replacing them by Muslims from lower classes as well as by deputies from the non-Muslim communities.[4] The next *vali*, Nuri Osman, followed his predecessor's line and exiled in 1851 ten more notables.

For a time it seemed that the power of the *eşraf* and Janissaries was completely broken while the Ottoman authorities fully controlled Aleppo and managed to carry out in it a considerable

[1] F.O. 195/302, Werry to Canning, No. 10, Aleppo, 8 Nov. 1850; Barker, ii. 293–4; Qarā'lī, op. cit., pp. 90–91.

[2] *Mühimme*, No. 258, p. 1, orders of Evail and Evahir M 1267; *Irade D.*, No. 13268/6, Gurre M 1267.

[3] *Takvim-i Vekayi*, No. 534, 6 L 1267; al-Ghazzī, ii. 382.

[4] F.O. 78/871, Werry to Palmerston, No. 1, Aleppo, 28 Feb. 1851; compare also Taoutel, iii. 146.

number of reforms.[1] But before long the new order of things was reversed; the chief leaders of both local groups were pardoned and allowed to return; Yūsuf Bey Sharīf was invested with the high rank of *mirmiran* and was allowed to return to his former position; the mufti also resumed his office in Aleppo.[2] Gradually, local notables were restored to the *meclis* and to its domination; the outbreak of the Crimean War, involving withdrawal of Ottoman troops, enabled the old local leaders to establish their position more firmly. Henceforth, the struggle for authority in Aleppo between the Ottoman *vali* and local forces was carried out mainly in the framework of the *meclis* and consequently the Aleppo notables, headed by Yūsuf Paşa Sharīf, were occasionally able to control both the Pasha and the local affairs.[3]

[1] F.O. 78/871, Werry to Palmerston, No. 20, Aleppo, 20 Dec. 1851.

[2] Al-Ghazzī, ii. 382. See also Barker, ii. 295; F.O. 78/871, Werry to Canning, No. 19, encl. in Werry to Palmerston, No. 6, Aleppo, 10 May 1851; *Irade M.V.*, No. 13688, 23 R 1271.

[3] See, for example, F.O. 78/1452, Skene to Bulwer, No. 11, encl. in Skene to Malmesbury, No. 20, Aleppo, 31 Mar. 1859; F.O. 78/1389, Skene to Bulwer, No. 25, encl. in Skene to Malmesbury, No. 38, Aleppo, 21 Aug. 1858; F.O. 78/1538, same to same, No. 27, encl. in Skene to Russell, No. 47, Aleppo, 4 Aug. 1860; A.E. Alep, iii, No. 3, 14 June 1859; Taoutel, iii. 163.

VIII

RULE IN THE MOUNTAIN DISTRICTS

'Abd ul Medjid is Sultan in Constantinople and I am Sultan here.'
(Sheikh 'Abd al-Raḥmān 'Āmir, chief in the Hebron mountains)[1]

In the Syrian countryside, particularly in the mountain districts, Turkish rule was much weaker than in the towns, and government administration was almost exclusively based on local chiefs: each village was led by a sheikh and the rural district was inspected by a local *nazır*. Being in the pay of the government and entitled to enlist a number of their men as irregular soldiers, these chiefs were entrusted with the performance of such functions as the keeping of village registers, collection of taxes, and maintenance of order.[2]

The centre of a mountainous region was the residence of a *müdir* or a *kaymakam*, usually also a native leader who had a wider range of duties to execute and who was assisted, as in the town, by a local council composed of chiefs and religious leaders of the district.[3] In practice, these local chiefs were petty autocrats in their respective regions and ruled them virtually independently of the Turkish government. Most attempts made by the government to replace them (particularly the *kaymakam*s and *müdir*s) with Turks proved impracticable,[4] largely owing to the unfavourable balance of power between the government and the mountain people. The Turkish troops in Syria were, as we know, relatively few in number and were deployed mainly in the cities; thus, while able to maintain their supremacy in the towns, they were inade-

[1] Cited in F.O. 78/839, Finn to Palmerston, No. 20, Jerusalem, 27 Apr. 1850.

[2] Aristarchi, iii. 373–7; *Irade D.*, No. 2580/53, 15 CA 1257; *Irade M.V.*, No. 8494, 12 Ş 1268; F.O. 78/1448, Finn to Malmesbury, No. 8, Jerusalem, 7 Feb. 1849; Segur, pp. 12–13.

[3] See, for example, Finn, i. 238–9; al-Nimr, p. 279; Robinson, p. 48.

[4] Compare *Cevdet D.*, No. 10155, 29 ZA 1261; F.O. 78/622, Wood to Aberdeen, No. 44, Damascus, 29 Dec. 1845; F.O. 78/1032, Finn to Clarendon, No. 17, Jerusalem, 3 Aug. 1845.

quate when it came to exerting a constant military pressure on the hilly districts. By contrast, the mountain chiefs could mobilize many thousands of armed warriors as well as numerous Bedouin allies and could, of course, use the natural protection of their strongholds to repulse Turkish encroachments. In these circumstances the authorities frequently resorted to the old policy of 'divide and rule' as a means of undermining the local military power and paving the way for direct rule. The Turks would revive and promote the local frictions and rivalries which existed on clannish, sectional, or religious grounds throughout the country, and would play off the rival factions against each other, aiming at weakening both sides and themselves keeping a local balance of power.[1] In addition, the government would occasionally rally large bodies of armed mountain warriors from one area to help in subduing those of another district which had shown signs of open rebellion.[2] These methods which were accompanied from time to time by direct military efforts to impose central control, although promoting frequent hostilities in the country, contributed indeed to weakening the mountain peoples and gradually to advancing Turkish direct rule in their areas. One such example was to be found in Jabal Ansariyya.

A. *Jabal Ansariyya*

The Nusayris, or ʿAlawis, had been for a long time notorious not only for their internal strife, but also for their disobedient and turbulent behaviour. Not only were they reluctant to pay taxes and submit to Ottoman rule, but they were also frequently engaged in acts of murder and robbery against neighbouring villages and passing caravans.[3] Ibrāhīm Paşa, as already mentioned, managed to subdue them and keep them in check, but when the

[1] Compare F.O. 78/497, Werry to Bidwell, No. 1, Aleppo, 23 Apr. 1842; F.O. 78/499, Wood to Aberdeen, No. 79, Damascus, 16 Nov. 1842; F.O. 195/234, Rose to Aberdeen, No. 75, 9 Dec. 1843, encl. in Rose to Canning, No. 2, Beirut, 6 Jan. 1844; Finn, i. 219–20, 393, 407–10; Lyde, pp. 208–9; Porter, *Damascus*, ii. 5–6.

[2] See, for instance, F.O. 78/538, Wood to Aberdeen, No. 36, Damascus, 6 Oct. 1843; F.O. 78/618, Rose to Canning, No. 42, encl. in Rose to Aberdeen, No. 33, Beirut, 13 May 1845; see also below, p. 126.

[3] See Burckhardt, pp. 141, 152–3; F.O. 195/274, Rose to Cowley, No. 46, Broumana, 25 Aug. 1847; Lyde, pp. 194, 219; Murray, ii. 620; *Rambles*, p. 177; Walpole, iii. 146.

Egyptians withdrew in 1840, the 'Alawis recovered their autonomy and were able virtually to maintain it over a long period.[1] Only infrequently did the Turkish authorities manage to collect certain amounts of taxes, and this by dispatching punitive military expeditions or by getting the co-operation of Khayrī Bey, the great Nusayri chief who was nominated as local governor.[2]

In 1852, the Ottomans took their first big step towards the subjection of the 'Alawis: while exploiting the internal rivalries and gaining the co-operation of certain local chiefs, they dispatched to the area a big military force which succeeded in quelling a large-scale resistance to conscription and managed to take recruits from most parts of the Jabal.[3] In the following years, however, the situation was reversed. Taking advantage of the government's weakness, owing, apparently, to the Crimean War, the 'Alawis revolted again in 1854; they refused to pay taxes, attacked government troops, and put the whole area into complete disorder; they even dared to raid the town of Latakia where they killed the local Turkish governor and freed a number of their hostages.[4] The authorities, unable to overcome the fresh uprisings, appointed Khayrī Bey in 1855 as *müdir* of Safita, the centre of local unrest. But the latter, who succeeded in rallying the support of most Nusayri clans, remained for some years the actual ruler of the area, and who would neither yield to Turkish control nor pay his taxes in time. This was largely due to his ambition to become the official governor of the whole Jabal, in parts of which the Ottomans had posted Sunni and other non-'Alawi governors whom they supported against Khayrī Bey[5]. Subsequently the area was again in flames as a result of the intense fighting between the Nusayris

[1] See, for example, F.O. 78/447, Wood to Aberdeen, No. 30, Damascus, 4 Nov. 1841; F.O. 195/195, Moore to Canning, No. 12, Beirut, 17 May 1842; F.O. 78/714, Wood to Palmerston, No. 26, Damascus, 10 Nov. 1847; A.E. Damas, i, from Beaudin, No. 3, 29 July 1843.

[2] F.O. 78/538, Wood to Aberdeen, No. 30, 30 Aug. 1843; F.O. 78/714, Wood to Palmerston, No. 28, Damascus, 8 Dec. 1847; Walpole, iii. 89, 366.

[3] *Irade D.*, No. 15452/1, 10 B 1268; *Ceride-i Havadis*, No. 636, 18 ZA 1269; F.O. 78/910, Elias to Werry, Latakia, 29 Mar., encl. in Werry to Malmesbury, No. 7, Aleppo, 29 Apr. 1852; Lyde, p. 194.

[4] F.O. 78/1033, British Vice-Consul in Latakia to Werry, 18 Nov., encl. in Werry to Clarendon, No. 20, 30 Nov. 1854; Wortabet, i. 26.

[5] F.O. 78/1116, Lyde to Moore, Latakia Mountains, 1 Sept. 1855, encl. in Moore to Clarendon, Beirut, 4 Sept. 1855; A.E. Damas, v, from Outrey, No. 43, 14 Jan. 1851; Muḥammad Ṭawīl, *Ta'rīkh al-'Alawiyyīn* (Latakia, 1924), p. 399.

and the neighbouring Muslim-Sunnis.[1] The authorities not only encouraged the latter, but sent, in May 1858, a military expedition against the rebels who succeeded, however, in repelling it.[2] A more powerful military expedition, including thousands of regular troops and supported by a Turkish warship, launched a fresh offensive in October 1858; it was able to crush the revolt after Khayrī Bey was betrayed and killed by one of his relatives.[3] The latter was nominated in the place of Khayrī Bey and for the time being Ottoman rule was established in Jabal Ansariyya.[4]

B. *Anti-Lebanon: Ba'albek*

A similar pattern of relations existed also between the Turkish authorities and another heterodox Islamic minority group, namely, the Ḥarfūsh Mutawali (Shi'i) family of Ba'albek. During the period under survey, the Ottomans kept playing the various factions of the Ḥarfūsh family against each other in order to break their power and control their district. But not until the end of the 1850s were the Turks able to rule the area without the help of the various Ḥarfūsh Amirs.

The withdrawal of Ibrāhīm Paṣa (who himself could govern Ba'albek only by using the above methods) saw two branches of the Ḥarfūsh family struggling for authority in the region. They were headed by Amir Ḥanjar and Amir Qablān respectively, both of whom had revolted against the Egyptian government and helped the Turks to expel Ibrāhīm Paṣa. The Ottoman authorities appointed first Ḥanjar as governor of Ba'albek, but in 1842 they replaced him by Amir Ḥamīd, the son of his rival, Qablān. But since neither of the rival chiefs could satisfy the high financial demands of the Turks and also remit the area's tax-arrears, the government promoted a third local faction against the other two:

[1] *Irade D.*, No. 27058/14, 3 ZA 1274; F.O. 78/1386, Moore to Malmesbury, No. 60, Beirut, 27 Oct. 1858.

[2] *Irade D.*, No. 27058/7, 10, and 14, of 22 and 27 ZA and 3 Z 1274; A.E. Damas, v, from Outrey, No. 52, 10 May 1858; F.O. 78/1386, Moore to Malmesbury, No. 60, Beirut, 27 Oct. 1858.

[3] F.O. 78/1388, Brant to Bulwer, No. 53, 25 Oct., encl. in Brant to Malmesbury, No. 13, Damascus, 26 Oct. 1858; *Rambles*, pp. 119–20.

[4] In later years the 'Alawis continued from time to time to revolt against the government; the latter would then send powerful punitive expeditions to quell the uprisings, arrest local chiefs, burn down villages, and levy a double amount of taxes and conscripts. See, *al-Jinān*, xi (1870), pp. 324–5; xii (1870), p. 357; *Rambles*, p. 177. Compare Ṭawīl, pp. 392 ff.

in 1845 it nominated Amir Muḥammad, head of a young branch of the Ḥarfūsh family, as governor of Baʿalbek. The old rival Amirs, opposing this nomination, united their forces and defeated government troops which had been dispatched to install Muḥammad in his office.[1] The matter was then referred to the provincial council of Damascus, whose Sunni members apparently seized this opportunity to destroy the Shiʿi Amirs: they ordered the governors of Homs, Hama, Rashāyā, and Ḥasbāyā to assemble their forces under the command of the ruler of Ḥasbāyā, Amir Saʿd al-Dīn, in order to attack the Ḥarfūshes. The latter prepared themselves to fight back and were supported in this aim by some Druze forces from the Lebanon. The Pasha of Damascus, however, wishing to avoid a military clash, sought the mediation of the English consul Wood, who was indeed able to achieve a truce: the rebellious Amirs laid down arms and were each given small districts from Baʿalbek and the eastern part of al-Biqāʿ.[2]

By 1850, the Turkish authorities were strong enough to make another attempt to deprive the Ḥarfūshes of their authority in Baʿalbek; Timor Paşa, a Turkish official, was appointed to govern the area of al-Biqāʿ with the intention of extending his control over Baʿalbek.[3] This step was followed by another unpopular measure—conscription—which aimed at destroying the power of the Ḥarfūsh Amirs. The latter once again united to resist the government troops, but were defeated and in large part arrested; Baʿalbek was then placed under direct Turkish rule.[4] For some three years the area remained tranquil and continued to be governed mainly by Turks.

In 1853, however, Turkish rule in this area was challenged by Amir Salmān Ḥarfūsh, who had managed to survive the 1850 defeat while taking refuge with some Bedouin tribes. Gathering many followers and exploiting the government's weakness at the time of the Crimean War, Salmān established his authority in the area and created serious trouble for the authorities and certain

[1] Mīkhāʾīl Alūf al-Baʿalbakī, *Taʾrīkh Baʿalbak* (Beirut, 1908), pp. 84–87; F.O. 195/226, Wood to Canning, No. 16, Damascus, 4 July 1844.

[2] F.O. 78/622, Wood to Aberdeen, No. 3, Damascus, 14 Jan. 1845; al-Baʿalbakī, p. 87.

[3] F.O. 195/291, Calvert to Canning, No. 23, Damascus, 20 Sept. 1850; compare also *Irade D.*, No. 13183, 24 Z 1266.

[4] *Irade D.*, No. 13183, 24 Z 1266; F.O. 195/219, Calvert to Canning, No. 26, Damascus, 9 Oct. 1850; al-Baʿalbakī, pp. 87–88.

sections of the neighbouring population. The Turks, unable to crush him, appointed Salmān, under pressure from Consul Wood and in opposition to the French attitude, as head of two hundred irregular cavalry, with orders to maintain order in the area.[1] For the next four years, Salmān and his men were engaged in performing their official duties which included also tax-collection in the area of Baʿalbek; but at the same time, they occasionally committed acts of aggression against the inhabitants of the vicinity.[2] The authorities, waiting for an opportunity to destroy Salmān, used the occasion of his defeat by a powerful body of Bedouin which invaded the area, and discharged him from his position at the end of 1858.[3] Yet the Ḥarfūsh chief revolted again, but was arrested in 1859; this was also the fate of his rival, Amīr Muḥammad Ḥarfūsh, who had been allowed to return from exile a year previously. It appears that henceforth the family of Ḥarfūsh lost its power, and although Salmān managed to escape from prison in the early 1860s and resumed his lawless behaviour, the area of Baʿalbek was finally put under direct Turkish rule.[4]

C. *Jabal Nablus*

Another area that was conspicuous for its internal friction as well as for its resistance to direct Turkish rule, was Jabal Nablus in central Palestine. All government efforts in the pre-reform era to play off the local factions against each other in order to install its own governor, proved a failure. For the rival parties would usually unite against the external threat, drive out their new governor, and return to their inner strife.[5] Thus, even Napoleon[6] and al-Jazzār failed to dominate Nablus,[7] whereas ʿAbdullāh Paşa was able, only with Bashīr's help, to take Nablus's stronghold of Ṣanūr in 1829–30, but failed to keep the mountain under his direct control.[8]

[1] F.O. 78/1029, Wood to Clarendon, No. 42, Damascus, 15 Aug. 1854; A.E. Damas, iii, from de Barrère, No. 6, 10 Oct. 1853; al-Baʿalbakī, p. 88.

[2] Letter from the *vali* of Damascus, dated 4 CA (?) 1271, in A.E. Damas, iii. 295; A.E. Damas, iii, from de Barrère, No. 13, 6 May 1854; F.O. 78/1388, Brant to Alison, No. 15, 23 Mar., encl. in Brant to Malmesbury, No. 3, Damascus, 25 Mar. 1858.

[3] F.O. 78/1388, Brant to Bulwer, No. 58, 19 Nov., encl. in Brant to Malmesbury, No. 15, Damascus, 22 Nov. 1858.

[4] F.O. 78/1454, Brant to Malmesbury, No. 1, Damascus, 15 Jan. 1859; al-Baʿalbakī, pp. 89–90.

[5] Cf. al-Bāshā, p. 100; al-Nimr, pp. 219, 235–6.

[6] Burckhardt, p. 42; al-Nimr, p. 161.

[7] Ibid., pp. 171–5, 184.

[8] Al-Dibs, viii. 645–8; Manṣūr, p. 61; al-Nimr, pp. 243–5.

The internal rivalry in the Jabal at that period involved chiefly the families of Ṭuqān, al-Jarrār, and al-Rayyān, who belonged to the Qaysi federation, and the families of al-Nimr, Qāsim, and ʿAbd al-Hādī, who claimed to be Yamanis. The warfare took place in almost every part of the area either between single families or coalitions, sometimes irrespective of their Qaysi or Yamani origin, and involved also corresponding Bedouin tribes on each side. Thus, for example, the first quarter of the nineteenth century saw a struggle for power between two Qaysi families—the Ṭuqāns, who had then begun to emerge as a powerful element, and the Jarrārs, who strove to maintain their old position in the district.[1] A third leading family which fought to reinforce its declining position was the Yamani family of al-Nimr: at first it supported the Ṭuqāns against their rivals, but in the second decade of the nineteenth century, it sided with the Jarrārs, and later even led a coalition of local families in a war against the Ṭuqāns.[2] The latter, however, despite occasional setbacks, managed to establish their supremacy in the Jabal for a long period of time; but on the eve of the Egyptian occupation they were faced with the emerging challenge of the Yamani families of ʿAbd al-Hādī and Qāsim, which were replacing the Jarrārs as their chief rivals.[3]

When Ibrāhīm Paṣa occupied the country, he appointed the leaders of the new Yamani coalition to govern Nablus as well as other Palestinian districts, thus further consolidating their position.[4] The course of the following years enabled the family of ʿAbd al-Hādī to deprive most local leaders, including even the Qāsims, of their power and to establish themselves as governors of Nablus and other parts of the area.[5] It was chiefly the 1834 revolt that helped the ʿAbd al-Hādīs, who remained completely loyal to the Egyptians, finally to shift the local balance of power in their favour. By contrast, the Qāsim family which took the leadership of this unsuccessful revolt was crushed, as were all other participating families, except for the al-Nimrs who, by remaining neutral, managed to improve their position.[6] The family of ʿAbd al-Hādī, assisted by the al-Nimrs, continued to rule Nablus until the end of

[1] Al-Nimr, pp. 159, 181 ff. [2] Ibid., pp. 186 ff. [3] Ibid., pp. 244, 248.

[4] Ibid., p. 261; Rustum, *Maḥfūẓāt*, i. 128–9, No. 342.

[5] Compare, Manṣūr, pp. 70–71; al-Nimr, p. 261. See also Abir pp. 28–29.

[6] Al-Bāshā, pp. 108–9; al-Nimr, pp. 252–6, 268; Rustum, op. cit. i. 220, No. 497; ii. 231, No. 549; p. 419, No. 3536; p. 424, No. 3556; p. 425, No. 3564; Spyridon, pp. 78, 94.

the Egyptian occupation, with a certain degree of autonomy which sometimes was at variance with Egyptian orders.[1]

When the Ottomans restored their authority in Palestine in 1840–1, the disfavoured families recovered their power and the old struggle for authority was resumed along the traditional pattern of Qays against Yaman. On the one side there stood the ʿAbd al-Hādīs backed by the al-Nimrs and supported by the now reconciliated Qāsim family, as well as by other Yamani families. On the other side, the alignment of the Qaysi faction was led by the Ṭuqāns and seconded by the families of Jarrār and Rayyān. During the 1840s and 1850s, local warfare flared up from time to time between rival families or knots of families, involving also corresponding factions of Bedouin and causing great destruction and loss of life.[2] The major object of this strife was again the governorship of the Nablus region, for which ʿAbd al-Hādīs and the Ṭuqāns competed. Neither element would, however, agree to concede this position to the Ottomans who constituted a third force seeking to establish its direct authority in Jabal Nablus. And in this struggle the Turks were again basically inferior to the united local elements: against the local militia (*jarūd*) which consisted of more than 20,000 armed peasants in addition to numerous Bedouin,[3] the government forces were generally not sufficient to support a Turkish official as governor. Under these circumstances, the authorities were bound to appoint as governor one of the local chiefs who would help them to maintain a certain degree of control and particularly to collect taxes from the district which was regarded as 'one of the very best portions of the Turkish Empire'.[4] At the same time, however, the choice of the local chiefs as governors was occasionally influenced by factors that were not always compatible with the ultimate Turkish goal of imposing direct rule in Nablus. For one thing, some nominations were put forward as a result of bribing the Pasha of Jerusalem or his *meclis*, while others were obtained by exploiting the friction between the Pasha of Jerusalem and his superior, the *vali* of Sidon.[5]

[1] Al-Nimr, pp. 261–2.

[2] Ibid., pp. 274–5, 277–9, 282–8; Finn, i. 239–40, 242 n, 409; Rogers, *Notices*, pp. 13 f.; Wortabet, ii. 120, 134.

[3] Finn, i. 237; F.O. 78/836, Finn to Rose, Safed, 31 Oct., encl. in Rose to Palmerston, No. 48, Beirut, 3 Nov. 1850; al-Nimr, pp. 288 ff.

[4] F.O. 78/1217, Finn to Clarendon, No. 51, Jerusalem, 15 Aug. 1856.

[5] See, for example, F.O. 78/1032, Finn to Clarendon, No. 14, Jerusalem,

The rivalry between the British and the French was another significant factor; the former supporting the Ṭuqāns and the latter the ʿAbd al-Hādīs.[1] The Ottoman authorities for their part preferred, on the whole, the Ṭuqān family, which was regarded as pro-Turk, for the governorship of the Jabal. But when unable to control the area either through the Ṭuqāns or by means of their own governor, the authorities would resort to the powerful and wealthy family of ʿAbd al-Hādī, despite its pro-Egyptian record.

Accordingly, the Ottomans, on their return to Palestine, reappointed members of the ʿAbd al-Hādī family to the governorship of Nablus and its adjacent village of Jenin, as well as to other places in the country. This step was partly motivated by the Turkish desire to continue the regular Egyptian system for a transitional period and partly was a result of bribery; it aroused, however, the dissatisfaction and resistance of all the rival local families.[2] Consequently the government removed Maḥmūd ʿAbd al-Hādī from the governorship of Nablus at the end of 1842, and appointed in his place Sulaymān Bey Ṭuqān as *kaymakam*. The latter, unable or unwilling to collect taxes, was arrested and replaced by two successive Turkish governors, who were also unable to control the area.[3] The renomination of Sulaymān Ṭuqān in 1845, following a fresh local opposition to a new Turkish governor, did not, however, bring a change in the unsettled state of affairs in Nablus. Military expeditions were sent from time to time during the next two years to put down disturbances and enforce tax-collection.[4] In 1847, Sulaymān was once more replaced by a Turkish governor, but following a new local uprising, he was again restored to his position which he occupied until 1851.

In that year, hostilities between the rival factions of ʿAbd al-Hādī and Ṭuqān were resumed with great intensity, involving a number

27 July 1854; Finn, i. 397; Rogers, op. cit., p. 14; compare also al-Nimr, p. 264.

[1] Finn, ii. 431 ff.; compare also F.O. 78/836, Finn to Rose, Safed, 31 Oct., encl. in Rose to Palmerston, No. 48, Beirut, 3 Nov. 1850; *Irade D.*, No. 14609, 2 Z 1267.

[2] F.O. 78/449, Moore to Palmerston, Beirut, 29 June 1841; F.O. 78/447, Wood to Palmerston, No. 16, Damascus, 4 Oct. 1841.

[3] F.O. 78/499, Wood to Aberdeen, No. 7, Damascus 17 Feb. 1843; A.E. Jérusalem, i, from Lantivy, 10 July 1844; ibid., ii, from de Barrère, No. 4, 18 Feb. 1845.

[4] See, for example, *Irade D.*, No. 6523, 10 L 1262; ibid., No. 7691/20, 24 C 1263.

of Bedouin tribes on each side. The Turks, while refraining from stopping the disturbances, exploited the mutual bloodletting to arrest the leaders of both factions;[1] the chiefs of the ʿAbd al-Hādī family were, however, released shortly afterwards, and their leader, Maḥmūd, was nominated *kaymakam* of Nablus. These steps were presumably adopted to pave the way for the unpopular measure of conscription which followed in 1852: unlike under Egyptian rule, it was now carried out with unexpectedly great facility.[2] But once this measure was accomplished, the government renewed its attempts to install a Turkish governor in the Jabal in place of Maḥmūd ʿAbd al-Hādī. This was made possible only at the end of 1853 after Maḥmūd was replaced by a member of the Ṭuqāns, and the latter—shortly after—by a Turkish *kaymakam*. The new governor was, however, still unable to master the district since he had insufficient military forces under his command, and for the next two years the post of local governor changed hands among the three contestants, namely, Turkish delegates, Maḥmūd ʿAbd al-Hādī, and ʿAlī Bey Ṭuqān. The termination of the Crimean War saw Sheikh ʿAbd al-Hādī again in office, which he occupied from 1856 to 1858, partly by bribing government quarters in Jerusalem, and partly as a result of the continuing military weakness of the government.[3]

Only at the end of 1858 were the Ottomans able to impose a radical change in the government of Jabal Nablus and bring it under their control. This was on the one hand due to the gradual weakening of the local forces, and on the other, a result of European pressure which followed serious anti-European disturbances in Nablus in 1856.[4] Above all, a number of decisive administrative and military steps were now for the first time taken by the authorities: the district of Nablus was transferred from the jurisdiction of Jerusalem and placed under the *vali* of Sidon with the same footing as Jerusalem; an energetic Turkish governor, Ziya Bey, was nominated as *mutasarrıf* of the district, and a great military force was posted in the area and arrested the powerful local

[1] *Irade D.*, No. 14609/14, 2 Z 1267; *Irade M.V.*, No. 7891, 6 R 1268; F.O. 78/872, Wood to Palmerston, No. 25, Damascus, 28 July 1851; al-Nimr, p. 268; Rogers, op. cit., p. 36.

[2] *Irade D.*, No. 14759/1, 3, of 12 and 19 M 1268.

[3] F.O. 78/1219, Moore to Clarendon, No. 12, Beirut, 17 Mar. 1856; F.O. 78/1217, Finn to Clarendon, No. 10, Jerusalem, 21 Feb. 1856.

[4] Finn, ii. 430; al-Nimr, pp. 268–9. See also below, pp. 226–7.

chief, Maḥmūd ʿAbd al-Hādī.[1] But other members of the ʿAbd al-Hādī family, secure within their stronghold of ʿArāba, organized and carried out yet another uprising. It was not until April 1859 that the government was able to overcome this last pocket of resistance. With the help of the Ṭuqāns and the Jarrārs, Turkish troops attacked the village of ʿArāba, sacked and destroyed it, and killed many of its inhabitants, although some managed to escape across the Jordan.[2] This firm action, which had 'not been taken by the Turkish government since its re-establishment in 1840', was followed by a series of further administrative and social reforms which provoked a fresh popular uprising at the end of 1859; it was eventually suppressed by reinforcements which arrived from other parts of Palestine.[3]

Henceforth, Jabal Nablus was permanently governed by Turkish officials who, on the whole, were able to keep the area in tolerable order, although local hostilities between the rival factions flared up again from time to time. The struggle for authority was now conducted, however, on more advanced lines; it was mainly concentrated in the local *meclis* where the heads of families, including the former rebels, constituted a dominant force which was occasionally able to challenge the Ottoman authority.[4]

D. *Judean Mountains*

South of Jabal Nablus, in the Judean hills around Jerusalem, the major centres of local power were the region around Hebron controlled by the violent chief ʿAbd al-Raḥmān ʿĀmir at the village of Durra, and Qaryat al-ʿAnab, a hilly village north-west of Jerusalem which was the stronghold of the Abū-Ghūsh family. The latter was a formidable family which for many years before the Egyptian occupation remained virtually autonomous, while dominating the main roads to Jerusalem and robbing the travellers

[1] F.O. 78/1383, Finn to Malmesbury, No. 26, Jerusalem, 9 Oct. 1858; F.O. 78/1454, Moore to Bulwer, No. 1, 12 Jan., encl. in Moore to Malmesbury, No. 2, Beirut, 20 Jan. 1859; al-Nimr, pp. 268–9, 293–5.

[2] *Irade D.*, No. 28545, 13 L 1275; F.O. 78/1454, Finn to Malmesbury, No. 10, Jerusalem, 26 Apr. 1859; al-Nimr, pp. 295 ff.

[3] Al-Nimr, pp. 268, 300–3; compare Manṣūr, p. 92; F.O. 78/1521, Finn to Russell, No. 1, Jerusalem, 4 Jan. 1860; *Irade D.*, No. 27620, 10 RA 1275.

[4] See, for example, F.O. 78/1588, Finn to Russell, No. 7, Jerusalem, 1 Mar. 1861; al-Nimr, pp. 299–300.

who passed there.[1] Only Ibrāhīm Paṣa was able to subdue this family, though he retained its chief in the official position of governor of the district and warden of the Jerusalem road.[2]

Unlike the Abū-Ghūshes who yielded to the Egyptian supremacy almost without a battle, the Hebronites, notorious for their disobedience, bitterly resisted the Egyptian régime. Hebron constituted, in fact, one of the major focuses of the 1834 revolt against Ibrāhīm Paṣa; after a severe fight, it was taken by the Egyptian army who sacked and partly destroyed the town, killing many of its inhabitants and conscripting many others.[3] The local chief, ʿAbd al-Raḥmān, managed, however, to escape to the bordering Judean desert, taking refuge among his Bedouin allies. On the eve of the Egyptian withdrawal from Palestine, this chief, with English encouragement, resumed his rebellion against Ibrāhīm: returning to Hebron, he slew the Egyptian-nominated governor and proclaimed himself governor of the town.[4] Having been confirmed by the Ottomans in this position with the title of *muhassıl* (tax-collector) of Jabal Khalīl (Hebron Mountain), ʿAbd al-Raḥmān established himself as an independent autocrat of the district, oppressing and extorting from its population, Muslims and non-Muslims alike.[5]

In the hilly area near Jerusalem, a similar situation emerged on the restoration of the Turkish rule: the Ottomans confirmed Muṣṭafā Abū-Ghūsh as governor and tax-collector of the district as well as warden of the Jerusalem road. But instead of maintaining order in the region, the Abū-Ghūshes resumed their disobedient activities; and as leaders of the regional Yamani faction, they were engaged in a fierce warfare with their Qaysi rivals led by the Samḥān family.[6] For more than five years both hilly districts of Jerusalem and Hebron were in a semi-rebellious state:

[1] Baedeker, p. 139; Finn, i. 231–2; Spyridon, pp. 38–39.

[2] Baedeker and Finn, op. cit.; Rustum, *Maḥfūẓāt*, ii. 243, No. 3548; Spyridon, p. 96.

[3] Al-Bāshā, pp. 111–12; Spyridon, pp. 99–100; Abū ʿIzz al-Dīn, p. 177; Rustum, op. cit. ii. 438, No. 3625.

[4] Wood's Papers, letter from A. Jochmus to Ahmed Zecharias, 13 Jan. 1841; Finn, i. 236–7.

[5] F.O. 78/447, Wood to Rifat Pasha, No. 2, Damascus, 18 Oct. 1841; Finn, i. 237.

[6] *Irade M.V.*, No. 1016, 8 ZA 1259; F.O. 78/581, Young to Canning, No. 25, Jerusalem, 3 Aug. 1844; A.E. Jérusalem, ii, from de Barrère, 29 Dec. 1844; Finn, i. 232–4; Spyridon, p. 138.

taxes were irregularly paid, travellers on the roads were subject to attack and plunder, and peasant factions revived their bloody strife.[1]

Only in mid-1846 were the Turks able to crush these rebellious chiefs and for a while subject the whole area to direct rule. These measures were accomplished by Mehmed Kıbrıslı Paşa, then Pasha of Jerusalem, who launched a series of military assaults against the numerous local chiefs, arresting most of them, demolishing their petty village strongholds, and disarming their followers.[2] During these operations Hebron was attacked and sacked, and 'Abd al-Raḥmān and his rival brother, Muḥammad, were both arrested and banished; this was also the fate of some chiefs of the Abū-Ghūsh family.[3] For about a year the whole area was kept under complete Turkish control by army units posted in key positions; 'perfect safety' prevailed everywhere, taxes were collected regularly, and other measures introduced.[4]

But when in 1847 Kıbrıslı Paşa was recalled to Istanbul, the area was again in revolt and disorder; it was being virtually controlled by the two great chiefs, each having under his command about 2,000 armed peasants in addition to numerous Bedouin allies.[5] 'Abd al-Raḥmān, who was allowed to return to Hebron in 1848, expelled the local governor by force and nominated himself in his place; the new Pasha of Jerusalem not only endorsed this action, but also bestowed on 'Abd a-Raḥmān a 'robe of honour'.[6] This chief then 'resumed his career of oppressing the peasantry, plundering the helpless Jews in Hebron and even employing agents to rob travellers upon the road'.[7] He was, in addition, engaged in an intense warfare with his rival brothers, which the authorities tried unsuccessfully to exploit in order to weaken both parties and control the town of Hebron.[8]

[1] *Irade D.*, No. 6275, 11 B 1262; F.O. 78/581, Young to Aberdeen, No. 37, Jerusalem, 23 Oct. 1844; F.O. 78/664, Finn to Aberdeen, No. 13, Jerusalem, 3 Sept. 1846; Finn, i. 233, 237.

[2] *Irade D.*, No. 6326, 25 B 1262; ibid., No. 24 C 1263; F.O. 195/210, Finn to Canning, No. 5, 27 Aug. 1846; Kibrizli, pp. 71–79.

[3] *Irade D.*, No. 6680, 10 ZA 1262; A.E. Jérusalem, ii, from Jorelle, No. 15, 16 Aug. 1846; F.O. 195/210, Finn to Canning, No. 3, Jerusalem, 30 May 1846.

[4] F.O. 78/664, Finn to Aberdeen, No. 13, Jerusalem, 3 Sept. 1846; F.O. 78/705, Finn to Palmerston, No. 13, Jerusalem, 13 Mar. 1847.

[5] F.O. 78/705, Finn to Palmerston, No. 7, Jerusalem, 5 Feb. 1847.

[6] F.O. 78/755, Finn to Palmerston, No. 22, Jerusalem, 17 July 1848.

[7] Finn, i. 237.

[8] F.O. 78/839, Finn to Palmerston, No. 20, Jerusalem, 27 Sept. 1850; Finn, ii. 42.

In 1852, following an imperial firman, ʿAbd al-Raḥmān was dismissed from his post as *müdir* of Hebron district, and was arrested by the Pasha of Jerusalem and charged with rebellion against the government. But before long he managed to escape from prison, returned to Hebron, and once again expelled the Turkish governor as well as the local mufti, while reappointing himself governor and nominating one of his followers as mufti.[1]

The mountainous district round Jerusalem underwent at the same time a similar course of events. Following the recall of Kıbrıslı Paşa from Jerusalem, a certain member of the Abū-Ghūsh family was allowed to fill the official posts of Muṣṭafā Abū-Ghūsh (who returned from exile only later, in 1851); and his men then resumed their turbulent activities along the Jerusalem road, levying excessive tolls on the travellers and even robbing and killing some passengers.[2] In addition, the Abū-Ghūshes revived their fierce hostilities against the Qaysi faction, causing heavy bloodshed and destruction.[3] As in other areas, this local warfare was indirectly encouraged by certain quarters in the city. Firstly, the members of the provincial *meclis* of Jerusalem would support, by means of their *mazbata*, the party whose bribe was the largest.[4] Secondly, the European consuls, particularly the French and the English, would occasionally support a certain rival chief as it suited their policy of protecting their Christian protégés in villages near Jerusalem.[5] Above all, the Turkish authorities themselves, militarily weak and unable to subdue the mountain peoples, often played off the rival groups against each other, aiming at balancing and weakening their power.[6]

In 1854 the Turks made a fresh attempt to pacify and subdue

[1] *Irade M.V.*, No. 8124, 3 C 1268; Finn, i. 248–55. According to Consul Finn, ʿAbd al-Raḥmān was strongly supported by Kıbrıslı Paşa, then *serasker* in Damascus, who regarded him as 'a loyal subject', see F.O. 78/913, Finn to Malmesbury, No. 2, Jerusalem, 29 May 1852.

[2] F.O. 78/1032, Finn to Redcliffe, No. 40, encl. in Finn to Clarendon, No. 21, Jerusalem, 28 Nov. 1854; Finn, i. 388–9; Wortabet, ii. 164.

[3] F.O. 78/755, Finn to Palmerston, No. 22, Jerusalem, 17 July 1848; F.O. 78/962, Finn to Redcliffe, No. 25, encl. in Finn to Clarendon, No. 12, Jerusalem, 12 Aug. 1853; Finn, i. 235, 298–9, 398.

[4] See F.O. 78/1032, Finn to Redcliffe, No. 40, encl. in Finn to Clarendon, No. 21, Jerusalem, 28 Nov. 1854; Finn, i. 266, 305, 313, 321, 324–5.

[5] A.E. Jérusalem, i, from Lantivy, No. 56, 22 Apr. 1844; F.O. 78/1032, Finn to Clarendon, No. 13, Jerusalem, 7 July 1854; Finn, i. 312.

[6] F.O. 78/618, Rose to Canning, No. 42, encl. in Rose to Aberdeen, No. 33, Beirut, 13 May 1845; Finn, i. 219, 231, 393, 407–10.

both districts of Hebron and Jerusalem. The province of Jerusalem was promoted to a status of *eyalet* and was directly subject to Istanbul. The new *vali*, Yakub Paşa, was an able governor despite his eighty-four years of age, and, unlike his predecessors, was entitled to employ regular troops without asking the *serasker*'s permission. And indeed, the Pasha, by employing his adequate garrison, succeeded in restoring order in his province,[1] although he was unable to destroy the two powerful local chiefs, ʿAbd al-Raḥmān in particular, whom he was forced to nominate as *nazır* (inspector) of the rural area of Hebron.[2] But following the death of Yakub Paşa, ʿAbd al-Raḥmān resumed his lawless campaign of oppressing the population of Hebron, Jews and Muslims alike, and committing new murders and robberies; furthermore, he refused to raise the district's taxes and incited its inhabitants to revolt against the government.[3] To quell this uprising which spread throughout the region, Turkish troops were sent against Hebron in 1855. ʿAbd al-Raḥmān retreated to the village of Idna, where he fortified himself with his peasant and Bedouin partisans. But the government forces were able to capture the village and to put down the rebellion; all local chiefs hurriedly expressed their submission by paying their tax-arrears, and only ʿAbd al-Raḥmān again managed to escape to the desert.[4]

Henceforth the area of the Judean mountains was kept in tolerable order and further steps were adopted there to exert direct Turkish rule. This process was intensified especially during the last two to three years of the 1850s when another energetic Turkish governor, Süreyya Paşa, succeeded in arresting an additional number of local chiefs and replacing them by Turkish governors.[5] Nevertheless, the Ottoman authorities could not at this stage, completely do away with the two principal chiefs of the Judean hills. The family of Abū-Ghūsh continued to control its

[1] F.O. 78/1032, Finn to Clarendon, No. 6, Jerusalem, 17 Apr. 1854; Finn, i. 454, 472 ff.

[2] F.O. 78/1032, Finn to Clarendon, No. 16, Jerusalem, 27 July 1854.

[3] *Irade D.*, No. 21422/17, 16 M 1272; *Irade M.M.*, No. 173, 24 L 1271; F.O. 78/1120, Finn to Clarendon, No. 11, Jerusalem, 26 May 1855; Finn, ii. 33–34, 41–43.

[4] *Irade D.*, No. 21422/17, 16 M 1272; F.O. 78/1120, Finn to Clarendon, No. 23, Jerusalem, 6 Aug. 1855; A.E. Jérusalem, v, No. 118, 18 Aug. 1855; Finn, ii. 286 ff.

[5] F.O. 78/1383, Finn to Clarendon, No. 1, Jerusalem, 1 Jan. 1858; A.E. Jérusalem, vi, from de Barrère, No. 9, 1 July 1858.

mountainous district and to commit occasional acts of lawlessness,[1] while 'Abd al-Raḥmān was allowed to return from the wilderness in 1858, and was reappointed *nazır* of the Hebron district although the town itself was governed by a Turkish *müdir*.[2] Only at the end of 1859 was 'Abd al-Raḥmān's power finally broken: a military expedition arrested him and his followers and the district was placed under military supervision.[3]

E. *Jabal Druze*

> 'These people have completely lost all respect for the government to which they no longer furnish any troops or taxes.'
>
> (Midhat Paşa)[4]

From what has been said up to now, it emerges that the Ottoman government succeeded, during the 1850s, in accomplishing some of its aims with regard to the administration of the mountainous areas: it was able to carry out measures of conscription and taxation as well as to impose a certain degree of direct rule in most hilly districts of Syria and Palestine. The only conspicuous exception was Jabal Druze of Houran, whose Druze inhabitants managed to maintain complete autonomy, despite successive Turkish attempts to subdue them, not only throughout the Tanzimat period, but also until the end of the century.

The source of the Druzes' strength was to be found in the combination of their social structure, features of character, and the topography of their stronghold. Ardently attached to their communal system and eager to live in isolation, the Druzes formed the most solid ethnic group in Syria. Unlike the other mountain people, they were less subject to internal conflict and so were less vulnerable to exploitation by the authorities in order to weaken them; at any rate they were always able to close their ranks tightly against any external encroachment. Their outstanding bravery and warlike spirit which derived from their sense of particularism and was forged in endless battles, enabled the Druzes of Houran to fight off not only formidable government expeditions, but also the

[1] See A.E. Jérusalem, vi, from de Barrère, No. 9, 20 July 1858; F.O. 78/1588, Finn to Russell, No. 9, Jerusalem, 23 Mar. 1861.

[2] F.O. 78/1383, Finn to Malmesbury, No. 17, Jerusalem, 23 June 1858.

[3] *Irade M.V.*, No. 18653/5, 11 CA 1276.

[4] From a cable by Midhat Paşa, the *vali* of Damascus, to the Grand Vezir, dated 18 Oct. 1879, in Midhat, p. 183.

attacks of local Bedouin tribes who vied with them for control in the Houran. Finally, the inaccessible nature of the Druze stronghold of Leja served further to strengthen their position and to make them undefeatable and virtually independent.

Thus the Druzes of Houran had succeeded in maintaining their autonomy not merely during the disorderly pre-Egyptian period, but also under the iron hand of Ibrāhīm Paşa. For, as already noted, the powerful Egyptian army which had been able to subdue and crush all local forces in Syria failed completely to subject the Druzes to government control.[1]

The position of the new Ottoman régime *vis-à-vis* the Druzes, was even worse than that of the Egyptians. Being militarily weaker than the Egyptians, not only were the Turks unable to master the Jabal, but they were also exposed to a Druze threat to their authority and interests in large neighbouring areas. Thus, for example, the Druzes, when disturbed, would descend from their mountain and ravage the plains of Houran, cutting the wheat supply to Damascus and threatening the safety of the Ḥajj caravan. They would, in addition, create grave disorders in a vast area ranging from Tiberias to the gates of Damascus and from Damascus to South Lebanon where their brethren constituted a dominant element.

In fact, the Turkish government faced its first rebuffs from Jabal Druze immediately on its restoration to Syria in 1840–1. Promptly, the Druzes, as well as other inhabitants of the Houran and Ajlun, demonstrated their independence by refusing to pay taxes. When the Pasha of Damascus remitted a part of the tax, some inhabitants paid small portions while others continued to refuse and even expelled a governor sent by the *vali*.[2] The latter then adopted further conciliatory steps: he bestowed upon some local chieftains 'robes of honour' while appointing the Druze chief, Shiblī al-ʿAryān, governor of the Houran and head of irregular troops drawn from his men. Yet this chief, in fact, used his troops to help the Lebanese Druzes in 1841 to fight their Christian rivals, and tried also to blackmail the government financially, threatening it that he would otherwise instigate a revolt in Damascus and its vicinity, attack Turkish troops, and provoke the

[1] See above, p. 4.

[2] F.O. 78/447, Werry to Palmerston, No. 1, Damascus, 21 Jan. 1841; F.O. 195/196, Wood to Bankhead, No. 30, Damascus, 6 Apr. 1842.

Bedouin to raid the pilgrimage caravan.[1] At first the authorities apparently agreed to fulfil his demands, but when these grew wider and included also political claims, the government dispatched a great military force to attack Shiblī and his men; the Druze force was ambushed and defeated and their leader surrendered. But thousands of other Druze warriors with Bedouin support massed in the Leja and repelled a new Turkish assault.[2] After a year of unwritten armistice, during which the Druzes remained unchallenged, the Ottomans renewed their preparations to attack the Jabal; but in view of a fresh alliance between the Druzes, Bedouin, and the inhabitants of Ajlun, this offensive was abandoned.[3] Henceforth, and for some seven years, the Druzes were left to conduct their own affairs without Turkish interference except for occasional demands for taxes. The districts of Houran and Ajlun were at this period nominally governed by natives of Syria, usually Muslims from Damascus who possessed, in fact, very little authority in these regions.[4]

It was only in the early 1850s that the Turks renewed their efforts to overcome Jabal Druze and its adjacent districts, in an attempt to carry out a general conscription in the country. Again the whole area rose against the government: the inhabitants of Ajlun showed armed resistance, while the Druzes and the Bedouin joined forces and defeated a Turkish detachment sent to the Leja to enforce recruitment. The latter place became, furthermore, the main shelter for Syrian Muslims and Lebanese Druzes who fled from conscription;[5] and the Turks, who could no longer tolerate such a centre of opposition lest it damage their prestige, now resolved to overcome it once and for all. Firstly, they tried vainly to create dissension between the Druzes and the Bedouin and among the Druzes themselves. Secondly, the government sent to the Houran several peace missions in an attempt to persuade the

[1] F.O. 78/447, Wood to Aberdeen, No. 3, Damascus, 3 Nov. 1841; F.O. 78/499, same to same, No. 77, Damascus, 5 Nov. 1842.

[2] F.O. 195/196, 'Literal translation, letter of Shibly al-Aryan to Mr. Wood under date 3rd November 1842', encl. in Wood to Canning, No. 57, Damascus, 14 Nov. 1842.

[3] F.O. 78/579, Wood to Aberdeen, No. 11, Damascus, 5 Apr. 1844.

[4] Compare F.O. 78/498, Wood to Aberdeen, No. 20, Damascus, 23 Feb. 1844; F.O. 78/801, Wood to Palmerston, No. 5, Damascus, 26 Feb. 1849.

[5] F.O. 78/837, Calvert to Canning, No. 26, encl. in Calvert to Palmerston, No. 24, Damascus, 29 Oct. 1850; F.O. 78/910, Wood to Canning, No. 9, encl. in Wood to F.O., No. 9, Damascus, 20 Mar. 1852.

insurgents to disperse and return home. But the Druze peasants kept insisting on exemption from conscription on the plea that their men were needed to defend the area from Bedouin raids, a function which the government neglected. They claimed also that conscription would affect their agricultural work on which they lived; instead they offered to the government an increased sum in taxes and occasional military assistance.[1]

The authorities declined to accept these offers and made unprecedentedly large preparations to launch a military offensive against the Houran. By September 1852, conscription had been completed elsewhere in the country so that the Turks were able to concentrate near the Houran foothills the major bulk of their regular army in Syria, namely, 8,000 troops of infantry, cavalry, and artillery. An additional 4,000 irregulars from all over the land, including armed peasants from Jabal Nablus, Mutawali warriors from the south Lebanon, and Bedouin mercenaries from Galilee, were called out to the battlefield.[2] At the head of this formidable expedition there stood the Syrian *serasker*, Mehmed Kıbrıslı Paşa, who had become notorious for crushing, a year previously, the Aleppo revolt and subduing the powerful chiefs near Jerusalem in 1846–7. This time, however, Kıbrıslı's harsh methods against the neighbouring population of the area were not so successful; they only served to consolidate further the alliance between the Druzes, Sunni peasants, and Bedouin and encouraged them to resist the government troops.[3] The first round of the encounter turned indeed in favour of the rebels; not only were they able to repel the Turkish attacks, causing the government troops heavy losses, but they also made a number of successful raids on army camps and supply caravans, killing soldiers and capturing quantities of ammunition.[4] In the frame of these activities the inhabitants of Houran also took steps to stop the wheat supply to Damascus, thus

[1] F.O. 78/872, 'Memo. by Houran notables to Consul Wood', of 21 L 1267, encl. in Wood to F.O., No. 29, Damascus, 26 Aug. 1851; Porter, *Damascus*, ii. 69.

[2] F.O. 78/910, Wood to Rose, No. 26, encl. in Wood to Malmesbury, No. 28, Damascus, 14 Sept. 1852; F.O. 78/913, Finn to Malmesbury, No. 12, Jerusalem, 27 Oct. 1852.

[3] Compare F.O. 78/910, Wood to Rose, No. 27, encl. in Wood to Malmesbury, No. 29, Damascus, 28 Sept. 1852; F.O. 78/959, Wood to Malmesbury, No. 1, Damascus, 3 Jan. 1853; Midhat, p. 33.

[4] F.O. 78/910, Wood to Malmesbury, No. 30, Damascus, 7 Oct. 1852; Finn, i. 262–3; Mishāqa, MS. p. 334; Porter, op. cit. i. 373.

exerting a new pressure on the authorities.[1] The effect of the Druze rebellion was, furthermore, felt in other parts of the country: bodies of Druze rebels and Bedouin raiders ravaged parts of Galilee and of the southern districts of Syria and Lebanon, cutting communications, attacking towns and villages, and causing bloodshed and destruction.[2]

Towards the end of October 1852, Kıbrıslı Paşa made fresh preparations for a second offensive, while more reinforcements and supplies were poured into the scene of war.[3] The decisive battle, which took place this time in the village of Azraʿ, ended again with a great Druze victory; several hundreds of Druzes managed to repulse a big force composed of thousands of *Nizam* troops, Albanian soldiers, and irregular cavalry, fighting under the personal command of the *serasker*; many soldiers were killed and several guns as well as a great deal of equipment captured by the rebels.[4] This serious defeat forced the *serasker* to seek peace negotiations with the Druzes: upon the *Porte*'s instructions, Kıbrıslı offered to exempt the Druzes from conscription by ballot, demanding instead that a certain number of substitutes should be recruited.[5] The Druzes, taking advantage of their strong position and under incitement from some Damascene leaders, not only refused to raise a single conscript, but put forward fresh demands for further tax concessions.[6] The authorities then took an unusual step and turned to Richard Wood, the English Consul in Damascus, who had special relations with the Druzes, requesting him to try to win over the rebels to the government proposals.[7] Consul Wood, being assisted in his mission by Lebanon Druze leaders, particularly Saʿīd Bey Jumblāṭ, managed to reach a settlement which was more in line with the Druze demands. According to this agreement,

[1] F.O. 78/910, Wood to Rose, No. 27, encl. in Wood to Malmesbury, No. 29, Damascus, 28 Sept. 1852.

[2] *Irade D.*, No. 15676/2, 14 Ş 1268; ibid., No. 16409/8, 11 B 1269; F.O. 78/910, Wood to Malmesbury, No. 30, 7 Oct. 1852; No. 33, 26 Oct. 1852; Velde, ii. 393, 427; Porter, i. 283–4, 309, 392, 394.

[3] *Irade D.*, No. 16115/5, 10 M 1269; F.O. 78/910, Wood to Malmesbury, No. 33, Damascus, 26 Oct. 1852; F.O. 78/913, Finn to Malmesbury, No. 12, Jerusalem, 27 Oct. 1852.

[4] F.O. 78/910, Wood to Malmesbury, No. 31, Damascus, 1 Nov. 1852; Finn, i. 263.

[5] F.O. 78/910, Wood to Malmesbury, No. 35, Damascus, 3 Nov. 1852.

[6] F.O. 78/910, Wood to Malmesbury, No. 38, Damascus, 7 Dec. 1852.

[7] *Irade D.*, No. 16409/17 and 20, 14 and 22 Saf. 1269; F.O. 78/910, Wood to Malmesbury, No. 38, Damascus, 7 Dec. 1852.

the Druzes were exempted from conscription altogether, but were to raise, in return, the taxes and the tax-arrears due from themselves and from their neighbouring Bedouin tribes for the last three years. The rebel leaders were, in addition, granted an amnesty but were to return the guns they had captured in the battle of Azraʿ.[1]

For the next five years, the Turkish authorities refrained from challenging the Druzes directly; instead, while changing the nominal governors of Houran every now and then, the Turks took to supporting and inciting the local Bedouin tribes against their traditional rivals, the Druzes. From time to time these factions were indeed engaged in fierce warfare; but when a fresh threat of conscription appeared, as in 1857, both parties would enter again into an alliance against the government.[2]

In the ensuing years and up to the end of the Tanzimat era, the Ottomans made more large-scale military efforts to subdue the Druzes and conscript their men; but all in vain.[3] The Druzes continued during this period to conduct their own life virtually independently of the authorities: they furnished no conscripts and raised almost no taxes for the government. Moreover, not only were they opposed to Turkish rule in their area, but they also continued to constitute a serious threat to peace and order in the adjacent regions: bodies of Druze brigands were frequently engaged in raiding villages and caravans in the neighbourhood, causing great disorder and destruction.[4] In the critical year of 1860, for example, the Houran Druzes were those who took a very active part in the massacres of Christians in both Lebanon and Damascus.

[1] F.O. 78/1028, Wood to Clarendon, No. 10, 24 Feb. 1854; A.E. Damas, iii, from de Barrère, No. 6, 10 Oct. 1853.

[2] F.O. 78/1298, Misk to Clarendon, No. 5, Damascus, 24 Apr. 1857.

[3] Porter, *Bashan*, p. 47; compare *Irade D.*, No. 26417/1, 9 Ş 1274; Jessup, i. 271; Midhat, pp. 183–4; Oliphant, pp. 57–58.

[4] Baedeker, pp. 412–13; Midhat, pp. 183–90; *P.E.F.*, July 1877, p. 144.

IX

THE STRUGGLE AGAINST THE BEDOUIN

'To uproot the Bedouin lawlessness and to check and prevent them from hurting the people.'

(Necib Paşa, *vali* of Damascus in 1841)[1]

'One year they are attacked and another subsidized. Promises are made and broken . . .'

(Consul Skene of Aleppo in 1858)[2]

THE struggle of government against the Bedouin is one of the oldest themes of Middle Eastern life, being basically the perpetual conflict between the nomad and the settled in the region. In Syria and Palestine, the lands lying at the edges of the three great deserts of Arabia, Syria, and Sinai, this conflict was particularly intense. Occasional waves of immigrant nomads from these deserts and from Egypt had pressed heavily against the borders of the Syrian provinces, challenging frequently and seriously the authority of the government; for the most part the Bedouin were in control of the steppe area south of Aleppo and great tracts of the countryside were constantly ravaged and sacked.

The Ottoman government almost from the beginning of its rule in the Syrian provinces and up to the Egyptian occupation of 1831, was on the whole unable to curb the vigorous sons of the desert and prevent the destruction they inflicted.[3] This was partly because of the Ottoman military weakness in the area, especially during the seventeenth and eighteenth centuries, and partly because of the lack of a firm Turkish policy towards the nomads. Many Turkish Pashas not only refrained from fighting the Bedouin tribes, but actually flattered them and even occasionally co-operated with their chieftains to share the fruits of their misdeeds.[4]

[1] From a declaration before the *meclis* of Damascus; *Irade D.*, No. 2117/4, 25 CA 1257.

[2] F.O. 78/1452, Skene to Bulwer, separate, encl. in Skene to Russell, No. 65, Aleppo, 30 Sept. 1858.

[3] See Burckhardt, pp. 31, 147, 300–2; Gibb and Bowen, i. 203, 233–4; Heyd, *Documents*, Docs. No. 2, 44; Manṣūr, p. 67; al-Nimr, p. 21.

[4] Al-'Awra, p. 139; Burckhardt, pp. 233–4, 302; Gibb and Bowen, i. 203, 233–4; Volney, ii. 342–3.

It is true that a small number of energetic rulers, such as Aḥmad al-Jazzār in northern Palestine, and As'ad al-'Aẓm in central Syria, succeeded during certain periods of the eighteenth century in restraining by force the Bedouin in their respective provinces.[1] But even these governors could only achieve partial and temporary domination of the Bedouin within their territories; outside, the tribes in the great desert remained as militant and unrepentant as ever.

It was not until the nineteenth century, in the 1830s, when Ibrāhīm Paşa occupied Palestine and Syria, that the first really successful measures were taken to subdue the powerful nomads in the Syrian provinces including some Bedouin strongholds across the Jordan.[2] Not that this success was long-lasting: in 1840, after the Egyptian withdrawal, the Ottoman government was faced with an intensified and aggressive Bedouin challenge.

It is perhaps useful here to distinguish some of the major Bedouin tribes which played a considerable role in Syrian life between 1840 and 1861.

The greatest threat to both the Ottoman authorities and the Syrian rural population alike came from the 'Anaza. This was a confederation of nomadic tribes who had emigrated from Najd during the eighteenth century and gained control over the area from the Euphrates to the Jordan and from Aleppo to Najd. The main tribes of the confederation along the Syrian borders were the Rwala and Wuld 'Alī, each maintaining many thousands of mounted and armed warriors;[3] their sphere of influence was in and around the *paşalık* of Damascus. In the province of Aleppo the 'Anaza were represented by the tribal factions of Dahām and Jud'an of the Fad'an tribe; and in Palmira—by the tribe of Banu Sba'a. South of the 'Anaza there lay another big tribe, the Banū Ṣakhr, who had emigrated in the eighteenth century from north Hijaz towards the area east of the Jordan, depriving the great 'Adwān tribe of its local predominance. By mid-nineteenth century the Banū Ṣakhr dominated most of the area east of the Jordan, leaving merely the district of Balqā' to the 'Adwān.[4] Both these tribes were engaged in frequent raids into Palestine,

[1] See above, p. 5. [2] See above, p. 14.

[3] F.O. 78/1297, Skene to Redcliffe, No. 28, encl. in Skene to Clarendon, No. 13, Aleppo, 28 July 1857; Baedeker, p. 84; Murray, ii. 537; *Rambles*, p. 29.

[4] Baedeker, p. 84; Burckhardt, p. 368; Finn, i. 241, 375–6; ii. 187; M. F. Von Oppenheim, *Die Beduinen* (Leipzig, 1843), ii. 232 ff.

particularly in the areas of Samaria (Nablus) and Jerusalem, where they created havoc and occasionally supported local peasant factions in their violent warfare.[1] A local small tribe, the Taʿāmra, roving in the area between Bethlehem and the Dead Sea, also supported these peasant factions and often disturbed the peace near Jerusalem.[2] South Palestine, the Negeb and Sinai were controlled by the tribes of Tiyāha, Tarābīn and ʿAzāzma, whose major activities concentrated around Gaza and Beersheba, but included also occasional incursions northward.[3] Other tribes who played a certain part in mid-nineteenth-century Syrian life were some Turkoman tribes in the Antioch plain (ʿAmq).

Apart altogether from all these marauding tribes, there were a number of warlike tribes usually half-sedentary, who, as we shall see later, were traditionally employed by the government as a police force to protect the country from encroachments of other Bedouin. Those were chiefly the Mawālī, who served in many parts of Syria, and the Hanādī, who were employed in northern Palestine as well as in northern Syria. There were, in addition, several dozens of smaller tribes within the boundaries of Syria and Palestine:[4] a few of these, particularly the sedentary or the semi-nomadic Bedouin, were generally submissive and orderly; but the great bulk of them followed the example of the big tribes who, unless restrained, were constantly engaged in ravaging the countryside, extorting money from the peasants, endangering the roads, and pillaging caravans.

A. *Bedouin turbulence and aggression*

Indeed, after a short period of peace and order under the Egyptians, the Syrian provinces became again a vulnerable target of Bedouin

[1] F.O. 78/962, Finn to Palmerston, No. 15, Jerusalem, 29 Aug. 1853; J. L. Farley, *The Massacres in Syria* (London, 1861), p. 72; Finn, i. 241–2; ii. 5–9, 22, 170–1; H. B. Tristram, *The Land of Israel* (London, 1876), pp. 478–80.

[2] F.O. 78/755, Finn to Palmerston, No. 22, Jerusalem, 17 July 1848; Murray, i. 185; Tristram, op. cit., pp. 227, 479.

[3] Burckhardt, p. 560; Finn, i. 241, 265; Murray, i. 185.

[4] For a detailed description, consult the following works: Oppenheim, op. cit.; F. G. Peake, *A History of Jordan and its Tribes* (Miami, 1958); M. Sharon, *ha-Beduim be-Eretz Israel ba-me'ot ha-18 ve ha-19* (unpublished M.A. thesis, Hebrew University, Jerusalem, 1964). For brief surveys of various Bedouin areas within the Syrian provinces, see Baedeker, p. 84; C. M. Doughty, *Travels in Arabia Deserta* (London, 1926), i. 16–17; Finn, i. 241, ii. 187; Murray, i. 185, ii. 499–500, 537; Tristram, op. cit., pp. 189, 227, 778 ff.

aggression and turbulence; as in the pre-reform era, the main victim was the peasant. Bedouin tribes driven in spring from the desert to find pasture for their flocks, would periodically raid villages and lay them waste:

> like locusts they spread over the land and their camels only too glad to revel upon the luxury of green food, . . . leaving bare, brown desolation where years of toil had made smiling fields and vineyards. Nor is this all, for the cattle and flocks are swept off to the desert by the marauders who leave behind for the unfortunate peasant nothing that they can carry away.[1]

In addition to these incursions, Bedouin chieftains would levy on villages within their reach an annual sum of money or quantity of grain as a protection-duty. But this duty would rarely protect the peasants from raids or blackmail by other Bedouin tribes, nor immunize them from greater demands by the 'protector' who, when refused, would sack the village and demolish parts of it.[2] It is true that a considerable number of villages, particularly in the mountains (and also the towns of Karak and Salt, east of the Jordan), were able to defend themselves against the nomads and repulse their attacks.[3] But on the other hand, the Bedouin, while exploiting the constant warfare between the peasant factions, would occasionally invade the hilly areas, usually on invitation of the rival parties, and complete the work of destruction.[4] Furthermore, the Bedouin threat was extended to villages on the outskirts of towns and even to a number of towns themselves. Places like Homs, Hama in Syria, Bethlehem, Jericho, and Gaza in Palestine, were almost constantly surrounded by nomads and sometimes even besieged by them.[5] In one instance at least nomadic elements invaded the city of Aleppo in order to join the 1850 uprising of the Aleppines against the authorities and to sack

[1] Finn, i. 315; compare F.O. 78/1118, Wood to Clarendon, No. 11, Damascus, 12 Feb. 1855; *Irade M.V.*, No. 18653/5, 11 CA 1276.

[2] F.O. 78/1297, Barker to Redcliffe, No. 3, encl. in Barker to Clarendon, No. 3, Aleppo, 10 Feb. 1857; F.O. 78/1586, Rogers to Bulwer, No. 37, encl. in Rogers to Russell, No. 24, Damascus, 26 Aug. 1861; Farley, *Syria*, p. 318; Finn, ii. 36; Murray, ii. 500; Segur, pp. 10–12.

[3] Finn, i. 265, 316; Segur, p. 22.

[4] F.O. 78/755, Finn to Palmerston, No. 25, Jerusalem, 28 Oct. 1848; Farley, *The Massacres*, p. 72; Finn, i. 312 ff., 378; *P.E.F.* (1906), pp. 33, 41–43, 47, 49.

[5] F.O. 78/962, Finn to Clarendon, No. 25, Jerusalem, 28 Oct. 1854; F. O. 78/1029, Wood to Clarendon, No. 40, 27 July 1854; Murray, ii. 591; J. L. Porter, *The Giant cities of Bashan* (London, 1867), p. 312

the Christian quarter.[1] As a result of Bedouin inroads and oppression, large portions of the Syrian countryside, notably the plains and valleys, were desolated, while a great number of villages were deserted and ruined during the Tanzimat period.[2]

Another major target of Bedouin assault were the roads. Almost no road in Syria or Palestine was free from this menace: travellers and caravans were, as in the past, constantly subject to Bedouin attack and pillage.[3] These occasionally included also official couriers as well as international caravans; the periodical Baghdad–Damascus commercial caravan was attacked and pillaged from time to time, for example in 1843 and 1857.[4] In certain areas, especially in the area east of Jordan and the desert, passengers and caravans had to pay to the local tribes a road protection-fee, a toll which became customary and was acknowledged *de facto* by the Turkish authorities.[5]

Moreover, the Turkish government itself continued to pay, as in the past, the annual fee (*sürre*) to certain big tribes for allowing the Ḥajj caravan from Damascus to pass peacefully to Mecca. Even this holy caravan would otherwise have been attacked and pillaged;[6] and the Ottomans obviously could not have afforded to expose it to such dangers, because 'the interruption of the pilgrimage is looked upon as a great national calamity inasmuch as it directly

[1] See above, p. 105; also A.E. Damas, i, No. 18, from Segur, 12 June 1851; Segur, pp. 19–20.

[2] F.O. 78/1118, Wood to Clarendon, No. 11, Damascus, 12 Feb. 1855; *Irade D.*, No. 29174/3, 7 Saf. 1276; Finn, i. 422; *Rambles*, p. 183. The areas which suffered most from nomadic infestation were the coastal areas, the Sharon plain and the valley of Esdraelon in Palestine, the plain of Houran and the valleys of the Orontes and the Euphrates in Syria.

[3] F.O. 78/456, Report by Major Wilbraham, encl. in Rose to Palmerston, No. 71, Beirut, 15 July 1841; F.O. 195/207, Werry to Canning, No. 7, Aleppo, 12 Apr. 1843; F.O. 78/226, Wood to Canning, No. 16, Damascus, 4 July 1844; F.O. 78/1521, Finn to Russell, No. 1, Jerusalem, 4 Jan. 1860; Jaffa *Sijill*, No. 13, order registered in 17 R 1258. It should be noted here that many travellers' books are full of frightful accounts of crimes committed by the Bedouin on the roads; these accounts, although exaggerated, are not without foundation.

[4] See F.O. 78/538, Wood to Bidwell, No. 1, Damascus, 28 Feb. 1843; F.O. 78/1388, Brant to Alison, No. 8, encl. in Brant to Clarendon, No. 10, Damascus, 29 Jan. 1858.

[5] F.O. 78/713, Rose to Palmerston, No. 56, Broumana, 30 Sept. 1847; Finn, i. 463–4; ii. 174–5, 316–17; *Rambles*, pp. 203, 206; Tristram, *Israel*, pp. 189–90, 263.

[6] F.O. 78/498, Wood to Aberdeen, No. 8, Damascus, 5 Jan. 1842; F.O. 78/1627, Dufferin to Russell, No. 43, Beirut, 21 Dec. 1860; A.E. Damas, i, No. 2, 26 Sept. 1843; al-Bāshā, p. 245; Segur, pp. 10, 31.

affects the stability of the Turkish government itself by destroying the 'prestige' of the Mahomedan Religion.'[1]

B. *Ottoman Bedouin policy*

The latter issue might, of course, indicate the basic weakness in the Ottoman position *vis-à-vis* the Bedouin. Lacking the modern inventions of railway, car, telegraph, and aeroplane in its struggle against the nomads, the government of that day could not easily gain the upper hand over the powerful and mobile nomads. (And indeed the Turks did not manage to protect the Ḥajj caravan until the construction of the Hijaz railway in 1908, and were compelled up to that time to buy its passage from the Bedouin tribes.)[2] Nevertheless, the major cause of the Ottomans' failure to accomplish during the 1840s and the 1850s what the Egyptians had succeeded in achieving in the 1830s, lay in their ambivalent and unsystematic Bedouin policy in the Syrian provinces. On the one hand, the Turkish authorities took a number of firm military measures which, however, being sporadic and incomplete, proved ineffective; on the other hand, they continued to use the old methods of conciliation and flattery alongside the indirect system of divide and rule. In practice this profusion of contradictory policies failed to restrain the Bedouin and often made them even more defiant. Only during the 1850s did there emerge the first signs of a firmer and planned Bedouin policy which paved the way for the final subjection of the nomads in the area.

1. USE OF FORCE

In marked contrast to pre-reform times, the Ottoman authorities made, during the Tanzimat period, great military efforts to curb the activities of the unruly Bedouin tribes of Syria and Palestine. But never during this period did the Ottomans succeed in obtaining a sufficiently decisive military superiority over the nomads which would have enabled them to destroy the Bedouin's strength. For one thing, the relatively small Turkish *Nizam*, which had many

[1] F.O. 78/622, Wood to Aberdeen, No. 23, Damascus, 10 July 1845.

[2] See Doughty, i. 10, 88; Jessup, ii. 407–8; I. Burton, *The inner life of Syria* (London, 1875), ii. 407–8; S. Merrill, *East of Jordan* (London, 1881), pp. 339–40; L. Oliphant, *The Land of Gilead* (N.Y., 1880), pp. 121–2.

other duties to perform in the country, was faced with numerous and vigorous Bedouin warriors, mostly mounted on camels or horses. And although the nomads were, to a certain extent, inferior to the regular troops in military equipment and training, they were lighter and more mobile than the regulars, and had that most valuable asset, an intimate knowledge of the country in which they were fighting. It is therefore not surprising that some military expeditions would return empty-handed from their missions after having failed to pursue the swift nomads, while others would occasionally even suffer heavy blows by the nomadic 'hit and run' tactics.[1] Yet on the whole the Turkish *Nizam* had the upper hand in face-to-face encounters with the nomads, and the latter would normally withdraw in the face of an approaching army in order to avoid an open clash.[2] But during long periods of time, the military expeditions dispatched against the nomads were usually too sporadic to effect the Bedouin subjection; in critical times, such as the Crimean War, hardly any regular forces were employed against them.

In such periods, as well as in ordinary times, the *başıbozuk*s were assigned to deal with the nomads; but they were not at all able to deter the vigorous Bedouin, and were frequently even defeated by them when there were direct encounters.[3] Indeed, as already pointed out, the *başıbozuk*s usually preferred to avoid challenging the nomads directly, and sometimes would secretly cooperate with them in lawless activities.[4] The only effective irregular troops who could cope successfully with the nomads were the bodies of Kurdish mercenaries and Druze mountain warriors.[5] But while the former units were often unreliable in carrying out their duties, the latter confined themselves to the protection of their

[1] See F.O. 195/170, Werry to Ponsonby, Aleppo, 2 Aug. 1841; F.O. 78/713, Rose to Palmerston, No. 28, Beirut, 1 June 1847; F.O. 78/1033, Werry to Redcliffe, No. 30, encl. in Werry to Clarendon, No. 17, Aleppo, 13 Oct. 1854; *Rambles*, pp. 29–31; Taoutel, iii. 122.

[2] See F.O. 78/621, Werry to Canning, No. 15, encl. in Werry to Aberdeen, No. 10, Aleppo, 3 June 1845; *Irade D.*, No. 8020, 27 N 1263.

[3] See F.O. 78/447, Wood to Rifat Pasha, Damascus, 18 Oct. 1841; F.O. 78/713, Rose to Cowley, No. 53, 25 Sept., encl. in Rose to Palmerston, No. 57, Beirut, 7 Oct. 1847; F.O. 78/1389, 'General Report on Syria' in Skene to Malmesbury, No. 25, Aleppo, 17 June 1858.

[4] F.O. 78/1586, Rogers to Bulwer, No. 37, 20 Aug., encl. in Rogers to Russell, No. 24, Damascus, 26 Aug. 1861. See also above, p. 57.

[5] See, for example, F.O. 78/447, Werry to Ponsonby, No. 5, Aleppo, 6 May 1841; F.O. 78/536, Rose to Aberdeen, No. 42, Beirut, 6 May 1843.

own territory and interests; thus the Druzes would, as we know, even enter into an alliance with certain Bedouin tribes when both parties were exposed to a common threat by the authorities.[1]

2. USE OF BEDOUIN AGAINST BEDOUIN

There was also another method by which the government tried to solve the problem of Bedouin aggression, and this was by employing other Bedouin tribes against them. This practice, which was quite common in Syrian history, had, it was argued, three merits: firstly, it kept the tribes in government pay obedient; secondly, the countryside was defended against nomad raids from the desert; and thirdly, the Bedouin tribes could be set against each other, thus weakening all of them. In fact, however, most of these aims were not accomplished, particularly when the government was weak. To begin with, the tribes employed by the authorities would frequently pillage caravans and plunder the villages they were assigned to protect.[2] In addition, the mercenary nomads would often fight other Bedouin tribes only if the latter were their own rivals and threatened their interests. Nor were they particularly successful; occasionally the government-paid tribes were defeated by their enemy-Bedouin; sometimes, indeed, in spite of the military support they received from the authorities.[3] If this happened, the government would periodically replace the defeated tribe by a more powerful one as its regional police force.[4] But peace did not follow, because the unfavoured nomads would be driven to commit lawless activities, while the newly-appointed tribe would sooner or later follow the same course. Consequently, peace and order were precarious, as far as the Bedouin were concerned, and the only obvious Ottoman 'success' from this

[1] See F.O. 78/761, Wood to Aberdeen, No. 14, Damascus, 8 Apr. 1848; see also above, pp. 126, 128.

[2] See, for example, F.O. 78/538, Wood to Aberdeen, No. 42, Damascus, 29 Nov. 1843; F.O. 78/960, Werry to Redcliffe, No. 17, encl. in Werry to Clarendon, No. 12, Aleppo, 23 Aug. 1853; A.E. Alep, iii, No. 18, 22 Mar. 1860; Farley, *Syria*, pp. 317–18.

[3] F.O. 78/622, Wood to Aberdeen, No. 18, Damascus, 9 June 1845; F.O. 78/1118, Barker to Redcliffe, No. 29, encl. in Barker to Clarendon, No. 22, Aleppo, 9 Oct. 1855; Finn, ii. 5.

[4] See F.O. 195/226, Wood to Canning, No. 15, Damascus, 26 June 1844; F.O. 78/1388, Brant to Bulwer, No. 51, encl. in Brant to Malmesbury, No. 13, Damascus, 26 Oct. 1858.

policy was the promotion of strife between Bedouin tribes, causing great bloodshed among themselves.[1]

One of the chief tribes which was employed by the Ottomans during some two centuries to check other Bedouin from the desert, was the Mawālī tribe. By mid-eighteenth century, their main task had become that of guarding the desert frontier between Aleppo and Damascus against the ʿAnaza nomads who had newly arrived from Najd, pushing the Mawālī westwards towards Aleppo and Hama. With this assignment the Mawālī remained in government service until the early 1850s,[2] when they resigned on grounds of a conflict with the authorities. It seems that the real background for this resignation and the subsequent aggressive behaviour of the Mawālī was their declining power which had apparently led the authorities to replace them by the more vigorous ʿAnaza tribes. For, about that time, the authorities of Aleppo began to employ intermittently the ʿAnaza factions of Adhām and Judʿān as a police force on the desert line;[3] and a similar policy was adopted by the Pashas of Damascus with regard to the ʿAnaza rival factions of Rwala and Wuld ʿAlī who were employed in turns to protect the borders and escort the Ḥajj caravans.[4]

Another Bedouin tribe with a long record of government service in the defence of the desert borders against other nomads was the Hanādī. Their history as mercenaries in the Syrian provinces goes back to the end of the eighteenth century, at which time parts of the Egyptian Hanādī tribe emigrated to Palestine and entered the service of al-Jazzār Paṣa, the *vali* of Sidon. Henceforth there was a sporadic stream of Hanādī factions from Egypt to Syria who followed the example of their predecessors. In 1831 thousands of these tribesmen came with the Egyptian invaders and were employed with great success in curbing the Bedouin

[1] See, for example, *Irade M.V.*, No. 12529, 3 Ş 1270; F.O. 78/1538, Skene to Russell, No. 70, Aleppo, 11 Dec. 1860; A.E. Damas, v, from Outrey, No. 53, 23 May 1858.

[2] See F.O. 195/170, Moore to Ponsonby, No. 1, Aleppo, 15 Dec. 1841; F.O. 78/871, Werry to Canning, No. 30, encl. in Werry to Palmerston, No. 11, Aleppo, 30 July 1851.

[3] *Irade M.V.*, No. 12529, 3 Ş 1270; F.O. 78/910, Werry to Canning, No. 9, encl. in Werry to F.O., No. 6, Aleppo, 10 Apr. 1852.

[4] See and compare F.O. 195/226, Wood to Canning, No. 15, Damascus, 26 June 1844; F.O. 78/872, Wood to Canning, No. 8, encl. in Wood to Palmerston, No. 13, Damascus, 28 Apr. 1851.

tribes of the Syrian desert.[1] When Ibrāhīm Paşa withdrew, a large number of them stayed and continued to serve the Ottomans in many parts of Syria.

Among the chiefs of these Hanādī bodies of irregulars the most remarkable was ʿAqīl (or ʿAqīla) *ağa* who acted, throughout the period under review, as head of Bedouin cavalry in northern Palestine.[2] His history in the service of the Ottoman government is relevant as it throws light on the position of a powerful chief of irregular Bedouin *vis-à-vis* the Turkish authorities in Syria.

ʿAqīl's father, Mūsā al-Ḥāsa, came from Egypt to Gaza in about 1814 and entered the service of the local Pashas as a head of mercenary troops. When he died in 1830, ʿAqīl succeeded him in the service of ʿAbdullāh Paşa, but when a year later the Egyptian army invaded Syria, ʿAqīl and his men defected to Ibrāhīm Paşa. In 1834, however, ʿAqīl joined the peasants' revolt against Ibrāhīm's rule, but when the uprising was quelled, his troops were dispersed. On the return of the Ottomans to Syria, ʿAqīl *ağa* again became head of a small body of irregular cavalry, but in 1845 he was discharged by Mehmed Kıbrıslı Paşa, then *muhafiz* of Acre, who was concerned about his increasing influence in the Nazareth area. The *ağa* and his followers then crossed the Jordan, joined the Bedouin tribe of Banū Ṣakhr, and led a revolt against the Turkish authorities. As a result ʿAqīl was recalled to Acre, and nominated commander of eighty Hanādī troops;[3] with these and with his other tribesmen he managed to restrain the turbulent Bedouin from across the Jordan and to establish order and peace in the whole of Galilee. In subsequent years ʿAqīl's semi-independent position in Palestine consolidated, and his fame grew wider, both at home and abroad, when in 1848 he successfully escorted the British expedition of Commander Lynch. This again aroused the jealousy and concern of the Turkish authorities: in 1852 ʿAqīl was sent at the head of a large body of Bedouin against the revolting Druzes of the Leja with apparently the concealed hope that he would

[1] See, for example, *Rambles*, p. 2; F.O. 78/580, Werry to Aberdeen, No. 12, Aleppo, 31 Dec. 1844.

[2] Many stories and legends were told of this hero of Galilee by European travellers. The following remark by Revd. Zeller, the Protestant missionary in Nazareth, is typical: 'The history of this man (ʿAqīl) contains some coincidences with the history of David'. See CM/072, Nazareth, 6 July 1860. On the life and activities of ʿAqīl *aga*, see also al-ʿĀrif, pp. 187–8; Finn, i. 410 ff.; Manṣūr, pp. 73–91; Oppenheim, ii. 30 ff.; cf. Sharon, 88–93.

[3] *Cevdet Z.*, No. 4510, 21 Kanun I 1265.

either help in taking this stronghold or find there his death. ʿAqīl *ağa* managed, however, to survive, but only to find himself accused by the authorities of conspiracy with the rebels; he was arrested in 1853 and sent into exile in Turkey and Bulgaria. He managed to escape and returning to Palestine, ʿAqīl reassembled his followers and other dissatisfied men, and in 1854 restored his authority in Galilee in revolt against the Turkish government.[1] The latter incited against him the Nablus chief, Muḥammad ʿAbd al-Hādī, but having failed, it reappointed ʿAqīl as commander of two hundred irregular troops from among his Hanādī tribe. Henceforth ʿAqīl *ağa* became virtually the ruler of Northern Palestine where he maintained complete security and peace. He protected the villages from Bedouin raids though not without an annual tribute paid to him by the inhabitants.[2] He was known likewise as a saviour of the Christian and Jewish population of Galilee, since he defended them against attacks by their Muslim and Druze neighbours during the 1850s and particularly in the course of the 1860 events;[3] thus, even the French and English consuls in Palestine sought ʿAqīl's assistance in protecting their respective Christian and Jewish protégés in the area.[4]

The increasing power and prestige of the *ağa* continued deeply to worry the authorities and they made every effort to destroy him. In 1856 they transferred a strong body of Kurdish irregulars from Syria and invested them with the same command over the district as that held by ʿAqīl, hoping to undermine his position.[5] However, the inevitable encounter between the Kurdish chief and ʿAqīl *ağa* which took place in April 1857 near the Horns of Hittin, ended with the decisive defeat of the Kurds.[6] Henceforth, until his death in 1870, ʿAqīl was either in government service—keeping the Bedouin in check and maintaining tranquillity in the area—or, if in disfavour, settled in the wilderness inciting the Bedouin to

[1] F.O. 78/1032, Finn to Redcliffe, No. 4, encl. in Finn to Clarendon, No. 2, Jerusalem, 8 Feb. 1854; CM/072 from Zeller, Nazareth, 6 July 1860; Finn, i. 411.

[2] CM. op. cit.; Tristram, *Israel*, pp. 108–9; Farley, *Syria*, p. 317.

[3] CM. op. cit.; Manṣūr, p. 91. Napoleon III granted him a medal as a reward and the Prince of Wales paid him a visit.

[4] Finn, i. 424–5.

[5] Ibid. 421; F.O. 195/524, Finn to Redcliffe, No. 12, Jerusalem, 8 Apr. 1857; Manṣūr, pp. 75–76.

[6] *Irade M.M.*, No. 398, Ṣ 1273; F.O. 195/524, op. cit.; Manṣūr, pp. 76–77; al-ʿĀrif, p. 188.

ravage Galilee.[1] His tactics in those days may be summarized in the words of a Nazarene historian: 'Kāna yuhawwil ʿalā al-dawla bi'lʿarab, wa-yuhawwil ʿalā al-ʿarab bi'ldawla.' (He threatened the government with the Bedouin, and the Bedouin with the government.)[2]

3. FORTIFICATION OF THE DESERT BORDER

With its military expeditions ineffective and Bedouin irregular forces unreliable, a government which insisted on the protection of the country from nomadic raids was bound to resort to more trustworthy defensive measures, primarily fortification of the desert border. Up to the Tanzimat era, such methods were hardly introduced in Syria and Palestine; not even by Ibrāhīm Paşa, who was satisfied by merely posting his Hanādī irregulars at key-points along the desert line.

The Ottoman government of the Tanzimat was, in fact, the first one to embark upon a great scheme of fortification of Syrian borders, though the actual execution of the plan did not take place before the late 1850s.[3] It was not until 1844 that the Ottoman authorities in Syria started to consider this issue; at the end of that year the newly-appointed *serasker*, Namık Paşa, drew up a plan to defend Syria from the Bedouin by erecting 'martello towers' on the desert border at regular intervals. These towers were to be garrisoned by detachments of infantry and artillery, while peasants and sedentary Bedouin of the vicinity were to act as auxiliaries.[4] But although this scheme was endorsed by the *Porte*, no further action was taken to execute it for several years. A similar state of affairs prevailed also in Palestine, where in 1847 Kıbrıslı Paşa, the governor of Jerusalem, prepared a plan to build fortresses in Jericho, Jabal Mūsā, and Petra; but none were constructed at the time.[5] Imperial firmans arriving in 1848 and 1849 and ordering once more the fortification of the desert

[1] Manṣūr, pp. 78–79; Tristram, *Israel*, p. 408; *Rambles*, p. 220.

[2] Manṣūr, p. 76.

[3] It should be noted, however, that a number of forts had been erected in earlier years (cf. Heyd, *Documents*, p. 102), but they were later abandoned by the authorities.

[4] F.O. 78/580, Werry to Aberdeen, No. 12, Aleppo, 31 Dec. 1844; A.E. Alep, i, from Guys, No. 19, 16 Jan. 1845.

[5] F.O. 78/705, Finn to Palmerston, No. 13, Jerusalem, 13 Mar. 1847.

borders,[1] resulted merely in additional plans which proposed the occupation of the abandoned forts of Palmira and Bozra, and the construction of a new Damascus–Baghdad road protected by military posts.[2]

The years 1851 and 1852, which were marked by the effective rule of Kıbrıslı Paşa in Aleppo and Damascus, saw at last some practical steps towards the fortification of the desert borders. Dayr al-Zūr was chosen as the starting point of this scheme and military preparations were made for its occupation; but the Druze rebellion in 1852 caused these arrangements to be postponed.[3] The preparations were resumed in 1854; Dayr al-Zūr was organized as a separate *sancak* in the *eyalet* of Aleppo and Yūsuf Bey Sharīf, the notable of Aleppo, was appointed to govern the area.[4] After a number of military offensives which were only partly successful, the district was put under government control and, in 1855, Yūsuf Paşa began the fortifications.[5] During the following years more military posts were established along the north-eastern desert border (but not near Damascus or in Palestine), all of which proved to be most effective in preventing Bedouin depredation.[6]

4. SETTLEMENT OF NOMADS

Another important way of restraining the Bedouin and indeed incorporating them to a certain extent in the defensive system of the desert line (again notably near Aleppo) was by settling them

[1] *Irade M.V.*, No. 2954, CA 1264; F.O. 78/801, Wood to Palmerston, No. 21, Damascus, 30 Aug. 1849.

[2] F.O. 78/761, Wood to Palmerston, No. 12, Damascus, 8 Mar. 1848; F.O. 78/837, same to same, No. 1, Damascus, 28 Jan. 1850.

[3] *Irade D.*, No. 15661, 22 ZA 1267; F.O. 78/871, Werry to Palmerston, No. 3, Aleppo, 10 Apr. 1851; A.E. Damas, ii, No. 40, from Segur, 2 Mar. 1852. Note, however, that a document from the beginning of 1848 mentions the erection of a fortress near the village of Dayr (= Dayr al-Zūr?) for the purpose of repulsing Bedouin attacks in the vicinity of Aleppo and Damascus; see *Cevdet D.*, No. 27805, 26 CA 1264.

[4] *Irade M.V.*, No. 13688, 23 R 1271; F.O. 78/1033, Werry to Redcliffe, No. 11, encl. in Werry to Clarendon, No. 6, Aleppo, 17 Apr. 1854.

[5] *Irade M.V.*, No. 14389, 16 L 1271; F.O. 78/1118, Barker to Redcliffe, No. 33, encl. in Barker to Clarendon, No. 25, Aleppo, 16 Dec. 1855; Taoutel, ii. 89.

[6] F.O. 78/1118, Barker to Redcliffe, No. 28, encl. in Barker to Clarendon, No. 13, Aleppo, 30 July 1856; F.O. 78/1389, Skene to Malmesbury, No. 17, Aleppo, 8 Apr. 1858; compare also *Rambles*, p. 275.

on the land. This practice, which was seldom followed during the pre-reform period, was one of the chief instruments of Ibrāhīm's Bedouin policy. His colonies, however, were not very long lived, and when he withdrew, many of these nomad settlements collapsed under the revived pressure of the desert Bedouin.

In the first four to five years after the Ottoman restoration there was apparently no official central policy of colonization. In the province of Aleppo, for example, groups of the Walda tribe, pushed by stronger tribes from across the Euphrates, asked in 1841 for permission to settle near the city. But the *vali* hesitated to grant this request on the grounds that 'a firman is required for such a thing'.[1] By contrast, the Pasha of Damascus made a personal appeal to some Houran tribes in 1842 to 'change their roving life and establish themselves in the deserted and ruined villages' of that neighbourhood.[2] No further steps were taken, however, to put this request into practice, and it was not until 1845 that there appeared the first signs of a central policy of colonization. Areas were then allocated in various parts of the country for the nomads to settle, build houses, and form villages.[3]

Yet settlement was still only sporadic and limited mainly to the province of Aleppo: for example, certain Turkoman tribes of the area were settled by the government in the ʿAmq plain,[4] though elsewhere no such measures were adopted. Then, in 1851, another colonization project was started in Aleppo by Mehmed Kıbrıslı Paşa: some thirty small nomad tribes settled in new villages in the *paşalık* having been granted land, seeds, and tools.[5] Again, in the late 1850s, the authorities of Aleppo encouraged more tribes, Arabs and non-Arabs alike, to settle in the area, allocating them pieces of land and exempting them from taxes over a certain period.[6] In the early 1860s a further step was taken

[1] F.O. 195/170, Werry to Ponsonby, Aleppo, 2 Aug. 1841.

[2] F.O. 78/498, Wood to Aberdeen, No. 32, Damascus, 18 Apr. 1842.

[3] F.O. 195/207, Werry to Canning, No. 17, Aleppo, 17 June 1845; F.O. 78/660A, Wood to Aberdeen, No. 17, Damascus, 10 Sept. 1846.

[4] *Cevdet D.*, No. 10965, 19 Z 1261; ibid., No. 13483, ZA 1262; note also Ottoman efforts to cause the settlement of Turkoman tribes in the plain of Bursa; MacFarlane, i. 164.

[5] *Irade D.*, No. 13794, 5 CA 1267; ibid., No. 19788, 13 Saf. 1271; F.O. 78/910, Werry to Malmesbury, No. 17, Aleppo, 16 Oct. 1852.

[6] F.O. 78/1452, Skene to Bulwer, No. 37, encl. in Skene to Russell, No. 74, Aleppo, 29 Oct. 1859; F.O. 78/1538, Skene to Bulwer, separate, encl. No. 1 in Skene to Russell, No. 14, Aleppo, 5 Apr. 1860; *Rambles*, pp. 143, 178–9.

in this direction through the colonization of the desert fringes by Circassian refugees from Russia; the first Circassian families arrived in Syria at the beginning of 1861 and were settled on the bank of the Euphrates and near Antioch.[1]

But although in the province of Aleppo the process of settlement seemed to go forward, it was defective in other Syrian provinces.[2] Not only did their authorities neglect to settle new tribes, but they contributed indirectly to discouraging existing nomad settlements. For one thing, the Ottoman government was unable to protect the sedentary tribes against the big and aggressive tribes of the desert.[3] Moreover, government troops, particularly the *başıbozuk*s, would occasionally attack sedentary Bedouin either for the purpose of pillage, or as a substitute target after an unsuccessful operation against a strong Bedouin tribe.[4] Consequently, colonization of nomads was kept back in many regions, while some settled Bedouin turned once more to disobedience and lawlessness.[5]

5. OTHER FEATURES OF THE OTTOMAN NOMAD POLICY

Other features of the Ottoman nomad policy appeared also to be inconsistent and ambivalent. Such a line was, for example, adopted with regard to the commercial intercourse between the nomads and the urban population, which in fact was of considerable economic importance,[6] and could also have been used to restrain the Bedouin. But some Turkish Pashas would gravely

[1] F.O. 78/1603, Skene to Russell, No. 12, Aleppo, 21 Jan. 1861; *Rambles*, p. 295. Note also that a small number of families from North Africa arrived in Syria in 1859 and were settled near the Lake of Hula; F.O. 78/1448, Finn to Russell, No. 47, Jerusalem, 19 Dec. 1859.

[2] See, for example, Segur, p. 24; J. Wilson, *The Lands of the Bible* (London, 1847), ii. 321.

[3] See F.O. 78/500, Moore to Aberdeen, No. 4, Aleppo, 27 Jan. 1842; F.O. 78/760, Notes from Consul Wood, encl. in Rose to Palmerston, No. 39, Beirut, 28 Aug. 1848.

[4] See F.O. 78/622, Wood to Aberdeen, No. 18, Damascus, 9 June 1845; F.O. 78/1297, Barker to Redcliffe, No. 11, encl. in Barker to Clarendon, No. 6, Aleppo, 19 May 1857; *Rambles*, pp. 27, 275.

[5] See, for example, F.O. 78/1118, Barker to Redcliffe, No. 29, encl. in Barker to Clarendon, No. 22, Aleppo, 9 Oct. 1855.

[6] See F.O. 78/1297, Skene to Redcliffe, No. 4, encl. in Skene to Clarendon, No. 1, Aleppo, 8 June 1857; F.O. 78/1383, Finn to Clarendon, No. 24, Jerusalem, 9 Oct. 1858; *Rambles*, p. 143; Segur, pp. 9–10. The Bedouin tribes were also useful as a source of information concerning events across the desert.

damage such peaceful communication by occasionally forbidding trade with the nomads, or suddenly arresting Bedouin who came to trade in the city. Equally treacherous was the notorious Ottoman trick whereby a Turkish Pasha would summon certain Bedouin chiefs upon an amnesty pledge (*aman*) and then put them under arrest.[1] Such steps, usually taken as punitive measures against disobedient tribes, not only often failed to check the Bedouin, especially the powerful ones, but sometimes made them even more aggressive.[2]

Another old method which was resumed during the Tanzimat period and proved again to be shortsighted, was the flattering and conciliatory line the authorities often adopted towards the lawless and powerful tribes. For example, Imperial *nişan*s (medals), high titles, and 'robes of honour' were frequently conferred by the government upon turbulent Bedouin chieftains.[3] Similarly, Bedouin tribes were occasionally bribed by the authorities and were allowed to draw the pay of irregular troops without any justification.[4] All these approaches, which aimed at appeasing and curbing the nomads, were regarded by the Bedouin as signs of weakness, and accordingly encouraged their defiance.[5]

C. *Stages in the struggle against the Bedouin*

In the early 1840s the Turkish Bedouin policy in Syrian provinces was largely dominated by such conciliatory approaches. As in other areas of administration, this was partly due to the government's wish to gain Bedouin co-operation in the expulsion of Ibrāhīm Paşa, and partly it was a result of Ottoman mili-

[1] F.O. 78/714, Wood to Palmerston, No. 26, Damascus, 10 Nov. 1847; Finn, i. 320.

[2] See, for example, F.O. 78/1297, Skene to Redcliffe, No. 21, encl. in Skene to Clarendon, No. 7, Aleppo, 15 July 1857; A.E. Alep, i, from Guys, No. 41, 27 June 1846; *Rambles*, pp. 27–28, 32; Walpole, i. 276–7.

[3] See *Cevdet D.*, No. 11852, 14 M 1257; *Irade M.V.*, No. 2818, RA 1264; *Accounts and Papers*, LX (1843), pt. ii, No. 128, from Wood, Damascus, 19 Apr. 1842; F.O. 78/799, Werry to Canning, No. 1, Aleppo, 7 Apr., encl. in Moore to Palmerston, No. 18, Beirut, 30 Apr. 1849.

[4] F.O. 195/226, Wood to Canning, No. 15, Damascus, 26 June 1844; F.O. 78/1389, 'General report on Syria', in Skene to Malmesbury, No. 25, Aleppo, 17 June 1858; F.O. 78/137, Finn to Russell, No. 22, Jerusalem, 30 May 1860.

[5] Finn, i. 382; see also *Rambles*, p. 28; F.O. 78/622, Wood to Aberdeen, No. 26, Damascus, 9 Aug. 1845; F.O. 78/1452, Skene to Bulwer, No. 11, encl. in Skene to Malmesbury, No. 20, Aleppo, 31 Mar. 1859.

tary weakness and financial difficulty.[1] Thus, for example, when Bedouin help was required to cut the supplies of the retreating Egyptians in 1840–1, an official promise was made to certain tribes granting them 'all the *miri* or Government Tithes of produce yearly collected at Maon provided they would remove them and other stores out of the way of Ibrahim's march'.[2]

After Ibrāhīm's withdrawal, there followed more conciliatory steps of the above-mentioned sort, which failed, however, to restrain the powerful nomads; and for some four years after the return of Turkish rule almost the whole countryside of Syria and Palestine was under Bedouin control. Villages were attacked and sacked, roads cut and caravans pillaged, and bodies of irregular troops which were sent against the disobedient nomads were defeated, while other military expeditions preferred to come to peaceful terms with the vigorous Bedouin, rather than to fight them.[3]

Only towards the end of 1844, following the reorganization of the army and the arrival of the new *serasker*, Namık Paşa, was there a certain change in the Turkish nomad policy. For the next four years, a considerable amount of punitive expeditions were dispatched against the disobedient tribes of Syria and Palestine, notably the ʿAnaza and Banū Ṣakhr.[4] But a certain number of these expeditions were unable to pursue the swift nomads and beat them; other military missions, although successful in overcoming Bedouin tribes, failed to destroy their strength by means of disarmament or conscription. Instead, the army would seize from the tribe camels in lieu of taxes, and take some tribesmen as hostages.[5] Moreover as well as the occasional lack of co-ordination between adjacent *paşalık*s in the struggle against the Bedouin,[6] there was also, at this stage, a shortage in long-range proceedings to

[1] F.O. 78/447, Werry to Palmerston, No. 9, Damascus, 20 May 1841; F.O. 195/226, Wood to Canning, No. 15, Damascus, 26 June 1844.

[2] See copy of a letter from Lieut.-Gen. A. Jochmus to *serasker* Zakariyya Paşa of 13 Jan. 1841, in Wood's papers.

[3] Cf. above, pp. 135–6. [4] Cf. above, pp. 134–5.

[5] *Irade D.*, No. 6275, 11 B 1262; A.E. Alep, i, from Guys, No. 44, 9 Dec. 1846; F.O. 78/714, Timoni to Palmerston, No. 13, Damascus, 30 June 1847; Kibrizli, pp. 81–82.

[6] See, for instance, F.O. 78/538, Wood to Aberdeen, No. 18, Damascus, 10 June 1843; F.O. 78/872, Wood to Canning, No. 6, encl. in Wood to Palmerston, No. 10, Damascus, 29 Mar. 1851; compare F.O. 78/1538, Skene to Russell, No. 70, Aleppo, 11 Dec. 1860.

solve the nomadic problem, for example, the authorities made great efforts to keep the tribes off the cultivated land, but at the same time failed to provide other pasture when they arrived in the spring to graze their animals.[1]

Consequently, despite some sporadic pauses in Bedouin aggression and, possibly, a slight improvement in comparison with the previous years, nomadic violence was by no means checked during the second half of the 1840s. In South Palestine, the powerful Sinai–Negeb tribes, the ʿAzāzma, Tiyāha, and Tarābīn, made deep incursions into the area, attacking and robbing villagers and travellers.[2] Further north 'all the most fertile country between Lake Tiberias and the Dead Sea . . . is completely in the hands of Beni Sakher' who ravaged large portions of it.[3] In Syria, the various ʿAnaza clans infested great parts of the countryside between the chief towns, raiding and extorting money and supplies from many villages in the area; they pillaged also the Baghdad–Aleppo or Baghdad–Damascus commercial caravans almost yearly.[4] The situation in those years can be summarized in the words of the English Consul-General in Syria, in his dispatch at the end of the term of office of Namık Paşa in 1849:

> Namik Pasha with the whole of what is called the Army of Arabia has not, after five years' command, brought into subjection the Arab tribes who infest Syria from the Euphrates to the Dead Sea. Worse than this, he has not been able to protect the cultivated vicinity of the great towns of Aleppo, Hama, Homs, Damascus and Jerusalem from their hordes.[5]

The succession of Namık Paşa by a new *serasker*, Emin Paşa, who occupied the office during 1849 and 1850, did not bring about any noticeable improvement: Bedouin invasions of the settled area were carried on in many places throughout the country.[6]

[1] F.O. 78/660A, Wood to Aberdeen, No. 7, Damascus, 9 Mar. 1846; F.O. 78/799, Werry to Canning, No. 1, Aleppo, 7 Apr., encl. in Moore to Palmerston, No. 18, Beirut, 30 Apr. 1849.

[2] *Irade D.*, No. 5138/6, 5 RA 1261.

[3] F.O. 78/760, Rose to Canning, No. 18, encl. in Rose to Palmerston, No. 39, Beirut, 28 Aug. 1848.

[4] *Irade D.*, No. 5297/2, 9 C 1261.

[5] F.O. 78/760, Rose to Canning, No. 18, encl. in Rose to Palmerston, No. 39, Beirut, 28 Aug. 1848.

[6] F.O. 78/799, Werry to Moore, No. 1, Aleppo, 7 Apr., encl. in Moore to Palmerston, No. 18, Beirut, 30 Apr. 1849; F.O. 78/801, Wood to Palmerston, No. 9, Damascus, 28 Apr. 1849; Segur, pp. 19–21; Taoutel, iii. 138.

A decisive shift in the position of the Ottoman government *vis-à-vis* the Bedouin came only in 1851 and 1852 when Kıbrıslı Paşa served as *vali* of Aleppo and *serasker* of Syria; for the first time after a great many years Turkish nomad policy became more systematic and consistent. Successive military expeditions encountered and punished the powerful tribes and in some cases forced nomads to provide recruits for the army.[1] This firm line, which was accompanied by a tactful policy of reward and punishment, brought about the submission of many tribes: they raised taxes and co-operated with the authorities and consequently the countryside became tolerably tranquil as never before under the new Ottoman régime.[2] Yet Kıbrıslı was not satisfied with merely offensive warfare, and started also to adopt practical steps towards the fortification of the desert borders and the settlement of nomad tribes on the land.[3]

This short phase of effective nomad policy suffered, however, a serious setback at the end of 1852, when the Druze revolt broke out and all government efforts were diverted in order to crush it. The situation further deteriorated during the following years as the great bulk of the Army of Arabistan was transferred to the Crimean battlefield. The nomads threw off control and intensively resumed their aggression in the rural areas and along the roads, reaching again the outskirts of some towns. According to Consul Wood of Damascus, 'the towns of Homs and Hama are besieged by the Bedouins', while Consul Finn reported from Jerusalem that 'never before had we known wild desert plunderers to exercise their vocation under the very walls of Jerusalem'.[4]

It was not until the end of the Crimean War and the return of regular troops to the country that the authorities were able to resume the firm nomad policy of the early 1850s; but the major

[1] *Irade M.V.*, No. 6119, 17 RA 1267; F.O. 78/871, Werry to Canning, No. 15, encl. in Werry to Palmerston, No. 2, Aleppo, 29 Mar. 1851; F.O. 78/872, Wood to Palmerston, No. 8, Damascus, 26 Feb. 1851.

[2] F.O. 78/871, Werry to Canning, No. 48, encl. in Werry to Palmerston, No. 21, Aleppo, 29 Dec. 1851; F.O. 78/910, Wood to Canning, No. 19, encl. in Wood to Malmesbury, No. 18, 14 June 1851; Walpole, i. 276–7.

[3] *Irade D.*, No. 13794, 5 CA 1267; cf. also above, p. 142.

[4] F.O. 78/1029, Wood to Clarendon, No. 40, Damascus, 27 July 1854; Finn, i. 355. During that time, however, the Pasha of Aleppo managed to conduct a tactful policy towards the Bedouin which resulted in a relative tranquillity around Aleppo; see F.O. 78/1033, Werry to Ward, No. 2, encl. in Werry to Redcliffe, No. 3, Aleppo, 17 Feb. 1854.

scene of the struggle against the Bedouin was the province of Aleppo. In this province military expeditions succeeded in punishing disobedient tribes, notably the 'Anaza;[1] posts and fortresses were set up, as already mentioned, along the desert borders commencing with Dayr al-Zūr, and further measures were taken to encourage the settlement of nomads.

Yet in other parts of the country the government was unable to gain the upper hand over the nomads. Thus, for example, key points in the Syrian desert such as Palmira and Bozra could not be held by the Turks over a long time;[2] so was the case with respect to the Negeb in South Palestine.[3] Another vast nomadic area which the Ottomans did not manage to subdue and control during the whole period was the area east of Jordan,[4] nevertheless they succeeded in establishing certain footholds in this region during the 1850s: in 1851 a Turkish *kaymakam* was installed in Irbid,[5] while Karak was brought under a certain degree of Ottoman control towards the late 1850s.[6]

In conclusion, the era of reform between 1840 and 1861 admittedly did not bring about a solution to the old and difficult nomadic problem in all Syrian provinces. Yet, this period, and particularly the 1850s, was a very significant stage in the Ottoman struggle against the Bedouin, as it produced the beginnings of more systematic and fruitful policies which gradually helped to settle some aspects of the nomadic issue in the area.

[1] *Irade D.*, No. 26448, 20 Ş 1274; ibid., No. 29174/3, 7 Saf. 1276; F.O. 78/1297, Skene to Redcliffe, No. 26, encl. in Skene to Clarendon, No. 13, Aleppo, 15 July 1857; F.O. 78/1538, Skene to Bulwer, separate, encl. in Skene to Russell, No. 14, Aleppo, 5 Apr. 1860; Taoutel, ii. 89, 92.

[2] See and compare F.O. 78/714, Timoni to Palmerston, No. 7, Damascus, 8 May 1847; F.O. 78/801, Wood to Palmerston, No. 26, Damascus, 20 Oct. 1849.

[3] 'Ārif al-'Ārif, *Ta'rīkh Bīr al-Sab' wa-qabā'ilahā* (Jerusalem, 1934), pp. 243–4.

[4] See F.O. 78/705, Finn to Palmerston, No. 30, 4 Oct. 1847; F.O. 78/1383, Finn to Clarendon, No. 1, Jerusalem, 1 Jan. 1858; Finn. i. 376, 463–4; ii. 174; Murray, i. 60.

[5] F.O. 195/368, Wood to Canning, No. 36, Damascus, 25 Oct. 1851; Peake, p. 91; N. Lewis, *The Frontier*, p. 53.

[6] A.E. Jérusalem, vi. from de Barrère, No. 19, 29 Aug. 1858; F.O. 78/1538, Finn to Russell, No. 21, Jerusalem, 24 Sept. 1861.

PART IV

Social and Economic Welfare

'Ever since the happy day of our accession to the throne, were our benevolent thoughts concentrated only in the public welfare, the building of the provinces and districts and improving the state of the people and the poor.'

(From the Gülhane edict of 1839)

IT has been stated already that the two great Tanzimat edicts, the *hats* of 1839 and 1856, were concerned with the basic human rights to security of life, honour, and property, and with the improvement in social and economic conditions of the subjects throughout the Ottoman Empire. According to the edicts these ends were to be achieved in various ways: by reforming the legal administration, the prison system, and the police force; by abolishing the ruinous and iniquitous *iltizam* and revising the tax system; and by a fiscal and economic policy designed to encourage agriculture and trade. And indeed a series of laws were promulgated during the Tanzimat period, and from time to time the local authorities in Syria and Palestine would receive Imperial firmans instructing them in both general and specific terms to maintain and improve the well-being of the population.[1]

It would be advisable to try and examine the conditions of life of the Syrian population during the period 1840–61, in the light of the conditions which had prevailed in Syrian provinces in the pre-reform era. The Ottoman régime in the Arab provinces in that era was definitely

[1] See, for example, *Irade D.*, No. 6275, 11 B 1262; Jaffa *Sijill*, No. 13, order registered on 27 N 1256; ibid., No. 18, 9 CA 1268; F.O. 78/761, Wood to Canning, No. 26, encl. in Wood to Palmerston, No. 26, Damascus, 18 Oct. 1848; compare also F.O. 78/1116, Moore to Clarendon, No. 5, Beirut, 25 Jan. 1855; this dispatch indicates the '. . . respect for the authority of the Sultan in Syria, whose benevolent intention as regards the welfare of all classes of His subjects is generally acknowledged and invariably spoken of in terms of praise and gratitude.'

> a system of exploitation, injurious to the social and economic welfare of the subjects . . . it not only lacked any guarantee for life and property against the violence, cupidity or caprice of the soldiery, but in effect made agriculture, industry and commerce their helpless victims. Legal redress . . . could not be looked for from courts whose officers were a byword for venality and corruption and whose decrees, moreover, were illusory, since they depended for enforcement upon the good will of the very administration and soldiery against whom they were directed.[1]

The consequences of this system were total insecurity and great injustice; there were mass poverty and class distinction, a marked fall in the size of the population, and a steady decline in the economy.[2]

The short term of Egyptian rule in Syria and Palestine during the 1830s proved, however, that it was possible to change radically the conditions of the people. Life and property became secure in the countryside and in the towns; greater justice and more equal taxation were administered, public services were introduced, and the economy flourished. But the Syrians had to pay for all this: they lost the measure of personal freedom and regional autonomy they had enjoyed under the previous anarchy; they were conscripted, compelled to pay regular taxes, give forced labour, and yield to a direct centralized rule. Tyranny and oppression were by no means a thing of the past, but became more regular and systematic under the iron hand of Ibrāhīm Paṣa.[3] Consequently the Syrian population overlooked the substantial benefits of Ibrāhīm's reforms and revolted against his cruel methods, looking forward to the restoration of the Ottoman régime. Thus, when the Egyptians withdrew in 1840, both their honey and their sting were removed, and a new era started in Syrian life.

[1] Gibb and Bowen, i. 208; compare Bodman, pp. 111 ff.; *Ḥasr al-lithām*, pp. 31–34; Heyd, *Documents*, p. 47; al-Munajjid, pp. 4–5, 7.

[2] Ibid.; see also above, pp. 8–10.

[3] See above, pp. 15 ff..

X

RIGHTS OF THE PEOPLE

A. *Security of life, honour, and property*

'The essential objects of these important laws are the security of life, and the preservation of honour and fortune.'

(From the Gülhane edict)

A STUDY of conditions prevailing in the Syrian provinces during the pre-reform period, shows that security, or the lack of it, was the most important single factor determining the degree of prosperity enjoyed by the local inhabitants. During that period none of the basic human rights of security of life, property, and fortune were preserved either in the countryside or in the towns. The peasants were daily exposed to attack, oppression, and extortion by vigorous Bedouin, offensive soldiers, or rapacious tax-collectors; travellers and caravans were under a constant threat of pillage and murder by outlaws, nomads, and soldiers alike; and many villagers throughout the area were engaged in a perpetual bloody warfare without restraint.[1] In the Syrian towns murders and robberies were openly committed, and Janissary factions like other military bodies, while frequently fighting each other, would spread rape, death, and destruction.[2]

The Tanzimat régime, though able to effect a considerable improvement in the anarchical state of affairs of the Syrian towns, failed to bring about an essential change in the countryside. From the last chapter it clearly emerges that, except for brief periods, the Syrian countryside was constantly exposed to the nomadic danger throughout the years 1840–61. Reports and accounts of contemporary consuls, missionaries, and travellers repeat the same theme in different ways, namely, that 'life and property in the country are becoming daily more insecure'; that there prevailed 'insecurity from robbery on the high roads up to the very gates of the city'; or that 'every man in the country districts has

[1] See, above, pp. 8–9.

[2] See Bodman, pp. 111 ff.; al-Munajjid, pp. 4–5, 7; Shamir, *The 'Azm*, p. 254.

to go armed and to defend his life and property for himself'.[1] Indeed, the Turkish government failed to protect either the rural areas or the roads from the aggression of the nomads and the outlaws. This failure was due to both the inefficiency of the police force and the weakness and apathy of the local authorities. Firstly, the country police were, as already pointed out, generally unreliable and ineffective. Not only did the *başıbozuk*s refrain from performing their duties, but they were frequently engaged in extorting money from the peasants and in highway robbery.[2] Secondly, the Turkish Pashas were usually unconcerned with lawless activities in the countryside and took no great pains to fight the highwaymen. For example, when the English consul in Jerusalem, James Finn, complained before the military governor about the activities of a certain brigand, the Pasha, simply unaware of his duties, cheerfully replied: 'Very good: you catch him and bring him here, and I shall cut his throat'.[3] Similarly the Turkish authorities were unwilling to stop—sometimes they even encouraged—the perpetual warfare between the various local groups such as the Qays and Yaman peasant factions in Palestine, the Druzes and Maronites in the Lebanon, the Kurds and Druzes near Damascus, the 'Alawis and Sunnis around Latakia, and rival Bedouin tribes all over the place.[4]

This neglect and omission caused much suffering to the local rural population: agriculture and commerce were seriously harmed, large portions of the countryside were ravaged, and the population steadily decreased.[5]

In sharp contrast to this gloomy picture was the one in the towns. Here the Ottoman government was more successful and there was significant improvements in conditions. As already mentioned, the Ottomans were able, in the course of the early Tanzimat, to prevent the revival of the pre-reform urban military

[1] See F.O. 195/210, Young to Canning, No. 4, Jerusalem, 30 Jan. 1844; Finn, p. 464 n; Lyde, p. 209.

[2] See above, pp. 57 ff.

[3] The sentence brought by Finn is a mixture of colloquial Turkish and Arabic and reads as follows: 'pek eyu! enti b'emsek boraya guestursen, ana be'kesser', Finn, ii. 144–5. A similar reply was given by the Pasha of Aleppo to a similar case; See Taoutel, iii. 108.

[4] See above, p. 58.

[5] See, for example, F.O. 78/1118, summary of Wood's notes to 'Arif Paşa, encl. in Wood to Clarendon, No. 11, Damascus, 12 Feb. 1855; F.O. 78/1627, Dufferin to Russell, No. 43, Beirut, 21 Dec. 1860; Bazili, i. 139 ff.; Finn, i. 315; Lyde, p. 216; *Rambles*, pp. 173–4, 182, 222; Segur, pp. 10–12; Tristram, *Israel*, p. 483.

organizations and thus to check their bloody feuds. Turkish military supremacy became predominant, and except for a few cases, notably that of Aleppo in 1850, no more hostilities took place within the cities. But although there was almost no danger from attack by the soldiery, there were still many robberies and murders in the towns.[1]

One of the major factors which helped to encourage crime in the towns as well as in the countryside was the lack of either proper means of redress or adequate punishment for such lawlessness. While only a few cases were properly punished,[2] many crimes were either ignored or lightly punished, partly because of bribery or pressure exercised by the criminals or their influential relatives;[3] mainly because of the inadequate legal powers of the Pasha to punish criminals. Under the Tanzimat decrees corporal punishment was abolished and the local authorities were strictly forbidden to exercise capital punishment without authority from the Sultan.[4] And although there was an extension of the Pasha's legal powers in 1852, he never became again the autocrat of the pre-Tanzimat era, and was thus somewhat restricted in his campaign against crime.[5]

B. *Human and legal rights*

'. . . to reconcile the rights of humanity with those of justice.' (From the *Hatt-ı Hümayun* of 1856)

The considerable decrease in the autocratic powers of the Pasha

[1] See, F.O. 78/447, Wood to Aberdeen, No. 33, Damascus, 20 Nov. 1841; F.O. 195/210, Young to Canning, No. 4, Jerusalem, 30 Jan. 1844; F.O. 78/1219, Moore to Clarendon, No. 62, Beirut, 19 Dec. 1856.

[2] See, for example, F.O. 78/622, Wood to Aberdeen, No. 12, Damascus, 7 Apr. 1845; F.O. 195/292, Finn to Palmerston, No. 21, encl. in Finn to Canning, No. 19, Jerusalem, 20 July 1848; Finn, i. 297.

[3] See F.O. 78/444, Young to Rose, Jerusalem, 25 May 1841; F.O. 78/538, Wood to Aberdeen, No. 37, Damascus, 24 Oct. 1843; F.O. 78/1521, Finn to Russell, No. 1, Jerusalem, 4 Jan. 1860.

[4] F.O. 78/498, Wood to Aberdeen, No. 19, Damascus, 3 Feb. 1842; F.O. 78/911, Moore to Rose, encl. No. 5 in Moore to Malmesbury, No. 20, Beirut, 30 Aug. 1852; A.E. Damas, i, from Beaudin, No. 16, 30 Sept. 1842; compare Bailey, p. 200; Engelhardt, i. 109; MacFarlane, i. 29. But according to Consul Finn, capital punishment of criminals acknowledging the crime of murder was permitted by a firman issued in 1848; see F.O. 195/292, Finn to Canning, No. 19, encl. in Finn to Palmerston, No. 21, Jerusalem, 20 July 1848.

[5] See F.O. 78/1588, Finn to Russell, No. 7, Jerusalem, 1 Mar. 1861; cf. Midhat, pp. 181–2. On the firman of 1852, see above, p. 36.

during the Tanzimat period, despite its disadvantages in the criminal field, had a unique effect on the human and legal rights of the population.

It has already been stated that in the time of the 'Pashas' rule', the Syrian people, notably the peasants, were deeply crushed and oppressed, and had no legal means by which to seek redress. On the one hand *vali*s, military commanders, and police officers would arbitrarily tyrannize their subjects and order punishment and execution without the semblance of a trial. On the other hand, the courts were unable to protect the citizen against this injustice and oppression since they depended on the local administration for the execution of their verdicts. Moreover, the *mahkeme*, which administered almost every branch of law, was often itself a scene of injustice and violence. This was partly a result of certain serious loopholes in the court's judicial procedure, and partly because the unsalaried judges frequently accepted bribes from the better-payer even if he were guilty.[1]

The Ottoman reformers made great efforts to uproot all these abuses and to preserve the human rights of the Ottoman subjects on a solid legal basis. They issued a series of decrees which aimed at restricting the Pasha's judicial powers, and at reorganizing the administration of justice and reforming its proceedings. Thus the Gülhane decree promised fair and public trial for suspects, forbade capital punishment without authority, and eliminated arbitrary interference with the legal rights of the subjects. The *Hatt-ı Hümayun* of 1856 confirmed the abolition of corporal punishment and other means of torture against suspects and called for a reform in the prison system. The Penal Codes of 1840, 1851, and 1858 elaborated these general decrees providing legal sanctions for their various clauses.[2]

The reform edicts and the Penal Codes, in addition to their system of checks on the civil administration, also laid down the lines for a far-reaching reorganization of the judicial administration. The Muslim *Şeriat* court (*mahkeme*) was now deprived of many of its former judicial functions and left to administer only

[1] Bodman, pp. 46 ff.; Gibb and Bowen, i. 208; ii. 126–32; *Ḥasr al-lithām*, p. 31; Shamir, *The 'Aẓm*, pp. 241–2; Ubicini, i. 184–5. On the structure of the Ottoman judicial system before the Tanzimat, see Gibb and Bowen, ii, ch. X; Heyd, *Documents*, p. 42; Ubicini, i, letter VIII.

[2] For text of the revised Penal Code, see *Düstur*, i. 527 ff.; Lûtfi, *Mirat*, pp. 128–46. English trans. in Bucknill and Utidjian.

matters of personal status, *vakf*, inheritance, and the like.[1] All other cases were transferred to the newly established provincial *meclis*, which acted also as a court of appeal against the *mahkeme*'s decisions.[2] In the mid-1850s the provincial *meclis* was, as already described, split into two separate bodies, administrative and judicial; the kadi was appointed an *ex officio* member of the *meclis* but his position was considerably diminished.

Criminal cases between foreign subjects or between them and Ottoman subjects were at the same time dealt with by mixed courts which were established in 1847 in the chief cities of the Empire and were composed of equal numbers of foreign delegates and local nominees, using rules of evidence and procedure drawn from European, rather than Islamic, practice.[3] In the Syrian provinces similar courts were set up only in the early 1850s; the *meclis-i ticaret* for commercial suits and the *meclis-i cinayet* or *meclis-i zaptiye* for criminal cases.[4]

All these comprehensive reforms in the administration of justice brought indeed great benefits to the Syrians, notably the urban population; they enjoyed greater freedom and were much less subject to government arbitrariness and abuse.[5] Capital punishment was, in fact, not carried out without the Sultan's verdict,[6] while the use of corporal punishment and torture, although still occasionally found, was gradually reduced.[7]

Nevertheless the major fault in the administration of justice

[1] Jaffa *Sijill*, No. 18, 13 Ş 1270; Ubicini, i. 47–49, 167–70. For examples, see Navon Collection, suits from Gurre B 1271 and 28 ZA 1271; Abū Shaqrā', pp. 195–6; see also Finn, i. 412.

[2] Ubicini, i. 49, 170; see also F.O. 195/291, Wood to Canning, No. 17, Damascus, 2 Aug. 1848; Lûtfi, *Mirat*, pp. 131–2, 155.

[3] Engelhardt, i. 83; Lewis, *Emergence*, p. 112; Madden, i. 460; Ubicini, i. 172–9.

[4] See *Irade D.*, No. 16420, 28 RA 1269; F.O. 78/871, letter from Vamık Paşa to Consul Moore, in Moore to Palmerston, No. 12, Beirut, 1 Oct. 1851; F.O. 78/1033, Werry to Redcliffe, No. 7, encl. in Werry to Clarendon, No. 5, Aleppo, 30 Mar. 1854; F.O. 195/458, Wood to Canning, No. 20, Damascus, 14 June 1854; compare Ubicini, i. 175–6; Davison, *Reform*, p. 52.

[5] See A.E. Damas, i, No. 10, 30 Dec. 1843; F.O. 78/871, Werry to Palmerston, No. 21, Aleppo, 29 Dec. 1851; Bazili, ii. 14–15, 20–21; Finn, i. 184; ii. 268 n. Compare Davison, op. cit., p. 50; *Rambles*, p. 61; Temperley, pp. 231–2.

[6] A.E. op. cit.; F.O. 195/292, Finn to Palmerston, No. 21, encl. in Finn to Canning, No. 19, Jerusalem, 20 July 1847; F.O. 78/911, Moore to Rose, encl. No. 5 in Moore to Malmesbury, No. 20, Beirut, 30 Aug. 1852.

[7] See F.O. 195/207, Werry to Canning, No. 3, Aleppo, 11 Feb. 1843; Finn, i. 184; Melek Hanum, pp. 98–99, 102; Walpole, iii. 327.

was not completely removed: as yet it was very difficult to get justice in the courts. The *mahkeme*, which still attracted a great many cases brought by Muslim litigants, continued to retain its old vices, mainly as a result of its defective procedures. For the kadis, like the other courts' functionaries, still did not get fixed salaries but received fees from the winner on every legal suit as well as on every document they issued. Out of these fees the kadi had also to pay the Chief Kadi of Istanbul a certain sum of money as rent for the *mahkeme*. These arrangements combined with the fact that the kadi was appointed for only one year, encouraged the judges to sell justice in order to cover all the expenses and secure present and future maintenance.[1] Such abuses were possible because there was yet inadequate control over the kadi's court and because there were many opportunities for dishonest dealing: it was, for example, very easy to obtain a false witness. Consequently favouritism and venality were rife and great injustice was done to large sections of the population.[2]

As for the new secular courts which had been established by the Tanzimat; though able to administer greater justice owing to their sound modern procedure and tighter central control,[3] they also suffered from serious defects. Firstly, they failed to exercise their jurisdiction on all the population; the most notable omissions being the peasants, Bedouin, and mountain people who continued to administer their own traditional laws and usages.[4] Secondly, the non-Muslim citizens were discriminated against by the *meclis*es.[5] Above all, the members of the *meclis*, local 'Ulema and notables were frequently corrupt and dishonest in their conduct of both the administrative and judicial functions.[6]

[1] A.E. Jérusalem, ii, from Jorelle, No. 34, 1 July 1847; F.O. 78/872, 'Memo. from Wood to the Grand Vezir', encl. in Wood to Palmerston, No. 6, Damascus, 29 Jan. 1851; F.O. 78/1452, Skene to Malmesbury, No. 20, Aleppo, 31 Mar. 1859; Finn, i. 175; Paton, p. 205; compare Ubicini, i. 184–6.

[2] See F.O. 78/447, Werry to Palmerston, No. 5, Damascus, 20 Feb. 1841; F.O. 78/622, Wood to Canning, No. 13, encl. in Wood to Aberdeen, No. 21, Damascus, 24 June 1845; F.O. 78/1588, Finn to Russell, No. 1, Jerusalem, 1 Jan. 1861; Finn, i. 91, 92 n., 175–6; *Rambles*, pp. 66–67; compare Ubicini, i. 182–5.

[3] A.E. Damas, i, No. 10, 30 Dec. 1843; Finn, i. 175; compare Davison, op. cit., p. 50.

[4] Finn, i. 220; E. Finn, 'The Fellaheen of Palestine', *The Survey of Western Palestine* (London, 1881), ii. 345–7; W. M. Thomson, *The Land and the Book* (N.Y., 1863), p. 291.

[5] See below, pp. 197 ff.

[6] See F.O. 78/538, Wood to Aberdeen, No. 39, Damascus, 6 Nov. 1843;

In fact, the councillors as well as other local notables emerged during the early Tanzimat period as the chief oppressors of the people, thus replacing, in a sense, the old tyranny of the Pasha which the era of reform did manage to uproot. This oppression was particularly evident with respect to the peasantry.

F.O. 78/872, Wood to Canning, No. 22, encl. in Wood to Palmerston, No. 28, Damascus, 12 Aug. 1851; F.O. 78/1220, Werry to Redcliffe, No. 35, encl. in Werry to Clarendon, No. 15, Aleppo, 24 Jan. 1856; F.O. 78/1330, Rogers to Moore, 26 Sept., encl. in Moore to Clarendon, No. 41, Beirut, 14 Oct. 1857; F.O. 78/1588, Finn to Russell, No. 1, Jerusalem, 1 Jan. 1861. See also above, p. 98.

XI

THE PEASANTRY: TAXATION, LAND TENURE, AND AGRICULTURE

A. *Taxation and land tenure*

> 'It is necessary that henceforth each member of [the] Ottoman society should be taxed for quota of fixed tax according to his fortune and means, and that it should be impossible that anything more could be exacted from him.'
>
> (From the Gülhane edict)[1]

FROM the texts of both Tanzimat edicts it is apparent that one of the chief handicaps to the peoples' well-being had been the previous wrong taxation system. Thus a comprehensive reform in the Ottoman system of taxation was much needed not only to increase the state's revenue, but also to abolish the various unjust exactions (*avanias*) and other forms of extortion which, in the pre-reform period, had been the source of great distress to the population, notably the peasants, and also a great obstruction to the economy.[2]

Primarily the Ottoman reformers strove to bring an end to the 'ruinous system of *iltizam*', which for long periods had depressed both the peasantry and agriculture.[3] But as already pointed out, despite official orders and some practical steps taken to abolish the *iltizam*, it continued to flourish in Syria and Palestine, as in other Ottoman provinces, throughout the Tanzimat era.[4] The authorities made a number of efforts to make the *iltizam* less harmful, firstly by placing the *mültezims* under the strict control of the local authorities and the *meclis*, and secondly, by offering the villages a

[1] Quoted from Hurewitz, i. 114.

[2] See above, p. 8; compare Bodman, pp. 40 ff.; Heyd, *Documents*, p. 47; Madden, i. 454–5.

[3] See the passages in the *hats* of 1839 and 1856; also Lûtfi, *Tarih*, vi. 68, 155; Ubicini, i. 281. On the history of the *iltizam* and its vices, see Gibb and Bowen, i. 205, 255; A. Granott, *The Land System in Palestine* (London, 1952), pp. 28, 29, 32, 57–58; A. N. Poliak, *Feudalism in Egypt, Syria, Palestine and the Lebanon, 1250–1900* (London, 1939), pp. 45 ff.; Ubicini, i. 278–83.

[4] On the damage caused to the state revenue by this system during the Tanzimat, see above, pp. 70–71.

prior option to farm their tithe through their sheikhs.[1] But all was in vain: the village sheikh would usually decline such an arrangement and prefer to be in league with the powerful *mültezim* in exploiting the peasants, for which he would receive a share in the tax-collection and sometimes even a special grant.[2] As for the authorities and the local *meclis*, they not only overlooked the misdeeds of the *mültezim*s, but often backed them and granted them administrative and military powers in return for the liberal bribes they received from these tax-farmers.[3] Moreover, it was frequently the case that the councillors themselves, or their relatives, were the *mültezim*s of the rural area.[4] The tax-farmer would thus oppress the peasant without fear of punishment on inspection; he squeezed from the fellah a much higher tax-rate than the fixed tenth, either by arbitrarily rating a higher price for his crops, or when receiving the tithe (*uşr*) in kind, by forcing the peasant to give him the wheat at a rate lower than the market price. If the peasant refused to yield to these demands, the tax-farmer could employ any of the following means against him. He could deprive a peasant of the necessary quantity of grain required to sow his field for the next year, or impose on him heavy fines, or even subject him to corporal punishment. Finally, the tax-farmer, with the help of the irregular soldiers under his command, could impound any part of the crops in question.[5] The tax-gatherer and his irregular cavalry were seldom content with the mere collection of taxes, and would privately extort money or foodstuffs from the peasant;[6] so also

[1] F.O. 195/210, Young to Canning, No. 2, Jerusalem, 22 Aug. 1842; F.O. 195/207, Werry to Canning, No. 3, Aleppo, 10 Feb. 1844; F.O. 78/660A, Wood to Canning, No. 4, encl. in Wood to Aberdeen, No. 8, Damascus, 21 Mar. 1846.

[2] Granott, pp. 57–58; F.O. 78/910, Werry to Granville, No. 5, Aleppo, 16 Mar. 1852.

[3] F.O. 78/499, Wood to Aberdeen, No. 56, Damascus, 20 July 1842; F.O. 78/577, Rose to Canning, No. 29, encl. in Rose to Aberdeen, No. 20, Beirut, 10 May 1844; F.O. 78/714, Timoni to Palmerston, No. 23, Damascus, 8 Sept. 1847; Finn, i. 162–4, 281–2; Granott, pp. 57–58; Kibrizli, p. 82; *Rambles*, pp. 55–56; Walpole, i. 353; compare MacFarlane, ii. 92–93; Oliphant, pp. 127–8.

[4] See above, p. 98; Werry's report in *M.E.J.* 16 (1962), pp. 511–12; compare also with the clause in the *Hatt-ı Hümayun* of 1856 strictly forbidding state officials and members of the *meclis* to be involved in farming *iltizam*s.

[5] F.O. 78/499, Wood to Aberdeen, No. 44, Damascus, 1 June 1842; Werry's Report in *M.E.J.*, op. cit., pp. 509–12; Finn, i. 284–5.

[6] F.O. 78/801, Wood to Canning, No. 13, encl. in Wood to Palmerston, No. 15, Damascus, 21 June 1849; F.O. 78/803, Finn to Canning, No. 20, encl. in Finn to Palmerston, No. 26, Jerusalem, 21 May 1849; Finn, i. 162, 164, 171; Lyde, p. 214; Kibrizli, p. 82.

did the village sheikh or the regional *nazır* (inspector) when charged by the government with the collection of tax, or with other duties affording a convenient pretext.[1]

Apart from the *uşr* (or *miri*) collected by *iltizam*, other taxes were also levied on the peasant, such as the *ferde* (personal tax) and sometimes the *salyane* (annual tribute) which were mostly collected directly by government officials.[2] These taxes, like the former, if levied justly and according to the official rates, could perhaps have been not particularly burdensome.[3] But here again the *Porte*'s orders were not kept by its local delegates. The Tanzimat edicts and many other firmans prohibited the exacting of unjust taxes and required the local authorities to assess and levy taxes justly and to revise the tax-rates every five years according to the changing agricultural conditions.[4] But government officials, either from sheer arbitrariness, or a desire to prove their zeal, would, for example, fix high rates for the *miri* (up to 1/5th instead of 1/10th of production) regardless of the fact that the actual area of land under cultivation had diminished or was producing less crops.[5] In addition, special rates and loans were occasionally levied on the villages to cover such expenses as Ḥajj caravans or the Crimean War.[6] From time to time also two other obligations, made illegal by the Tanzimat, were imposed on the peasants: these were the duty to provide men and animals for forced labour, and food and supplies for troops.[7]

[1] See, for example, F.O. 195/292, Finn to Canning, No. 20, Jerusalem, 22 May 1849; F.O. 78/872, Wood to Canning, encl. No. 2 in Wood to Palmerston, No. 17, Damascus, 29 May 1851; Robinson, p. 59.

[2] See F.O. 78/447, Werry to Ponsonby, No. 5, Damascus, 6 May 1841; F.O. 78/535, Rose to Aberdeen, No. 24, Beirut, 7 Mar. 1843; F.O. 78/1450, Brant to Bulwer, No. 23, encl. in Brant to Malmesbury, No. 12, Damascus, 20 June 1859; F.O. 78/1521, Finn to Dufferin, encl. No. 1 in Finn to Russell, No. 46, Jerusalem, 23 Nov. 1860. Compare MacFarlane, i. 158, 242; ii. 3. On the *salyane* see Sertoğlu, p. 283; Gibb and Bowen, i. 134; Bodman, pp. 43–44.

[3] F.O. 78/1383, Finn to Malmesbury, No. 25, Jerusalem, 9 Oct. 1858; Finn, i. 172; *Rambles*, p. 59. See also Ubicini, i. 267–8; *al-Jinān*, iii (1873), pp. 80–82.

[4] See F.O. 78/801, Wood to Palmerston, No. 20, Damascus, 30 Aug. 1849; F.O. 78/871, Werry to Palmerston, No. 1, Aleppo, 28 Feb. 1851.

[5] F.O. 78/499, Wood to Aberdeen, No. 44, Damascus, 1 June 1842; F.O. 195/292, Finn to Canning, No. 20, Jerusalem, 22 May 1849; A.E. Jérusalem, ii, from Jorelle, No. 34, 1 July 1847; Finn, i. 172. Compare MacFarlane, ii. 144; Young, p. 302.

[6] F.O. 78/910, Elias to Werry, No. 6, Latakia, encl. in Werry to Malmesbury, No. 7, Aleppo, 29 Apr. 1852; F.O. 78/1029, Wood to Clarendon, No. 36, Damascus, 6 July 1854; Finn, i. 437; ii. 45; Lyde, p. 218.

[7] F.O. 78/910, Elias to Werry, No. 6, Latakia, encl. in Werry to Malmesbury,

Hence although certain villages—notably in the mountains—were occasionally able to resist the payment of taxes while some peasants managed sometimes to evade it,[1] the Syrian peasant on the whole was normally overtaxed. This situation, combined with Bedouin oppression, naturally caused the impoverishment of the peasant and drove him to obtain loans in order to pay his taxes and buy seeds for the following year's crops. The moneylender from the town (who was frequently the *subaşı*, the *mültezim*'s delegate) would then add to his misery by lending the peasant money at an interest amounting sometimes to fifty per cent. per annum.[2] The authorities tried in vain to save the fellah from the moneylender: a firman issued in 1851 fixed a rate of eight per cent. interest on loans made to the peasants and ordered the *meclis* to supervise such loans and protect the villagers against extortion.[3] However, these regulations were by no means observed and only served to aggravate the situation: the moneylender refused to lend money at eight per cent. interest, and tended even to raise his former rate because of the new risk involved.[4] Consequently the peasant fell head over heels into debt, endless distress, and eventually was bankrupted and ruined. There were hence only two solutions available for his problem: to desert his land and try

No. 7, Aleppo, 29 Apr. 1852; F.O. 78/1454, Brant to Bulwer, separate, encl. in Brant to Russell, No. 9, Damascus, 8 Oct. 1859; Werry's report, M.E.J., 16, p. 510; Kibrizli, p. 70; Taoutel, iii. 168; compare MacFarlane, i. 158, 177.

1 See, for example, *Cevdet D.*, No. 5575, R 1274; F.O. 78/447, Werry to Ponsonby, No. 6, Damascus, 10 June 1841; F.O. 78/444, Young to Ponsonby, No. 15, Jerusalem, 14 July 1841; Lyde, p. 218. It is common knowledge that the peasant of Syria and Palestine would never pay his taxes unless forced to do so, and would do everything in his power to escape tax payment; compare E. Finn, 'The Fellaheen', op. cit. ii. 351 n.; Werry's report, *M.E.J.* 16, 512.

2 F.O. 78/622, Wood to Aberdeen, No. 44, Damascus, 29 Dec. 1845; Paton, p. 40; compare MacFarlane, i. 157; Ubicini, i. 329–31. The term *subaşı* had various meanings in Ottoman history (see Gibb and Bowen, i. 154–9, 250, 279, 325–6). It was sometimes given to a police superintendent whose duty was also to collect taxes (see Sertoğlu, p. 298). In Syria of the 1840s it was given to the person who superintended the *mültezim*'s interests and collected the taxes in the villages (Werry's report, *M.E.J.*, 16, p. 509). It seems that this person was later engaged also in lending money to the peasants independently of the *mültezim*.

3 Jaffa *Sijill*, No. 18, 9 CA 1268; F.O. 78/910, Wood to Canning, No. 3, encl. in Wood to Palmerston, No. 2, Damascus, 28 Jan. 1852. Cf. G. Aristarchi, *Législation Ottomane* (7 vols., Constantinople, 1873–88), i. 45.

4 F.O. 78/910, Wood to Canning, No. 9, encl. in Wood to Palmerston, No. 9, Damascus, 20 Mar. 1852; ibid., Werry to Granville, No. 5, Aleppo, 10 Mar. 1852.

his fortune in another area or in the city,[1] or to place himself under his tax-collector, the usurer, or any other influential townsman and become his tenant. The second alternative was sometimes more attractive: the fellah continued to cultivate his land while sharing the crops with his landlord. The latter would usually advance to the peasant seeds, pay the taxes, and protect him from the oppression of tax-collectors, government officials, and the like.[2]

Such was, for example, the position of peasants who lived in villages belonging to a *malikâne* (life tenancy). The peasantry of these villages are 'born in debt are held thereby in a kind of servitude during their whole life and die in debt'; but at the same time they enjoyed a certain degree of protection by their influential *malikânecis*.[3] And when in 1851 the Ottoman authorities decided to abolish the *malikâne* in Syria, compensate their proprietors, and make their peasants pay their taxes directly to the government from whom they were to receive seeds, this reform 'created dissatisfaction both among the peasantry and *malekanigis*'.[4]

Yet from his position of servitude it was only a small step for the peasant to lose the right to his land altogether; and indeed it was not infrequently that the fellah would sell his land to his protector, the tax-farmer, or other effendi and remain his tenant.[5] This again was at variance with the principles of the Tanzimat as described by Bernard Lewis: 'The general trend of the reformers was to abrogate the earlier agrarian relationship and progressively to extend and confirm the rights of use, of possessions and of ownership.'[6] Moreover, the Land Law of 1858 which originally aimed at checking the rise of large landownership, in fact reinforced this tendency: many peasants, unwilling to register their land for fear that it would involve more taxation or conscription, registered it in the name of their chiefs or powerful urban notables. Consequently, the latter acquired freehold ownership of lands with

[1] Segur, pp. 13–17; Tristram, *Israel*, p. 578; Walpole, iii. 117–18; Wortabet, p. 165; compare *al-Jinān*, vii (1870), p. 227; Granott, pp. 59–61.

[2] Compare F.O. 78/872, Wood to Canning, encl. No. 2 in Wood to Palmerston, No. 17, Damascus, 29 May 1851; F.O. 78/1389, General Report on Aleppo, encl. in Skene to Malmesbury, No. 25, Aleppo, 17 June 1858; Granott, pp. 58–60.

[3] Werry's report, in *M.E.J.*, 16, p. 511.

[4] F.O. 78/871, Werry to Canning, No. 35, encl. in Werry to Palmerston, No. 14, Aleppo, 10 Sept. 1851.

[5] See above, n. 2.

[6] Lewis, *Emergence*, p. 117. Compare Urquhart, ii. 171, 346. On the agrarian relationship and land tenure before the Tanzimat, see Gibb and Bowen, i, ch. v; Ubicini, i, letter 12.

full rights of disposal and succession confirmed by the government, whereas the peasants—the actual cultivators—lost their true rights and became sharecroppers or hired labourers at the mercy of their new landlords.[1]

B. *Agriculture*

It is perhaps paradoxical that the above forms of large ownership, in which the peasant was a mere tenant, were sometimes more beneficial to his economic conditions as well as to position of cultivation, than the small private holdings. The landowner, admittedly, would share the crops with the peasant, but the latter's share was at least safe from further intruders. The landlord, as already mentioned, was usually strong enough to protect his tenant from both the tax-gatherer's extortion and the Bedouin oppression; he would pay the tax due from the land and often advance to the peasant seeds and agricultural implements as well as loans.[2]

By contrast the government did comparatively little to encourage agriculture which, as it were, constituted the major basis of the Syrian economy. It is evident that the reformers were indeed concerned with the promotion of agriculture: following the general declaration of the Gülhane edict regarding the improvement of the provinces, a council of agriculture (*meclis-i ziraat*) was set up by the *Porte* in 1844; its mission was to promote and encourage agriculture in the provinces with the help of regional commissions of improvement.[3] In addition, agricultural officers were appointed in each province and district in connexion with the local *meclis*: a *ziraat müdiri* (agricultural officer) in each *eyalet* and *sancak* and a *ziraat vekili* (agricultural agent) in each *kaza* and *nahiye*. While responsible to the council of agriculture in Istanbul, these functionaries were assigned to supervise and instruct the peasants, settle their disputes, and advance to them various facilities.[4]

In Syria and Palestine such agricultural officers appeared in the course of the 1840s on the list of the *meclis* members, but their activities were unnoticed.[5] Instead, a certain number of Pashas

[1] Lewis, op. cit., p. 117; Granott, pp. 74–77; Davison, *Reform*, pp. 99–100; Oliphant, p. 206; for the text of the Land Law, see *Düstur*, i. 165 ff.; French text in Aristarchi, i. 57 ff.; Young, vi. 45 ff.; English text in S. Fischer, *Ottoman Land Laws* (London, 1919).

[2] See above, p. 162.

[3] Ubicini, i. 321–2; MacFarlane, ii. 145.

[4] *Takvim-i Vekayi*, No. 274, 11 Ş 1260; Lûtfi, *Tarih*, pp. 90, 120; F.O. 195/226, Wood to Canning, No. 1, Damascus, 4 Jan. 1845.

[5] Ibid.; cf. MacFarlane, ii. 145.

were occasionally engaged in the promotion of agriculture: steps were taken to rebuild ruined and deserted villages and resettle their former inhabitants,[1] seeds and implements were granted, locusts were fought with government help, and other measures were taken to encourage cultivation.[2] However, these reforms were carried out sporadically and, at any rate, formed only a few drops in the ocean of appalling difficulties which were encountered by the Syrian peasantry.

The government not only refrained from assisting the peasant financially to maintain and develop his land,[3] but was also, as we know, unable to protect him against the ruinous interest demanded by his usurer. Moreover, the authorities not only abstained from justly assessing tax-rates or adjusting them in a poor year, but they would often, in fact, fix low prices on agricultural production and even occasionally raise the tax-rates in a good year.[4] Above all, the Turkish government could not defend the peasant against the aggression and blackmail of the *mültezim* and the nomads.

Consequently many peasants would diminish their agricultural produce while others would choose to desert their farms altogether. Indeed, almost every foreign consul and European traveller in Syria and Palestine during the 1840s and the 1850s was aware of the mass emigration of peasants from their villages to safer places like the mountains, towns, and even to Egypt.[5] Consul Wood, for example, reported in 1843 that out of about 100 villages in the Houran area, seventy-five had been deserted during the

[1] F.O. 78/622, Wood to Aberdeen, No. 26, Damascus, 9 Aug. 1845; F.O. 78/621, Werry to Aberdeen, No. 13, Aleppo, 3 Sept. 1845.

[2] *Cevdet D.*, No. 14011, 26 Saf. 1264; A.E. Alep, i, from Guys, No. 37, 29 Jan. 1846; F.O. 195/207, Werry to Canning, No. 9, Aleppo, 12 Apr. 1845; F.O. 195/226, Wood to Canning, No. 1, Damascus, 4 Jan. 1845; F.O. 78/803, Finn to Canning, No. 20, encl. in Finn to Palmerston, No. 26, 21 May 1849; Taoutel, iii. 79.

[3] Compare F.O. 78/705, Kayat to Palmerston, No. 9, Jaffa, in Dec. 1847; F.O. 78/1031, Moore to Clarendon, No. 62, Beirut, 19 Dec. 1854; F.O. 78/1297, Report on wheat prices encl. in Skene to Clarendon, No. 6, Aleppo, 15 July 1857; Guys, *Esquisse*, pp. 38–39.

[4] F.O. 195/207, Werry to Canning, No. 3, Aleppo, 10 Feb. 1844; F.O. 78/1452, Skene to Bulwer, separate, encl. in Skene to Malmesbury, No. 42, Aleppo, 30 June 1859; Werry's report, *M.E.J.* 16, p. 509; compare *al-Jinān*, vii (1870), p. 227.

[5] F.O. 78/499, Wood to Aberdeen, No. 71, Damascus, 28 Sept. 1842; F.O. 78/803, Finn to Canning, No. 20, encl. in Finn to Palmerston, No. 26, Jerusalem, 21 May 1849; F.O. 78/1452, Skene to Bulwer, separate, encl. in Skene to Russell, No. 65, Aleppo, 30 Sept. 1859.

previous year because of tax-gatherers' oppression, Bedouin violence, and invasion of locusts. And although a number of these villages were resettled in later years, partly with government help, in 1849 more than fifty villages were still deserted.[1] According to a report of 1860, nine villages east of Damascus had been abandoned since 1856; and in 1861 Consul Rogers reported that 'within the Pashalik of Damascus are more than two thousand ruined and deserted villages of which about a thousand were cultivated and have been deserted within the memory of man'.[2] Other rural areas in Syria and Palestine, notably in the plain, also underwent this process of depopulation which continued to affect the countryside and local agriculture throughout the Tanzimat period.[3]

The lands that survived and flourished because they could better defend themselves against both nomads and tax-collectors were mainly those adjacent to mountain areas such as Jabal Nablus, Houran, al-Biqā' (and Lebanon), and the large estates near the main cities.[4] These areas would normally yield rich crops, usually sufficient to cover local consumption and occasionally even to export great quantities abroad.[5] Yet the country's total agricultural production at the period under survey formed only a part of her potential capacity; moreover, from time to time, especially in bad years, the Syrian provinces could not supply their own needs in grain and had to import it in order to prevent famine in towns and villages.[6]

[1] See and compare F.O. 78/538, Wood to Aberdeen, No. 25, Damascus, 30 July 1843; F.O. 78/801, Wood to Palmerston, No. 20, Damascus, 30 Aug. 1849.

[2] F.O. 78/1586, Rogers to Bulwer, No. 37, encl. in Rogers to Russell, No. 24, Damascus, 26 Aug. 1861; cf. F.O. 78/1627, Dufferin to Russell, No. 43, Beirut, 21 Dec. 1860.

[3] See, for example, F.O. 78/705, Kayat to Palmerston, No. 9, Jaffa, Dec. 1847; F.O. 78/803, Finn to Canning, No. 20, encl. in Finn to Palmerston, No. 26, Jerusalem, 21 May 1849; F.O. 78/1297, Skene to Redcliffe, No. 3, encl. in Skene to Clarendon, No. 2, Aleppo, 5 June 1857; *al-Jinān*, xx (1870), p. 688; Manṣūr, p. 88; Murray, ii. 11, 591, 618.

[4] Compare F.O. 78/755, Finn to Palmerston, No. 36, Jerusalem, 22 Nov. 1848; F.O. 78/874, Finn to Canning, No. 20, encl. in Finn to Palmerston, No. 9, Jerusalem, 5 Dec. 1851.

[5] F.O. 78/705, Kayat to Palmerston, No. 10, Jaffa, 31 Dec. 1847; F.O. 195/302, Werry to Canning, No. 1, Aleppo, 2 Feb. 1850; F.O. 78/914, Finn to Palmerston, No. 5, Jerusalem, 30 Jan. 1852; Taoutel, iii. 164–5.

[6] F.O. 195/207, Werry to Canning, No. 2, Aleppo, 14 Feb. 1846; F.O. 78/964, Kayat to Clarendon, No. 20, Jaffa, 19 Dec. 1853; F.O. 78/1452, Skene to Bulwer, No. 31, encl. in Skene to Russell, No. 60, Aleppo, 17 Sept. 1859; F.O. 78/1605, Finn to Russell, No. 15, Jerusalem, 1 Mar. 1861; Polk, pp. 225–6; *Rambles*, pp. 173–4; Taoutel, iii. 99, 101, 164–5; Urquhart, ii. 362; compare Manṣūr, p. 98.

XII

MEASURES OF ECONOMY AND FINANCE

A. *Public works and utilities*

> 'Sound facilities shall be made . . . with the opening of roads and canals . . . and with the preventing of the factors which impede the expansion of agriculture and commerce.'
>
> (From the *Hatt-ı Hümayun* of 1856)

> 'Les travaux publics en effet ont occupé de tout temps une place très secondaire dans le programme gouvernemental.'[1]

THE growth of agricultural activities in the Syrian provinces was hampered not only by insecurity and heavy taxation but also by the lack of roads and other public works.

Theoretically, the Ottoman reformers seemed to have been aware of the need for public works to encourage economic development. In the same year that the Gülhane edict declared the Sultan's desire to 'build up the provinces', a ministry of works was set up in Istanbul to promote economic activities, especially agriculture and commerce.[2] By the *hat* of 1856 and subsequent regulations, further emphasis was laid upon expenditure and powers of the local authorities for carrying out public works.

But in practice it could be stated that works connected with agriculture and commerce, such as roads and canals, were generally neglected, while facilities for administrative and military purposes and for prestige, received preferential treatment.

The latter works included mainly military barracks and hospitals, guard houses and forts, government buildings, and Pashas' residences, many of which were built or repaired during the period under survey.[3] Similar care was taken with facilities along the Ḥajj

[1] Engelhardt, ii. 312; cf. Longrigg, p. 294.

[2] Lewis, *Emergence*, p. 366; Ubicini, i. 294.

[3] See, for example, *Irade D.*, No. 8526, 11 M 1264; No. 25750, 25 RA 1274; *Iarde M.V.*, No. 4040, 8 Ş 1265; No. 17525, 18 Saf. 1275; *Cevdet D.*, No. 10874, 28 RA 1262; F.O. 78/1448, Finn to Russell, No. 44, Jerusalem, 17 Nov. 1859; Finn, i. 274.

route as well as with other religious institutions such as mosques and courts.[1]

Post and telegraph services were accordingly also established in the Syrian provinces, although about half a decade later than in Turkey proper. The postal system which was first set up in Turkey in 1834 and then reorganized in 1840,[2] was introduced into Syria and Palestine towards the mid-1840s, some four years after the Egyptian post had withdrawn.[3] Through it Istanbul and the Syrian centres were regularly connected, and it operated also once or twice a week between the cities of Aleppo, Damascus, Beirut, Tripoli, Homs, Hama, Acre, Jaffa, and Jerusalem.[4] The postal system was 'tolerably rapid and not expensive' and apparently reliable too, since it was occasionally used to transfer dispatches of foreign consuls.[5] The telegraph came to Syria only in the early 1860s after it had been first introduced into Turkey in 1855.[6] Aleppo, Beirut, and Damascus were connected in 1861,[7] and in the following years the telegraph service was gradually extended to the coastal towns of Tripoli, Acre, and Jaffa, though it did not reach the interior until a decade later.[8]

Health services were another major enterprise which the Ottomans endeavoured to promote, partly to encourage foreign trade and gain prestige in the West. Like their Egyptian predecessors in Syria, the Turks took great care to prevent infectious diseases from entering the country. Following the quarantine laws of 1838 and 1840[9] a great number of quarantine stations and lazarettos were set up, notably along the borders and in sea ports; their

[1] *Irade D.*, No. 3210, 10 B 1258; No. 16969, 16 B 1269; *Irade M.V.*, No. 1710, 25 ZA 1262; No. 16698, 18 RA 1274.

[2] Karal, *Tarih*, v. 160–1; Young, iv. 256.

[3] On its operation under the Egyptians, see Rustum, *Maḥfūẓāt*, i. 163, Nos. 423, 527; ii. 178, No. 2250.

[4] *Salname* 1263; F.O. 78/621, Rose to Aberdeen, No. 10, Beirut, 10 Nov. 1845; Murray, i. lviii; Robinson, p. 32; Taoutel, iii. 134, 138. But the interior towns of Palestine were in the mid-1850s still not connected to the system: Finn, i. 422–3.

[5] Robinson, op. cit.; F.O. 78/754, Timoni to Bidwell, Damascus, 28 Feb. 1848; Paton, p. 269.

[6] *Irade H.*, No. 6959, 12 M 1273; *Ceride-i Havadis*, No. 830, 13 Ş 1273; Young, iv. 345. On the preparatory step to introduce the telegraph into Syria, see *Mühimme*, No. 360, p. 45, Evahir N 1274.

[7] *Irade H.*, No. 9954, 4 CA 1277; *Ceride-i Havadis*, No. 36, 6 C 1277; F.O. 78/1586, Moore to Russell, No. 10, Beirut, 20 June 1861; Taoutel, ii. 102.

[8] Baedeker, pp. 38, 355, 509.

[9] *Mühimme*, No. 254, pp. 181–3, year 1856; Young, iii. 125, 135.

work was to issue bills of health to caravans and ships and to supervise public health in the district.[1] Although some of these institutions were perhaps responsible for delays in commercial transactions, the whole system seems to have operated very efficiently. The quarantine stations, which were well built, provided useful services through a team of qualified and well-paid Europeans and Ottomans; each station had its doctor and inspector and was responsible to a regional Board of Health.[2] This system was also of great help to the native population in fighting the periodical outbreaks of cholera; for example, in 1841–2, a potential epidemic was successfully controlled. (But success was not always to be won, and in 1848 cholera destroyed thousands of lives, many of them among the peasants who refused to be treated in these European-like institutions.)[3] In addition to the quarantine system, the Ottoman authorities adopted various measures, both legislative and practical, to promote sanitary conditions among the Ḥajj pilgrims and to set up medical services in the chief cities.[4]

Public Works, however, were at the same time seriously disregarded. To begin with, little or nothing was done to develop port facilities so that by 1859, for example, the port of Beirut, which was the busiest on the Syrian coast, was still without harbour accommodation, breakwaters, or lighthouses. The port of Jaffa was without a lighthouse or quays until 1864; and not until ten years later were breakwaters constructed there.[5]

But the most neglected public works were roads and their ancillaries—bridges, and inns. From the beginning the Ottoman authorities showed no enthusiasm for the construction of the new roads that were vital for the Syrian economy. For example, the

[1] *Irade D.*, No. 7828, 20 B 1263; *Irade M.V.*, No. 6686, 21 C 1267; F.O. 78/803, Finn to Palmerston, 19 May 1849; F.O. 78/1449, Moore to Malmesbury, No. 16, Beirut, 28 May 1859.

[2] See 'Report on the Ottoman Board of Health at Beirut', encl. in F.O. 195/274, Moore to Rose, No. 2, Beirut, 6 Feb. 1847; F.O. 78/803, op. cit; Neale, i. 13–14. For criticism on this system, see F.O. 78/912, Moore to Granville, No. 8, Beirut, 20 Feb. 1852; Paton, pp. 52–53.

[3] *Irade D.*, No. 9056, 6 CA 1264; *Cevdet D.*, No. 11499, 25 C 1264; F.O. 195/274, op. cit. On the attitude of the Muslim population towards the quarantine, see also Heyd, *'Ulemā*, p. 66.

[4] *Mühimme*, No. 254, p. 183, dated 1256; ibid., p. 110, C 1262; A.E. Jérusalem, ii, from Jorelle, No. 33, 9 June 1847; Penal Code, para. 254, in Bucknill and Utidjian, p. 199; Young, iii. 167. But see Baedeker, p. 25.

[5] F.O. 78/1449, Moore to Malmesbury, No. 5, Beirut, 31 Jan. 1859; F.O. 78/1834, 15 Mar. 1864, in Tibawi, p. 144

important Beirut–Damascus road originally planned in 1851 and started in 1857, was not finished and opened by a French company until 1861.[1] Similarly, a plan for an Aleppo–Alexandretta road, which was proposed in 1846, and then reconsidered in 1852, was only put into practice in the early 1870s.[2] Or again, an offer by foreign investors made in 1860 to construct the Jaffa–Jerusalem road, had not materialized by 1870.[3] Moreover, not only were no new roads built in Syria and Palestine during the first two decades of the Tanzimat rule; neither were old roads and bridges, as well as other works, maintained by the local authorities, although funds were allocated and dues raised from the population for these ends.[4] The reasons for these delays and omissions were the corruption of the local authorities, and the indifference of the native population. Except for a few Pashas like Kıbrıslı who showed great zeal in repairing roads, bridges, and canals and in initiating other public works,[5] most Turkish governors would usually neglect, if not hinder, this task.[6] Some of them would embezzle the money allocated for such projects and while authorizing cheap or temporary substitutes would falsely report that their assignments had been carried out.[7] Consequently such works would usually collapse after a short time;[8] the central government was thus betrayed, and the Syrian population and its economic well-being were affected.

[1] F.O. 78/872, Wood to Palmerston, No. 7, Damascus, 29 Jan. 1851; F.O. 78/1300, Moore to Clarendon, No. 46, Beirut, 24 Nov. 1857; *Irade H.*, No. 7929, 15 RA 1274; *Irade D.*, No. 28574, 19 L 1275.

[2] A.E. Alep, i, from Guys, No. 44, 9 Dec. 1846; F.O. 78/910, Werry to Canning, No. 19, encl. in Werry to Malmesbury, No. 11, Aleppo, 30 June 1852; compare the situation in other parts of the Empire: Madden, i. 467; *al-Jinān*, xiii (1870), p. 398.

[3] F.O. 78/1521, Finn to Bulwer, No. 1, encl. in Finn to Russell, No. 2, Jerusalem, 4 Jan. 1860; Baedeker, pp. 14, 132. Frequently foreign initiative and investment in such schemes was suspect, and accordingly rejected.

[4] F.O. 78/836, Werry to Canning, No. 3, Aleppo, 16 Mar., encl. in Moore to Palmerston, No. 23, Beirut, 30 Apr. 1850.

[5] *Irade D.*, No. 8868, 13 R 1264; No. 15722, 11 L 1268; No. 29590, Gurre CA 1276; F.O. 195/302, Werry to Canning, No. 1, Aleppo, 2 Feb. 1850.

[6] F.O. 78/1383, Finn to Clarendon, No. 1, Jerusalem, 1 Jan. 1858; F.O. 78/1586, Rogers to Bulwer, Damascus, 10 Nov. 1861; Finn, ii. 17, 343–4; Murray, i. xlvi; ii. 615.

[7] See Barker, ii. 307–9; Jessup, i. 118; Walpole, i. 259–60; iii. 115–16; compare *al-Jinān*, i (1872), p. 1.

[8] F.O. 78/836, Werry to Canning, No. 3, Aleppo, encl. in Moore to Palmerston, No. 23, Beirut, 30 Apr. 1850; *Irade D.*, No. 8138, 23 L 1263; Murray, ii. 615; Walpole, iii. 116. Compare MacFarlane, i. 396–7; Oliphant, p. 99.

B. *Monetary measures*

> 'Measures like (the formation of) banks shall be taken to provide credit for the state's fiscal affairs, by reforming the monetary system.'
>
> (From the *Hatt-ı Hümayun* of 1856)

The prosperity of the people and of the local economy was for a long time also jeopardized by the instability of the Ottoman monetary system, namely, the inflation of the currency and the debasement of the coinage. During the reign of Mahmud II, for example, the form and name of the Ottoman coinage were changed dozens of times and the rate of the Turkish piaster or its equivalent to the pound sterling fell from 23 in 1814 to 104 in 1839. All this obviously affected the standard of living, damaged the integrity of the salaried civil servants, and undermined economic activities.[1] Under the rule of Abdülmecid, a series of measures, some of them unprecedented in Ottoman history, were taken to reform the monetary system, but ended in failure. In 1841 the first Ottoman paper money (*kaime-i mutebere* or simply *kaime*) was issued. It was in fact treasury bonds for over half a million pounds sterling carrying twelve per cent. interest, which in the following year was reduced to the rate of six per cent., while a part of the issue was redeemed; but new issues soon followed amounting, within a decade, to a total of one and a half million pounds sterling. However, since the *kaime* was not guaranteed and easily torn, it was unpopular and underwent a considerable depreciation.[2] Meanwhile, in 1843, new measures were adopted to safeguard the currency: the old currency was withdrawn, the circulation of foreign pieces was prohibited, and a new gold and silver coinage (*mecidiye*—after Abdülmecid) was issued.[3]

In Syrian cities the change of coinage caused at first a great uproar, as the authorities did not possess enough of the new currency to replace the old.[4] When, however, this was settled, there

[1] Lewis, *Emergence*, pp. 108–9; see also Ubicini, i. 298.

[2] Lewis, op. cit.; Madden, i. 553; Sertoğlu, p. 159; Temperley, p. 231; Ubicini, i. 298–9; White, ii. 71–72; Engelhardt, i. 72.

[3] Lewis, op. cit.; Sertoğlu, op. cit. Note that the *mecidiye* was issued in 1843 and not in 1844 as has sometimes been suggested; see *Mühimme*, No. 255, pp. 117–18, B 1259; F.O. 78/539, Moore to Canning, No. 2, encl. in Moore to Aberdeen, No. 16, Beirut, 9 Oct. 1843; Taoutel, iii. 46, 63.

[4] A.E. Damas, i, No. 7, 5 Dec. 1843; F.O. 78/538, Wood to Aberdeen, No. 44, Damascus, 8 Dec. 1843.

followed a short period of monetary stabilization and commercial revival.[1] But since the supplies of new currency were not sufficient to meet all the demands, the old coinage as well as foreign currency continued to circulate.[2] In addition, the different coins in circulation had no fixed rates and accordingly they varied considerably: for example, the rates of the new and the foreign coins, which were less debased than the old ones, became higher than the original standard; also the rates of exchange of the different coins varied from place to place, particularly from coastal towns to inland cities.[3] During the early 1850s further measures were taken by the government to unify and stabilize the currency: the circulation of old and foreign coins was prohibited and those still in use were to be exchanged for the new coinage at seventy-five per cent. of their value. At the same time the rate of the Turkish currency was officially fixed at 110 piasters for one pound sterling.[4] But in fact foreign currency without fixed rates continued to circulate as Ottoman money became more and more scanty[5] and continued to lose its value until, by 1861, the rate stood at 131 piasters to one pound sterling.[6] Consequently commercial and other economic transactions were much confused, and considerable distress was inflicted upon large sections of the population.[7]

The banking system which was set up to regulate and control the monetary system was also a complete failure. Following an Imperial firman of April 1840, the first Ottoman Bank—'The

[1] F.O. 195/207, Werry to Canning, No. 17, Aleppo, 23 Sept. 1843; F.O. 78/621, Moore to Aberdeen, No. 3, Beirut, 1 Feb. 1845; F.O. 78/714, Wood to Palmerston, No. 28, Damascus, 8 Dec. 1847.

[2] F.O. 78/802, Moore to Bidwell, No. 3, Beirut, 30 Jan. 1849; al-'Awra, p. 154 n. Note successive government orders regarding the change of the old coins to new ones; see *Mühimme*, No. 256, 1 C 1262; compare also Ubicini, i. 301.

[3] See F.O. 78/1521, Finn to Russell, No. 1, Jerusalem, 4 Jan. 1860; al-'Awra, p. 154 n.; Murray, pp. lvii–lix; compare Young, v. 1–2.

[4] Ubicini, i. 302; al-'Awra, p. 154 n.

[5] F.O. 78/1452, Skene to Bulwer, separate, encl. in Skene to Russell, No. 65, Aleppo, 30 Sept. 1854; F.O. 78/1521, Finn to Russell, No. 1, Jerusalem, 4 Jan. 1860.

[6] See and compare F.O. 195/170, Young to Ponsonby, No. 13, Jerusalem, 24 June 1841; F.O. 78/538, Wood to Aberdeen, No. 36, Damascus, 6 Oct. 1843; F.O. 78/1389, Skene to Bulwer, No. 29, encl. in Skene to Malmesbury, No. 41, Aleppo, 4 Sept. 1858; F.O. 78/1586, Rogers to Bulwer, No. 19, encl. in Rogers to Russell, Damascus, 10 June 1861.

[7] F.O. 78/1537, Brant to Bulwer, separate, encl. in Brant to Russell, No. 6, Aleppo, 8 Apr. 1860; A.E. Alep, ii, from Geofroy, No. 3, 23 June 1860; compare Taoutel, ii. 99.

Bank of Constantinople'—was established in 1844 and proved useless. It was succeeded in 1848 by the 'Imperial Bank of Constantinople', which was later dissolved in 1852 with a deficit of thirty-five million piasters, which the government had to meet. A third Bank, the 'Ottoman Bank', was established in 1853 and was assigned to withdraw the depreciated coinage from circulation and to remit the *kaime* money within fifteen years. To this end a series of foreign loans were raised, all of which led gradually to the bankruptcy of 1875.[1]

In Syria, the first bank, a branch of the 'Ottoman Bank', was established in 1856 at Beirut, but was unable to control and regulate the monetary system as well as to provide other financial facilities (such as sufficient credit) for local branches of the economy.[2] Instead, almost all monetary affairs were still in the hands of private bankers (*sarraf*) who arbitrarily monopolized the currency and transacted their business at an enormous rate of interest irrespective of the official rate of eight per cent. fixed in 1851.[3] Again the obvious victims of this system were the Syrian economy and the population.

[1] Barker, i. 148–9; Engelhardt, i. 102; Lewis, *Emergence*, p. 109; Madden, i. 553; Ubicini, i. 300–6. For additional factors involving the Ottoman financial crisis, see above, pp. 69 ff. See also Rodkey, p. 349.

[2] F.O. 78/1219, Moore to Clarendon, Beirut, 6 Oct. 1856; Farley, *Syria*, p. 36; *Tanzimat*, p. 255.

[3] F.O. 78/910, Wood to F.O., No. 10, Damascus, 2 Apr. 1852; F.O. 78/1452, Skene to Bulwer, No. 21, encl. in Skene to Malmesbury, No. 31, Aleppo, 2 June 1859; F.O. 78/1521, Finn to Bulwer, encl. in Finn to Russell, No. 21, Jerusalem, 19 July 1860.

XIII

COMMERCE AND INDUSTRY: THE CITY

As in other areas of economic life, the Tanzimat period failed to provide a suitable remedy for the serious decline which Syrian trade and industry had been undergoing for a long time.[1] Most of the causes of this decline remained unchanged during the era of reform, namely, the insecurity of the roads, the lack of public works, the heavy taxation, and the irregularity of the monetary system. And although Syrian foreign trade flourished during that period and stimulated, to a certain extent, commercial activities and agricultural production, it carried further the destruction of local industry, affecting as a consequence the traditional structure of Syrian urban society.

It is true that the Ottoman reformers were highly concerned with the promotion of trade as one of the chief ways of improving the conditions of life of the subjects. This policy was apparent from the relevant clauses in both reform edicts and, for Syria, it was expressed by the dispatch in 1841 of a special commercial adviser to Damascus, and by occasional firmans ordering the local authorities to encourage commercial activities in their respective districts.[2] But the substantial measures introduced during the Tanzimat in effect turned out to be beneficial mainly to foreign trade and actually harmful to internal trade and industry.

A. *Commercial Institutions*

The major reforms of the Tanzimat regarding commerce—the commercial legislation and institutions—were initiated largely under European pressure and direction, and served, in fact, to reinforce the foreign privileges as acquired by the capitulations.

The first Ottoman Commercial Code, based on Western legislation, was drawn up in 1840 under the inspiration of Reşid Paşa

[1] See Gibb and Bowen, i. 299–301; Hourani, *Arabic Thought*, p. 35; Taoutel, ii. 30–31; also Burckhardt, pp. 167–8.

[2] *Irade D.*, No. 1637, 7 M 1257; ibid., No. 6275, 11 B 1262; compare F.O. 78/638, Canning to Aberdeen, No. 44, 18 Mar. 1846, in Bailey, p. 216.

and aimed at facilitating commercial activities on modern lines.[1] This code, however, was not put into effect before 1850 due to strong opposition by the 'Ulema of Istanbul who regarded it as a serious breach of Islamic Law.[2] When eventually issued, the Commercial Code formed the basis for the proceedings of the newly established commercial tribunals, the first of which was set up in Istanbul in 1848 on the foundations of the old Ottoman Chamber of Commerce, and consisted of an equal number of Ottoman and European members.[3]

In Syria the first commercial courts had already been established by Ibrāhīm Paşa in the 1830s but collapsed when the Egyptians withdrew;[4] and until such courts were reinstated by the Ottomans a decade later, commercial suits were tried by the provincial *meclis* and sometimes in the *mahkeme*.[5] In the *meclis* the legal proceedings in commercial cases were based on usage and 'equity', while in certain instances the *Şeriat* Law was still enforced.[6] In the early 1850s the first Ottoman-styled commercial tribunals were set up in the chief Syrian cities, following the example of the metropolis and after pressure by foreign emissaries in Syria. In Damascus and Beirut, the *meclis-i ticaret* were set up in 1850; that in Damascus was composed of seven Ottoman subjects (four Muslim merchants, two Christians, and a Jew) appointed by the authorities, and seven foreign merchants chosen by the consuls.[7]

[1] For text of the Commercial Code, see *Düstur*, i. 375 ff. French text in Aristarchi, i. 275 ff.; Young, vii. 55 ff. On the Code, see Engelhardt, i. 40; Ubicini, i. 166; Temperley, p. 232. Note that in 1860 the Code was complemented; *Düstur*, i. 445 ff.; Lûtfi, *Mirat*, p. 123.

[2] See above, pp. 23–24.

[3] *Ceride-i Havadis*, No. 372, 8 RA 1264; MacFarlane, ii. 641–3; Temperley, pp. 232–3; Ubicini, i. 173–4; Young, i. 225. On the former commercial tribunal in Istanbul, see Lûtfi, *Tarih*, vi. 102. In 1860 the commercial courts were reorganized on the basis of the new supplement to the Commercial Code which *inter alia* destroyed the numerical equality of the native and foreign elements. See *Irade M.V.*, No. 20049/1 and 2, 20 ZA and 15 Z 1277; F.O. 78/1586, Moore to Bulwer, No. 52, encl. in Moore to Russell, No. 34, Beirut, 5 Dec. 1861; Young, i. 226.

[4] See F.O. 78/412, Werry to Ponsonby, Aleppo, 21 Jan. 1840; see also above, pp. 91–92.

[5] F.O. 195/170, letter by Zakariyya Paşa, in Werry to Ponsonby, Damascus, 5 Mar. 1841; Paton, p. 269.

[6] F.O. 78/800, Moore to Canning, No. 53, encl. in Moore to Palmerston, No. 41, Beirut, 31 Oct. 1849; F.O. 78/801, Wood to Canning, No. 10, encl. in Wood to Palmerston, No. 10, Damascus, 1 May 1849.

[7] A.E. Damas, ii, No. 6, 28 May 1850; F.O. 78/837, Calvert to Palmerston, No. 13, Damascus, 15 June 1850.

In Beirut the tribunal consisted of four members each of Muslims, non-Muslims, and foreign merchants;[1] a similar pattern was given to the commercial *meclis* of Aleppo when it was inaugurated in 1853.[2] In small towns commercial suits continued to be heard in the local council.[3]

The new tribunals conducted their proceedings according to the Commercial Code but were put under the control of the provincial *meclis*es which had to confirm their verdict. This caused much friction between the two councils; the chief issues being the active interference of the provincial *meclis* and its attempts to subject the native members of the commercial council to its directions.[4] In addition the tribunals' work was occasionally upset by dissensions among the foreign members or between them and the authorities, and by various other irregularities.[5] Consequently the commercial courts were from time to time divided or paralysed or even ceased to operate.[6] In ordinary times, however, these courts helped to remove old prejudices and to facilitate commercial transactions,[7] though the main beneficiaries were non-Muslim and foreign merchants, rather than local Muslim traders.[8]

[1] *Irade M.V.* No. 4564, 21 Saf. 1265; F.O. 78/836, circular by Vamık Paşa of 8 R 1266, encl. in Moore to Palmerston, No. 15, Beirut, 1 Mar. 1850; see also Urquhart, ii. 345–6; Wortabet, i. 83.

[2] *Irade M.V.*, No. 10164, 11 C 1269; A.E. Alep, ii, from Geofroy, No. 5, 7 May 1853; *Rambles*, p. 67.

[3] See, for example, Jaffa *Sijill*, No. 18, order of 9 CA 1268.

[4] See F.O. 78/1381, Brant to Bulwer, No. 59, encl. in Brant to Malmesbury, No. 53, Damascus, 14 Dec. 1858; F.O. 78/1454, Moore to Bulwer, separate, encl. in Moore to Malmesbury, No. 15, Beirut, 3 May 1859.

[5] F.O. 195/368, Wood to Canning, No. 17, Damascus, 27 June 1851; F.O. 78/960, Werry to Clarendon, No. 9, Aleppo, 3 June 1853; F.O. 78/1031, Moore to Clarendon, No. 22, Beirut, 1 July 1854; F.O. 78/1520, Brant to Bulwer, separate, encl. in Brant to Russell, No. 1, Damascus, 5 Jan. 1860. Compare MacFarlane, ii. 643.

[6] See F.O. 78/1454, Moore to Bulwer, separate, encl. in Moore to Malmesbury, No. 15, Beirut, 3 May 1859; F.O. 78/1630, Memo. by Vice-Consul White, encl. in Dufferin to Russell, No. 113, Beirut, 10 May 1861; *Rambles*, pp. 67–68. In Aleppo, for example, the commercial court ceased to operate from 1857 to 1860; see F.O. 78/1538, Skene to Bulwer, No. 27, encl. in Skene to Russell, No. 47, Aleppo, 4 Aug. 1860.

[7] F.O. 78/872, Wood to Palmerston, No. 6, Damascus, 29 Jan. 1851; F.O. 78/1031, Moore to Clarendon, No. 22, Beirut, 1 July 1854; compare F.O. 78/1297, Barker to Redcliffe, No. 2, encl. in Barker to Clarendon, No. 2, Aleppo, 27 Jan. 1857; Ubicini, i. 174.

[8] Cf. F.O. 78/1031, op. cit.; Temperley, p. 232; Young, i. 225.

B. *Monopolies and customs*

Another major economic measure which proved to be beneficial to foreign trade, though not to internal commerce, was the Commercial Treaty of 1838.[1] It was originally signed with England and subsequently accepted by all European powers including Russia (though the latter country, by virtue of earlier conventions, enjoyed a far better position). According to the treaty, all monopolies and various dues that had been imposed during previous years were abolished, and a uniform customs system was introduced whereby a total duty of five per cent. was levied on imported goods and twelve per cent. on exports by foreign merchants. Local merchants, however, did not enjoy these concessions nor were they granted similar conditions in European countries.[2] In fact they continued to be subject to a number of burdensome monopolies and excessive duties. For even after the restoration of the Ottoman rule in Syria, not all the former monopolies were abolished at once; most were gradually replaced by customs duties during the 1840s[3] and some still existed during the whole period under survey causing embarrassment to internal trade.[4] The new customs duties themselves were fairly high and exorbitant, contrary to the *Hatt-ı Hümayun*'s instructions;[5] they were farmed out to private individuals who, lacking government control, would levy excessive duties on local goods, thus affecting native merchants and consumers.[6]

This factor together with the factors already discussed—inade-

[1] For text, see Hurewitz, i. 110–11.

[2] Temperley, p. 212; Ubicini, i. 348–50.

[3] A.E. Damas, i, from Beaudin, No. 16, 30 Sept. 1842; F.O. 78/705, Kayat to Palmerston, No. 9, Jaffa, Dec. 1847; F.O. 78/872, firman of 16 M 1267, encl. in Wood to Palmerston, No. 9, Damascus, 19 Mar. 1851.

[4] F.O. 78/1388, Brant to Alison, No. 4, encl. in Brant to Clarendon, No. 6, Damascus, 28 Jan. 1858; Tristram, *Israel*, p. 594. Compare Engelhardt, i. 309.

[5] Jaffa *Sijill*, No. 18, order of 23 L 1265; A.E. Damas, i, from Beaudin, No. 16, 3 Sept. 1842; F.O. 78/659, Rose to Wellesley, encl. No. 2 in Rose to Palmerston, No. 35, Beirut, 8 Sept. 1846; F.O. 78/1388, Brant to Alison, No. 4, encl. in Brant to Clarendon, No. 6, Damascus, 28 Jan. 1858; F.O. 78/1521, Finn to Dufferin, encl. No. 1 in Finn to Russell, No. 46, Jerusalem, 23 Nov. 1860.

[6] F.O. 78/872, Wood to Palmerston, No. 9, Damascus, 19 Mar. 1851; F.O. 78/1521, Finn to Dufferin, encl. No. 1 in Finn to Russell, No. 46, Jerusalem, 23 Nov. 1860; Consul Werry's report, in *M.E.J.* 16, p. 510; Finn, i. 281, 284–6; Urquhart, i. 288; ii. 441.

quate public works, the wrong monetary system, and, above all, insecurity of roads—all served to impede Syrian internal trade. Indeed, throughout the period under review, this trade was on the whole in a state of stagnation, and although sometimes it revived for short periods,[1] it occasionally came to a complete standstill.[2]

C. *Foreign Trade*

Yet the most significant aspect of Syrian trade of the Tanzimat era, and the most determinative to the local economy, was the trade with Europe. This trade, which had its roots in the pre-reform time and became important under the Egyptian rule, developed further during the 1840s and 1850s and was shared by many European countries, notably England. Syria imported from Europe cotton and wool manufactures, iron, copper and steel, sugar, coffee, and other goods, and exported to European countries grain, raw cotton, wool and silk, tobacco, and dried fruits.[3] Imports from the West, chiefly Britain, increased rapidly owing to the light customs duty of five per cent. and other favourable conditions, one of which was the growing number of local consumers, especially in the towns.[4] Thus, for example, imports to the port of Beirut rose from £66,748 in 1841 to £546,266 in 1848, to £722,864 in 1853, and to £1,162,676 in 1856, reaching £1,448,860 in 1860.[5] Similarly, European imports at Aleppo, which in 1841 amounted to

[1] See, for example, F.O. 78/660B, Werry to Palmerston, No. 12, Aleppo, 30 Oct. 1846; F.O. 195/302, Werry to Canning, No. 1, Aleppo, 2 Feb. 1850; F.O. 78/1603, Skene to Russell, No. 45, Aleppo, 1 July 1861; Farley, *The Massacres*, pp. 185–6.

[2] A.E. Jérusalem, ii, from Jorelle, No. 34, 1 July 1847; F.O. 78/836, Werry to No. 2, Moore, Aleppo, encl. in Moore to Palmerston, No. 23, Beirut, 30 Apr. 1850; F.O. 78/1537, Report on trade, encl. in Brant to Russell, No. 17, Damascus, 13 Aug. 1860.

[3] Details in F.O. 78/1121, Finn to Clarendon, No. 22, Jerusalem, 31 Dec. 1855; F.O. 78/1388, 'Report on the Trade of Damascus', in Brant to Malmesbury, No. 41, Damascus, 12 Aug. 1858; F.O. 78/1603, 'Report on the Trade of Aleppo', encl. in Skene to Russell, No. 6, Aleppo, 15 Jan. 1861.

[4] See F.O. 78/535, Rose to Aberdeen, No. 22, Beirut, 5 Mar. 1843; F.O. 78/1389, Skene to Clarendon, No. 10, Aleppo, 9 Mar. 1858; Farley, *Syria*, pp. 26, 29; *Rambles*, pp. 180–1; Urquhart, ii. 191–2.

[5] Farley, *The Massacres*, p. 185. Compare the growth of the British imports to Beirut in F.O. 78/754, Moore to Bidwell, No. 4, Beirut, 9 Dec. 1848; F.O. 78/1221, Moore to Clarendon, No. 22, Beirut, 31 Mar. 1850; see also tables in Farley, *Syria*, p. 370.

about £232,000, were doubled by 1851 and stood at £1,414,059 in 1854.[1]

Exports from Syria to Europe likewise steadily increased, particularly after the Crimean War: goods exported from Beirut rose, for instance, from £25,128 in 1841 to £253,648 in 1848, to £624,544 in 1853, and £983,318 in 1857;[2] from Aleppo they were £115,000 in 1841, £993,630 in 1854, and £1,254,130 in 1855.[3] Yet although the Syrian export trade was growing remarkably, it was not sufficient to balance the large import from Europe. It is true that in secondary seaports such as Sidon, Acre, Haifa, and Jaffa, the exports usually exceeded the imports,[4] but this was by no means the case in the major ports of Beirut and Aleppo (namely, Alexandretta, Latakia, and Tripoli) where the greater part of the foreign trade was handled. In Beirut, except for the years 1851–2 in which exports equalled the value of imports,[5] there was a continuing trade gap (especially with Britain); it amounted to about £100,000 in 1853 and £60,000 in 1856 and 1857.[6] Aleppo's foreign trade gap was even larger being about £117,000 in 1841, and though falling to £80,000 in the following years, by 1844 it amounted to about £160,000, and thereafter rose to £170,000 in 1858, falling again to £150,000 in 1860.[7] Potentially, it was alleged, Syria's chief export item, its agricultural produce, could have been sufficient to cover the value of the

[1] F.O. 78/497, Werry to Bidwell, 1 June 1842; F.O. 78/1221, Barker to Clarendon, No. 11, Aleppo, 7 Apr. 1856; Farley, *The Massacres*, p. 185.

[2] Farley, ibid., pp. 185–6; id., *Syria*, p. 370; compare, Murray, ii. 403; Robinson, p. 627; Urquhart, ii. 191–2.

[3] F.O. 78/497, Werry to Bidwell, Aleppo, 1 June 1842; F.O. 78/1221, Barker to Clarendon, No. 11, Aleppo, 7 Apr. 1856; Farley, *Syria*, p. 185.

[4] See and compare F.O. 78/803, Kayat to Palmerston, No. 11, Jaffa, 30 June 1849; F.O. 78/1218, Finn to Clarendon, No. 51, Jerusalem, 31 Dec. 1856; F.O. 78/1387, Kayat to Malmesbury, No. 21, Jaffa, 31 Dec. 1858.

[5] F.O. 78/873, Moore to Bidwell, No. 1, Beirut, 1 Mar. 1851; see also F.O. 78/961, Moore to Clarendon, No. 6, Beirut, 24 Mar. 1853.

[6] Farley, *Syria*, p. 370; compare Murray, ii. 403; Robinson, p. 627. Note, moreover, that a certain portion of the exports from Beirut (one-seventh in 1843) was composed of silk manufactures from the English and French factories in Lebanon; see F.O. 78/802, Moore to Bidwell, No. 3, Beirut, 30 Jan. 1849. Note also that a certain part of the Syrian foreign trade was a transit trade between Europe and Iraq, Persia, and India.

[7] F.O. 78/497, Werry to Bidwell, No. 4, Aleppo, 1 June 1842; F.O. 78/1221, Barker to Clarendon, No. 11, Aleppo, 7 Apr. 1856; F.O. 78/1452, 'Report on the Trade of Aleppo', encl. in Skene to Malmesbury, No. 25, Aleppo, 5 May 1859; F.O. 78/1603, 'Report on the Trade of Aleppo', encl. in Skene to Russell, No. 6, Aleppo, 15 Jan. 1861.

imports if it had not been for the unfavourable conditions already described.[1] But as things were, there was a steady drain of Syrian gold to Europe to pay for these excess imports.[2]

D. *Industry*

Another grave result of the growing import of foreign goods to the Syrian provinces was the destruction of local industry and crafts. European manufactures (being largely produced from raw materials imported from Syria and other Ottoman provinces) flooded the local markets and since they were cheaper and usually of better quality than the home manufactures, they were preferred by the native population.[3]

The most affected industry was textiles—cotton, wool, and also to a lesser extent silk—which had been for long the chief Syrian manufacture.[4] Thus, for example, the number of Aleppo's textile looms, which had reached in the past a record of 40,000, diminished to about 5,500 in 1856 and rose back to only 10,000 in 1859.[5] Similarly the number of looms in Damascus fell from some 34,000 in the recent past to about 4,000 in the late 1850s.[6] The local silk industry was also not immune from this decline, although it enjoyed an initial revival during the 1850s, partly owing to the establishment of several new factories in Lebanon owned by English and French investors.[7] Moreover, while the consumption

[1] F.O. 195/302, Werry to Canning, No. 1, Aleppo, 2 Feb. 1850; F.O. 78/1539, Moore to Russell, No. 5, Beirut, 7 Feb. 1860; A.E. Jérusalem, ii, from Jorelle, No. 34, 1 July 1847; Finn, i. 281; Murray, ii. 597; Urquhart, ii. 441.

[2] F.O. 78/535, encl. No. 1 in Rose to Aberdeen, No. 22, Beirut, 5 Mar. 1843; Bazili, ii. 7–11; Paton, p. 267; *Rambles*, pp. 59–60. Note, for example, that in 1848 Beirut paid £70,000 in specie and bullion for its imports from England which amounted to £150,000; see F.O. 78/802, Moore to Bidwell, No. 3, Beirut, 30 Jan. 1849.

[3] F.O. 78/1389, 'General Report on Aleppo', encl. in Skene to Malmesbury, No. 25, Aleppo, 17 June 1858; Baedeker, p. 566; Guys, *Esquisse*, pp. 38–39; Paton, p. 14; Walpole, i. 94; compare Engelhardt, ii. 308; Gibb and Bowen, i. 295–6; MacFarlane, i. 145–6; Mardin, p. 165; Ubicini, i. 339–40.

[4] On the textile industry in the eighteenth century, see Gibb and Bowen, i. 297.

[5] F.O. 78/1221, Skene to Bidwell, No. 11, Aleppo, 7 Apr. 1856; F.O. 78/1389, op. cit.; compare Ubicini, i. 340; Qarā'lī, *Ḥalab*, p. 71.

[6] F.O. 78/1586, Rogers to Bulwer, No. 38, encl. in Rogers to Russell, No. 24, Damascus, 26 Aug. 1861; Urquhart, ii. 71. According to Bazili there were in 1840 50,000 looms in all Syrian cities and within a decade they were reduced to only 2,500; Bazili, ii. 7.

[7] F.O. 78/754, Moore to Bidwell, No. 4, Beirut, 8 Feb. 1848; F.O. 78/1603,

of European textiles was increased every year, partly owing to reform in the dress which introduced Western fashions,[1] nothing was done by the authorities to encourage local textile industry either by financing it or by modernizing its methods.[2] Not only did the government refrain from protecting the local industry by a calculated customs policy, but it even imposed heavy taxation on local crafts and factories.[3]

At the same time, however, the local industries of soap and oil and tobacco, which had no foreign competition, remained outside the process of decline. Furthermore, although they were sometimes heavily taxed by the authorities,[4] these industries managed to flourish, particularly the soap manufacture which often even received considerable support from the authorities.[5]

E. *The impact on the city*

The big economic changes which occurred in Syria and Palestine during the Tanzimat period—the huge increase of foreign trade and the decline of local industry and commerce—had a great impact on the development of the Syrian city and on its social structure.

One of the major effects of the flourishing foreign trade was the rapid growth of Syrian coastal towns which were engaged in this trade. The unique example was Beirut, a town which had been encouraged to grow under the Egyptian régime but which made its most substantial progress during the early Tanzimat. From a village of 5,000–6,000 inhabitants in the mid-1820s, Beirut became a town with a population of 12,000 in 1840, and in the late 1850s

Skene to Russell, No. 6, Aleppo, 15 Jan. 1861; cf. *al-Jinān*, ii (1870), p. 50; *Tanzimat*, pp. 427, 438; Wortabet, i. 199.

[1] Ubicini, i. 341; Taoutel, iii. 138; Paton, pp. 190–1. On the question of European dress in the Syrian provinces in the nineteenth century, see R. Tresse, 'L'évolution du costume Syrien depuis un siècle', in *Entretiens sur l'évolution de pays de civilisation Arabe* (Paris, 1938), pp. 87–96.

[2] Guys, *Esquisse*, pp. 38–41; cf. *al-Jinān*, xii (1870), p. 372; Merrill, p. 7.

[3] F.O. 78/456, Wilbraham's report, encl. in Rose to Palmerston, No. 71, Gazir, 23 July 1841; Bazili, i. 7; see also below, p. 182.

[4] Jaffa *Sijill*, No. 18, 23 L 1265; F.O. 78/962, Finn to Clarendon, No. 10, Jerusalem, 19 July 1853; Farley, *The Massacres*, p. 83; Merrill, p. 7.

[5] *Irade M.V.*, No. 7516, 16 CA 1263; No. 15582, 25 L 1272; F.O. 78/958, Moore to Rose, No. 13, encl. in Moore to Clarendon, No. 7, Beirut, 16 Apr. 1853; F.O. 78/1389, 'General Report on Aleppo', encl. in Skene to Malmesbury, No. 25, Aleppo, 17 June 1858; CM/017, from Bowen, No. 21, Nablus, 6 Aug. 1855.

it was a prosperous city of 50,000 inhabitants. This growth was due in some part to its safe location near Mount Lebanon, and in some part to its position as the seat of government and of the foreign quarters; but mainly it was a consequence of its growing trade. Indeed, Beirut became the biggest port along the Syrian coast with commercial transactions amounting yearly to more than two million pounds in the 1850s.[1] It conducted *inter alia* a considerable part of the Damascus foreign trade thus making the Syrian capital for the first time dependent to some extent upon it for the supply of various manufactures.[2]

South of Beirut, Haifa began to develop after the restoration of the Turkish rule and particularly during the 1850s, mainly because it was one of the major ports through which grain was exported to Europe, notably England (this led the British government to establish a vice-consul there in 1853).[3] Other sea ports which made great progress during that period, because of the increasing foreign trade, were Latakia, north of Beirut,[4] and Jaffa on the Palestinian coast.[5] But on the other hand, the growth of these towns, particularly Beirut, caused the decline of the old ports of Sidon, Acre, and Tripoli, although they continued to retain a certain export of grain and tobacco.[6]

In the interior, there were also a few places like Nablus which, being relatively safe and very fertile, managed to produce and export large quantities of soap and grain, and thus to flourish.[7] Other towns, such as Jerusalem and Nazareth, benefited economically

[1] See Farley, *Syria*, pp. 27–28; Finn, i. 276; *Ha-Karmel*, i, No. 3 (1860), p. 19; Jessup, i. 265; Murray, ii. 403; Thomson, p. 37; Urquhart, ii. 190–2; Walpole, i. 50–51; Wortabet, i. 42–43; on the growth of Beirut under the Egyptian régime, see Polk, pp. 162 ff. On its growth after 1861 see Baedeker, pp. 438–41.

[2] Compare F.O. 78/1398, 'Report on Damascus', encl. in Brant to Malmesbury, No. 41, Damascus, 12 Aug. 1853; Wortabet, i. 199–200.

[3] Finn, i. 352; for more details on the development of Haifa, see F.O. 78/963, Finn to Malmesbury, separate, Jerusalem, 1 Jan. 1853; Neale, i. 155–6; M. E. Rogers, *Domestic Life in Palestine* (London, 1863), p. 85; see also Baedeker, p. 349.

[4] Neale, i. 278, 296; Walpole, i. 45–46, iii. 364.

[5] F.O. 78/803, Kayat to Palmerston, No. 6, Jaffa, 7 Mar. 1849; F.O. 78/1459, Kayat to Russell, No. 19, Jaffa, 31 Dec. 1859; Baedeker, p. 128; Finn, i. 173; Thomson, pp. 515–16; Wortabet, ii. 155.

[6] F.O. 78/962, Finn to Clarendon, No. 10, Jerusalem, 19 July 1853; F.O. 78/1218, same to same, No. 51, Jerusalem, 31 Dec. 1856; Murray, ii. 582–3; Neale, i. 189; Robinson, p. 91; Thomson, p. 109.

[7] See, for example, F.O. 78/705, Kayat to Palmerston, No. 9, Dec. 1847; compare Tibawi, p. 180.

from the foreign and missionary activities which were increasing during the Tanzimat period.[1]

More significant, however, was the impact of the foreign trade on the social structure of the traditional big Syrian cities of Damascus and Aleppo. For one thing, most of the flourishing foreign trade was concentrated in the hands of non-Muslim minorities who enjoyed the protection of both European consuls and Ottoman commercial legislation, and conducted their transactions directly with Europe, mainly through Beirut.[2] While these Christian and Jewish merchants were prospering, Muslim traders were far from enjoying the new trade boom and some of them were probably also affected by the decreasing internal trade. Secondly and more acute was the blow which foreign manufacturing goods inflicted on local industry, as we have already seen. A considerable number of native craftsmen and manufacturers, being unable to find a market for their traditional products, were consequently impoverished.[3] The decline of local industry and commerce was also accompanied by the disintegration of their professional and social organizations—the guilds—a process that was encouraged by the Ottoman authorities who endeavoured to deprive the guilds of the certain authority they possessed over their members.[4] All this had deep repercussions on Syrian Muslim urban society, whose backbone had for a long time been the middle class of artisans and traders.

A further blow to this middle class, as well as to the lower classes of the urban population, came from the new Ottoman taxation system. It is true that the taxes levied in the towns were generally lighter than those imposed on the peasants, and except for occasional exactions, such as the *salyane* and compulsory loans, no excessive taxes were demanded.[5] However, the

[1] See Finn, i. 174; Robinson, p. 161; Tibawi, p. 180; Tristram, *Israel*, p. 117.

[2] See F.O. 78/1388, 'Report on the Trade of Damascus', encl. in Brant to Malmesbury, Damascus, 12 Aug. 1858; Neale, ii. 110–11; Robinson, p. 457; Tristram, op. cit.

[3] See F.O. 195/207, Werry to Canning, No. 2, Aleppo, 14 Feb. 1846; F.O. 78/661A, Moore to Bidwell, No. 4, Beirut, 2 Feb. 1846; F.O. 78/1028, Wood to Clarendon, No. 16, Damascus, 15 Mar. 1854; Bazili, ii. 7.

[4] See Taoutel, ii. 50. Compare Mardin, p. 167; on the position of the guilds see, Elia Qoudsi, 'notice sur Les Corporations de Damas', *Actes du sixième congrès International des Orientalistes*, II (Leiden, 1885).

[5] See F.O. 78/801, Wood to Palmerston, No. 29, Damascus, 29 Dec. 1849; F.O. 78/1452, Skene to Bulwer, No. 11, encl. in Skene to Malmesbury, No. 20, Aleppo, 31 Mar. 1859.

taxes which the authorities did demand were not levied progressively on the population: whereas the rich managed to evade the payment of their full portion, by means of their local influence and membership in the *meclis*, the major burden fell upon the lower and middle classes,[1] as well as on the non-Muslim communities (although the latter, unlike the Muslims, frequently enjoyed foreign protection against such exactions).[2]

This practice can be illustrated by the way in which the chief urban tax—the *ferde* (personal tax)—was levied. On their return to Syria, the Ottomans considered first the possibility of abolishing this tax, which, under the Egyptian régime, had constituted one of the major causes for popular uprisings against Ibrāhīm.[3] Instead, they intended to impose a property tax at the rate of ten per cent.[4] Eventually, however, the *ferde* was revived in a considerably reduced form; the total levy on each city was only a half or two-thirds of that demanded by the Egyptians.[5] The city of Damascus enjoyed even further concessions, by which its inhabitants were exempted from the *ferde* until 1843, and afterwards were required to pay only one-third of the Egyptian rate. But the authorities in Damascus as well as in other towns agreed to an unjust distribution of the tax by which the Muslim majority had to pay a relatively smaller portion than the non-Muslim minorities.[6] Yet the distribution of the *ferde* within the Muslim community itself was by no means equitable; whereas the rich paid a comparatively small share, the lower and middle classes had to bear the main load. Consequently outbreaks of popular violence occurred in Syrian cities in reaction to the *ferde*, and in Aleppo this levy constituted, as we know, one of the main causes of the 1850 revolt.[7]

[1] See F.O. 78/447, Wood to Aberdeen, No. 33, Damascus, 20 Nov. 1841; F.O. 78/1118, White to Barker, Antioch, 15 Mar., encl. in Barker to Clarendon, No. 9, Aleppo, 3 Apr. 1855; F.O. 78/1450, Brant to Bulwer, No. 23, encl. in Brant to Malmesbury, No. 12, Damascus, 30 June 1859; Wortabet, i. 348; Taoutel, ii. 50. See also above, p. 98.

[2] See below, pp. 217 ff. Compare MacFarlane, ii. 93; Mardin, pp. 18; Oliphant, p. 128.

[3] See, above pp. 16 ff.

[4] *Accounts and Papers*, LX (1843), pt. i, No. 7, from Wood, Therapia, 22 May 1841.

[5] Ibid., pt. ii, No. 5, Rose to Palmerston, Beirut, 22 May 1841; A.E. Alep, i, from Guys, No. 68, 16 Oct. 1841; Taoutel, iii. 41, 73.

[6] A.E. Damas, i, from Devoizy, No. 12, 7 Feb. 1844; F.O. 78/714, Timoni to Palmerston, No. 21, Damascus, 8 Sept. 1847.

[7] A.E. op. cit.; F.O. 78/448, Moore to Aberdeen, No. 2, Aleppo, 25 Nov. 1841;

The Muslim urban masses demanded from the Turkish authorities the removal of these inequalities by converting the *ferde* from a personal tax to a property tax, a practice which was compatible with the Tanzimat concepts and common in other Ottoman provinces. But the rich notables who dominated the local councils and helped the government to levy and collect the tax, objected to this reform and were indeed able to block it for many years.[1] Only in 1852 and 1853, despite the *âyan*'s opposition, did the *ferde* become, by the *Porte*'s orders, a property tax and changed accordingly its name to *vergi* (tax on immovables).[2] Even then the rich councillors who were still in charge of assessing the tax rates and enjoyed the authorities' support, managed to evade a full payment of their taxes, while throwing the major burden on the lower and middle classes as well as on the non-Muslim communities.[3]

The unequal distribution of taxes constituted in fact one feature of the new framework of Syrian urban life during the period 1840–61; it was characterized, as already analysed, by an illicit co-operation between the local Turkish authorities and the rich *âyan* to control and oppress the people, and helped to encourage social and economic distinction in Muslim society.[4] Thus, while the lower and middle classes were affected and impoverished by this injurious régime as well as by the foreign economic penetration, the higher classes of landowners and big proprietors were growing in power and wealth. They not only dominated the *meclis* and other branches of the administration, but also used these positions to enrich themselves at the expense of the masses whom

F.O. 195/207, Barker to Werry, Suedia, 15 Jan., encl. in Werry to Canning, No. 3, Aleppo, 11 Feb. 1843; A.E. Alep, i, from Guys, No. 68, 16 Oct. 1841; A.E. Damas, i, from Beaudin, No. 7, 8 Dec. 1843; al-Bāshā, p. 245; al-Jundī, p. 284; Taoutel, iii. 41. See also above, pp. 103 ff.

[1] F.O. 195/207, Werry to Canning, No. 2, Aleppo, 14 Feb. 1846; F.O. 78/714, Timoni to Palmerston, No. 21, Damascus, 8 Sept. 1847; A.E. Alep, ii, from Geofroy, No. 5, 7 May 1853; Taoutel, iii. 109, 159, 161.

[2] *Irade D.*, No. 15556, 7 Ş 1268; *Irade M.V.*, No. 12122/4, 4 ZA 1269; F.O. 78/910, Wood to Canning, No. 14, encl. in Wood to Malmesbury, No. 13, Damascus, 27 Apr. 1852.

[3] F.O. 78/1538, Skene to Bulwer, No. 40, encl. in Skene to Russell, No. 76, Aleppo, 15 Dec. 1860. Compare also, F.O. 78/872, Wood to Palmerston, No. 9, Damascus, 19 Mar. 1851.

[4] See above, pp. 98–99 ff. See also, F.O. 78/499, Wood to Aberdeen, No. 74, Damascus, 6 Oct. 1842; F.O. 78/1118, summary of some remarks from Consul Wood to *serasker* Arif Paşa, encl. in Wood to Clarendon, No. 11, Damascus, 12 Feb. 1855; one remark indicates that 'the Governors conspire with the notables against the people'.

they were supposed to represent. They would, for example, farm large *iltizams* in the surrounding rural districts; and with the silent approval of the local authorities, who were usually bribed, the *âyan* would squeeze and oppress the peasants. Similarly, the alliance of councillors and Pashas would occasionally impose a monopoly on wheat and arbitrarily raise its sale prices so that the great landowners who produced wheat could make a great profit, and other councillors who had managed to accumulate large quantities of grain at negligible prices, would be able to speculate with it.[1] The high prices of bread as well as the shortage (sometimes artificial) of wheat occasionally caused great distress and hunger and even provoked bread riots among the urban masses.[2] Other deeds of oppression by the *âyan* would likewise from time to time produce outbursts of popular resentment and violence among the lower classes in the cities.[3] This phenomenon, although not completely new in Syrian life—it had sporadically happened in the pre-reform period—indicates nevertheless the growing social gap in this society, a tendency which was enforced during the Tanzimat era.

[1] F.O. 195/207, Werry to Canning, No. 10, Aleppo, 11 July 1846; F.O. 78/1120, Finn to Redcliffe, No. 45, encl. in Finn to Clarendon, No. 49, Jerusalem, 19 Dec. 1855; Finn, i. 438, 447–8; Taoutel, iii. 99–101.

[2] A.E. Alep, i, from Guys, No. 68, 16 Oct. 1841; F.O. 195/207, op. cit.; F.O. 78/1028, Wood to Clarendon, No. 18, Damascus, 3 Apr. 1854; Finn, op. cit.; *Rambles*, pp. 47–48, 173–4; Taoutel, op. cit.

[3] See above, n.1.

PART V

The State of the Christians and Jews and the Muslims' attitude towards them

'The Muslims and the other communities who are among the subjects of our Sublime Sultanate shall be the objects of our imperial favours without exception.'

(From the Gülhane edict of 1839)

THE most outstanding and remarkable reform of the Tanzimat was, without question, the fundamental change it tried to effect in the status of the non-Muslim population within the Ottoman Empire. Never before had any attempt been made by an Islamic state officially to treat its Muslim, Christian, and Jewish subjects as equals.

Until the Gülhane edict of 1839, Christians and Jews alike, although enjoying a certain degree of autonomy within their *millets* and allowed to practice their religions, had been regarded as second-class citizens and as such were subjected to various discriminatory laws and practices. Firstly, they had to pay special poll-tax (*cizye* or *harac*) for the protection (*zimmet*) granted to them by the Muslim ruler. Secondly, the administration of justice was weighted heavily against the *zimmis*; for example, their evidence was not accepted in a court of law against a Muslim, and in a case of murder of a non-Muslim by a Muslim, the latter was usually not condemned to death. In addition, Christians and Jews were not eligible for appointments to the highest administrative posts; they were forbidden to carry arms (i.e. they could not serve in the army), to ride horses in towns, and to wear Muslims' dress. Even in purely ecclesiastical matters the *zimmis*, or *reaya*, were unequally treated; they were not permitted to build places of worship, to hang or ring church bells, or to carry crosses in public.[1]

This was basically the position of both Christians and Jews in pre-reform Syria and Palestine. And although in some places and

[1] Davison, *Turkish Attitudes*, p. 845; Gibb and Bowen, ii. 208. For the original use of the terms *harac* and *reaya*, see ibid. ii, 10 n.; i. 48 n., 158.

under certain rulers the Syrian *reaya* were tolerated and esteemed, some of their members even being employed in senior administrative posts,[1] they were generally exposed to insults by, and oppression and violence from, both the local authorities and the Muslim population. Many governors would, for example, demand excessive taxes from the non-Muslims or impose on them various illegal tributes and dues. Similarly, Muslims would often assault and humiliate Christians and Jews, force them to sweep the streets or carry burdens, or would even dishonour their dead.[2]

It is true that the first reforming Sultans, notably Mahmud II, tried, albeit in vain, to prevent the maltreatment of the non-Muslims in Syria and Palestine as well as in other Ottoman provinces.[3] But no attempt was made to change their inferior legal status and make them equal to the Muslims.

The first ruler who, as already mentioned, de facto placed the non-Muslims of Syria and Palestine on the same footing as their Muslim countrymen, was the Egyptian Ibrāhīm Paşa. Under his rule Christians and, to a lesser extent, Jews, enjoyed full equality with Muslims. They were appointed to the local *meclis*es, accepted by the civil service in greater numbers, and some of them, notably Christians, occupied high positions in the new Syrian administration. The non-Muslims were also allowed to build and repair their places of worship almost without limit and were permitted to ride horses in towns and wear the same dress as Muslims. But, and it was an important proviso, this equality enjoyed by the Syrian *reaya*, was dictated and imposed from above, markedly in opposition to the wishes of the Muslim majority, and only Ibrāhīm's iron hand could prevent this majority from violating the minorities' rights.[4]

The reforms of the Tanzimat, which were first proclaimed in the Syrian provinces on the Ottoman restoration there, formally provided the *reaya* with essentially the same status and privileges they had actually enjoyed under the Egyptian régime.[5] But the

[1] Al-'Awra, pp. 50, 159–66, 227; Burckhardt, pp. 14, 180, 292, 329, 332, 381, 652; Bodman, pp. 45, 98; Shamir, *The 'Aẓm*, p. 244.

[2] See above, p. 10.

[3] See, for example, firman of Z 1246 (May–June 1831) ordering the protection of Jewish pilgrims to Jerusalem against excessive taxes; L. A. Mayer, 'Le-qorot ha-Yehudim be-Eretz-Israel', *Zion*, i, No. 4, pp. 5–7. See also firman of N 1223 (1808) in al-'Awra, pp. 95–96. See also, Bazili, i. 171; Temperley, pp. 40–41.

[4] See above, pp. 17–18.

[5] But cf. above, p. 20.

attempt by the Turkish government to re-establish these privileges was now met with a more effective Muslim opposition, which produced considerable prejudice.

Syrian Muslim opposition to the *reaya*'s new status was evident in all aspects of life, its main expression being again the use of violence: Christians and Jews were, as in the pre-reform period, occasionally subjected to insult and threat, robbery and attack, and sometimes even to murder by their Muslim countrymen.[1] But in addition to these acts of oppression, Muslim aggression against the Christians found a new and horrible form of violence. For the first time there were a number of anti-Christian riots or massacres, the principal of which occurred in 1850 in Aleppo, in 1856 in Nablus, and finally, and most seriously, in Damascus in 1860. In these events a great number of Christians were massacred, but Jews were untouched.[2]

In trying to examine the state of the non-Muslims in the various aspects of life and to analyse the factors behind the Muslims' divergent attitude towards Christians and Jews, we shall see that while the traditional religious attitude towards all *reaya* communities was basically unchanged during the Tanzimat, new rivalries had entered the scene, especially on the Christian front. Social and economic forces, and particularly political considerations, were now also at stake. And the Christians by their proud conduct and open enjoyment of their new privileges in almost every area of life, as well as by their strong links with foreign powers, formed a more provoking target for Muslim aggression than the humble and discreet Jews.

[1] See, for example, A.E. Jérusalem, i, from Lantivy, No. 16, 10 Aug. 1843; A.E. iv, from Botta, No. 51, 18 July 1853; collection of various files from the Germau Consulate in Jerusalem (1838–1939), Report from Gaza, dated 27 July 1855; F.O. 195/207, Werry to Canning, No. 1, Aleppo, 13 Jan. 1844; F.O. 78/1217, Finn to Clarendon, No. 62, Jerusalem, 15 Sept. 1856; Manṣūr, p. 88; Murray, ii. 333; Neale, pp. 278–9; Taoutel, ii. 102; iii. 163.

[2] On these events see below, pp. 226 ff..

XIV

THE RIGHTS OF THE NON-MUSLIMS *VIS-À-VIS* MUSLIM OPPOSITION

A. *Religious rights*

It is evident that the Tanzimat reformers were greatly concerned with the religious freedom of their non-Muslim subjects. The *hat* of 1856 as well as many other firmans which were sent to the Syrian provinces both before and after 1856, insist on full freedom of worship for the *reaya*, going so far as to make interference a punishable offence.[1]

In fact, however, the religious liberty of the non-Muslims, although growing considerably during the period under survey was still far from being complete, chiefly because of the Muslims' vigorous opposition. In certain cases the *reaya* were not allowed by the Muslim population to build or repair places of worship; some churches and synagogues were closed by force or were converted into mosques and others were violated by conservative Muslims and sometimes even by soldiers.[2] Another privilege which was not always preserved was that 'no one shall be compelled to change his religion or faith'.[3] A noticeable number of

[1] See, for example, firman to Tayyar Paşa, governor of Jerusalem and Gaza of Evail CA 1257, in *Accounts and Papers*, LX (1843), pt. i, No. 8, Ponsonby to Palmerston, Therapia, 21 June 1841 (also in Khazin, i. 52–53); firman of Evahir B 1257 in H. Z. Hirshberg, 'Ha-mifneh be-ma'amada shel Yerushalayim' in *Yad Yosef Yizhak Rivlin* (Ramat Gan, 5724), pp. 95–98; firman of Gurre L 1268 in Jaffa *Sijill*, No. 18; firman of June 1853 in Robinson, p. 24; Penal Code, Paras. 132, 133, in Bucknill and Utidjian, p. 101; see also Finn, i. 157; Muḥammad Farīd, *Ta'rīkh al-dawla al-'Uthmāniyya* (Egypt, 1893), pp. 294–5; Taoutel, iii. 128.

[2] F.O. 195/234, Rose to Canning, No. 13, Beirut, 8 Mar. 1844; F.O. 78/801, Wood to Palmerston, No. 27, Damascus, 29 Oct. 1849; F.O. 78/1383, Finn to Clarendon, No. 13, Jerusalem, 20 July 1858; F.O. 78/1538, Skene to Bulwer, No. 4, encl. in Skene to Russell, No. 16, Aleppo, 14 Apr. 1860; A.E. Jérusalem, vi, from de Barrère, No. 12, 3 Aug. 1858; A.E. Damas, v, from Outrey, No. 77, 14 Aug. 1859; *Irade H.*, No. 9507/9, 28 B 1276. Note that more cases of violation of churches occurred during the events of 1850 in Aleppo and those of 1860 in Damascus.

[3] See the *Hatt-ı Hümayun* of 1856; compare firman to the Jewish *Hahambaşı*, in Jerusalem, Evahir B 1257, in Hirshberg, *Rivlin*, pp. 95–98; Manṣūr, p. 90.

Christians and Jews, particularly children, were forced to adopt Islam, and only a small proportion of these returned to their original faith after intervention by the Pasha (usually under a consul's pressure).[1] Similarly, although the Imperial order of March 1844, that apostasy from Islam would not be punished by death, was generally kept in Syria,[2] Muslim converts to Christianity were usually persecuted and forced to leave their homes in order to save their lives.[3]

But while anti-religious activities against Jews did not go beyond these traditional acts of intolerance, Christians were subject to further aggression because of the new privileges they were not tardy to practise in public: in several towns church bells were rung, crosses carried in processions, wine shops opened in market places, and corpses carried by men instead of on animals. Such deeds strongly irritated the Muslims almost everywhere, and in some places they provoked anti-Christian outbreaks.[4] The conspicuous event of this kind was the grave massacre in Aleppo during the 1850 revolt, in which many Christians were killed and their houses and churches sacked and burnt. That these riots were largely caused by Christian demonstration of their religious privileges is apparent from the following evidence; firstly, according to Consul-General Rose: 'The Greek Catholic Patriarch Maximos is accused of having excited the ill will of the Mussulmans by a sort of triumphant entry which he made not long since into Aleppo with much pomp and great display of costly church ornaments.'[5]

[1] F.O. 195/196, Wood to Canning, No. 42, Damascus, 26 June 1842; F.O. 195/207, Moore to Canning, No. 1, Aleppo, 5 Feb. 1842; compare A.E. Alep, i, from Guys, No. 68, 16 Oct. 1841; A.E. Damas, iii, from de Barrère, No. 24, 27 May 1855.

[2] F.O. 78/1220, Barker to Clarendon, No. 3, Aleppo, 25 Feb. 1856; compare Davison, *Reform*, p. 55; Young, ii. 11. But see also Temperley pp. 225–9.

[3] F.O. 78/622, Wood to Aberdeen, No. 28, Damascus, 3 Sept. 1845; F.O. 78/863, Kayat to Moore, encl. No. 1 in Moore to Palmerston, No. 1, Beirut, 2 Jan. 1850; CM/041 from Klein, 2 Feb. 1852; Manṣūr, pp. 89–90; Velde, i. 133–4; compare Davison, *Attitudes*, p. 860; Doughty, ii. 372–3.

[4] *Irade M.V.*, No. 5184, 19 R 1266; F.O. 78/705, Finn to Palmerston, No. 36, Jerusalem, 3 Dec. 1847; F.O. 78/836, Rose to Canning, No. 48, encl. in Rose to Palmerston, No. 49, Beirut, 5 Nov. 1850; *Aḥwāl al-Naṣārā ba'da al-ḥarb al-qrīm* (MS. No. 66, A.U.B.), pp. 26–27; Finn, ii. 424–5; Taoutel, iii. 133; Walpole, iii. 419–20; Urquhart, ii. 68–69.

[5] F.O. 78/836, Rose to Canning, No. 48, encl. in Rose to Palmerston, No. 49, Beirut, 5 Nov. 1850; see also *Rambles*, p. 241; Wortabet, ii. 81. For details on the riots, see A.E. Alep, ii, from de Lesseps, No. 9, 29 Oct. 1850. See also above, pp. 105–6 ff.

Secondly, some of the conditions made by the Aleppo rebels for laying down their arms speak for themselves: 'Bells must not be rung, neither must the cross be carried in procession.'[1] Thirdly, there is the fact that the Jews of Aleppo were not affected at all during these events.[2]

Indeed, the gravity of the 1850 riots in Aleppo, a city traditionally famous for its tolerance,[3] clearly indicates how intense was Muslim opposition to the Christians' new liberties.

Yet, despite this vigorous opposition, the Syrian non-Muslims did enjoy on the whole, particularly during the 1850s, greater freedom of worship than ever before within the Ottoman Empire, thanks mainly to the government's protection.[4] A considerable number of churches, convents, and synagogues, as well as other religious institutions, were repaired or built by permission from Istanbul.[5] Christian Patriarchs and Jewish Rabbis were held in great esteem and a few were honoured with Imperial medals.[6] Religious education was given to children in an increasing number of missionary schools, bringing about enlightenment and cultural revival especially among the Christian communities.[7]

B. *Social and Economic Conditions*

Better education and competence made the Christians and Jews also more acceptable to public administration; their share in the

[1] See list of conditions in *Irade D.*, No. 13185/14, 26 Z 1266—the document facing p. 105 above. See also a petition by Aleppo notables in *Irade D.*, No. 13268/6, Gurre M 1267.

[2] *Irade D.*, No. 13185, 14 Z 1266; F.O. 195/302, Werry to Rose, No. 43, encl. in Werry to Canning, No. 8, Aleppo, 26 Oct. 1850.

[3] Cf. Gibb and Bowen, i. 309–10. On the change of atmosphere in Aleppo towards intolerance, see F.O. 78/500, Moore to Aberdeen, No. 5, Aleppo, 27 Jan. 1842; Paton, pp. 260–1; *Rambles*, p. 43; Taoutel, iii. 31, 45.

[4] See F.O. 78/1217, Finn to Clarendon, No. 1, Jerusalem, 7 Jan. 1856; F.O. 78/1538, Skene to Bulwer, No. 29, encl. in Skene to Russell, No. 51, Aleppo, 23 Aug. 1860; A.E. Damas, ii, from Segur, No. 30, Oct. 1851; Finn, i. 222; ii. 449–50; Manṣūr, p. 88; Wortabet, ii. 282–3.

[5] See, for example, *Mühimme*, No. 257, p. 54, firman of Evahir N 1264; No. 258, p. 25, Evahir C 1267; No. 260, p. 219, Evasit Saf. 1276; *Irade H.*, No. 4094, 12 R 1268; No. 6965, 15 M 1273; No. 8822, 12 B 1275; F.O. 78/622, Wood to Aberdeen, No. 24, Damascus, 20 July 1845; F.O. 195/302, Werry to Canning, No. 4, Aleppo, 8 Sept. 1849; al-Dibs, viii. 786–7; Finn, ii. 462; Manṣūr, pp. 87, 90, 95; Paton, p. 25; Schwartz, *Tevu'ot*, p. 491; Taoutel, ii. 79, 86; iii. 129–34.

[6] See, *Irade H.*, No. 659, 3 N 1257; No. 9957, 5 CA 1277; *Ceride-i Havadis*, 26 C 1277.

[7] See, for example, *Aḥwāl*, MS., pp. 27–28; *Ḥasr al-lithām*, p. 223; see also Hourani, *Fertile Crescent*, p. 50.

Ottoman civil service was indeed considerable, although admittedly not in all departments were they fairly represented[1] and from time to time they were still arbitrarily dismissed from their offices.[2] Many Syrian Christians served, for example, as clerks and scribes in various government departments, in the *meclis*es, and as private secretaries to Turkish Pashas.[3] Some of them managed to reach comparatively high positions, particularly after 1856 at the time when the first Christian public officials in Syria were granted the titles of *Bey* and *Efendi*.[4] In a number of towns Christians and Jews managed to control, as in the past, the local financial administration, namely, the offices of accountants, customs officers, and the like.[5] And although the great Jewish and Christian Bankers (*sarraf*) had been deprived, under the new administration, of their old *berat*s (patents or warrants) as heads of the provincial treasury, other members of their communities continued to occupy senior offices in this department, particularly in Damascus and Aleppo.[6] In Damascus, for example, the government financial administration was apparently based almost entirely on Christian officials, who became thus indispensable: 'The persons who managed the affairs of the Pashalik were Christians, they kept the public accounts and grew richer in the

[1] F.O. 78/1521, Finn to Bulwer, encl. No. 1 in Finn to Russell, No. 21, Jerusalem, 19 July 1860; Wortabet, i. 34–35; compare al-Ḥuṣrī, p. 92; Karal, v. 260; Mardin, p. 15.

[2] F.O. 78/456, Major Wilbraham's Report, encl. No. 2 in Rose to Palmerston, No. 71, Beirut, 23 July 1841; F.O. 78/622, Wood to Aberdeen, No. 38, Damascus, 10 Nov. 1845; F.O. 195/219, Calvert to Canning, No. 10, Damascus, 2 May 1850; compare *al-Jinān*, ii (1872), pp. 27, 38.

[3] See, for example, *Irade D.*, No. 5, ZA 1263; *Irade M.V.*, No. 18868/5, 21 C 1276; Jaffa *Sijill*, No. 13, 27 N 1256; F.O. 78/837, Wood to Palmerston, No. 3, Damascus, 6 Mar. 1850; F.O. 78/1217, Finn to Clarendon, No. 38, Jerusalem, 26 May 1856; Nawfal, *Ṭarāblus*, pp. 53, 63–65, 88, 91–92; Velde, i. 362; Taoutel, iii. 130–1; al-Shidyāq, i. 226; compare Karal, v. 260.

[4] *Irade D.*, No. 27934, 20 CA 1275; F.O. 78/1219, Moore to Clarendon, No. 25, Beirut, 2 June 1856; F.O. 78/1217, Finn to Clarendon, No. 38, Jerusalem, 26 May 1856; al-Ba'albakī, p. 106; al-Dibs, viii. 741–2; Nawfal, op. cit., pp. 65–66; on the titles *Efendi* and *Bey*, see Sertoğlu, pp. 39, 87.

[5] See *Irade D.*, No. 10667, 16 R 1265; *Irade M.V.*, No. 7013, 13 Ş 1267; *Cevdet D.*, No. 15561, 11 CA 1265; Jaffa *Sijill*, No. 13, 27 L 1256 and 27 N 1256; A.E. Damas, i, from Munton, No. 1, 3 Feb. 1842; al-Ba'albakī, p. 105; Paton, p. 39; Walpole, iii. 174.

[6] *Cevdet D.*, Maliye No. 19213, L 1261; Y. Levton, *Sefer nokhaḥ ha-shulḥan* (Izmir, 5628 (1867/8)), p. 112*b*. Compare F.O. 195/170, Werry to Ponsonby, No. 1, Damascus, 14 Jan. 1841; Nawfal, op. cit., p. 62; Taoutel, iii. 33. On the term *berat*, see Sertoğlu, p. 42.

employment'; and when, during the critical days of June 1860, they failed to attend to their duties, government offices became idle.[1]

Another economic field which was dominated by Christians and Jews was the country's major commerce; as already pointed out, they controlled the growing foreign trade of Syria and thus were more flourishing than ever.[2]

Hence it emerges that the Syrian *reaya* not only managed remarkably to improve their economic and social conditions under the Tanzimat,[3] but in many respects became more advanced than, or gained advantage over, their Muslim countrymen, who for their part felt themselves affected or deprived of their due. 'The Christian traders were more prosperous than the Mussulmans';[4] Christian tax-collectors and customs officials levied from Muslims taxes and duties which sometimes were above the official rate;[5] Jewish and Christian moneylenders would lend money to Muslims at an exorbitant interest.[6] Even Muslim notables in some places found themselves in debt since they could no longer extort money from rich Christians and Jews as they had done in the past.[7]

Muslim reaction to this state of affairs varied; in certain circles it was one of retaliation. According to Consul Finn, 'Difficulties are put in the way of Christians exercising some trades which have been of old time in the hands of the Moslems'.[8] In Damascus,

[1] See F.O. 78/1520, Brant to Bulwer, No. 40, encl. in Brant to Russell, No. 17, Damascus, 6 Sept. 1860; Mishāqa, MS., p. 350.

[2] See above, p. 182. Cf. *Birjīs Barīs*, No. 36; Temperley, pp. 240–1.

[3] Compare F.O. 78/1454, Finn to Palmerston, No. 1, Jerusalem, 1 Jan. 1859; F.O. 78/1538, Skene to Bulwer, No. 27, encl. in Skene to Russell, No. 47, Aleppo, 4 Aug. 1860; CM/041, from Klein, 2 Feb. 1852; Finn, i. 202.

[4] F.O. 78/1520, Brant to Bulwer, No. 40, encl. in Brant to Russell, No. 17, Damascus, 6 Sept. 1860; see also F.O. 78/1452, Skene to Bulwer, separate, encl. in Skene to Malmesbury, No. 42, Aleppo, 30 June 1859; F.O. 78/1383, Finn to Clarendon, No. 1, Jerusalem, 1 Jan. 1858; *Aḥwāl*, MS., pp. 27–28; Edwards, pp. 82–83; *Ḥasr al-lithām*, p. 223; Jessup, i. 165; compare Farley, *Turkey*, pp. 36–37; MacFarlane, ii. 258–9.

[5] See Finn, i. 286; F.O. 78/958, Calvert to Clarendon, No. 12, Beirut, 29 June 1853; compare *Irade D.*, No. 10349, 3 Saf. 1265.

[6] F.O. 195/207, Werry to Canning, No. 16, Aleppo, 9 Sept. 1843; Segur, pp. 14–15.

[7] See F.O. 78/1452, Skene to Bulwer, separate, encl. in Skene to Malmesbury, No. 42, Aleppo, 30 June 1859; *Rambles*, p. 241. But in a number of places, notably the Jerusalem area, local notables and chiefs continued to extort money from Jewish communities and Christian convents; see F.O. 195/369, Finn to Redcliffe, No. 26, Jerusalem, 11 Aug. 1853.

[8] F.O. 78/1521, Finn to Bulwer, encl. No. 1 in Finn to Russell, No. 21, Jerusalem, 19 July 1860.

for example, the Muslim weavers, who were apparently affected by the import of European-manufactured goods, tried to undercut the livelihood of their Christian colleagues: under their pressure the local *meclis* issued an order in 1842 forbidding the Christian craftsmen from producing a certain kind of silk material.[1] As for the reaction of the general Muslim public, here again elements of demonstration were not missing from the Christians' conduct, and accordingly they produced strong ill-feeling among the Muslims. Thus Christians riding horses in certain towns or wearing Muslim dress were occasionally assaulted;[2] 'The splendid houses built by the rich class of Christians excited jealousy and their general prosperity tended to create in the Mussulmans feelings of envy',[3] as well as 'vicious passions' to loot and sack, all of which was actually expressed when the opportunity occurred as in Aleppo in 1850 and in Damascus in 1860.[4]

But with the exception of these cases, the Syrian Christian and Jewish subjects did enjoy now, on the whole, greater security of life and property as well as economic prosperity, than during the pre-reform era,[5] and this again chiefly owing to government protection and foreign support.

C. *Political inequality*

Yet, in one major aspect of life, in the area of political rights, the Syrian *reaya* did not reach the same advanced position as in the religious and social-economic spheres.

Christians and Jews continued, during the early Tanzimat period, to be unequal before the law of the state and its institutions. For one thing, they had still to pay the discriminatory poll-tax (*cizye*), although the method of its collection was not as harsh as in the past;

[1] F.O. 78/499, Wood to Canning, No. 45, Damascus, 12 July 1842.

[2] F.O. 78/449, Moore to Palmerston, No. 25, Beirut, 4 May 1841; F.O. 78/801, Wood to Palmerston, No. 7, Damascus, 13 Mar. 1849; A.E. Alep, iii, from Geofroy, No. 2, 23 Aug. 1860; al-Bāshā, pp. 234 ff.; Bazili, ii. 4; Farley, *The Massacres*, p. 75; *Ḥasr al-lithām*, p. 71; Khazin, i. 78; Jessup, i. 28; Porter, *Damascus*, i. 143; Taoutel, iii. 26, 31. But see F.O. 78/1217, Finn to Clarendon, No. 1, Jerusalem, 7 Jan. 1856; Walpole, i. 98–99; Wortabet, i. 178.

[3] See F.O. 78/1520, Brant to Bulwer, No. 40, encl. in Brant to Russell, No. 17, Damascus, 6 Sept. 1860.

[4] F.O. 78/836, Rose to Canning, No. 48, encl. in Rose to Palmerston, No. 49, Beirut, 5 Nov. 1850; see also *Aḥwāl*, MS., p. 28; Finn, i. 218.

[5] Cf. Finn, i. 195–6 n., 202; CM/041, from Klein, 2 Feb. 1852; *Ḥasr al-lithām*, p. 50; Paton, p. 260; see also F.O. 78/1538, Skene to Bulwer, No. 27, encl. in Skene to Russell, No. 47, Aleppo, 4 Aug. 1860.

it was now collected by the heads of the communities, rather than by the oppressive tax-collectors.[1] It is true that on 7 May 1855 the *cizye* was finally abolished, together with another discriminatory measure against the *reaya*, the prohibition to carry arms. But in fact the non-Muslims were not conscripted even then, but were required to pay instead an exemption tax called *bedel*. This tax was levied in the same way as the abolished poll-tax, and was, of course, regarded as such by the *reaya* of the Empire including those in the Syrian provinces.[2] The Muslims admittedly were also allowed now to buy exemption from military service, but for a much higher sum than the *bedel* paid by the *reaya*; and unlike the Muslims, the non-Muslims did not have any choice but to pay the tax. In this sense inequality between the two groups was further maintained.

Another old restriction on the legal rights of the Christians and Jews, which was revived during the Tanzimat, was that they were forbidden to own Muslim (men and women) slaves.[3] In addition the *reaya* in certain parts of Syria were not allowed to own certain kinds of land while in other parts they would face great difficulties when trying to buy it.[4] Moreover, and very significantly, government orders were periodically received in some places forbidding Muslims to sell land and immovables to non-Muslims.[5] Also contrary to the Tanzimat instructions was the interference of the Muslim *mahkeme* in cases of inheritance by Christian minors;[6]

[1] *Takvim-i Vekayi*, p. 238, 3 M 1258; Lûtfi, *Tarih*, vi. 69; Engelhardt, i. 40, 51; F.O. 78/872, Wood to Palmerston, No. 11, Damascus, 29 Mar. 1851; Taoutel, iii. 49, 89, 160.

[2] F.O. 78/1220, Barker to Redcliffe, No. 28, encl. in Barker to Clarendon, No. 13, Aleppo, 30 July 1856; F.O. 78/1218, Finn to Clarendon, No. 32, Jerusalem, 7 Nov. 1856; A.E. Damas, iv, from Outrey, No. 14, 16 Aug. 1856; Finn, i. 172–3; Manṣūr, p. 287; *Rambles*, pp. 58–59. Compare Lewis, *Emergence*, p. 114; Young, v. 275–6. On the *bedel*, see also *Badal* in EI²; *Bedel-i Askeri*, in IA.

[3] F.O. 195/207, Werry to Canning, No. 17, Aleppo, 23 Sept. 1843; Taoutel, ii. 102; iii. 64; see also Young, ii. 171–5.

[4] F.O. 78/1521, Finn to Bulwer, encl. No. 1 in Finn to Russell, No. 21, Jerusalem, 19 July 1860; F.O. 78/1538, Skene to Bulwer, No. 27, encl. in Skene to Russell, No. 47, Aleppo, 4 Aug. 1860; *Rambles*, p. 42.

[5] '*Manʿ al-muslim min bayʿī arāḍihi wa-sāʾir amlākihi ilā al-dhimmiyyīn al-raʿāyā*', Jaffa *Sijill*, No. 18, orders of Evail Saf. and 14 Saf. 1268; see also A.E. Alep, i, from Guys, No. 34, 28 Sept. 1845; letter from the Greek Catholic community in Aleppo to Canning, dated 12 Azar 1846, encl. in F.O. 195/207; Paton, p. 32.

[6] F.O. 78/1220, Wood to Redcliffe, No. 2, encl. in Wood to Clarendon, No. 3, Damascus, 18 Jan. 1856; F.O. 78/1219, Moore to Redcliffe, No. 40,

this interference which, incidentally, was not applied to Jews, became apparently so troublesome that in 1861 the *Porte* issued a special decree prohibiting the Muslim court from taking any part in such cases.[1]

Rather more harmful to the legal rights of the *reaya* was the *mahkeme*'s practice of rejecting in all circumstances evidence by a Christian or a Jew against a Muslim.[2] Furthermore, up to the early 1850s, non-Muslims' testimony was utterly discounted also in the *meclis*[3] which would sometimes refer a case to the *mahkeme* where non-Muslims' evidence was essentially invalid.

It is true that in 1847 validity was granted to non-Muslims' testimony in the newly established Ottoman mixed courts.[4] But these courts for criminal and commercial cases were not established in Syria for some years: at Beirut in 1851 and at Damascus and Aleppo in 1854.[5] The new tribunals would then usually accept *reaya*'s evidence against Muslims and thereby do justice to many non-Muslims.[6] Nevertheless there were still instances in which the criminal and commercial courts would reject such evidence; in one case, for example, 'the court endeavoured to persuade the (Muslim) offender to plead guilty and to submit to a slight punishment, rather than to establish a precedent opposed . . . to their faith'. When the Muslim refused, the court denounced him but would not accept any evidence.[7] Sometimes these courts

encl. in Moore to Clarendon, No. 35, Beirut, 14 July 1856; A.E. Alep, iii, No. 23, 14 Sept. 1861.

[1] See Law of 7 Saf. 1278, in Düstur, i. 298–300. As for the Jews, see firman to the Jewish *Hahambaşı* in Jerusalem, of Evahir B 1257, in Hirshberg, *Rivlin*, pp. 95 ff.; compare Young, i. 321.

[2] F.O. 78/622, Wood to Canning, No. 13, encl. in Wood to Aberdeen, No. 21, Damascus, 24 June 1854; F.O. 78/1116, Moore to Redcliffe, No. 12, encl. in Moore to Clarendon, No. 20, Beirut, 8 Mar. 1855; F.O. 78/1521, Finn to Bulwer, encl. No. 1 in Finn to Russell, No. 21, Jerusalem, 19 July 1860; Finn, i. 177; Urquhart, p. 259.

[3] *Accounts and Papers*, LX (1843) pt. i, No. 7, Wood to Rifat, encl. in Ponsonby to Palmerston, Therapia, 27 May 1841; F.O. 195/320, Rose to Cowley, No. 2, Beirut, 19 Jan. 1848. Compare MacFarlane, i. 184, 334, 337.

[4] Engelhardt, i. 83–84; Ubicini, i. 175.

[5] See above, p. 155. On the firman making the non-Muslims' evidence in these courts valid, see F.O. 195/369, Finn to Rose, No. 4, Jerusalem, 3 Feb. 1853; F.O. 195/458, Wood to Canning, No. 20, Damascus, 14 June 1854.

[6] F.O. 78/871, Rose to Canning, No. 5, encl. in Rose to Palmerston, No. 6, Beirut, 4 Feb. 1851; A.E. Damas, iii, from de Barrère, No. 18, 15 Dec. 1854; F.O. 78/1630, Memo. by Vice-Consul White encl. in Dufferin to Russell, No. 113, Beirut, 10 May 1861.

[7] F.O. 78/1029, Wood to Clarendon, No. 50, Damascus, 6 Sept. 1854; see

were induced to decline, by the provincial *meclis* to whom they were subordinated, non-Muslims' evidence.[1] The *meclis* itself, while acting as a judicial body, continued during the 1850s, as in the 1840s, only occasionally to receive *reaya*'s testimony against Muslims, normally under pressure exerted on it by a foreign consul through the Pasha.[2] In many cases the council would reject such evidence, particularly when it was presided over by the kadi.[3] Instead, the *meclis* would frequently 'rather condemn at once a Mussulman in favour of a Christian without recording testimony than accept non-Muslim evidence'.[4]

Thus, although Christians and Jews in certain parts of Syria, notably the province of Beirut, began gradually, in the course of the 1850s, to enjoy greater equality and justice in the judicial administration,[5] this was by no means complete, nor were the new legal privileges applied everywhere in the country. Consul Skene, for example, reports from Aleppo in 1859 that: 'The evidence of Christians is not yet received by any court notwithstanding all that has been said, written and proclaimed on the subject.'[6]

The non-Muslims of Syria and Palestine were subject to unequal treatment not only in the administration of justice, but also in other government institutions. The provincial *meclis*, apart from cases of misjudgement would, in effect, occasionally discriminate against Christians and Jews in matters of taxation, in economic affairs, and sometimes even in religious matters.[7]

also F.O. 78/1388, Brant to Bulwer, encl. No. 2 in Brant to Malmesbury, No. 53, Damascus, 14 Dec. 1858.

[1] See, for example, F.O. 78/1388, Brant to Bulwer, encl. No. 1, in Brant to Malmesbury, No. 53, Damascus, 14 Dec. 1858.

[2] See, for example, F.O. 78/1038, Moore to Clarendon, No. 38, Beirut, 28 Aug. 1854.

[3] See F.O. 78/1116, Moore to Redcliffe, No. 1, encl. in Moore to Clarendon, No. 2, Beirut, 2 Jan. 1855; F.O. 78/1519, Moore to Bulwer, No. 69, encl. in Moore to Russell, No. 42, Beirut, 10 Sept. 1860.

[4] F.O. 78/1521, Finn to Bulwer, encl. No. 1 in Finn to Russell, No. 21, Jerusalem, 19 July 1860.

[5] See F.O. 78/1031, Moore to Redcliffe, No. 69, encl. in Moore to Clarendon, No. 61, Beirut, 16 Dec. 1854; *The Times and recent events in Turkey* (London, 1853), p. 258, in Urquhart's Papers, No. 257; compare Jessup, i. 269; Davison, *Reform*, p. 97.

[6] *Rambles*, p. 67; F.O. 78/1452, Skene to Malmesbury, No. 20, Aleppo, 31 Mar. 1859; see also F.O. 78/1220, Werry to Redcliffe, No. 35, encl. in Werry to Clarendon, No. 15, Aleppo, 24 Jan. 1856.

[7] See F.O. 78/499, Wood to Canning, No. 45, Damascus, 12 July 1842; A.E. Damas, i, from Devoizy, No. 7, 5 Dec. 1843; F.O. 78/714, Timoni to Cowley,

The non-Muslim members of the *meclis* were by no means in a position to avoid or check such acts of unequal treatment against members of their communities, since they were themselves mistreated and under-represented in the *meclis*. Indeed, with the exception of the provincial *meclis* of Beirut whose seats were equally shared by Muslims and Christians,[1] all other provincial councils in Syria and Palestine allotted few seats to the *reaya* deputies. The *meclis* of Jerusalem consisted, for instance, of about seven to ten Muslim members as opposed to four to five non-Muslim ones, representing a Jewish and Christian population which greatly outnumbered that of the Muslims.[2] In Aleppo no *reaya* deputy was admitted to the *meclis* during the first years of the 1840s; later on two Christian members were admitted, but not a Jewish one.[3] The *meclis-i eyalet* of Damascus included two Christians and a Jew, as against thirteen to twenty Muslim members; but the former were compelled to withdraw because of molestation within the first years of the 1840s and were not restored before 1850.[4]

Ill-treatment of *reaya* deputies was not restricted to Damascus; it was to be observed in all other areas. The English consuls in the Syrian centres described the position of the non-Muslim members of the *meclis* as follows:

> they 'rarely attend and when they are called, they are seated on the extreme end of the mat but not on the Divan . . .'; 'their Mussulman colleagues made them light their pipes . . .'; 'they take no part in the deliberations and are treated with utter disregard, never venturing to express dissent in any decision even though it be calculated to injure their

No. 26, encl. in Timoni to Palmerston, No. 21, Damascus, 8 Sept. 1847; F.O. 78/910, Wood to Malmesbury, No. 13, Damascus, 27 Apr. 1852; F.O. 78/1538, Skene to Bulwer, No. 40, encl. in Skene to Russell, No. 76, Aleppo, 15 Dec. 1860; see also Finn, ii. 167; Taoutel, iii. 163.

[1] See *Irade M.V.*, No. 5184, 19 R 1266; F.O. 78/499, Moore to Palmerston, No. 43, Beirut, 19 June 1841.

[2] F.O. 78/1521, Finn to Bulwer, encl. in Finn to Russell, No. 21, Jerusalem, 19 July 1860; compare *Irade D.*, No. 21422/7, Z 1271; *Cevdet Z.*, No. 2703, Kanun II. 1277; Finn, i. 178.

[3] F.O. 195/207, Moore to Aberdeen, encl. No. 2 in Moore to Canning, No. 1, Aleppo, 5 Feb. 1842; cf. *Irade M.M.*, No. 219, 25 Ş 1271; *Cevdet D.*, No. 7367, 17 N 1273; *Irade M.V.*, No. 17507/4, 13 Z 1274.

[4] F.O. 78/622, Wood to Canning, encl. No. 1 in Wood to Aberdeen, No. 21, Damascus, 24 June 1845; F.O. 195/219, Calvert to Canning, No. 10, Damascus, 2 May 1850.

> brother Christians . . .'; 'sometimes . . . placing their seals falsely to Mazbattas merely from fear of displeasing the Mussulman members'.[1]

Nevertheless, it is worthy of notice that the mere presence of Christian and Jewish deputies in local councils was a big step forward; moreover, in some places and under certain liberal and firm Pashas, non-Muslim councillors were treated well and were sometimes allowed to take a more active part in the *meclis*'s works.[2] Yet it remains true to say that during the years 1840–61 the status of the non-Muslim deputies in the *meclis*, like the general political position of the communities they represented, in fact continued to be unequal and inferior to their fellow Muslim subjects, and this despite the Tanzimat decrees.

In this context it should, however, be emphasized that it was not really so easy to create within only two decades full political equality between Muslims and non-Muslims, in a state which for centuries had been predominantly Muslim and in which inequality of the *reaya* had been a basic principle. Indeed, to give up this principle of inequality and segregation required of the Ottoman Muslims a much greater effort of renunciation than they were prepared to make.

[1] See respectively: F.O. 195/207, Werry to Canning, No. 23, Aleppo, 16 Dec. 1843; F.O. 78/622, op. cit.; F.O. 78/1538, Skene to Bulwer, No. 27, encl. in Skene to Russell, No. 47, Aleppo, 14 Aug. 1860; F.O. 78/1521, op. cit.

[2] See, for example, Jaffa *Sijill*, No. 18, 3 CA 1267; F.O. 78/872, Wood to Palmerston, No. 12, Damascus, 17 Apr. 1851; F.O. 78/1294, Finn to Clarendon, No. 1, Jerusalem, 1 Jan. 1857, in Hyamson, i. 246; Finn, ii. 359.

XV

MUSLIM–CHRISTIAN ANTAGONISM: THE POLITICAL MOTIVES

If the Ottoman Muslims in general were unwilling to put up with the new equal status granted to the *reaya*, the Syrian Muslims who had experienced a similar situation under the Egyptian rule were even more reluctant to accept the non-Muslims as equals. Hence their reaction to the Gülhane decree soon after it was proclaimed in the country, as Consul-General Rose described in 1841:

> It is a curious fact that only a little more than half a year after the reading and proclamation of the Hatti Sheriff of Gülhane in this country there has been a general reaction in favour of the Koran and of the exclusive privileges of the Mahometans over Christians in diametrical opposition to the doctrine of equality of all before the law which is the essence of the Hatti Sheriff.[1]

This reaction, which represented also the Muslims' protest against the previous pro-Christian Egyptian régime,[2] was expressed by a wave of intense anti-Christian and, to some extent, anti-Jewish violence which swept the country for a while, and was in some places encouraged by the Druze–Maronite hostilities in Lebanon or by the weakness of the Turkish authorities.[3]

In later years and up to 1856 the degree of Muslim opposition varied from place to place. Being largely based on religious beliefs, Muslim political animosity was particularly intense in conserva-

[1] F.O. 78/457, Rose to Aberdeen, No. 110, Beirut, 12 Oct. 1841; see also F.O. 78/449, Wood to Ponsonby, Beirut, 17 Feb. 1841.

[2] In several places, for example, Muslims threatened to destroy churches which had been built or repaired during the Egyptian period; see F.O. 78/447, Wood to Aberdeen, No. 33, Damascus, 20 Nov. 1841; A.E. Alep, i, from Guys, No. 57, 15 Apr. 1841; al-Bāshā, p. 248.

[3] F.O. 78/447, Wood to Aberdeen, No. 33, Damascus, 20 Nov. 1841; F.O. 195/170, Young to Rose, encl. in Young to Ponsonby, No. 12, Jerusalem, 4 June 1841; A.E. Alep, i, from Guys, No. 51, 20 Jan. 1841; al-Bāshā, pp. 234 ff.; Bazili, ii. 4; *Ḥasr al-lithām*, p. 71; Khazin, i. 78; Paton, p. 35; Taoutel, iii. 24–31; compare also *Irade D.*, No. 2117/2, 29 CA 1257.

tive circles; and it was also bitter in areas where Muslims were faced with Christian rivalry or superiority in the economic field. Thus, for example, in a city like Damascus, which was very conservative and whose population was jealous of, if not affected by, the local Christians' prosperity, Muslim animosity was particularly strong and conspicuous.[1] But in towns where religious sensitivity was not great and where the economic circumstances were different, the Muslim attitude was milder. A report of June 1853 points out, for example, that 'thirteen years of peace, commercial emulation and industry had contributed to soften down the intolerance and hatred which the Mussulman of Beyrout were wont to exhibit towards their Christian countrymen and the foreigners'.[2] Even in a conservative town like Jerusalem, we are told 'old prejudices are abating and liberality of sentiment greatly increased . . . inasmuch as the Moslems live by the trade created by pilgrimage and by letting houses to Europeans'.[3]

But at the same time we are reminded that 'the feeling is merely dormant and that a very slight pretext will be sufficient to rouse it into dangerous action.'[4] Such a pretext was sometimes supplied, as already noted, by the Christians themselves who behaved in some places in a provocative manner.

Yet it seems that on the whole Muslim opposition to the *reaya* and to their new official status was still immature and did not reach its peak during the *Hatt-ı Şerif* era. This was firstly because 'the Hatti Shereef of Gulhaneh . . . and the rules known as Tanzimat . . . were only accepted by the bigoted part of the Moslem population as temporary regulations of the Turks in their mistaken system dictated by the exacting Europeans'.[5] Secondly, not only did the Gülhane edict speak in broad and cautious terms on the subject of equality, but in practice, during that period, Christians continued to be in general unequal to the Muslims while not everywhere did they dare to exercise all their new privileges. For

[1] On the strong anti-Christian feelings of the Muslim Damascenes during the period under survey, see, for instance, F.O. 195/194, Rose to Canning, No. 35, Beirut, 27 May 1842; A.E. Damas, ii, No. 24, 14 July 1851; Baedeker, p. 467; Wortabet, i. 179–80.

[2] F.O. 78/958, Calvert to Clarendon, No. 12, Beirut, 29 June 1853.

[3] F.O. 78/1217, Finn to Clarendon, No. 1, Jerusalem, 7 Jan. 1856; see also F.O. 78/962, same to same, No. 8, Beirut, 29 June 1853; Finn, ii. 448. In a few places Muslim–Christian relations were even cordial: al-Jundī, pp. 251–2; Murray, ii. 359; compare also Farley, *The Massacres*, pp. 69–70.

[4] See above n. 2.

[5] Finn, ii. 446–7.

example, the *reaya*, as we know, did not stop paying the poll-tax and their evidence before the courts was still invalid; in a number of places they also continued to wear distinctive clothing and refrained from ringing church bells or from enjoying their other new religious liberties.

A. *The* Hatt-ı Hümayun*: the turning point*

A decisive change in the relations between Muslims and Christians came on the promulgation of the *Hatt-ı Hümayun* of February 1856. Unlike the Gülhane edict, the 1856 decree granted, for the first time and categorically, full equality of status to the 'Christian communities and the other non-Muslim subjects'. Its provisions openly provided the *reaya* with complete freedom of worship, equality in the administration of justice and in taxation; they also officially abolished the two major discriminatory measures which for centuries had indicated the inferior status of the non-Muslims: the poll-tax and the prohibition to carry arms.[1]

It is therefore not surprising that the proclamation of the *Hatt-ı Hümayun* caused a sharp reaction among virtually all Muslims throughout the Empire. According to the Ottoman historian, Cevdet Paşa: 'Many Muslims began to grumble: "Today we have lost our sacred national rights which our ancestors gained with their blood; while the nation used to be the ruling nation it is now bereft of this sacred right. This is a day of tears and mourning for the Muslim brethren." '[2]

In Syria and Palestine Muslim reaction was perhaps even more intense: not only was the *hat* received with great dissatisfaction throughout the country,[3] but, as will be seen later, there was anti-Christian rioting in several places, starting at Nablus in 1856 and reaching its climax in 1860 with the massacre in Damascus. The greater hostility of the Syrian Muslims was primarily due to the wider privileges now enjoyed by the local Christians;[4] it was also

[1] See above, p. 195; see also Cevdet, *Tezakir*, i. 67 ff.; Engelhardt, i. 126, 139 ff.

[2] Cevdet, op. cit. pp. 67–68; English translation taken from Mardin, p. 18; see also Davison, *Reform*, p. 58; id. *Turkish Attitudes*, pp. 858–61.

[3] F.O. 78/1220, Barker to Redcliffe, No. 14, encl. in Barker to Clarendon, No. 8, Aleppo, 10 Mar. 1856; F.O. 78/1217, Finn to Redcliffe, No. 40, encl. in Finn to Clarendon, No. 42, Jerusalem, 23 June 1856; A.E. Damas, iv, from Outrey, No. 5, 25 Mar. 1856; CM/045 from Kruze, Jaffa, 1856; id. annual letter, Jaffa, 12 Feb. 1857; *Aḥwāl*, MS. p. 22; Finn, ii. 443; Taoutel, ii. 90–92.

[4] See above, pp. 191 ff.

a result of the way the Christians reacted after the proclamation of the 1856 *hat*. On the one hand, large sections of the Christian population were greatly dissatisfied with the *Hatt-ı Hümayun* or with its implementation. The clergy opposed the *hat* because it diminished their authority in the *millet*;[1] certain circles resented the idea of sharing equal rights with Jews whom they deeply despised and with whom they were engaged in economic rivalry;[2] and some Christian elements, desiring the downfall of the Empire, feared lest the reform programme should strengthen the declining Ottoman state.[3] And as time went on there were many grievances about the actual results of the *Hatt-ı Hümayun*: 'The Christians complain that they are insulted by language in the streets—that they are not placed in equal rank at public courts with Moslem fellow subjects—are ousted from almost every office of government employment.'[4]

But on the other hand, the Christians lost no time in displaying their liberties in places where previously they had not dared to do so: church bells were hung and rung and feasts celebrated in public,[5] and on a number of occasions they even went so far as to insult and attack Muslims.[6] Above all, it was the question of military service over which the Christians behaved in a conspicuously ambivalent, if not provocative manner. Up to 1856 they were officially exempted from military service (nor in some instances could they conceal their joy and mockery when their

[1] A.E. Damas, iv, from Outrey, No. 5, 25 Mar. 1856; F.O. 78/1217, Finn to Clarendon, No. 22, Jerusalem, 10 Apr. 1856; cf. Engelhardt, i. 141, 147, 150; Karal, vi. 10–11.

[2] Cf. Cevdet, *Tezakir*, i. 68; S. Dubnow, *Divrey yemey ʿam ʿolam* (Tel-Aviv, 1952), p. 648.

[3] Compare Davison, *Turkish Attitudes*, p. 853; see also Oliphant, p. 497.

[4] F.O. 195/524, Finn to Redcliffe, No. 29, Jerusalem, 22 July 1857; see also A.E. Damas, iv, from Outrey, No. 19, 24 Oct. 1856; CM/045 from Kruze, Jaffa, 1856; CM/063d from Sanreczki, Gaza, 19 July 1858; Mishāqa, MS., pp. 343–7; Edwards, p. 168; *Rambles*, pp. 111–12.

[5] See F.O. 195/458, Wood to Redcliffe, No. 34, Damascus, 10 Oct. 1856; A.E. Damas, iv, from Outrey, No. 58, 1 Aug. 1858; F.O. 78/1383, Finn to Clarendon, No. 28, Jerusalem, 12 Oct. 1858; F.O. 78/1520, Brant to Bulwer, No. 40, encl. in Brant to Russell, No. 17, Damascus, 6 Sept. 1860; Finn, ii. 443; compare *Birjīs Barīs*, i, No. 23, 25 Apr. 1860.

[6] See *Irade M.V.*, No. 17595/5, 17 ZA 1274; F.O. 78/1294, Finn to Clarendon, No. 30, Jerusalem, 30 July 1857; F.O. 78/1389, Skene to Alison, No. 20, encl. in Skene to Malmesbury, No. 33, Aleppo, 7 Aug. 1858; Iskandar ibn Yaʿqūb Abkāriūs, *The Lebanon in Turmoil* (New Haven, 1920), pp. 26–27; Muḥammad Abū Saʿūd al-Ḥasībī, *Ḥādithat al-sittīn* (MS. No. (4) 4668, Ẓāhiriyya Library, Damascus).

Muslim neighbours were conscripted).[1] But when it was proclaimed in May 1855 that Christians too were liable to serve in the army, many expressed great dissatisfaction. However, subsequently it turned out that the *reaya* could not be admitted to the army and were instead required to pay an exemption tax—*bedel*; and while in many parts of the Empire this arrangement was generally accepted by the non-Muslim subjects, it was opposed by the Syrian Christians. They regarded the *bedel* as a renewal of the poll-tax which they had already ceased to pay a year or two previously, and alleged that this was at variance with the *Hatt-ı Hümayun* and its conception of equality.[2] In most parts of Syria and Palestine Christians declared their readiness to furnish recruits and refused to pay the *bedel*;[3] only in Aleppo did the Christians, under a threat of arrest, consent to pay the tax,[4] but with the proviso that it should not be levied at that time as there was no conscription among the Muslims.[5] In other places the *bedel* was collected by force,[6] while in Damascus the continuing reluctance of the Christians to pay it constituted, as we shall see later, one of the major causes of the 1860 outbreak.

By contrast, the Syrian Jews who did pay the *bedel* almost without objection[7] were by no means affected during the massacres of 1860 in Damascus. They were similarly untouched both in the course of the Aleppo events in 1850, as already mentioned,[8] and during the anti-Christian riots at Nablus in 1856, which will be described later. Indeed, in this respect the position of the Jews in Syria and Palestine during the period under discussion was far safer than that of their Christian fellow-subjects; and a brief

[1] See petition by Aleppo notables in *Irade D.*, No. 13268/6, Gurre M 1267; see also F.O. 78/836, Rose to Palmerston, No. 47, Broumana, 14 Oct. 1850; compare A.E. Damas, ii, No. 6, 5 Dec. 1852.

[2] See above, p. 195 and below, pp. 232–3.

[3] F.O. 78/1220, Misk to Clarendon, No. 14, Damascus, 27 Aug. 1856; F.O. 78/1219, Moore to Clarendon, No. 37, Beirut, 18 Aug. 1856; F.O. 78/1218, Finn to Clarendon, No. 32, Jerusalem, 7 Nov. 1856; A.E. Damas, iv, from Outrey, No. 14, 10 Aug. 1856.

[4] F.O. 195/416, Barker to Redcliffe, No. 37, Aleppo, 10 Nov. 1856.

[5] F.O. 78/1452, Skene to Bulwer, No. 11, encl. in Skene to Malmesbury, No. 20, Aleppo, 31 Mar. 1859; *Rambles*, pp. 58–59.

[6] F.O. 78/1218, Finn to Clarendon, No. 33, Jerusalem, 10 Nov. 1856.

[7] A.E. Damas, iv, from Outrey, No. 14, 16 Aug. 1856; ibid., v, No. 63, 27 Sept. 1858; F.O. 78/1219, Moore to Clarendon, No. 37, Beirut, 18 Aug. 1856; Mishāqa, MS., pp. 344–7.

[8] See above, p. 191.

survey of this position is relevant not only to show the significant impact of that era on the Syrian Jews, but to confirm further, by way of comparison, the major causes for Muslim–Christian antagonism.

B. *The position of the Jews*

> 'The Muslims and Jews do not hate each other . . . but to the Christians the Muslims bear hate.'
>
> (A Jewish traveller in Syria in 1859)[1]

The several thousands of Jews, mainly town-dwellers, were perhaps the most depressed community in Syria and Palestine during the pre-reform period. They were frequently subject to a great deal of aggression and oppression by the local authorities and the Muslim population as well as by their Christian neighbours.[2] It is true that under the Egyptian régime the position of the Jews became noticeably better: they enjoyed greater security, justice, and religious freedom than in the past,[3] but at the same time they were far from being equal to their Muslim or Christian fellow-subjects, nor did they enjoy the same measure of safety as the rest. They continued occasionally to be maltreated and persecuted by Muslims, Christians, and some government officials alike;[4] and in certain occurrences—in Safed and Hebron—a great number of them were massacred and their property sacked by Muslim and Druze rioters as well as by Egyptian soldiers.[5]

It was only during the Tanzimat period that the position of the Jews in Syria and Palestine was remarkably improved and in certain respects it represented a turning point in their history.

[1] A. Ya'ari, *Massa'ot shliaḥ Tzfat* (Jerusalem, 1942), p. 19. See also A.E. Damas, i, from Munton, No. 5, 18 Jan. 1841; *Birjīs Barīs*, No. 32 (1860).

[2] See A. Y. Braver in *Zion*, i (5690), No. 1, pp. 5, 168–76, 186; L. A. Mayer in *Zion*, i, No. 4, pp. 5–7; A. Shoḥaṭ in *Zion* (new series), i (5696), pp. 380–6; Schwartz, *Tvu'ot*, ii. 47–48; Schulman, *Ariel*, pp. 72–73; see also Burckhardt, p. 317.

[3] F.O. 78/283, Campbell's Report: Rustum, *Maḥfūẓāt*, ii. 336, No. 3077; p. 394, No. 3420; iii. 123, No. 4583; pp. 294–5, No. 5178; Frumqin, in *Zion*, ii. 147; Schulman, *Ariel*, p. 69.

[4] F.O. 78/368, Young to Palmerston, No. 13, Jerusalem, 25 May 1839, in Hyamson, i. 6–8; F.O. 78/410, Werry to Palmerston, No. 6, Damascus, 22 May 1840.

[5] M. Abir, 'Tvi'ot Yehudey Tzfat', in *Sefunot*, No. 7 (Jerusalem, 5723), pp. 269–70; Y. Ben-Zvi, 'Me, ora'ot Tzfat', in *Sefunot*, No. 7, pp. 277–80; al-Dibs, viii. 649; Schulman, op. cit., p. 76; Spyridon, p. 100.

In 1840, following the Damascus 'blood libel', a special Imperial firman was issued by Sultan Abdülmecid upon the request of Sir Moses Montefiore, confirming the rights of the Jews in accordance with the Gülhane edict, and guaranteeing their complete security.[1] A similar attitude was expressed in other firmans sent to Syria in 1841, immediately after its restoration to the Ottomans; in one order, for example, which dealt with the protection of the Christians, a special reference was made by the Sultan on the need to protect also the Jews.[2] In the same year the first Jewish *Hahambaşı* (Chief Rabbi) was nominated in Jerusalem by an Imperial order and was granted an official position and considerable authority over his community.[3]

Another firman of 1841 was concerned with the preservation of the status of the Jews in the public administration;[4] and about the same time, Raphael Farḥi, a member of the well-known Jewish family, resumed his senior position as the Banker of the provincial treasury of Damascus.[5] When this office was subsequently abolished and Farḥi was superseded by an official sent from Istanbul,[6] other members of the Jewish community, both in Damascus and in Aleppo, continued to hold (alongside Christian officials) a considerable number of posts in the new financial administration.[7] Like their Christian fellow-subjects, the Jews of Syria, notably those living in the commercial centres, were engaged also in the country's foreign trade and were thus prospering economically.[8]

[1] See text in F.O. 78/416; M. Montefiore, *Diaries* (London, 1890), i. 278–9.

[2] See *Irade H.*, No. 527, 3 CA 1257 (on the facing page); see also ibid., No. 532, 9 CA 1257; F.O. 195/181, Palmerston to Ponsonby, No. 95, 21 Apr. 1841, in Hyamson, i. 40.

[3] See *Irade H.*, No. 532, op. cit.; see also firman of Evahir B 1257, in Hirshberg, *Rivlin*, pp. 95–98; A. Almaliḥ, 'Ha-rishonim le-Zion bi-Yerushalayim', in *Ozar Yehudey Sefarad*, iii, p. 63; compare *Ha-magid*, ii, No. 36, p. 144, 16 Sept. 1858.

[4] *Maliyeden Müdevver*, No. 9061, p. 3, para. 9, dated 1257 (1841).

[5] F.O. 78/447, Werry to Bidwell, private, Damascus, 21 Aug. 1841; al-Bāshā, p. 242; Paton, p. 39; Taoutel, iii. 23.

[6] *Cevdet D.*, Maliye, No. 19123, L 1261; F.O. 78/447, op. cit.

[7] Levton, p. 112*b*; G. W. Curtis, *The Wanderer in Syria* (London, 1852), p. 303; Paton, p. 39; Wilson, *The Lands*, ii. 333; see also *Irade D.*, No. 10607, 16 R 1265; F.O. 195/207, Werry to Canning, No. 16, Aleppo, 9 Sept. 1843.

[8] Israel Ben Yosef Binyamin, *Sefer massa'ey Israel* (Lyck, 1859), pp. 12 ff.; *Ha-Karmel*, No. 27, 29 Ṭevet 5621 (1861), p. 212; Lyall, p. 101; Porter, *Damascus*, i. 147; Wilson, op. cit., ii. 333–4, 364; Ya'ari, *Tzfat*, pp. 13–19. See also F.O. 78/622, Wood to Canning, No. 13, encl. in Wood to Aberdeen, No. 21, Damascus, 24 June 1845.

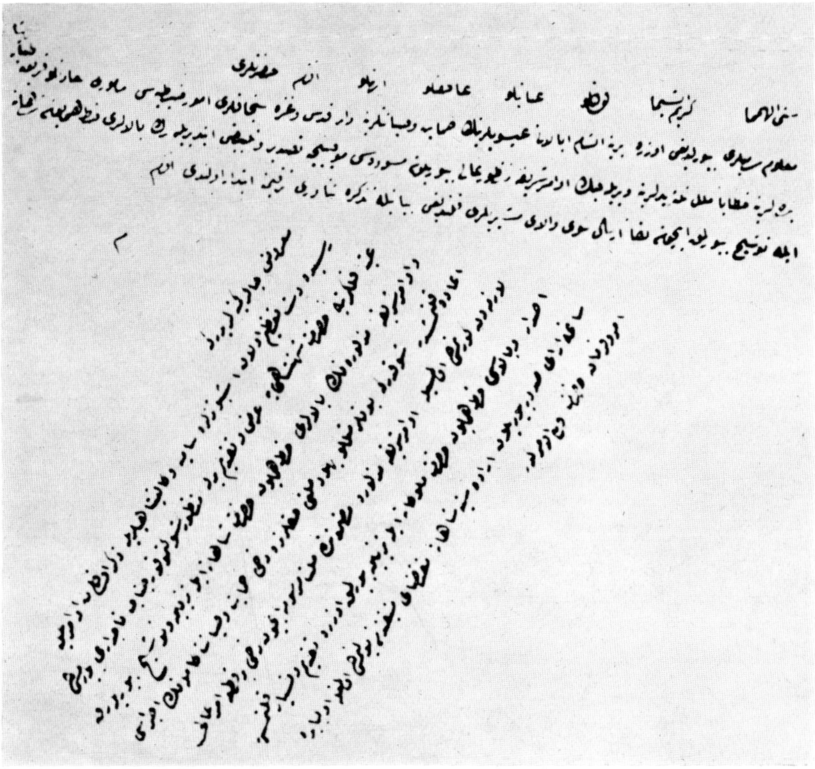

FIG. 3. An Imperial firman on the need to protect the Jews as well as the Christians

On the other hand, however, as already described, the Jews together with the Christians continued to be unequal to the Muslims before the law and in the public institutions. In addition, they were still occasionally insulted and attacked, sometimes to death, by their Muslim neighbours as well as by soldiers and policemen.[1] Such cases occurred particularly in Palestinian towns, where the Jews were largely foreign subjects; in these places they continued to be, especially in the 1840s, the major target for oppression by local Muslim notables and some government officials.[2]

Yet in comparison with the past, the situation of the Jews in Palestine was markedly better, and as time went on, it improved further. Reports of the 1850s indicate, for example, that 'Jews do obtain more redress from the local governors in Palestine', and that 'the oppression of the Turkish governors has considerably . . . almost . . . completely ceased'.[3]

The growing security of the Jews in Palestine, which was largely due to the protection granted by the European consuls, particularly the English,[4] helped to attract to Palestine a considerable number of Jewish immigrants from Europe, who came and settled mainly in Jerusalem, Hebron, Safed, and Tiberias.[5] Thus, for example, the Jewish population of Jerusalem, which in 1839 had amounted to some 5,000, had almost doubled by the late 1850s to

[1] F.O. 195/194, Rose to Aberdeen, No. 55, encl. in Rose to Canning, No. 54, Beirut, 7 Aug. 1842; F.O. 78/837, Calvert to Canning, No. 20, encl. in Calvert to Palmerston, No. 19, Damascus, 29 Aug. 1850; F.O. 78/1538, Skene to Bulwer, No. 4, encl. in Skene to Russell, No. 16, Aleppo, 14 Apr. 1860; A.E. Jérusalem, i, from Philibert, No. 44, 28 Jan. 1844.

[2] F.O. 78/498, Wood to Bidwell, No. 3, Damascus, 3 Jan. 1842; F.O. 78/839, Finn to Palmerston, No. 20, Jerusalem, 27 Sept. 1850; Binyamin, pp. 8–9; Finn, ii. 59 ff.; M. Raysher, *Sefer sha'arey Yerushalayim* (Lemberg, 1866), p. 17; Wortabet, i. 110.

[3] See respectively, F.O. 78/874, Finn to Canning, No. 10, encl. in Finn to Palmerston, No. 6, Jerusalem, 24 July 1851; *Jewish Intelligence*, xxii, No. 260, cited in F.O. 78/1217, Finn to Clarendon, No. 1, Jerusalem, 7 Jan. 1856; see also F.O. 78/2068, Moore to Palmerston, No. 45, Beirut, 1 Dec. 1849 in Hyamson, i. 156; Jessup, i. 269; Raysher, pp. 18, 28; G. Williams, *The Holy City* (London, 1845), p. 432.

[4] F.O. 78/836, Rose to Palmerston, No. 54, Beirut, 1 Dec. 1850; F.O. 78/963, Finn to Clarendon, No. 33, Jerusalem, 28 Dec. 1859; see also undated letter from the Russian Jews in Tiberias to Sir M. Montefiore, in Montefiore Papers, Ben-Zvi Institute, Jerusalem.

[5] F.O. 78/963, Finn to Clarendon, No. 33, Jerusalem, 28 Dec. 1853; F.O. 78/1454, Finn to Malmesbury, No. 1, Jerusalem, 1 Jan. 1859; F.O. 78/1521, Finn to Russell, No. 1, Jerusalem, 4 Jan. 1860; see also Braver in *Zion*, v (1939–40), p. 169; *V*inreb, in *Zion*, iii (1938), p. 76.

become half of the total population in the city.[1] They purchased land in and round Jerusalem,[2] and, with the help of Moses Montefiore, gradually learned 'to work for their own living instead of depending solely for subsistence upon the alms from Europe'.[3]

At the same time the position of the Jews in Syria, who were mainly Ottoman subjects, was even more secure and politically advanced; it was in fact better than ever before under Ottoman rule and safer than that of the local Christians.[4] This was partly due to foreign protection, but mainly it was because the Jews were now treated with greater respect both by the authorities and by the Muslim leaders. Indeed, a great number of Turkish Pashas would endeavour to protect their Jewish inhabitants against both Muslim ill-treatment and Christian vexation.[5] Muslim notables, among them members of the *meclis*, would likewise support Jews in their disputes with Christians,[6] and in at least one instance—the case of inheritance by a minor—the Jewish community enjoyed, as already mentioned, a more favoured status in the *mahkeme* than the Christian communities.[7]

This preferential attitude of Muslims towards Jews, although

[1] See and compare, Great Britain, *A Handbook of Syria (including Palestine)*, prepared by the Admiralty (1913?) p. 184; A.E. Jérusalem, ii, from Jorelle, No. 34, 1 July 1847; Finn, i. 101–2; F.O. 78/1388, Finn to Clarendon, No. 1, Jerusalem, 1 Jan. 1858; A. M. Hyamson, *Palestine* (London, 1917), ii. 331.

[2] See, for example, document of 24 R 1258 in the Archives of the Sephardi community in Jerusalem, Ben-Zvi Institute, Jerusalem; D. Yelin, *Zikronot le-ven Yerushalayim* (Jerusalem, 5684), pp. 52, 57; F.O. 195/292, Finn to Canning, No. 11, Jerusalem, 14 Aug. 1850.

[3] F.O. 78/1454, Finn to Malmesbury, No. 1, Jerusalem, 1 Jan. 1859; see also F.O. 78/874, Finn to Canning, No. 20, encl. in Finn to Palmerston, No. 9, Jerusalem, 5 Dec. 1851; Finn, ii. 321 ff., 408–9.

[4] See, for example, F.O. 78/448, Werry to Palmerston, No. 16, Aleppo, 28 July 1841; Binyamin, pp. 12–17; Lyall, p. 101; Neale, ii. 105; Porter, *Damascus*, i. 147; Ya'ari, *Shliaḥ Tzfat*, pp. 13 ff.

[5] F.O. 195/207, Werry to Canning, No. 10, Aleppo, 10 Apr. 1844; F.O. 78/714, Timoni to Wellesley, No. 11, encl. in Timoni to Palmerston, No. 9, Damascus, 31 May 1847; F.O. 78/1219, Moore to Clarendon, No. 33, Beirut, 14 July 1856; A.E. Jérusalem, i, from Philibert, No. 44, 20 Jan. 1844; A.E. Damas, iii, No. 24, 27 May 1855; see also Mishāqa, MS., pp. 356–7.

[6] See, for example, F.O. 78/658, Rose to Aberdeen, No. 25, Beirut, 7 June 1846; F.O. 78/1217, Finn to Moore, No. 42, encl. in Finn to Clarendon, Jerusalem, 7 July 1856; F.O. 78/1220, Misk to Clarendon, No. 17, Damascus, 29 Oct. 1856; 'Material from the Collection of Me'ir Naḥmad, Aleppo', in Ben-Zvi Institute, Jerusalem; compare *Ha-Karmel*, i, No. 29, p. 227, 14 Shvaṭ 5621 (1861).

[7] F.O. 78/1219, Moore to Redcliffe, No. 40, encl. in Moore to Clarendon, No. 35, Beirut, 14 July 1856; see above, p. 195–6.

not completely new in Islamic and Ottoman history,[1] became now more conspicuous in the light of the equality officially granted to the non-Muslim subjects under the Tanzimat reforms. Unlike the Christians, the Jews of Syria usually refrained from demonstrating their new liberties, and from behaving insolently towards Muslims; they continued to carry on their life more as a second-class minority than as an equal community. Related to this and more significant was the fact that the local Jews were a small religious group, who possessed no political aims and had 'an interest in the present and future welfare of the country'.[2]

By contrast, the Syrian Christians, who formed a large part of the local population,[3] firmly claimed to be equal to their Muslim fellow-subjects; and in view of their close links with the European Powers, they were regarded as a political danger by both the Muslim population and the Turkish authorities.

[1] See G. E. Von Grunebaum, *Medieval Islam* (Chicago, 1946), pp. 180–1; *Turkey*, in Jewish Encyclopaedia.

[2] F.O. 78/444, Young to Ponsonby, No. 11, Jerusalem, 11 June 1841; see also Almaliḥ, op. cit., p. 63; Finn, i. 408; L. A. Frankel, *Nach Jerusalem*, i. 366, cited in Braver, *Zion*, x–xii (1945–7), p. 99; Madden, ii. 28.

[3] There are no official figures on the numerical division of the Syrian population in the mid-nineteenth century. According to estimates by contemporary European observers, the population of Syria, Lebanon, and Palestine was composed of over a million Muslims (mostly Arabs), about half a million Christians (including some 200,000 Maronites, mainly in Mount Lebanon), and some 25,000 Jews. See and compare Edwards, pp. 12–13; Farley, *The Massacres*, p. 173; Thomson, pp. 166–7. See also R. F. Burton and C. F. Tyrwhitt Drake, *Unexplored Syria* (London, 1872), pp. 101 ff.; *Ḥasr al-lithām*, pp. 6–8.

XVI

EUROPEAN ACTIVITIES AND MUSLIM–CHRISTIAN RELATIONS

'... the European powers are hostile to the Turkish authority in Syria and ... in union with the Christians they wish to overset it.'

(A common belief of Syrian Muslims)[1]

THE association of local Christians with European powers was not completely new among the Muslim population of Syria and Palestine. For some centuries there had been certain religious and cultural connexions between Syrian Christians and Catholic centres in Europe,[2] as well as commercial ties between the Syrian *reaya* and European countries.[3] During the eighteenth century these relations expanded and grew closer and, coinciding with the strengthening of Christian Europe and the decline of the Ottoman power, they produced feelings of suspicion among Syrian Muslims.[4] In 1799 these feelings were intensified by the Napoleonic invasion of Palestine which threatened the integrity of Syria and the Empire; so strong had this mistrust become that in Damascus a Muslim mob rioted against the Christians,[5] and more than two decades later, when the Greek revolt broke out, Christians were attacked by Muslims in many parts of Syria and Palestine.[6]

Yet these anti-Christian outbursts were only sporadic and rather limited and did not indicate an essential change in the Muslim traditional attitude: the Christians, like the Jews, were still second-

[1] F.O. 195/194, Rose to Canning, No. 25, Beirut, 21 Mar. 1842.

[2] See Hourani, *Arabic Thought*, pp. 55–59.

[3] Gibb and Bowen, i. 308–10; Shamir, *The 'Aẓm*, p. 247.

[4] Compare Gibb and Bowen, ii. 258; Polk, p. 136.

[5] Mīkhā'īl al-Dimashqī, *Ta'rīkh hawādith al-Shām wa-Lubnān* (Beirut, 1912), p. 9; *Kitāb al-aḥzān fī ta'rīkh al-Shām* (MS., No. 956. 9, A.U.B.), pp. 48–50; see also Baedeker, p. 350.

[6] See F.O. 78/495, Rose to Canning, No. 36, Beirut, 29 May 1842; Baedeker, p. 350; Barker, ii. 19–21; Mishāqa, MS., pp. 170–1; Spyridon, pp. 18–29; Bodman, p. 138. Compare Heyd, *'Ulemā*, p. 91.

class citizens and on the whole were treated by the dominant Muslims with contempt rather than hostility. Similarly, European activities in Syria and Palestine, as well as their connexions with local Christian communities, were as yet comparatively limited, and being mainly restricted to the coastal areas, had hardly any political or military implications.

A decisive shift in this complexity of factors and relations took place during the era of reform, starting in the 1830s under the Egyptian régime,[1] and developing during the first two decades of the Tanzimat. In the course of this period, European religio-cultural and commercial activities increased greatly and spread into the Syrian hinterland, and while further strengthening the position of the Christian communities, caused great anger and anxiety among the Muslim population. As matters stood, the opening of taverns and the performance of dances, festivities and the like, by foreigners, deeply hurt the feelings of the Muslims;[2] the growing missionary activities likewise produced great dissatisfaction among orthodox Muslims.[3] Another major grievance expressed by the local Muslims was 'that the Europeans not only carried away their money, but had superseded the native industry, by which they had ruined and reduced to poverty the subjects of the Sultan'.[4]

Above all it was the expanding foreign political activities through a network of newly established consulates all over the country that gave the greatest anxiety to both the Muslim population and the Turkish authorities. This activity, which was connected with various internal matters, especially among the Christian subjects, provided quite good grounds for the belief that Christian Europe was aiming at occupying Syria and Palestine with the aid of the local Christians.

[1] See above, p. 17. On the pro-European policy of Muḥammad ʿAlī, see Rustum, *Maḥfūẓāt*, ii. 298, No. 2868. See also Polk, pp. 136–7.

[2] See F.O. 78/538, Wood to Aberdeen, No. 17, Damascus, 25 May 1843; Letter from the *kaymakam* of Aleppo to Consul Werry of 14 N 1258 in F.O. 195/207; F.O. 78/959, Wood to Russell, No. 9, Damascus, 7 Feb. 1853; F.O. 78/1454, Finn to Malmesbury, No. 13, Jerusalem, 23 May 1859; A.E. Damas, ii, 3 Feb. 1853.

[3] See *Irade D.*, No. 2670/18, 19 Z 1257; ibid., No. 14609, 2 Z 1267; A.E. Alep, ii, from de Lesseps, No. 1, 30 May 1851; compare Davison, *Reform*, pp. 74–75; Tibawi, p. 166.

[4] F.O. 78/761, Wood to Canning, No. 29, encl. in Wood to Palmerston, No. 30, Damascus, 25 Nov. 1848; see also Kibrizli, pp. 83–84.

A. *Foreign activities and intervention*

'Tous les consulats sont des États dans l'État, des pierres d'achoppement.'[1]

During the 1840s and the 1850s there was virtually no area of government administration, from finance and justice to affairs of the *reaya* and obvious political issues, in which the European consuls did not interfere.[2] The English took the leading role in this practice, being from the beginning convinced that 'without the aid of the British forces the Turks could not have regained possession of Syria . . . (and) without the continued aid of the British government . . . the Turks cannot govern Syria'.[3] This was especially the attitude of Consul Wood, who for several years behaved almost as if he were the Governor-General of Syria, as he himself stated: 'British influence of course was not only paramount but the country may be said to have been administered by us; . . . nearly all the Governors and public officers owed their nomination to me. . . . I nominated also to the various offices under them my own people to act as checks upon them.'[4] Wood was, admittedly, empowered by the Ottomans to supervise the affairs in the country in the first year after the restoration of Ottoman rule in Syria,[5] but he was certainly not authorized by the *Porte* to act as he and his colleagues did during the early 1840s and later on. Nor was Consul Wood or any other British consul ordered by their own government to do so: a Foreign Office dispatch sent to Ponsonby, the Ambassador in Constantinople, regarding the future of Syria after its restoration stated: 'Her Majesty's Government are not sufficiently conversant with the internal arrangements of Turkish Administration to be able to say what specified measures

[1] Edwards, p. 77; compare Wortabet, i. 347.

[2] See *Irade D.*, No. 2058/6, 3 CA 1257; *Irade H.*, No. 3923, 4 ZA 1267; F.O. 78/447, Wood to Bidwell, No. 8, Damascus, 21 Dec. 1841; F.O. 78/581, Young to Aberdeen, No. 18, Jerusalem, 29 June 1844; F.O. 78/1538, Skene to Bulwer, No. 5, encl. in Skene to Russell, No. 17, Aleppo, 19 Apr. 1860; Porter, *Damascus*, i. 135; Taoutel, iii. 153, 169.

[3] F.O. 78/444, Young to Palmerston, No. 5, Jaffa, 25 Jan. 1841.

[4] F.O. 78/499, Wood to Ponsonby, Beirut, 17 Feb. 1841.

[5] Compare F.O. 78/499, 'Plan proposé à la Sublime Porte pour le gouvernement de la Syrie', encl. in Wood to Ponsonby, Beirut, 17 Feb. 1841; see also F.O. 78/447, Wood to Aberdeen, No. 42, Damascus, 4 Dec. 1841; al-Qasatīlī, p. 90; Mishāqa, *Muntakhabāt*, p. 152.

would be best adopted for this purpose.'[1] And in its instructions to Colonel Rose on his appointment as Consul-General of Syria in 1841, the Foreign Office clearly stressed: 'You will be careful to abstain from meddling interference.'[2] But in spite of these instructions, Consul Wood was repeatedly accused by the Turkish authorities of 'interference and meddling'.[3]

It is true that a considerable part of these English activities in the Syrian provinces aimed at seeing that the reforms of the *hat* of Gülhane (in the promulgation of which the British had had a major share) were carried out; as Consul Wood pointed out: 'Her Majesty's consulate has been incessantly struggling for years with Her officers, and in Her interest for the maintenance and execution as far as its sphere of action will permit, of the provisions of the Tanzimat.'[4] Indeed, in certain instances the intervention of the English and French consuls, and sometimes even their mere presence in the province, helped to control abuses and to hasten the introduction of the reforms; in some cases their advice and help, which was occasionally sought by the Pashas, proved useful.[5] But on the other hand, foreign interference frequently made the task of the Ottoman authorities in Syria more difficult.

Firstly, many Turkish Pashas in the Syrian provinces, as well as in the *Porte*, were sceptical about the sincerity of British support for the Tanzimat, and were suspicious of British aims in the area. One idea common in Ottoman high circles was that England had been supporting the Ottomans against Muḥammad ʿAlī and the Russians only because this was compatible with her own interests; the Ottoman provinces, including those of Syria, were important to the British from the point of view of their position in India and their commercial interests in the area.[6] Secondly, and more important, the consuls' intervention contributed on many occasions to the damaging of Ottoman authority in the provinces, as

[1] F.O. 78/391, F.O. to Ponsonby, No. 266, 12 Dec. 1840.

[2] F.O. 78/454, F.O. to Rose, No. 6, 2 Nov. 1841.

[3] F.O. 78/535, Rose to Wood, encl. No. 1 in Rose to Aberdeen, No. 2, Beirut, 7 Jan. 1843; *Irade D.*, No. 2053/6, 3 CA 1257.

[4] F.O. 78/801, Wood to Canning, No. 20, encl. in Wood to Palmerston, No. 23, Damascus, 25 Sept. 1849; see also F.O. 78/391, F.O. to Ponsonby, No. 92, 12 Apr. 1841 in Temperley, p. 186.

[5] Farley, *Syria*, p. 300; Finn, i. 193, 340–2; ii. 21, 145–6; compare Oliphant, p. 337; Yelin, p. 33.

[6] Urquhart Papers, ii, MSS. C1 (6), 'Conversation with Namic Pasha on offering military aid to Turkey, 1854'; see also Karal, v. 215.

Mr. Bulwer, the British Ambassador to Constantinople, frankly wrote in 1859:

> Many of the foreign consuls including our own have been in the habit of assuming the functions of government, of dictating to the Pashas arbitrarily the line of conduct to be pursued in internal matters, of fostering partisans; . . . (all of which) has gone towards annihilating the power of the provincial Governors, of introducing a restless spirit of dissatisfaction amongst the native population.[1]

Thus, for example, French and English consuls, seeking to establish their influence in the country, would occasionally support rival mountain groups or other semi-autonomous elements. The principal scene of this struggle was, of course, Mount Lebanon, where the French supported their traditional allies, the Maronites, while the English sided with the Druzes.[2] In addition, the English and French consuls would, as already indicated, periodically back the rival families of Ṭuqān and ʿAbd al-Hādī in Jabal Nablus and those of al-Laḥḥām and Abū-Ghūsh in the Jerusalem mountains.[3] Such support was occasionally extended also to the Shihābi Amir of Ḥaṣbāyā Saʿd al-Dīn or to certain Ḥarfūsh Amirs of Baʿalbek in their relations with the Turkish authorities.[4] Even local elements such as the Druzes of Houran and the Bedouin chief ʿAqīl *ağa* of northern Palestine, who were notorious for their disobedience, were associated in one way or another with the British and French consuls respectively.[5] It is true that the consuls would from time to time use their contacts and influence with the various territorial groups in order to settle anti-government uprisings or local armed disputes.[6] But it is equally true that these

[1] F.O. 78/1637, Bulwer to Russell, Constantinople, 26 July 1859.

[2] *Irade D.*, No. 2058, 25 CA 1257; F.O. 78/500, Moore to Aberdeen, No. 33, Beirut, 4 Apr. 1842; Abū-Shaqrā', pp. 45–46; Karal, v. 214–17; Khazin, i. 66–67, 73; Ubicini, i. 348.

[3] See, for example, *Irade D.*, No. 14609, 2 Z 1267; F.O. 78/581, Young to Canning, No. 25, Jerusalem, 3 Aug. 1844; A.E. Jérusalem, i, from Lantivy, No. 56, 22 Apr. 1844; Finn, i. 314; ii. 400, 426, 431; al-Nimr, p. 269; see also above, pp. 112, 116.

[4] F.O. 78/498, Wood to Aberdeen, No. 6, Damascus, 3 Jan. 1842; F.O. 78/959, Wood to Clarendon, No. 23, Damascus, 11 May 1853; A.E. Damas, ii, from Segur, No. 21, 13 Aug. 1851; A.E. Damas, iii, from de Barrère, No. 15, 12 Aug. 1854.

[5] See above, pp. 127, 139.

[6] See, for example, F.O. 78/1028, Wood to Clarendon, No. 10, Damascus, 24 Feb. 1854; F.O. 78/1033, Werry to Redcliffe, No. 17, encl. in Werry to Clarendon, No. 10, Aleppo, 13 June 1854; Finn, i. 320–3; ii. 195, 286; Lyde, p. 216; see also above, pp. 127–8.

local warring elements drew much encouragement in their efforts to remain autonomous, from the links they maintained and the support they occasionally received from the foreign emissaries.

Foreign agents of various European powers were, furthermore, reported to have been directly engaged in subversive activities against the Turkish government.[1] Among those were also English military officers such as Major Churchill, whose activities were described by the Turkish authorities as aiming at 'agitating the provinces'.[2] French agents were apparently no less active: according to British consular reports they were periodically engaged in distributing arms among certain sections of the population and inciting them to rise against the government.[3] Such reports, which obviously indicated the contest for influence between the British and the French, became particularly accusatory after the Crimean War at the time when France was replacing England as the leading foreign power in the Syrian provinces.[4] Consul Moore reported, thus, in 1858: 'The French have succeeded in establishing a system of terror all over Syria by means of which they have become the virtual rulers of the country.'[5]

B. *European protection of the Christian communities*

'. . . Foreign Embassies have no title to interfere in matters concerning rayas and . . . the communities must declare whether they are Ottoman or foreign subjects.'

(A statement by the *meclis* of Damascus)[6]

Foreign intervention and rivalry were, of course, much more vigorous and more evident with regard to the local non-Muslims

[1] See F.O. 78/959, Wood to Clarendon, No. 46, Damascus, 26 Aug. 1853; F.O. 78/1383, Finn to Malmesbury, No. 6, Jerusalem, 13 Apr. 1858; A.E. Damas, iii, from de Barrère, No. 1, 15 July 1853; *Irade D.*, No. 2058, 25 CA 1257; ibid., No. 14609, 2 Z 1267; Finn, ii. 304, 306, 313–14.

[2] *Irade H.*, No. 2580, 6 N 1257; compare F.O. 78/457, Rose to Aberdeen, No. 108, Beirut, 7 Oct. 1841.

[3] F.O. 78/500, Moore to Canning, Beirut, 4 Apr. 1842; F.O. 78/959, Wood to Russell, No. 10, Damascus, 10 Feb. 1853.

[4] F.O. 78/1217, Finn to Clarendon, No. 15, Jerusalem, 14 Mar. 1856; F.O. 78/1219, Moore to Clarendon, No. 6, Beirut, 29 Dec. 1856; F.O. 78/1220, Wood to Redcliffe, No. 1, encl. in Wood to Clarendon, No. 2, Damascus, 18 Jan. 1856. On the English-French rivalry in Istanbul, see Cevdet, *Tezakir*, i. 26–27; Engelhardt, i. 49–50; ii. 316 ff.

[5] F.O. 78/1385, confidential memo. encl. in Moore to Clarendon, No. 8, Beirut, 19 Feb. 1858.

[6] F.O. 78/1298, Misk to Clarendon, No. 14, Damascus, 27 Sept. 1857.

and especially the Christian communities. In this area the chief contestants were France and Russia. The former continued to extend its traditional protection and support to the Maronites, Melkites, and Latins,[1] while the latter did the same thing with respect to the Greek Orthodox and Armenian communities, particularly after the Treaty of Hünkâr Iskelesi of 1833.[2] Both powers backed their respective protected communities in their endless rivalry and disputes, especially over the Holy Places in Palestine; this policy eventually, it may be said, led to the involvement of the Ottomans in the Crimean War.[3]

Apart from Russia and France other European powers were also engaged in the protection of the *reaya*. British and Prussian protection was granted to the small Protestant community, which was formed in Syria and Palestine in the late 1830s–early 1840s, and which was officially recognized as a *millet* in 1850.[4] English protection was also extended to a considerable number of Jews, particularly non-Ottoman subjects;[5] other Jews were under Russian, Prussian, Austrian, and French protection.[6]

[1] See, for example, F.O. 78/444, Young to Palmerston, No. 15, Jerusalem, 7 Apr. 1841; F.O. 78/964, Kayat to Clarendon, separate, Jaffa, 1 May 1853; Finn, i. 21 ff., 51 ff., 72 ff.; for more information on the history of French protection over the Catholics, see B. Homsy, *Les Capitulations et la Protection des Chrétiens au Proche-Orient* (Paris, 1956).

[2] For details on Russian protection over the Orthodox community in Syria and Palestine, see F.O. 195/226, Wood to Canning, No. 19, Damascus, 29 July 1844; Bazili, ii. 2–3, 21–22; *Birjīs Barīs*, i, No. 20, 13 Mar. 1860; for a study on the Russian activities in Syria and Palestine during that period see D. Hopwood, *Russian Activities in Syria in the Nineteenth Century*, D.Phil. Thesis (Oxford, 1964). See also T. G. Stavrou, 'Russian Interest in the Levant 1843–1848', *M.E.J.*, No. 17 (1963), pp. 91–103. On Russian protection over the Armenian community see, for example, *Irade H.*, No. 1335, 4 RA 1261. On the treaty of Hünkâr Iskelesi, see P. E. Mosley, *Russian Diplomacy and the Opening of the Eastern Question in 1838–1839* (Harvard, 1934).

[3] See F.O. 78/444, Young to Palmerston, No. 15, Jerusalem, 7 Apr. 1841; F.O. 195/226, Wood to Canning, No. 19, Damascus, 29 July 1844; Finn, i. 21 ff. On the rivalry over the Holy Places and its consequences, see also Temperley, Ch. XI.

[4] F.O. 78/872, Wood to Canning, encl. No. 2 in Wood to Palmerston, No. 18, Damascus, 29 May 1851; Finn, i. 148, 156 ff.; Porter, *Damascus*, i. 145; Robinson, p. 161.

[5] F.O. 78/391, F.O. to Ponsonby, No. 248, London, 24 Nov. 1840; F.O. 78/836, Rose to Palmerston, No. 54, Beirut, 1 Dec. 1850; F.O. 78/713, Malmesbury to Finn, No. 5, London, 8 Nov. 1852.

[6] See, for example, Letter from Jews in Tiberias under Russian protection, n.d. (1839?) in Montefiore Papers, Ben-Zvi Institute; F.O. 78/963, Finn to Clarendon, No. 33, Jerusalem, 28 Dec. 1853; Hopwood, p. 94; Hyamson, *Palestine*, pp. 52–53; Poujade, pp. 213–14; Temperley, pp. 443–4; Yelin, p. 9.

European consuls in the country, notably the English and French, would protect Christians and Jews alike, both Ottoman subjects and aliens, against persecution of all kinds—religious, economic, and political; and would similarly help them to achieve various benefits.[1] But in so doing the consuls frequently overstepped the bounds of discretion, while undermining government authority among the Christians and aggravating the relations between Christians and Muslims. Thus great embarrassment and financial loss were caused to the Turkish government by European consulates which misused their capitulatory privileges and enlisted a large number of Ottoman subjects as their protégés, exempting them from government jurisdiction and certain taxes.[2] Moreover, the Powers not only used their influence in the *Porte* to cause the dismissal of alleged anti-Christian Pashas in Syria, but they would occasionally also threaten the Turkish authorities and the Muslim population with military occupation were the Christian subjects to be maltreated. After the Aleppo riots of 1850, Palmerston wrote: 'If the Christian subjects of the Sultan are to be liable to become the victims of such abominable crimes, Christian Europe will come to the conclusion that the existence of the Ottoman Empire is an evil and that its overthrow would be conducive to the general interest of the human race.'[3] The French consul in Damascus expressed a similar idea in public while warning the local Muslims after a quarrel between a Frenchman and a Muslim: 'Is it necessary for them to witness a French army on the heights of Salhiyé to make them recollect that the French took Algiers and furnished it for a mere stroke of a fan?'[4] Nor were the European powers satisfied with purely verbal warnings: French and British warships would often patrol

[1] See, for example, F.O. 78/800, Moore to Palmerston, No. 30, Beirut, 31 Aug. 1849; A.E. Damas, iii, from de Barrère, No. 24, 27 May 1855; F.O. 78/1388, Brant to Malmesbury, No. 10, Aleppo, 10 June 1852; Wortabet, i. 351.

[2] F.O. 78/910, Werry to Canning, No. 16, encl. in Werry to Malmesbury, No. 10, Aleppo, 10 June 1852; F.O. 78/1538, White to Skene, Antioch, 18 Apr., encl. in Skene to Russell, No. 18, Aleppo, 30 Apr. 1860; Edwards, pp. 78–81; Wortabet, i. 345–50; compare Ubicini, i. 187; White, i. 133.

[3] F.O. 78/816, Palmerston to Canning, No. 321, 18 Dec. 1850 in Temperley, p. 198.

[4] Letter from the French consul to the Pasha at Damascus, encl. in F.O. 78/958, Wood to Russell, No. 10, Damascus, 10 Feb. 1853 ('Salhiyé'—a quarter in Damascus); see also F.O. 78/1120, Finn to Clarendon, No. 13, Jerusalem, 28 May 1855.

along the Syrian coast or call on coastal towns, particularly at times of anti-Christian tension.[1]

The outbreak of the Crimean War served as a decisive proof that the Christian threat to the Islamic state was indeed real; and the fact that England and France were on the side of the Turks did not, on the whole, undermine this belief. The termination of the Crimean War saw, furthermore, the intensification of Western pressure; the *Hatt-ı Hümayun* of 1856, which was issued after the war, was itself in fact a product of European intervention in favour of the Ottoman Christians.[2]

This foreign intervention on behalf of the *reaya* was so efficient —sometimes it overstressed the latter's rights and overfulfilled even their expectations—that they would frequently refer their grievances and other matters to the consuls rather than to the Turkish authorities.[3] It is true that the Christians could not feel great confidence in a government which did not protect them against the Muslims' aggression; they were, indeed, unable to forget such events as the 1850 riots in Aleppo.[4] But at the same time, various sections of this population did not show any readiness to integrate into a new Ottoman society, and from the beginning manifested a desire to be under the rule of European powers. In 1841, for example, a circular was issued by Syrian Christians (apparently with missionaries' inspiration) requesting Christian Europe to endeavour to bring Palestine under Christian rule.[5] The Greek Orthodox openly demonstrated from time to time their inclination towards Russia,[6] while the Maronites were allegedly

[1] F.O. 195/194, Rose to Canning, No. 55, Beirut, 30 Aug. 1842; F.O. 78/962, Finn to Redcliffe, No. 44, encl. in Finn to Clarendon, No. 30, Jerusalem, 7 Dec. 1853; F.O. 78/1219, Moore to Redcliffe, No. 67, encl. in Moore to Clarendon, No. 59, Beirut, 8 Dec. 1856; A.E. Damas, v, from Outrey, 27 Apr. 1858; see also *Aḥwāl*, MS., p. 29; Finn, i. 303.

[2] See text of the *hat*. Cf. Engelhardt, ii. 319–20; Mardin, p. 16; *Rambles*, p. 49. See also *Aḥwāl*, MS., p. 29.

[3] A.E. Jérusalem, v, No. 8, 2 Sept. 1857; F.O. 78/1383, Finn to Clarendon, No. 15, Jerusalem, 22 July 1858; Hopwood, pp. 123–4; see also F.O. 78/964, Kayat to Clarendon, separate, Jaffa, 1 Mar. 1853; Khazin, i. 114; cf. al-Ḥasībī.

[4] See and compare F.O. 78/1452, Skene to Bulwer, separate, encl. in Skene to Malmesbury, No. 42, Aleppo, 30 June 1859; F.O. 78/495, Rose to Canning, No. 36, Beirut, 29 May 1842; Wortabet, ii. 89–91.

[5] *Irade D.*, No. 462, dated 1257 (1841); 'Circular of a project for the erection of Palestine into an independent state' in CM/065, Schlien's Report (see appendix); see also Khazin, i. 114–15.

[6] See above, p. 216, n. 2; compare Poujade, p. 230.

in a secret alliance with France.[1] And according to a British source, there were also rumours in 1855 of a plan that France should occupy Palestine, this apparently being suggested by the Latin Patriarch of Jerusalem.[2]

In view of all these factors—the foreign intervention and threats, and the Christians' open intentions—it is not surprising that the common belief among the Syrian Muslim population and a large portion of the Ottoman administration, was that 'the European powers are hostile to the Turkish authority in Syria and (that) in union with the Christians they wish to overset it' and turn the country into a Christian state.[3] According to this belief, all foreign residents and visitors were spies,[4] and the local Christians were collaborators and informers. In Damascus, for instance, Christian and Jewish deputies were refused admission to the *meclis* on the grounds they they would pass its secrets to the foreign consuls.[5]

With these suspicions growing daily stronger, both Turkish officials and Arab Muslims tried wherever possible to check the foreign consuls or diminish the privileges of the Europeans and the Christian protégés.[6] Some of these restrictions were indeed imposed by orders from the *Porte*: imperial orders sent to Syria abolished, for instance, certain tax concessions for foreign subjects and local protégés,[7] and prohibited the sale of land to foreigners;[8] this prohibition continued in fact to be enforced in

1 F.O. 78/761, Wood to Palmerston, No. 14, Damascus, 8 Apr. 1848; compare *Ḥasr al-lithām*, pp. 107–8.

2 F.O. 78/1120, Finn to Clarendon, No. 13, Jerusalem, 28 May 1855.

3 See motto at the beginning of this chapter; see also F.O. 78/713, Rose to Palmerston, No. 28, Beirut, 1 June 1847; F.O. 195/292, Finn to Canning, No. 11, Jerusalem, 14 Aug. 1850; A.E. Alep, i, from Guys, No. 62, 1 July 1841; A.E. Damas, iv, from Outrey, No. 11, 23 May 1856; CM/063d, from Sanreczki, No. 514, Jerusalem, 1860; compare MacFarlane, ii. 678.

4 F.O. 78/803, Finn to Palmerston, No. 51, Jerusalem, 1 Oct. 1849; Doughty, ii. 374; Velde, i. 423–4.

5 F.O. 78/801, Wood to Canning, No. 5, encl. in Wood to Palmerston, No. 4, Damascus, 16 Feb. 1849.

6 See, for example, F.O. 195/171, Rose to Ponsonby, No. 27, Beirut, 3 June 1841; F.O. 78/1118, Wood to Redcliffe, Confidential, No. 33, encl. in Wood to Clarendon, No. 35, Damascus, 18 Aug. 1855.

7 See, for example, F.O. 78/498, Wood to Bidwell, No. 14, Damascus, 27 Jan. 1842; F.O. 78/801, Wood to Palmerston, No. 6, Damascus, 7 Mar. 1849; Taoutel, iii. 112, 115.

8 *Cevdet D.*, No. 3430, 25 Ş 1259; Jaffa *Sijill*, No. 13, 6 Z 1259; see also F.O. 78/839, Finn to Palmerston, No. 18, Jerusalem, 24 Sept. 1850; Urquhart papers, i, c (10) (4), 23 Jan. 1850

the Syrian provinces even after it was officially lifted by the 1856 *hat*.[1]

The years following the *hat* were indeed marked with a growing tendency on the part of the Ottoman authorities to check the consuls' activities and interference. Apparently to accomplish these aims the *Porte* nominated at the end of 1858 a certain Sadık *efendi* of the *Tercüme Odası* (translation office) in Istanbul as *politika memuri* (political officer) in Damascus, with orders to deal with the foreign consuls in the country.[2] Consul Brant reported at the same time from Damascus that 'the governors of provinces have secret orders to destroy the influence of European consuls',[3] while Consul Finn quoted the Pasha of Jerusalem as saying that: 'I will teach the English that they are not to treat this country as if it were India.'[4] This tendency which was accompanied by an anti-Christian attitude on the part of many Turkish Pashas can be summed up with the following statement by Consul-General Moore in April 1858:

> Within the last six months there has been a most complete and entire change of provincial ruling pashas everywhere, and in every single instance the appointed man is a religious fanatic of the first water. The old race of mild gentlemanly Turks ruling under the guidance of the European consuls seems to have vanished at a moment's notice. The Turkish functionaries have lately shewn a desire to diminish European influence and check native Christian interests.[5]

[1] F.O. 78/1298, Misk to Clarendon, No. 1, Damascus, 28 Jan. 1857; F.O. 78/1387, Kayat to Clarendon, Jaffa, 13 Jan. 1858; F.O. 78/1389, Report encl. in Skene to Malmesbury, No. 25, Aleppo, 17 June 1858.

[2] F.O. 78/1388, Brant to Bulwer, No. 63, encl. in Brant to Malmesbury, No. 17, Damascus, 29 Dec. 1858; F.O. 78/1450, same to same, No. 2, Damasus, 15 Jan. 1859.

[3] F.O. 78/1388, Brant to Malmesbury, No. 23, Damascus, 22 Apr. 1858; see also F.O. 78/1299, Moore to Redcliffe, encl. No. 2 in Moore to Clarendon, No. 2, Beirut, 21 Jan. 1857; F.O. 78/1387, Kayat to Clarendon, Jaffa, 13 Jan. 1858; F.O. 78/1389, Report from Latakia, encl. in Skene to Malmesbury, No. 52, Aleppo, 16 Oct. 1858. Cf. Davison, *Reform*, pp. 71–72; Young, ii. 231–2.

[4] F.O. 78/1537, Finn to Bulwer, No. 9, encl. in Finn to Russell, No. 8, Jerusalem, 27 Mar. 1860.

[5] F.O. 78/1385, Moore to Malmesbury, Nos. 17 and 18, Beirut, 28 Apr. 1858; see also F.O. 78/1298, Brant to Clarendon, No. 30, Beirut, 30 Dec. 1857; F.O. 78/1388, Brant to Malmesbury, No. 23, Damascus, 22 Apr. 1858; A.E. Damas, v, No. 60, 31 Mar. 1858.

C. *The authorities' attitude towards the Christians*

Unlike the Egyptian régime, which firmly sanctioned the equal rights it granted to the non-Muslims, the Turkish authorities in Syria and Palestine tended to show a lukewarm and sometimes even a hostile attitude towards Christian–Muslim equality. This was due not only to the personal views of the local Ottoman governors themselves, but was also influenced by the position taken within the *Porte* on the subject of equality. It is true that Reşid and his liberal followers succeeded, with British and French help, in bringing the Sultan to promulgate his reform edicts, despite the constant strong opposition by the powerful conservative element in Istanbul. But even Reşid himself, being aware of the popular dissatisfaction with the *reaya*'s equality, refrained from pushing this issue to extremes and preferred the gradual way. It was presumably owing to this cautious attitude that the statement on equality in the Gülhane decree was so indecisive and that certain discriminatory measures against non-Muslims, such as the *cizye*, were not removed at once. Similarly, many of the Imperial orders sent to Syria and Palestine during the Gülhane period (up to the Crimean War) dealt mainly with the security and well-being of the *reaya* as well as their religious rights, and not with substantial steps towards political equality.[1] And when in 1856 the *Hatt-ı Hümayun*, issued by Reşid's disciples Âli and Fuad, promised full equality to the *reaya*, it was criticized by Reşid himself as a product of foreign intervention and as going too far too fast in granting political privileges to the Christians.[2]

If this was the attitude of the architect of the Tanzimat, it is not surprising that the attitude of the Turkish Pashas in Syria, who were not always in favour of reform, was even more reserved. Admittedly, a considerable number of Turkish Pashas, mostly liberal but also some conservative, would endeavour, often under foreign pressure, to protect the *reaya* against molestation by the local Muslims;[3] they would likewise enforce, t[illegible] greater or lesser

[1] See *Irade D.*, No. 1402, 16 ZA 1256; *Irade H.*, No. 527, 3 CA 1257; Jaffa *Sijill*, No. 13, 11 ZA 1256; *Takvim-i Vekayi*, No. 235, 10 L 1257; F.O. 78/761, Wood to Canning, No. 26, encl. in Wood to Palmerston, No. 26, Damascus, 18 Oct. 1848; F.O. 78/871, Wood to Canning, encl. No. 2 in Wood to Palmerston, No. 17, Damascus, 28 May 1851; Khazin, i. 52–53. Cf. above, pp. 201–2.

[2] See Cevdet, *Tezakir*, i. 68–69, 76 ff.; see also Engelhardt, i. 140–1.

[3] See *Irade H.*, No. 462/4, 25 M 1258; *Irade M.V.*, No. 5184, 21 Ş 1266; F.O.

degree, the decrees granting religious rights to the non-Muslim communities, this despite Muslim intrusion.[1] Some of the reformist and able Pashas would also, on certain occasions, back non-Muslims in the administration of justice or occasionally make special gestures towards the *reaya*.[2] But hardly any of these officials would go much beyond the point of securing the safety, well-being, and religious rights of the non-Muslim subjects and grant them full equality. This was partly because of the reactionary pressure brought to bear on the Pashas, as already mentioned, by conservative elements either in Istanbul or in the province itself;[3] and in fact a few liberal governors in Syria were dismissed because they showed pro-Christian inclinations.[4] Not all the well-intentioned Pashas were able to stand against such pressure and reverse these reactionary trends; some governors were even forced to take a conservative position in order to win the goodwill of the Muslim population.[5]

Yet it seems that the major cause for the reserved attitude of the liberal Pashas on the subject of equality was that many regarded the Christians as an instrument of foreign encroachment and thus as a political danger to the Ottoman state. These reformist Pashas would therefore prefer to carry out reforms in other realms of life than to place the Christians on the same footing as the Muslims. The best example for such an attitude was perhaps Mehmed Kıbrıslı Paşa, who became the reformist Grand Vezir in 1853, and who, while serving previously in Palestine and Syria,

195/331, Moore to Canning, No. 55, Beirut, 4 Nov. 1849; F.O. 78/960, Werry to Redcliffe, No. 15, encl. in Werry to Clarendon, No. 12, Aleppo, 23 Aug. 1853; A.E. Damas, i, from Munton, No. 2, 6 Jan. 1841; A.E. Damas, ii, from de Barrère, No. 24, 14 July 1851; al-Bāshā, pp. 235–8; Manṣūr, p. 88.

[1] F.O. 78/579, Wood to Aberdeen, No. 20, Damascus, 26 June 1844; F.O. 78/872, Wood to Palmerston, No. 26, Damascus, 28 July 1851; A.E. Damas, iii, No. 24, 27 May 1855; CM/041 from Klein, 2 Feb. 1842; *Rambles*, pp. 77–79.

[2] F.O. 78/538, Wood to Aberdeen, No. 32, Damascus, 8 Sept. 1843; F.O. 78/801, Wood to Palmerston, No. 7, Damascus, 13 Mar. 1849; A.E. Damas, ii, from de Barrère, No. 6, 21 May 1850; al-Bāshā, pp. 237–9.

[3] See above, pp. 68–69.

[4] See F.O. 78/447, Werry to Bidwell, No. 5, Damascus, 6 May 1841; F.O. 78/622, Wood to Aberdeen, No. 39, Damascus, 10 Nov. 1845; F.O. 195/210, Young to Canning, No. 27, Jerusalem, 27 Aug. 1844; see also A.E. Damas, i, from Munton, No. 9, 27 Mar. 1842.

[5] F.O. 78/497, Werry to Aberdeen, No. 6, Aleppo, 2 Sept. 1842; F.O. 78/714, Timoni to Wellesley, No. 8, encl. in Timoni to Palmerston, No. 6, Damascus, 30 Apr. 1847; F.O. 78/1383, Finn to Redcliffe, No. 32, encl. in Finn to Malmesbury, No. 29, Jerusalem, 24 Oct. 1858; see also Bazili, ii. 3.

firmly carried out many administrative reforms and granted to the local Christians a considerable measure of security and religious freedom.[1] This Pasha, however, was reported to be 'decidedly anti-Christian and anti-European'; he expressed this by 'exalting the Moslem nationality and patriotism . . . accompanied it by reducing . . . the influence of the Europeans and with it the rights and equalities of the Christian Rayahs generally'.[2]

If this was the attitude of the prominent reformer Kıbrıslı Paşa, there is no doubt that the conservative Pashas who served in the Syrian provinces in great frequency were even less moderate over this issue. A considerable number of such officials indeed 'made themselves conspicuous, more or less, by their fanaticism, anti-Christian and anti-progressive policy'.[3] For example, some would support forced conversion of Christians (and Jews) to Islam;[4] others would occasionally impose various restrictions on the *reaya*, refer to them in offensive terms, or even engage themselves in maltreatment of non-Muslims.[5] Certain Turkish Pashas would, furthermore, promote anti-European and anti-Christian feelings among both the soldiers and the Muslim population, urging them 'to be ready to run to arms as soon as danger threatened Mahometanism'.[6] In small towns, where central control was less

[1] A.E. Damas, ii, from Segur, No. 30, Oct. 1851; Taoutel, iii. 148.

[2] F.O. 78/871, Werry to Canning, No. 34, encl. in Werry to Palmerston, No. 13, Aleppo, 30 Aug. 1850; see also Melek Hanum, pp. 78–79; compare F.O. 78/761, Wood to Palmerston, No. 10, Damascus, 4 Mar. 1848.

[3] F.O. 78/801, Wood to Canning, No. 20, encl. in Wood to Palmerston, No. 23, Damascus, 25 Sept. 1849; see also A.E. Damas, ii, from de Barrère, No. 6, 28 May 1850.

[4] See *Irade M.V.*, No. 1818, 27 L 1263; F.O. 78/660A, Wood to Aberdeen, No. 7, Damascus, 9 Mar. 1840; F.O. 78/713, Rose to Palmerston, No. 46, Broumana, 8 Dec. 1847; F.O. 78/761, Wood to Palmerston, No. 10, Damascus, 11 Mar. 1848.

[5] F.O. 78/456, Rose to Palmerston, No. 72, Gazir, 23 July 1841; F.O. 78/801, Wood to Palmerston, No. 29, Damascus, 29 Oct. 1849; *Accounts and Papers*, LX (1843), pt. i, No. 5, Grand Vezir to Necib Paşa, encl. in Ponsonby to Palmerston, Therapia, 15 June 1841; CM/028 from Bishop Gobat, 5 Aug. 1841; *Ḥasr al-lithām*, p. 71; Paton, p. 33; Taoutel, iii. 28. Christians and Jews were occasionally referred to by the authorities in offensive terms even after this practice was forbidden by the 1856 *hat*. See, for example, F.O. 78/1219, Moore to Clarendon, No. 62, Beirut, 19 Dec. 1856; F.O. 78/1298, Misk to Clarendon, No. 9, Damascus, 19 June 1857; F.O. 78/1383, Finn to Malmesbury, No. 34, Jerusalem, 11 Nov. 1858; Mishāqa, MS., p. 347.

[6] See F.O. 78/494, Rose to Aberdeen, Beirut, 5 Apr. 1842; see also F.O. 78/498, Wood to Aberdeen, No. 23, Damascus, 25 Feb. 1842; F.O. 195/320, Rose to Canning, No. 20, Beirut, 11 Aug. 1848; F.O. 78/871, Werry to Canning, No. 35, encl. in Werry to Palmerston, No. 14, Aleppo, 10 Sept. 1851.

effective, the authorities tended to violate more frequently the rights of the local *reaya*.[1]

A similar attitude was taken by government troops—both regular and irregular—who would from time to time insult and attack Christians and Jews,[2] (although admittedly not without being usually punished afterwards by their superiors).[3] One conspicuous case of such behaviour took place at the Christian village of Maʿlūla in Anti-Lebanon, where irregular soldiers killed and robbed a number of unarmed inhabitants while searching for rebels during October 1850.[4] Another such case occurred in August 1859 in the village of Maʿlaqa near Zahle, in which Turkish soldiers violated a church and insulted and attacked the priests.[5] The attitude of the city police, who were recruited from Syrian Muslims, was obviously even more hostile. When, for example, in the critical days of 1860 the military commander of Aleppo was giving the local police instructions and asking them what they would do if they saw a Muslim and a Christian quarrelling, 'one of the policemen replied with the utmost simplicity that he would take the Ghiaoor (infidel) to prison, of course'.[6]

In these circumstances it is not surprising that the Muslim masses themselves, who possessed, as we know, deep motives for disliking the Christians, were occasionally involved in anti-Christian hostilities which took place in the country during the period under survey. It is true that some Muslim leaders disapproved of the use of violence against Christians, and would sometimes protect members of the Christian communities against the mob's violence.[7] But even those notables were opposed

[1] See F.O. 78/455, Rose to Palmerston, No. 31, Beirut, 4 May 1841; F.O. 78/1389, Report from Latakia, encl. in Skene to Malmesbury, No. 52, Aleppo, 16 Oct. 1858; F.O. 78/1294, Finn to Clarendon, No. 1, Jerusalem, 1 Jan. 1857 in Hyamson, i. 245; A.E. Alep, i, from Guys, No. 66, 10 Sept. 1841.

[2] F.O. 78/444, Young to Palmerston, No. 5, Jaffa, 25 Jan. 1841; F.O. 78/1383, Finn to Malmesbury, No. 33, Jerusalem, 8 Nov. 1858; A.E. Jérusalem, i, from Lantivy, No. 53, 18 Apr. 1844; A.E. Damas, ii, from Bourville, No. 11, 20 Mar. 1848.

[3] See, for example, F.O. 78/455, Rose to Palmerston, No. 70, Beirut, 28 May 1841; F.O. 78/836, Moore to Palmerston, No. 21, Beirut, 1 Apr. 1850.

[4] See F.O. 195/291, Calvert to Canning, No. 29, Damascus, 23 Oct. 1850.

[5] *Irade H.*, No. 9507/9, 28 B 1276; A.E. Damas, v, from Outrey, No. 77, 14 Aug. 1859; F.O. 78/1454, Brant to Bulwer, No. 26, encl. in Brant to Russell, No. 7, Damascus, 24 Sept. 1859.

[6] *Rambles*, p. 251.

[7] See F.O. 78/448, Werry to Ponsonby, Aleppo, 29 Jan. 1841; F.O. 195/170, Wood to Bankhead, No. 16, Damascus, 15 Dec. 1841; F.O. 78/836, Rose to

to Christian equality in principle and would, alongside other 'Ulema, use their great influence and official positions as heads of the religious institutions and as councillors, to subvert the new privileges of the *reaya*.[1] On the other hand, a large portion of the Muslim leadership—'Ulema and members of the *meclis*—did foment, back, or direct virtually all anti-Christian riots of that period,[2] the gravest of which occurred in the period following the promulgation of the *Hatt-ı Hümayun* of February 1856.

Canning, No. 47, encl. in Rose to Palmerston, No. 48, Beirut, 3 Nov. 1856; A.E. Damas, iv, from Outrey, No. 24, 12 Jan. 1857; *Birjīs Barīs*, Nos. 33 and 40; Taoutel, iii. 31; Manṣūr, p. 89. See also below, p. 230.

[1] See, for example, A.E. Damas, i, from Munton, No. 2, 6 Jan. 1841; F.O. 195/207, Werry to Canning, No. 17, Aleppo, 23 Sept. 1843; F.O. 78/619, Wood to Canning, No. 30, encl. in Wood to Aberdeen, No. 41, Damascus, 4 Dec. 1845; F.O. 78/1217, Finn to Clarendon, No. 55, Jerusalem, 1 Sept. 1856; al-Bāshā, pp. 235 ff.; Finn, ii. 20; Paton, pp. 33–34. Note that Amir 'Abd al-Qādir, the great saviour of Christians during the 1860 events, was reported to have said that if he were to be the governor of Syria he 'would not allow Christians to enter the army nor to testify against Moslems as Christians can never be on an equality with Moslems'. See Jessup, i. 203.

[2] See *Irade M.V.*, No. 5184, 21 Ş 1266; F.O. 195/234, Rose to Canning, No. 20, Beirut, 8 Mar. 1844; F.O. 78/801, Wood to Palmerston, No. 7, Damascus, 13 Mar. 1849; A.E. Damas, iii, from de Jong, 6 Feb. 1853; F.O. 195/416, Barker to Redcliffe, No. 25, Aleppo, 28 June 1856; F.O. 195/524, Finn to Redcliffe, No. 29, Jerusalem, 22 July 1857; CM/034 from Revd. Jacob, Nazareth, 30 Sept. 1858; Taoutel, ii. 76; Urquhart, ii. 68–69; see also below, the incidents in Nablus, Gaza, and Maraş, pp. 226 ff.

XVII

THE EVENTS OF 1856–60

A. *The Nablus riots and the subsequent tension*

THE promulgation of the 1856 *hat*, which aimed at integrating all Ottoman subjects into one political community, achieved exactly the opposite—a complete rift between Muslims and Christians throughout Syria and Palestine. Hardly was this edict proclaimed in the country when in Nablus there were anti-Christian and anti-European riots, in which one Christian was killed, a church and several Christian houses sacked, and European consular agencies were attacked. The immediate events which led to this rioting were the following. A few days before the outbreak the Anglican Bishop of Jerusalem, on receiving the news of the proclamation of the *Hatt-ı Hümayun*, acted at once and on his own initiative, without the approval of the authorities, placed a bell in the Nablus local chapel and started ringing it. In the same manner, a day or two later, on 2 April 1856, the French, English, and Prussian consular agents hoisted their countries' flags on the occasion of the birth of the French Crown Prince. As if all this was not enough to inflame the feeling of the Nablus Muslims who were notorious for their conservative and intolerant spirit,[1] and who indeed felt so strongly that on the day following, 3 April, a Friday, they interrupted the noon service in the mosque to go out and demonstrate in protest; on the very day of the demonstration there occurred the shooting of a Muslim by an English missionary, the Reverend Lyde. According to the latter and to European sources, the Muslim, a deaf beggar, was killed by a shot accidentally fired from Lyde's rifle while the former was forcibly demanding charity.[2] A local Arabic source claims, however, that after Lyde had been walking about the town for some thirty

[1] See Finn, i. 207, 296–7; Murray, ii. 333; Tristram, *Israel*, p. 139; Wortabet, ii. 142–3.

[2] On the Nablus riots and their motives, see and compare F.O. 78/1217, Finn to Clarendon, No. 21, Jerusalem, 10 Apr. 1856; ibid., Young to Finn, encl. in No. 26, 14 Apr. 1856; ibid., No. 60, 11 Sept. 1856; A.E. Jérusalem, v, from de Barrère, No. 9, 17 May 1856; Finn, ii. 424–8, 434; Manṣūr, pp. 88–89.

days under suspicious circumstances and escorted by local Christian guards, he was attacked by the deaf Muslim who was then shot by one of the guards.[1] At any rate this accident became the signal for the anti-Christian riots led by the local 'Ulema which could easily have turned into a general massacre had not the local governor intervened and controlled the mob.[2] During the whole tumult, which involved also the destruction of the European and Ottoman flags, the local Jews and Samaritans remained unharmed.

The Nablus event has been described in some detail because both its causes and main characteristics are to be found underlying the factors and elements which were the source of Muslim–Christian tension during the years 1856–60, and which also helped to produce the 1860 massacres in Damascus.

In the first place anti-Christian feelings swelled as a result of the fundamental Muslim reluctance to give up their traditional superiority and to accept the Christians as equals—a principle which was stressed by the 1856 *hat*. Secondly, related to it and no less powerful, was the Muslim anxiety lest the country should 'be taken by the Europeans'[3] with the help of the local Christians—the two were now identical in the eyes of the Muslims and in some places were jointly called *naṣārā* (Christians).[4] Muslim feelings were now kept alive by the superficial symbols of Christian equality and foreign influence: the ringing of bells, the carrying of crosses, etc., and the hoisting of foreign banners. It should be noted here that up to the end of 1855, no European consulates flew their national flags except in one case in 1843 when the *tricolor* was hoisted at the French consulate in Jerusalem and, provoking a violent Muslim disturbance, was quickly lowered and stored away.[5] But after the Crimean War, European flags were hoisted in all Syrian towns and greatly irritated the Muslims;[6] in the southern town of Gaza, there was, for example, another anti-European and anti-Christian disturbance in April 1856

[1] Al-Nimr, pp. 270–1. [2] Ibid.

[3] CM/063d, from Sanreczki, No. 514, Jerusalem, 1860; A.E. Damas, iv, from Outrey, No. 11, 23 May 1856.

[4] See F.O. 78/1217, Finn to Clarendon, No. 37, Jerusalem, 26 May 1856.

[5] A.E. Jérusalem, i, from Lantivy, No. 4, 29 June 1848; F.O. 195/210, Young to Canning, No. 14, Jerusalem, 4 Aug. 1843.

[6] F.O. 78/1121, Finn to Clarendon, No. 37, Jerusalem, 27 Oct. 1855; F.O. 78/1298, Brant to Clarendon, No. 30, Damascus, 30 Dec. 1857; Finn, ii. 37. Note that even the Russian flag was hoisted in the town of Haifa by the end of 1856, F.O. 195/524, Finn to Redcliffe, No. 76, Jerusalem, 17 Dec. 1856.

following the hanging out of the Austrian flag by the local consular agent.[1]

Tension grew stronger as the conduct of the Christians, both European and Ottoman, became, in Muslim eyes, more defiant. Some ten days after the Nablus riots there occurred a similar outbreak in Maraş, a town across the northern border of Syria, in which the English consular agent (a local Christian) and his family were murdered by a Muslim mob. These murders occurred after Mr. Guarmani, the consular agent, had insulted the local kadi in the *mahkeme*.[2] The subsequent years saw a number of similar misdeeds by Christians and Europeans in places such as Damascus, Aleppo, Jerusalem, and Latakia: in these cases Muslims were insulted, their religious feelings affronted, and at least two Muslim notables were murdered.[3] Simultaneously, particularly in the second half of 1858 and onwards, rumours were rife throughout the country of the smuggling of French arms to Lebanon, of Christian plots against Muslims, and of European intentions to attack the Empire.[4] These stories were supported by old prophecies of an approaching conflict between Christianity and Islam and were confirmed by the news of events like the shelling of Jidda by French and English warships, the Christian uprising in Crete and the Balkans, and the anti-British insurrection in India.[5]

All this produced feelings of alarm and deep hatred among the Muslims of Syria and Palestine; great quantities of arms were purchased and the anti-Christian atmosphere intensified.[6] In

[1] F.O. 195/424, Kayat to Redcliffe, No. 3, Jaffa, 4 Apr. 1856.

[2] F.O. 78/1200, a letter from Maraş dated 13 Apr. 1856, encl. in Barker to Clarendon, No. 8, Aleppo, 2 Apr. 1856.

[3] A.E. Damas, v, from Outrey, No. 61, 14 Aug. 1858; F.O. 78/1388, Brant to Malmesbury, No. 11, Damascus, 21 Aug. 1858; F.O. 78/1294, Finn to Clarendon, No. 30, Jerusalem, 30 July 1857; F.O. 78/1452, Skene to Bulwer, separate, encl. in Skene to Malmesbury, No. 42, Aleppo, 30 June 1859.

[4] F.O. 78/1386, Moore to Malmesbury, No. 49, Beirut, 4 Aug. 1858; F.O. 78/1538, Skene to Bulwer, No. 18, encl. in Skene to Russell, No. 32, Aleppo, 12 June 1860; A.E. Alep, iii, from Bentivoglio, No. 5, 29 July 1858; Edwards, p. 171; Farley, *The Massacres*, pp. 108 ff.

[5] F.O. 78/1389, Skene to Alison, No. 20, encl. in Skene to Malmesbury, No. 33, Aleppo, 7 Aug. 1858; F.O. 78/1388, Brant to Malmesbury, No. 11, Damascus, 21 Aug. 1858; A.E. Damas, v, from Outrey, No. 62, 30 Aug. 1858; A.E. Alep, iii, from Bentivoglio, No. 5, 29 July 1858; CM/063d, from Sanreczki, No. 535, 1858.

[6] A.E. Damas, vi, from de Barrère, No. 12, 3 Aug. 1858; F.O. 78/1386, encl. in Moore to Malmesbury, No. 47, Beirut, 22 July 1858; F.O. 78/1389, Skene to

the second half of 1858 there even appeared some signs of an anti-Christian conspiracy throughout the country. In certain Palestinian towns, Muslim Dervishes were reported to have preached about the coming destruction of local Christians.[1] A report by a Protestant missionary alleged, at the same time, plots by the kadi of Nazareth and the 'Ulema of Tyre to slaughter their respective Christian townsmen.[2] Vice-Consul Abela of Sidon reported likewise on a great number of secret meetings between Muslims, Druzes, and Mutawalis in Lebanon, 'The object being a general massacre of Christians'.[3] From Aleppo a consular dispatch of July 1858 stated that 'Musulmans secretly announced to respectable European families with whom they were on friendly terms that a general massacre was about to commence'.[4] In the same month the English Consul-General in Syria informed Admiral Fanshaw, the commander of a British naval force near Syrian waters, that 'the large interior cities such as Damascus and Aleppo, as well as the sea coast towns, are liable at any moment to a Mahomedan rising against the Christians and Europeans residing thereat'.[5]

Similar signs of a general anti-Christian plot reappeared during the second quarter of 1860. In Aleppo, for example, placards were found at the end of April on the doors of local mosques inciting Muslims to attack the Christians in order to prevent the latter's designed assault.[6] Likewise in Latakia Muslims were reported to have said: 'We know that our country will be taken by the Europeans, but before that we will destroy as many Christians as we can.'[7]

It should be remembered here also that during those critical

Alison, No. 20, encl. in Skene to Malmesbury, No. 33, Aleppo, 7 Aug. 1858; F.O. 78/1383, Finn to Clarendon, No. 28, Jerusalem, 12 Oct. 1858; CM/063d, from Sanreczki, No. 535, 1858.

1 F.O. 78/1833, Finn to Malmesbury, No. 11, Jerusalem, 8 July 1858; CM/063d, No. 509, from Sanreczki, 22 May 1858; compare Madden, ii. 270–1.

2 CM/034, from Revd. Jacob, Nazareth, 30 Sept. 1858; ibid., 31 Dec. 1858.

3 F.O. 78/1383, Finn to Malmesbury, No. 30, Jerusalem, 8 Nov. 1858.

4 Skene to Alison, 31 July 1858, cited in Farley, *The Massacres*, p. 67; Taoutel, ii. 96.

5 F.O. 78/1386, encl. in Moore to Malmesbury, No. 47, Beirut, 22 July 1858; Farley, op. cit., p. 68. See also F.O. 78/1389, Report from Lataika, encl. in Skene to Malmesbury, No. 52, Aleppo, 16 Oct. 1858.

6 F.O. 78/1538, Skene to Bulwer, No. 8, encl. in Skene to Russell, No. 19, Aleppo, 30 Apr. 1860; A.E. Alep, iii, No. 1, 3 May 1860; *Birjīs Barīs*, ii, No. 25, 29 May 1860; *Ha-Karmel*, i, No. 2, 28 Apr. 1860; *Rambles*, pp. 242–4.

7 CM/063d, from Sanreczki, No. 514, dated 1860.

years, 1858–60, the Turkish authorities themselves showed a hostile attitude towards Europeans and to a certain extent also towards local Christians.[1] In addition, the Turkish military force in the country was relatively very small, was ill-paid and ill-trained, and contained also a number of local Muslim recruits.[2]

Nevertheless, in many places the Turkish authorities managed to avert a full-blooded slaughter of Christians by Muslims. In Aleppo, for example, prompt military action avoided a major outbreak in August 1858 and twice in mid-1860,[3] and in towns such as Jerusalem, Nablus, Homs, Hama, and Latakia too, the Turkish authorities were able to prevent or check Muslim attacks by taking strict military precautions.[4] Similarly, the appearance of European warships stopped Christian bloodshed at Sidon in the first week of June 1860,[5] and prevented similar outbreaks in other coastal towns such as Beirut, Acre, Haifa, and Jaffa.[6] In places like Aleppo, Beirut, Antioch, and Jaffa, local Muslim notables also endeavoured to restrain their co-religionists from attacking Christians;[7] and in Northern Palestine peace and order was maintained by the strict control of ʿAqīl *aǧa*, the famous Bedouin chief.[8]

[1] See above, p. 223, also *Aḥwāl*, MS., pp. 29–30. Note, for example, a remark by the Pasha of Jerusalem in October 1858, that during the rule of his predecessor 'the Christians had too much liberty and that now it is time to put all to rights'. F.O. 78/1383, Finn to Redcliffe, No. 32, encl. in Finn to Malmesbury, No. 29, Jerusalem, 24 Oct. 1858.

[2] See above, p. 54.

[3] See F.O. 78/1389, Skene to Alison, No. 20, encl. in Skene to Malmesbury, No. 33, Aleppo, 7 Aug. 1858; F.O. 78/1557, Skene to Bulwer, No. 21, encl. in Skene to Russell, No. 36, Aleppo, 28 June 1860; A.E. Alep, iii, from Geofroy, No. 4, 20 July 1860; *Rambles*, pp. 250–2.

[4] See F.O. 78/1521, Finn to Russell, No. 1, Jerusalem, 4 Jan. 1860; F.O. 78/1557, letters to Consul Finn from Haifa dated 29 June 1860, encl. in Finn to Russell, No. 20, Jerusalem, 17 July 1860; F.O. 78/1538, Skene to Bulwer, No. 11, encl. in Skene to Russell, No. 21, Aleppo, 1 May 1860; Edwards, pp. 160–2; L. Shaykhū, *Nubdha mukhtaṣara fī hawādith Lubnān wa'l-Shām* (Beirut, 1927), pp. 32–33.

[5] F.O. 78/1519, Moore to Russell, No. 11, Beirut, 7 June 1860; F.O. 78/1521, Finn to Bulwer, No. 21, encl. in Finn to Russell, No. 12, Jerusalem, 19 June 1860; Baedeker, p. 433; Shaykhū, op. cit., pp. 23–24.

[6] CM/045 from Kruze, Jaffa, 2 Aug. 1860; *Birjīs Barīs*, No. 34; *Ḥasr al-lithām*, p. 237; Manṣūr, p. 91.

[7] See F.O. 78/1537, Kayat to Russell, No. 13, Jaffa, 17 July 1860; F.O. 195/595, White to Skene, Antioch, 19 July 1860, encl. in Skene to Bulwer, No. 24, Aleppo, 21 July 1860; F.O. 78/1521, Finn to Russell, No. 25, Jerusalem, 31 July 1860; F.O. 78/1538, Skene to Bulwer, No. 29, encl. in Skene to Russell, No. 51, Aleppo, 23 Aug. 1860; CM/045 from Kruze, Jaffa, 2 Aug. 1860; F.O. 78/1627, Bulwer to Dufferin, No. 90, Beirut, 30 Dec. 1860; Shaykhū, op. cit., pp. 22, 34–35.

[8] F.O. 78/1521, op. cit., No. 26, 2 Aug. 1860.

B. *The Damascus Massacre*

Only in Damascus (and previously in Lebanon) events had taken a different course and in mid-July 1860 serious riots broke out in which thousands of Christians—men, women, and children—were massacred and many others injured; women violated or abducted, and children forced to adopt Islam. Most Christian houses, churches, and convents, were sacked, destroyed, or burnt down. Such was also the fate of a great number of European consulates (the Russian consulate was the first to be attacked) and even foreign subjects, including some consuls, were not spared by the rioters.[1]

The Damascus massacre was the culmination of the Muslim–Christian antagonism which developed from the Tanzimat reforms, notably the *Hatt-ı Hümayun* of 1856. The religious, economic and, especially, political motives underlying this enmity have already been described, but in Damascus these were more intense. No less disastrous was the provocative Christian behaviour which reached its peak on the eve of the outbreak. A number of other factors also played a critical part in starting the riots and in determining their huge size and great bitterness.

To begin with, the Muslim population of Damascus, a major centre of Islam, was no doubt more sensitive than other Muslims in the country to the change in the traditional orthodox character of the city.[2] Their feelings were therefore deeply hurt when the local Christians started to display their new religious privileges, particularly after 1856; as Consul Brant wrote, for example, in 1860: 'A large bell lately placed in the Maronite church gave great umbrage. The magnificent Lazarist convent was not seen with pleasure;' nor were the wine shops opened in market places or the green dress worn by Christians.[3]

[1] For more details on the Damascus massacre, see F.O. 78/1520, Brant to Russell, No. 8, Damascus, 16 July 1860; ibid., No. 12, 11 Aug.; Abkāriūs, p. 131; al-ʿAqīqī, p. 117; Farley, *The Massacres*, pp. 118–19; Mishāqa, MS., pp. 352 ff.; Porter, *Bashan*, pp. 346 ff. See also below, pp. 236–7.

[2] Safveti Paşa, who was the *vali* of Damascus in 1847, was reported, for example, to have said: 'I am aware of the sentiments of the inhabitants of the city who are not in the same state as in the other parts of the Empire.' See F.O. 78/714, Timoni to Wellesley, No. 13, encl. in Timoni to Palmerston, No. 11, Damascus, 9 June 1847; cf. A.E. Damas, ii, 30 Nov. 1843. See also F.O. 195/194, Rose to Canning, No. 35, Beirut, 27 May 1842; A.E. Damas, ii, No. 24, 14 July 1851; al- Ḥasībī.

[3] F.O. 78/1520, Brant to Bulwer, No. 40, encl. in Brant to Russell, No. 17, Damascus, 6 Sept. 1860; see also Abkāriūs, p. 127.

The economic motive behind the Muslims' animosity was equally powerful: while the Damascus Christians were, as already described, growing richer through foreign trade and in government employment, large sections of the local Muslim population were either suffering acute economic distress or did not find their prosperity increasing proportionately.[1]

Above all, the Muslim population of the Syrian capital was deeply concerned about the threat both to their dominant role in the country and to the integrity of the Muslim state, which had allegedly arisen from the political equality granted to the Christian and from the suspected Christian-European co-operation.[2] These feelings were confirmed and enforced not only by the recent events in Jidda, Crete, and India, but—more significantly—by the behaviour of the Christians of Damascus themselves. The latter apparently lost all sense of proportion and went too far too fast in interpreting and practising their new equal rights. Mishāqa, himself a local Christian, put it in the following way:

> It is necessary for them to know that the grandees of the land . . . its government and ministers and the army and all its senior people are Muslims, and that the Christians in Syria are the smallest portion in everything and in every respect; they ought to show utmost respect to the Muslims and complete obedience to the ruler.[3]

Indeed, from the Muslim point of view, the Christians of Damascus behaved with considerable defiance and insolence, particularly over the issue of the *bedel.* It has already been mentioned that the Damascus Christians, unlike those in other towns and unlike the local Jewish community, were reluctant to pay this tax, on the plea that it was high and burdensome and at variance with the principles of equality. They maintained this refusal even after some of their leaders had been arrested and agreed to pay, insisting on being conscripted instead.[4] This atti-

[1] See above, pp. 182–5; see also Baedeker, p. 467; *Nafīr Sūriyya*, No. 8 (1861).

[2] *Kitāb al-aḥzān*, pp. 252–3; Abkāriūs, p. 127; Nādir al-ʿAṭṭār, *Ta'rīkh Sūriyya* (Damascus, 1962), p. 213.

[3] Mishāqa, MS., pp. 343 ff. See also Abkāriūs, p. 127.

[4] A.E. Damas, v, from Outrey, No. 63, 27 Sept. 1858; ibid., No. 70, 14 Feb. 1859; Mishāqa, MS., p. 346; al-Ḥasībī; *Kitāb al-aḥzān*, p. 254.

tude, although justified in principle, was in practice not completely genuine. Firstly, the *bedel*, although bigger than the former *cizye*, was not levied on every adult but demanded from the community *en bloc* in lieu of a certain number of recruits (forty-eight in Aleppo, for example).[1] Secondly, the Christians were not sincerely willing to serve in the army, but pretended to be so, calculating that the government, unwilling to recruit them, would exempt them from the *bedel* too; if it did nevertheless conscript them, they could then pay the exemption fee as Muslim recruits, although this fee was bigger than the *bedel* for the *reaya*.[2] According to the French consul in Damascus, the local Christians were encouraged in their stand by the fact that they were situated near Mount Lebanon where the Maronites had also refused to pay the *bedel*. This consul, as well as his English colleague, strongly disapproved of the Christians' attitude and warned them that he would not protect them if they continued to disobey the *Porte*'s orders.[3]

The reaction of the Damascus Muslims was obviously more acute: in Muslim eyes the Christians who disobeyed the Sultan's orders and who had ceased to pay the *cizye* were rebels and were 'no longer entitled to their lives'.[4] The local *meclis* shared also the view that the Christians were revolting against authority and issued a *mazbata* in 1859 recommending the collection of the *bedel* by force.[5] Such was, moreover, the standpoint of Ahmed Izzet Paşa, the *vali* and the *serasker* in Damascus, who was said to have reported to his government in Istanbul that the local Christians were revolting.[6] The attitude of Ahmed Paşa in those critical days of 1860 carried indeed great weight since it played a decisive role in determining the development of events.

Ahmed Paşa had served as *vali* of Damascus for about a year in 1856–7 and at the end of 1858 he was appointed to the office of

[1] F.O. 78/1220, Barker to Redcliffe, No. 28, encl. in Barker to Clarendon, No. 13, Aleppo, 30 July 1856; F.O. 78/1219, Misk to Moore, Damascus, 14 Aug., encl. in Moore to Clarendon, No. 37, Beirut, 18 Aug. 1856; Finn, i. 172–3.

[2] Mishāqa, MS., p. 344; compare F.O. 78/1220, Misk to Clarendon, No. 14, Damascus, 27 Aug. 1856.

[3] A.E. Damas, iv, from Outrey, No. 14, 16 Aug. 1856; ibid., 16 Nov. 1856.

[4] F.O. 78/1521, Finn to Russell, No. 32, Jerusalem, 16 May 1860; Abkāriūs, p. 162; *Aḥwāl*, MS., p. 25; *Kitāb al-aḥzān*, pp. 51–52; Mishāqa, MS., p. 347; see also A.E. Damas, iv, from Outrey, No. 14, 16 Aug. 1856; ibid., v, No. 70, 14 Feb. 1859.

[5] A.E. Damas, v, from Outrey, No. 71, 28 Feb. 1859; Mishāqa, MS., p. 347; *Kitāb al-aḥzān*, pp. 51–52.

[6] Ibid., p. 254; Jurjī Zaydān, *Asīr al-Mutmahdī* (Egypt, 1901), p. 303.

Commander-in-Chief of the Syrian army. In each of these posts the Pasha showed great energy and competence and was able to maintain order, check local turbulent elements, and occasionally to protect Christians against Muslim maltreatment.[1] At the beginning of 1859 the *vali* of Damascus was recalled and *serasker* Ahmed Paşa was authorized to administer also the civil affairs of the *eyalet*, and in April 1859 he was officially nominated to the joint office of Commander-in-Chief and *vali* of Damascus.[2] But in the course of the subsequent months, Ahmed's attitude to his duties changed: he apparently lost interest in his office and ceased to carry out his functions with the same zeal as before. Consul Brant, who reported this, explained that the Pasha had been expecting to be transferred to another post in Rumelia or Baghdad but this appointment was cancelled for the time being; 'The uncertainty therefore of His Excellency's position seemed to have slackened his zeal and to have rendered him indifferent to the good government of a pashalik he was so soon to give up.'[3]

Another factor which presumably had a discouraging effect on Ahmed's position was the recall—in May–June 1859 and a year later—of a substantial number of his troops back to Istanbul: 'The Seraskeir is said to have represented that were his force diminished, he should not be able to maintain his authority.'[4]

Ahmed's authority in those days had been indeed challenged from a number of quarters. Firstly, he had aroused the opposition of the local *ağa*s who usually served in the irregular force: at the beginning of 1859, after a tumult in the Maydān (a Damascus quarter), Ahmed arrested forty *ağa*s and banished them to Acre; subsequently, the irregular troops were disbanded and a new force—the *avniye*—was organized.[5] Secondly, the Pasha was

[1] See F.O. 78/1298, Misk to Clarendon, Damascus, 25 Mar. 1857; F.O. 78/1454, Brant to Bulwer, No. 7, encl. in Brant to Malmesbury, No. 2, Damascus, 28 Jan. 1859; *Kitāb al-aḥzān*, p. 255; cf. *Irade M.M.*, No. 603, 20 Ş 1275; al-Bayṭār, i. 260–1.

[2] F.O. 78/1450, Brant to Bulwer, No. 1, encl. in Brant to Malmesbury, No. 2, Damascus, 15 Jan. 1859; ibid., No. 16, encl. to Malmesbury, No. 8, 23 Apr. 1859.

[3] F.O. 78/1454, Brant to Bulwer, separate, encl. in Brant to Malmesbury, No. 6, Damascus, 4 July 1859.

[4] F.O. 78/1454, Brant to Bulwer, No. 22, encl. in Brant to Malmesbury, Damascus, 20 June 1859.

[5] *Irade M.M.*, No. 603, 20 Ş 1275; F.O. 78/1454, Brant to Bulwer, No. 7, encl. in Brant to Malmesbury, No. 2, Damascus, 28 Jan. 1859; see also above, pp. 59–60.

criticized by large sections of the Muslim population for his inability to collect the *bedel* from the Christians and for his general misrule. The critics, who were backed by the prominent member of the local ʿUlema, Sheikh ʿAbdullāh Ḥalabī, even sent a petition against Ahmed to the *Porte*. In order to neutralize the effect of this petition, the Pasha had to obtain a *mazbata* in his favour from the *meclis*; this he managed to do only after he had succeeded in winning the support of Sheikh Ḥalabī himself, apparently by granting him, in return, a piece of government land at a negligible price.[1]

Against this background of the Pasha's precarious position, the Christians' provocative behaviour, and the Muslims' anger, rumours were spread in Damascus that the Empire was seriously threatened by European powers and that Muslims had been attacked by Christians in some parts of Syria.[2] At the same time, in June 1860, news came from the neighbouring areas of Lebanon and Hermon of the massacre of Christians by Druzes with government backing.[3] According to some European consuls, Ahmed Paşa himself did nothing to prevent the flow of men and arms from Jabal Druze and Damascus to the help of the Lebanese Druzes; nor did he try to protect the Christians of Rashāyā and Ḥaṣbāyā, villages under his jurisdiction, against the Druze attack; instead he was reported to have said that 'there were two great evils in Syria, the Christians and the Druzes and that the massacre of either party was a gain to the Turkish government'.[4]

Indeed, as tension grew daily in Damascus and Christians were being maltreated by Muslims, Ahmed's actions and omissions contributed to aggravate the situation further. He neither prevented

[1] F.O. 78/1454, Brant to Bulwer, No. 27, encl. in Brant to Russell, No. 8, Damascus, 4 Oct. 1859; see also A.E. Damas, v, from Outrey, No. 70, 14 Feb. 1859.

[2] See, for example, *Kitāb al-aḥzān*, pp. 39–40; Khazin, ii. 179; al-Ḥasībī.

[3] A.E. Damas, vi, from Lanusse, No. 85, 4 June 1860; F.O. 78/1625, 'Report by Mr. Robson', encl. in Dufferin to Russell, No. 9, Damascus, 23 Sept. 1860; Farley, *The Massacres*, p. 65; Khazin, ii. 179; *Kitāb al-aḥzān*, p. 34; Mishāqa, MS., p. 349; for more information on the events in Lebanon, their causes, and the attitude of the local authorities, see, Istanbul, Başvekâlet Arşivi, *Cebel-i Lübnan*, Docs. Nos. 138 and 139 of 20 L 1277; F.O. 78/1519, dispatches No. 9 and onwards from Moore to Russell, Beirut, 24 May 1860 and onwards.

[4] F.O. 78/1520, Brant to Bulwer, No. 40, encl. in Brant to Russell, No. 17, Damascus, 6 Sept. 1860; cf. F.O. 78/1586, 'Memo. of conversation with the Emir Abd-El Kadir', encl. in Moore to Russell, No. 19, Beirut, 8 Aug. 1861; A.E. Damas, vi, from Lanusse, No. 85, 4 June 1860; No. 86, 19 June 1860.

bodies of Druzes from entering the city nor did he permit Amir ʿAbd al-Qādir, the local Algerian notable, to employ his own men, under government inspection, to check those Druzes and to protect the Christian quarter.[1] (A similar rebuff was given to other Muslim notables as well as to some European consuls who warned the Pasha of the deteriorating situation.)[2] Instead, the force he dispatched to defend the Christian quarter against a possible attack consisted of soldiers who were themselves local Muslims, or who had been involved in the previous anti-Christian riots at Rashāyā and Ḥaṣbāyā.[3] Subsequent steps taken by the governor were even more disastrous. One of these was to station troops by the central mosque of Damascus in order—as Ahmed was reported to have said—to protect the Muslims against a Christian attack.[4] The Pasha's next move led, in fact, to the first outbreak of riots: on his orders a number of young Muslims who had painted crosses on pavements in the Christian quarter were arrested, put in chains, and were made to sweep the roads of that quarter. They were forcibly freed by an angry Muslim crowd who then turned to attack the local Christians.[5] At this point, Ahmed Paşa refrained from employing his troops, however limited they were, to quell the outbreak (as other Turkish Pashas had done elsewhere), thus ruling out the only chance of avoiding the massacres; or, in Consul Brant's words: 'The military force was small, it is true, but I have little doubt that had it been actively employed it could have mastered the outbreak and prevented the calamity.'[6]

For, as already pointed out, when a handful of soldiers did make one or two attempts to drive back the attacking mobs, the slaughter

[1] F.O. 78/1586, op. cit.; A.E. Damas, vi, No. 86, op. cit.; al-Bayṭār, p. 262; al-ʿAqīqī, p. 116.

[2] Mishāqa, MS., p. 349; F.O. 78/1520, Brant to Bulwer, No. 40, encl. in Brant to Russell, No. 17, Damascus, 6 Sept. 1860; compare A.E. Damas, op. cit.

[3] Abkāriūs, p. 123; Farley, *The Massacres*, p. 77; Jessup, i. 195; Madden, ii. 329–30; Zaydān, p. 303; see also above, p. 60.

[4] Mishāqa, MS., p. 347; *Kitāb al-aḥzān*, pp. 41–42, 254; compare al-ʿAṭṭār, p. 214; *Ḥasr al-lithām*, p. 226; Shaykhū, *Nubdha*, p. 25.

[5] F.O. 78/1557, Brant to Moore, Damascus, 10 June, encl. No. 3 in Moore to Russell, No. 20, Beirut, 13 July 1860; al-Bayṭār, i. 262–3; *Kitāb al-aḥzān*, pp. 46 ff.; al-ʿAṭṭār, pp. 214 ff.; *Ḥasr al-lithām*, pp. 228–9; Edwards, p. 175; Farley, *The Massacres*, pp. 75–76.

[6] F.O. 78/1520, Brant to Russell, No. 8, Damascus, 16 July 1860; cf. F.O. 78/1586, 'Memo. of conversation with the Emir Abd-El Kadir', encl. in Moore to Russell, No. 19, Beirut, 8 Aug. 1861; Mishāqa, MS., pp. 352–3, 356; *Kitāb al-aḥzān*, p. 115; see also al-Bayṭār, i. 262; Abkāriūs, p. 130; Madden, ii. 327; Porter, *Bashan*, p. 346.

was halted for a while; but such attempts were sporadic and short-lived.[1] Most of the regular troops remained passive, like their commander, Ahmed Paşa, and abstained from extending their help to Christian victims;[2] some even participating in the plunder and rape.[3] The most active part in the massacre was taken by the police and irregular soldiers—both Arabs and Kurds—including those of the new force *avniye*; they were followed by the local riffraff as well as by a number of Druzes and some small traders.[4]

As for the attitude of the local Muslim leaders: on the one hand a number of Muslim notables not only gave refuge to many Christians, but also made (especially ʿAbd al-Qādir) substantial efforts to avoid the approaching calamity; these being fruitless, they then tried to stop it and even to fight back the rioters.[5] efforts were, however, either ignored by the rioters or discouraged by the authorities as, for example, in the case of ʿAbd al-Qādir, who was accused of being a French protégé.[6] On the other hand,

[1] See above, p. 54; see also F.O. 78/1520, op. cit.; A.E. Damas, vi, No. 89, 28 July 1860; al-Bayṭār, i. 263; Farley, op. cit., pp. 77–78; Madden, ii. 329; Mishāqa, MS., p. 356.

[2] A.E. Damas, vi, No. 88, 17 July 1860; Khazin, ii. 181, 209; *Kitāb al-aḥzān*, pp. 66, 75–77; according to a report by an eye witness, a rioting mob was encouraged by the following cry: 'Fear not the soldiers, fear nothing. The soldiers will not meddle with you.' See F.O. 78/1557, Revd. Robson to Consul Brant, 9 July, encl. in Moore to Russell, No. 20, Beirut, 13 July 1860; compare Jessup, i. 196; Mishāqa, MS., p. 356.

[3] See *Irade D.*, No. 31571, 20 L 1277; F.O. 78/1520, Brant to Bulwer, No. 40, encl. in Brant to Russell, No. 17, Damascus, 6 Sept. 1860; A.E. Damas, vi, No. 89, 28 July 1860; see also *Ḥasr al-lithām*, p. 229; Khazin, ii. 182; Madden, ii. 329; Porter, *Bashan*, p. 347; Zaydān, p. 329.

[4] Cf. F.O. 78/1519, 'Copy of a letter from a Turkish Muslim in Damascus', encl. in Moore to Russell, No. 27, Beirut, 4 Aug. 1860; F.O. 78/1520, Brant to Bulwer, No. 34, encl. in Brant to Russell, No. 15, Damascus, 25 Aug. 1860; F.O. 78/1625, Report by Mr. Robson, encl. in Dufferin to Russell, No. 9, Beirut, 23 Sept. 1861; A.E. Damas, vi, from Lanusse, No. 88, 17 July 1860; al-Ḥasībī; Mishāqa, MS., p. 355; Jessup, i. 198–200; consult also lists of people convicted for taking part in the massacres, F.O. 78/1520, Fuad to Brant, 23 Aug., encl. in Brant to Russell, No. 16, Damascus, 25 Aug. 1860; see also F.O. 78/1628. There were, however, a few cases whereby irregular chiefs saved Christians; see *Irade M.V.*, No. 19910/3, 7 C 1277.

[5] See *Irade M.M.*, No. 864/1, 1 Saf. 1277; ibid., No. 872/3, 24 RA 1277; F.O. 78/1586, Wrench to Bulwer, No. 12, encl. in Wrench to Russell, No. 7, Damascus, 19 Apr. 1861; A.E. Damas, vi, from Lanusse, No. 86, 19 June 1860; ibid., from Outrey, No. 103, 31 Oct. 1860; al-ʿAqīqī, p. 118; al-Bayṭār, i. 264–5; al-Ḥasībī; Mishāqa, MS., pp. 349 ff.; Edwards, pp. 173–9.

[6] See above, p. 236; see also F.O. 78/1586, 'Memo. of conversation with the Emir Abd-El Kadir', encl. in Moore to Russell, No. 19, Beirut, 8 Aug. 1861; Madden, ii. 336; Mishāqa, MS., pp. 353, 356.

a number of Muslim notables, among them the chief 'Ulema of Damascus—the Shāfi'i mufti, Sheikh 'Umar al-Ghazzī, and Sheikh 'Abdūllah Ḥalabī—and most other members of the *meclis*, had a hand in instigating or backing the riots.[1]

In view of all that has been said, there are good grounds for assuming that behind this outbreak there was a concealed alliance between Ahmed Paşa and a number of local leaders to punish the Christians for their disobedience; and this by secretly instigating or at least tacitly directing the fatal course of events.[2] The fact that the Damascus Jews, who lived near the Christian quarter, remained untouched (some of them were even said to have given refreshment to the rioters) also suggests that the outbreak was not completely spontaneous.[3] At any rate the Muslim mob, whose anti-Christian feelings had reached their climax on the eve of the outbreak, from all the factors mentioned above, surely possessed every reason to believe that the punishment of the Christians was not only required by their religion but also sanctioned by both the local authorities and the religious leadership.[4]

[1] See *Irade M.V.*, No. 19505/2, 14 CA 1277; F.O. 78/1519, 'Copy of a letter from a Turkish Muslim in Damascus', encl. in Moore to Russell, No. 27, Beirut, 4 Aug. 1860; F.O. 78/1625, Report from Revd. Robson, encl. in Dufferin to Russell, No. 9, Beirut, 23 Sept. 1860; F.O. 78/1520, Brant to Bulwer, No. 48, encl. in Brant to Russell, No. 26, Damascus, 27 Sept. 1860; F.O. 78/1628, Extraits des sentences de fonctionnaires Ottomans et des Notables de Damas; A.E. Damas, vi, from Outrey, No. 91, 14 Aug. 1860; *Kitāb al-aḥzān*, p. 88; Edwards, pp. 178–9; *Birjīs Barīs*, No. 32. Note that some Muslim sources claim that Sheikh Ḥalabī did in fact save Christians; see al-Ḥasībī. This however, seems doubtful in the light of his previous record; cf. F.O. 195/368, Wood to Redcliffe, No. 48, Damascus, 11 Oct. 1853. See also *Ha-Karmel*, No. 13 (1861), p. 99.

[2] Cf. 'Abd al-Qādir's comment: '. . . the causes were the wish of the Government, the concurrence of the notables and the turbulent character of the populace', see F.O. 78/1586, op. cit.

[3] Cf. al-'Aqīqī, p. 117. See also Mishāqa, MS., p. 357; *Kitāb al-aḥzān*, pp. 116 ff.; F.O. 78/1520, Brant to Russell, No. 8, Damascus, 16 July 1860. Some sources claim, however, that the Jews were forced to hand refreshment under threat by the rioters. See *Ha-Magid*, iv, No. 33, p. 129; F.O. 78/1586, Rogers to Russell, No. 16, Damascus, 16 June 1861.

[4] According to certain sources Ahmed had prepared the plot and initiated into it some local 'Ulema and Druze chiefs of the Houran; A.E. Damas, vi, from Lanusse, No. 86, 19 June 1860; Mishāqa, MS., pp. 348–9; Baedeker, p. 46; Khazin, ii. 179; Shaykhū, pp. 24–25; Zaydān, p. 303; cf. F.O. 78/1520, Brant to Russell, No. 5, Damascus, 18 June 1860; F.O. 78/1586, op. cit.; al-Bayṭār, op. cit. It is not impossible, however, that the plot had been planned by local elements who initiated into it the *vali*, and the latter, in view of his precarious position and military weakness, had no other choice but to co-operate.

At the same time, however, in view of the previous massacres in Lebanon and the anti-Christian outbreaks in other parts of the country, there are some grounds for assuming that the Damascus events constituted part of a general conspiracy in which the Damascus conspirators played only a local role. Some of the sources which suggest this, claim that the *Porte* and the Sultan gave orders to exterminate the Christians of Syria;[1] this suggestion seems, however, far-fetched. Another assumption is that behind the plot there stood the reactionary circles in Istanbul who opposed the reforms and hoped, in this way, to cause the overthrow of Sultan Abdülmecid in favour of his conservative brother, Abdülaziz.[2] But although this suggestion seems less unreasonable, there is no direct evidence to support it, nor are documents available to prove the above assumptions.[3]

Yet the *Porte* cannot be entirely exempt from responsibility for what happened in Damascus; for while trying to introduce in the Syrian provinces a most difficult and unpopular reform such as placing Muslims and Christians on an equal footing, it failed to take the necessary precautions, despite the growing tension, to prevent the outbreak of Muslim opposition. The Turkish government in Syria was too weak to withstand the local reactionary pressure, and the military force was too small to provide an adequate sanction behind such a radical and undesired change.[4]

What they failed to do before 1860, the Ottomans tried to amend afterwards: immediately after the Damascus events, a

Cf. F.O. 78/1520, Brant to Bulwer, No. 40, encl. in Brant to Russell, No. 17, Damascus, 6 Sept. 1860; Edwards, p. 176; Abkāriūs, p. 166.

[1] *Aḥwāl*, MS., pp. 22–24; F.O. 78/1557, Extract of a letter by Revd. Cyril Graham, encl. in Dufferin to Russell, No. 1, Paris, 5 Aug. 1860; *Ḥasr al-lithām*, pp. 131–2, 138–9; Jessup, i. 176; F. Lenormant, *Les derniers événements de Syrie* (Paris, 1860), p. 16; Mishāqa, MS., p. 356; Porter, *Bashan*, p. 348; Shaykhū, *Nubdha*, p. 36 n.; Zaydān, p. 303.

[2] Barker, i. 43–44; *Birjīs Barīs*, No. 31; Madden, ii. 266 ff. Note the Kuleli affair in Istanbul of mid-September 1860; see Davison, *Reform*, pp. 100–2. Note also a report of September 1860 about anti-Christian plots by Muslims in two Bulgarian towns; *Ha-Magid*, iv, No. 35, p. 136, 5 Sept. 1860; see also *Ha-Karmel*, i, No. 2, p. 12, Aug. 1860; F.O. 78/1627, Dufferin to Bulwer, No. 106, 18 Jan. 1861. Cf. Arabic circular in Shaykhū, op. cit., p. 48.

[3] Cf. Sublime Porte, Affaires Étrangères, carton 256, Dossier No. 1, from Fuad Paşa, Beirut, 25 Aug. 1860; ibid., No. 4, Oct. 1860; F.O. 78/1520, Brant to Bulwer, No. 40, encl. in Brant to Russell, No. 17, Damascus, 6 Sept. 1860.

[4] See above, pp. 51 ff.; cf. F.O. 78/1220, Barker to Clarendon, No. 3, Aleppo, 25 Feb. 1856; Barker, i. 48–49; *Birjīs Barīs*, ii, No. 25, 29 May 1860; *Nafīr Sūriyya*, 22 Shubāṭ 1861.

large and well-equipped army was sent to Syria and the country was put under strict military control. Fuad Paşa, who led this operation, carried out in addition a great number of punitive measures: he arrested and executed a great many culprits, imposed disarmament and conscription, and levied a special tax on the non-Christian population to compensate the Christians for their losses.[1]

But although these strict and severe steps contributed to the averting of further anti-Christian outbreaks and perhaps to the easing of the tension in the long run,[2] they could not remove the cause of Muslim–Christian antagonism which continued to prevail in Syria and Palestine up to the end of 1861 and in later years.[3]

[1] Cevdet, *Tezakir*, ii. 109–11; *Bu defa şamişerif eyaleti ahalisi üzerine tarh olanan vergi ve ianeyi fevkaladenin kararnamesi* (Istanbul, A.H. 1277); N.B.V.K./OR, No. 279/98; al-Bayṭār, i. 267 ff.; Edwards, pp. 382 ff.; Mishāqa, MS., pp. 370 ff.; Shaykhū, op. cit., pp. 36 ff.

[2] Jessup, i. 206; al-Bayṭār, i. 279; Finn, i. 201; ʿAbd al-Raḥmān Sāmī, *Safar al-salām fī bilād al-Shām* (Egypt, 1896), p. 64.

[3] For example, the landing of the French military expedition in August 1860, strongly irritated the Muslims in many places throughout the country; see placard in Arabic in F.O. 78/1519, Rogers to Moore, Haifa, 29 Aug. 1860, encl. in Moore to Russell, No. 38, Beirut, 31 Aug. 1860; see also F.O. 78/1520, Brant to Russell, No. 11, Damascus, 28 July 1860; F.O. 78/1521, Finn to Russell, No. 32, Jerusalem, 16 Aug. 1860; F.O. 78/1538, Skene to Bulwer, No. 27, encl. in Skene to Russell, No. 49, Aleppo, 18 Aug. 1860; A.E. Damas, vi, from Outrey, No. 110, 21 Feb. 1861; Abkāriūs, p. 161, n.; *Birjīs Barīs*, No. 36; Madden, ii. 361; *Rambles*, p. 291; Taoutel, ii. 102.

XVIII

EPILOGUE: NEW TRENDS IN SYRIAN SOCIETY BY 1861

ONE major result of these tense relations between Syrian Muslims and Christians was a marked wave of emigration of Christians from Aleppo and Damascus to safer places in the Empire or abroad. Thus, after the 1860 events in Damascus (and those of 1850 in Aleppo) a considerable number of families, mainly from the upper and middle classes, left these cities and settled in Beirut, Egypt, Turkey, and Europe.[1]

The Ottoman government, while trying to check the waves of emigration, prepared some plans for the establishment of common institutions for Muslims and Christians such as hospitals and schools, hoping 'to lessen the mutual illfeeling . . . between the two sects'.[2]

The first modern government schools—*rüşdiye* (secondary schools)—were established in Aleppo in the late 1850s, and in Damascus in the early 1860s[3] (and this about a decade later than in Turkey proper).[4] But these schools accepted virtually only Muslim children,[5] and were, in addition, too scanty to replace the network of traditional Muslim schools—*mekteb*s and *medrese*s—which continued to form the main basis for the young Muslims' education.[6]

Yet though a better understanding between Muslims and

[1] F.O. 78/871, Werry to Canning, No. 40, encl. in Werry to Palmerston, No. 17, Aleppo, 30 Oct. 1851; F.O. 78/1603, Skene to Bulwer, encl. in Skene to Russell, No. 69, Aleppo, 3 Oct. 1861; A.E. Damas, vi, No. 114, 21 Mar. 1861; al-Bayṭār, i. 270; Edwards, p. 259; *Rambles*, p. 266; Taoutel, iii. 149.

[2] F.O. 78/1586, Brant to Russell, No. 1, Damascus, 10 Jan. 1861.

[3] *Irade D.*, No. 28913, 17 Z 1275; *Irade M.V.*, No. 17615, 12 RA 1275; al-Ghazzī, i. 165–6.

[4] Ubicini, i. 197–201; Engelhardt, i. 76; ii. 77, 297; Madden, i. 461–2; R. H. Davison, 'Westernized Education in Ottoman Turkey', *M.E.J.* (1961), pp. 296–7; Karal, v. 256; Lewis, *Emergence*, pp. 111–12; Temperley, p. 234.

[5] *Ḥasr al-lithām*, p. 11; Jessup, i. 221; ii. 512.

[6] Jessup, i. 221; *al-Jinān*, iii (1870), p. 70; ix (1870), p. 200; Midhat, pp. 51–52; Oliphant, p. 113; Sāmī, p. 83. See also F.O. 78/1521, Finn to Bulwer, encl. in Finn to Russell, No. 21, Jerusalem, 19 July 1860.

Christians could not be achieved by Ottoman educational efforts, it was accomplished in the long run and indirectly largely through the system of missionary education. This system, having existed in Syria for some time, was greatly expanded after the 1860 events, when the attention of Christian Europe was called sharply to the position of its Syrian co-religionists.[1] The missionary schools, which gave elementary, secondary, and higher education, included also a number of non-Christian students,[2] and despite their sectarian character helped to create a cultural atmosphere in the country and contributed to the revival of the Arabic language.[3] From these schools there emerged the first modern Arabic writers and journalists, all Christians; around them literary societies were formed, an Arabic theatre was set up, and printing presses were established, most of them in Beirut—the centre of the new cultural revival.[4]

The Ottoman government itself helped indirectly to encourage this revival either by granting prizes to Christian-Arab writers such as Fāris al-Shidyāq and Buṭrus al-Bustānī,[5] or by employing in its service people like Marūn al-Naqqāsh and Khalīl al-Khūrī, who were among the pioneers of this literary renaissance.[6]

The major themes of this cultural movement were Syrian patriotism—based on a common language, culture, and domicile—and secularism, principles which were to become in later years the basis for a new Syrian society and for Arab nationalism. This may be said to be an important outcome of the 1860 events; for a small number of Syrian Christians, who had suffered severely from these events, realized that a religious loyalty was a dangerous

[1] Al-Dibs, viii. 773–82; *Ḥasr al-lithām*, pp. 11–12; Jessup, i. 218, 221–2, 298–9; L. Shaykhū, *al-Ādāb al-ʿarabiyya fī'l-qarn al-tāsiʿ ashar* (Beirut, 1924–6), pp. 49–50.

[2] Prof. Fleischer, 'Michael Meschaka's cultur-statistik von Damaskus', *ZDMG*, viii (1854), pp. 352–3; Manṣūr, p. 84; Wortabet, ii. 208–9. See also *Irade D.*, No. 14609, 2 Z 1267.

[3] Fleischer, *ZDMG*, viii (1854), 352–3; Jessup, i. 218, 220–1; *al-Jinān*, ii (1870), p. 44; iii (1870), p. 70. See also Tibawi, pp. 178–9.

[4] Shaykhū, *al Ādāb*, pp. 47–48, 87; *al-Kulliyya*, xi. 410; Farley, *Syria*, p. 36. See, for example, F.O. 78/1294, Finn to Clarendon, No. 1, Jerusalem, 1 Jan. 1857; F.O. 78/1385, Moore to Alison, No. 74, encl. in Moore to Clarendon, No. 1, Beirut, 6 Jan. 1858. On the formation of the theatre in Beirut, see *Irade M.V.*, No. 5976, 23 Saf. 1267; *Mühimme*, No. 258, p. 46, CA 1268.

[5] On this prize to al-Shidyāq, see *Irade H.*, No. 28896, 8 Z 1275; to al-Bustānī, see Shaykhū, op. cit., p. 19.

[6] Ibid., p. 106; Nawfal, *Ṭarāblus*, pp. 65–66, 94.

basis for political life and sought to replace it by a secular common ground; and having, at the same time, acquired a certain national consciousness under the impact of European ideas, they were capable of applying it to their own environment.

Thus, during the very days of the 1860 crisis, the phrases *ḥubb al-waṭan* (love of the country), *abnā' al-waṭan* (fellow countrymen) were used in a modern sense for the first time in Syrian history by the leader of the cultural movement, Buṭrus al-Bustānī, in his appeal to the people of the country 'to open a new era in Syria' (*iftitāḥ 'aṣr jadīd li-Sūriyya*) within the Ottoman Empire.[1]

But these ideas of patriotism and secularism which in fact were similar to the principles of the Ottoman reform movement, were not acceptable to the Muslim population of Syria, who regarded them as subversive to the character of their society and state. In the eyes of the Muslims, the Ottoman Empire was primarily a religious state in which they alone formed the political community; any change in this basis would mean not only the end of their dominant position in the state, but also the collapse of the Empire.

Indeed, the question of the legal basis of the Empire constituted not only the motive of the Syrian Muslims' opposition to Christian equality, but also the source of a new local attitude of antagonism to the Ottoman government itself, which was to a certain degree another result of the Tanzimat reforms. The Muslim population of Syria and Palestine, like that of other parts of the Empire, strongly disapproved of the Tanzimat edicts which, for the first time in Islamic history, seriously challenged the Holy Law (particularly with regard to the equality issue). But whereas in Turkey such opposition was comparatively mild owing to the moderate attitudes taken by some chief 'Ulema[2] and because the population was not fully aware, for example, of the practical applications of the Gülhane edict, in Syria it seems that large sections of the population felt particularly strongly and bitterly about the reforms. After having endured the harsh secular and pro-Christian régime of Ibrāhīm Paşa for nine years, the Syrian Muslims hoped that the returning Ottomans would help them 'to maintain the ancient

[1] *Nafir Sūriyya*, 25 Oct. 1860; cf. Hourani, *Arabic Thought*, p. 101. See also *al-Jinān* xxii (1870), p. 674.

[2] Heyd, *'Ulemā*, pp. 88–89.

privileges and rights';[1] and accordingly they welcomed the new rulers and even the proclamation of the Gülhane decree which they had wrongly interpreted as meaning 'the abolition of Ferdeh conscription, statute labour and requisition and the restoration of the old order of Government, which is more or less congenial to the desire and feelings of the people'.[2] But when later they realized that the aims of the Ottomans were no different from those of the Egyptians, their attitude to the Ottomans was completely reversed; the masses resented the government because of the burdensome taxes and the hateful conscription, while the entire Muslim population, headed by the 'Ulema, opposed the new rights granted to the *reaya*. It is true that certain elements regarded the latter reforms as temporary concessions made by the Sultan to the European allies who had helped to drive out the Egyptians from Syria and Palestine.[3] But as these concessions were confirmed and even enlarged by the *Hatt-ı Hümayun* of 1856, they were taken not only as signs of weakness on the part of the Sultan, but also as a betrayal of Islam:

> The Arabs and other Moslems consider that the Sultan has forfeited their allegiance and that in fact the country no longer belongs to him on account of the unlawful concessions which he has made to Christians. Even officials in authority do not hesitate to cast reproaches upon the Padisha asserting that 'The Sultan eats melons and that His Majesty's officers and subjects are only bound to obey him so long as his orders are in conformity with the Law of the Prophet'.[4]

Along such statements there appeared also in at least one instance other signs of defiance: during the riots of April 1856 in Nablus,

[1] F.O. 78/620, Rose to Aberdeen, No. 55, Beirut, 7 Oct. 1845; cf. Bazili, ii. 1–2.

[2] F.O. 195/170, Werry to Ponsonby, No. 46, Damascus, 21 Jan. 1840. See also *Irade D.*, No. 1330, 24 L 1256; cf. *Aḥwāl*, MS., p. 18.

[3] A.E. Damas, i, No. 10, 30 Dec. 1843; F.O. 195/292, Finn to Canning, No. 17, Jerusalem, 20 Nov. 1850; *Aḥwāl*, MS., p. 18; al-Bayṭār, ii. 1030–1; Finn, ii. 497; Walpole, iii. 126.

[4] Farley, *The Massacres*, p. 69. ('To eat melons'—to talk nonsense); see also F.O. 78/1383, Finn to Malmesbury, No. 11, Jerusalem, 8 July 1858; F.O. 78/1521, Finn to Russell, No. 30, Jerusalem, 14 Aug. 1860; F.O. 78/456, Rose to Palmerston, No. 3, Gazir, 26 July 1841; cf. al-Bayṭār, ii. 1135; Manṣūr, p. 90; Shaykhū, *Nubdha*, p. 33; Taoutel, ii. 90; compare also Engelhardt, i. 44; Lewis, *Emergence*, p. 106; Temperley, pp. 200, 206, 214; W. S. Blunt, *The Future of Islam* (London, 1882), p. 78; Davison, *Reform*, p. 43; Madden, i. 443–4.

the Ottoman flag was torn down by Muslims and thrown away, together with European flags.[1] It would seem therefore that these reactions represented something more than merely a religious-inspired opposition to a Sultan who went astray; they were, perhaps, the first signs of local Arab opposition to Turkish rule as such.

It is apparent that throughout history the Arabs maintained a sort of 'Arab' consciousness about their language and special role in Islam. Hence their awareness of the difference between Turks and Arabs, which was possibly intensified in the course of the eighteenth and the beginning of the nineteenth centuries when the Ottoman Empire was disintegrating.[2] The Egyptian occupation of Syria in the 1830s had apparently also a certain effect in this direction:

> During the long and unrestrained dominion of Egypt over Syria the languages, sympathies, interests and prospects of the Turkish Empire were daily becoming more and more estranged from the minds of the people and it was no uncommon thing to hear inhabitants express their opinion that the Sublime Porte would never again have the Government of the country.[3]

The fact that the Turks were twice defeated by the Egyptian army in the battle over Syria and that they were able to recapture the country only with European aid, helped undoubtedly to diminish further the Syrians' respect for Turkish authority.[4]

All this, combined with the facts that the new Ottoman régime had imposed unpopular reforms and that in Muslims' eyes the

[1] F.O. 78/1217, Finn to Clarendon, No. 60, Jerusalem, 11 Sept. 1856; Manṣūr, p. 88. See also above p. 227.

[2] Cf. Hourani, *Arabic Thought*, pp. 260–1, 266–7. Note, for example, that in 1826, when Turkish troops besieged Jerusalem and demanded its surrender by order from the Sultan, local Muslim rebels declared, 'that they had repeatedly sworn never again to receive back into the town a foreigner or a stranger (i.e., an Ottoman or an Albanian), and for that reason they were ready to die as free men rather than accept the yoke of the stranger be he Moslem or otherwise'; Spyridon, pp. 39–40. According to an English traveller in Syria in the 1820s, who quotes a prominent Syrian—the population in Syria wanted a change in the Government; they preferred Englishmen or even Greeks. R. R. Madden, *Travels in Turkey, Egypt, Nubia and Palestine in 1824, 1825 and 1827* (London, 1829), ii. 71.

[3] F.O. 78/444, Young to Ponsonby, No. 11, Jerusalem, 11 June 1841.

[4] Cf. *Accounts and Papers*, LX (1843), pt. i, No. 7, from Wood, Therapia, 23 May 1841; *Irade D.*, No. 2837, 15 CA 1258.

Sultan had betrayed the cause of Islam, possibly made some elements within the Arab Syrian population wish to break from Turkish rule and be placed under an Arab rule.

Such tendencies were indeed observed by European consuls and travellers during the 1840s and particularly the late 1850s. Consul Finn, for example, who lived and travelled in Palestine from the mid-1840s to the early 1860s, claimed that the Arab natives not only 'speak of 'Abdu'l Mejeed el Khain' (the betrayer of trust) [and] detest and hate the Turks . . . due to difference of race and traditional remembrance of conquest',[1] but that they were also 'often heard to affirm that if they (the Arab-speaking population of Palestine) could but suppress their own dissensions, and unite under one leader, they were able to drive away the Turks from their presence with sticks and stones'.[2]

In this dispatch of September 1858, Consul Finn referred also to the:

> Constant use in public papers of all sorts of the term 'independence of the Turkish Empire'—*istiklāl* [sic]—which we have brought into use and which the natives understand in a different sense from us, namely, not the independent action of central Ottoman dominion in reference to European and other Powers, but independence of the natives from Turkish control over them, the Turks being now looked upon as Europeans—'one of the European family of nations'.[3]

About the same time—in August 1858—Consul Skene reported from Aleppo that: 'The Mussulman population of Northern Syria harbours hopes of a separation from the Ottoman Empire and the formation of a new Arabian state under the sovereignty of the Shereef of Mecca.'[4]

[1] Finn, i. 215. Cf. Hourani, *Arabic Thought*, pp. 266–7. See also Finn, ii. 24; Farley, *The Massacres*, pp. 68–69; F.O. 78/836, Rose to Palmerston, No. 47, Broumana, 14 Oct. 1850; Consul-General Rose writes that 'The Arab . . . entertains a national jealousy of the Turks from whom he differs besides in language manners and character'. See also Urquhart, ii. 69; Edwards, p. 18; Kibrizli, p. 57. Note that part of the Arab hatred of the Turks was motivated by the haughty and offensive attitude the Turkish officials showed towards the Arabs; see F.O. 78/447, Werry to Ponsonby, No. 5, Damascus, 6 May 1841; F.O. 78/456, Rose to Palmerston, Gazir, 23 July 1841; Lyall, p. 111.

[2] Finn, ii. 190.

[3] F.O. 78/1384, Finn to Malmesbury, No. 46, Jerusalem, 13 Sept. 1858.

[4] F.O. 78/1389, Skene to Alison, No. 20, encl. in Skene to Malmesbury, No. 33, Aleppo, 7 Aug. 1858; cf. *Rambles*, pp. 246–7. On the re-emergence of this concept in later years, see Hourani, op. cit., pp. 269 ff.

These separatist tendencies, which were also occasionally observed later in the 1860s,[1] were certainly significant. Yet, at the same time they were by no means either universal or mature; such feelings were furthermore far from outweighing the basic and ultimate loyalty of the Syrian Muslims to Islam and its political embodiment—the Ottoman Empire. As Consul Finn himself stressed: 'But the loyalty to Islam is a powerful and pervading principle which keeps in check every other feeling.'[2] And if the present Sultan has deviated from the true path and made a breach in Islam, he is after all not immortal as is the Holy Law; indeed, when in June 1861 Abdülmecid died and was succeeded by Sultan Abdülaziz, the Muslims of Syria burst out in cries: 'Islam is saved'.[3] At that stage and for many years to come, Syria and Palestine were in most respects still part of the Ottoman Islamic state, in which the local Muslims played a dominant role. Turkish rule in these lands was stronger than ever before; the Holy Law although challenged was nevertheless paramount; Muslim religious and educational institutions were maintained by the state;[4] government administration and the judicial system were largely staffed by Muslim Arabs, in various ranks, and local 'Ulema were highly esteemed by the state and its delegates.[5]

[1] H. B. Tristram, who travelled in Syria in the early 1860s, remarked that the local Arabs wished to see the Turks driven out from Syria and wanted Amir 'Abd al-Qādir as Caliph of Arabia; see Tristram, *Israel*, p. 554. Mrs. I. Burton, who lived in Damascus for several years during the late 1860s, wrote that 'the Moslem Syrians . . . hate the Turkish rule, and they wish to be free from their yoke'. See I. Burton, *Inner Life*, i. 112. See also King 'Abd Allah's *Mudhakkirat*, p. 318, cited in Hourani, *Arabic Thought*, p. 297.

[2] Finn, i. 215–18; cf. Hourani, op. cit., p. 267. See also F.O. 78/836, Rose to Palmerston, No. 47, Broumana, 14 Oct. 1850. Compare Bernard Lewis, *The Middle East and the West* (London, 1964), pp. 71–72. Note that when, for example, the Crimean War broke out, thousands of Muslims from Syria and Palestine volunteered to go to the jihad against Christian Russia; many others contributed great sums of money as well as equipment to the military effort; prayers were said and poems composed to the victory of Islam and the Sultan over the infidels. See, for example, *Ceride-i Havadis*, No. 657, 21 Saf. 1270; *Irade M.V.*, No. 12825/4, 6 L 1270; *Irade D.*, No. 18785, 19 B 1270; F.O. 78/1028, Wood to Clarendon, No. 4, Damascus, 17 Jan. 1854; Finn, ii. 43–44; al-Ghazzī, ii. 388; Nawfal, *Tarāblus*, p. 246.

[3] F.O. 78/1603, Skene to Bulwer, No. 14, encl. in Skene to Russell, No. 54, Aleppo, 9 July 1860; A.E. Damas, vi, No. 125, 3 July 1861.

[4] See, for example, *Irade D.*, No. 1330, 24 Saf. 1256; ibid., No. 6549, 26 Saf. 1262; *Irade M.V.*, No. 3197, 7 B 1258; ibid., No. 14364, 11 L 1271; *Irade M.M.*, No. 440, 16 Saf. 1274; Jaffa *Sijill*, No. 13, 19 CA 1258.

[5] See above, pp. 88–89 ff.

The two divergent and mutually contradictory streams of Muslim-Arab separatism and of Christian-Arab secularism and patriotism, each having emerged largely under the impact of the Tanzimat, were to meet only at the end of the century in one national movement.

BIBLIOGRAPHY

A. TURKISH SOURCES

Unpublished Official Documents

Istanbul, Archives of the Prime Minister's Office. All documents for the years A.H. 1256 to A.H. 1277 from the following series:

Cevdet, Dahiliye.
Cevdet, Zaptiye.
Iradeler, Dahiliye.
Iradeler, Hariciye.
Iradeler, Meclis-i Mahsus.
Iradeler, Meclis-i Valâ.
Mühimme Defteri.

Also selected documents from the series:

Cebel-i Lübnan.
Maliyeden Müdevver.

Sofia, Vasil Kolarov National Library. Selected documents from the series:

N.B.V.K./OR, Nos. 279, 282, 283, 285, 287.

Published Official Documents, Periodicals, and Books

Cevdet Paşa, Ahmed, *Tarih-i Cevdet*, 12 vols., Istanbul, A.H. 1301–9.
——, *Tezakir*, ed. C. Baysun, vols. i–ii, Ankara, 1953–60.
Ceride-i Havadis, Istanbul, weekly (first published in 1840).
Islam Ansiklopedisi, Istanbul, 1941– .
Karal, Enver Ziya, *Osmanlı Tarihi*, v–vii, Ankara, 1947–56.
Karaspan, Celal Tevfik, *Filistin ve Şark-ül-Ürdun*, 2 vols., Istanbul, 1942.
Lûtfi, Ahmed, *Mirat-i Adalet*, Istanbul, A.H. 1304.
——, *Tarih-i Lûtfi*, 8 vols., Istanbul, A.H. 1290–1328.
Süreyya, Mehmed, *Sicill-i Osmanı*, 4 vols., Istanbul, A.H. 1308–15.
Sertoğlu, Midhat, *Resimli Osmanlı Tarihi Ansiklopedisi*, Istanbul, 1958.
Turkey, Sublime Porte, *Bu defa şamişerif eyaleti ahalisi üzerine tarh olanan vergi ve ianeyi fevkaladenin kararnamesi*, Istanbul, A.H. 1277.
Ministry of Justice, *Düstur*, Istanbul, 1871–1928.
Sublime Porte, *Mani irtikaba dair kanunnamesi*, Istanbul, A.H. 1271.
Salname, Istanbul (annual, started A.H. 1263).
Takvim-i Vekayi, Istanbul (weekly, started 1831).
Ministry of Education, *Tanzimat*, i, Istanbul, 1940.

B. ARABIC SOURCES

Unpublished Documents and Manuscripts

(Anon.) *Aḥwāl al-naṣārā baʿda al-ḥarb al-qrīm*, MS., No. 66, American University, Beirut.
al-Ḥasībī, Muḥammad Abū Saʿūd, *Ḥādithat al-sittīn*, MS., No. (4) 4668, Ẓāhiriyya Library, Damascus.
Jaffa, Muslim Shariʿa Court, *Sijill*, A.H. 1256–77.
(Anon.) *Kitāb al-aḥzān fī ta'rīkh al-Shām wa-jabal Lubnān, wa-mā yalīhimā bi-mā aṣāba al-masīḥiyyīn min al-durūz wa'l-islām fī 9 tammūz 1860*, MS., No. 956. 9 K. 62 KA, American University, Beirut.
Mishāqa, Mīkhā'īl, *Al-jawāb ʿalā iqtirāḥ al-aḥbāb*, MS., No. 956. 9, M 39 JA, 48532, American University, Beirut.

Periodicals

ʿAṭārid, Marseille, 1858.
Birjīs Barīs, Paris, 1859–61.
Al-Jinān, Beirut, 1870–85.
Al-Majmaʿ al-ʿilmī al-ʿarabī, Damascus, 1921– .
Al-Mashriq, Beirut, 1898– .
Nafīr Sūriyya, Beirut, 1860–1.

Contemporary sources, Published Documents, and Works

Abū ʿIzz al-Dīn, Sulaymān, *Ibrāhīm Bāshā fī Sūriyya*, Beirut, 1929.
Abū al-Naṣr, ʿUmar, *Sūriyya wa-Lubnān fī'l-qarn al-tāsiʿ ashar*, Cairo, 1954.
Abū Shaqrā', Yūsuf Khaṭār, *Al-ḥarakāt fī Lubnān 'ilā ʿahd al-mutaṣarrifiyya*, Beirut, 1952.
Al-Adhanī, Sulaymān, *Kitāb al-bākūra al-Sulaymāniyya fī kashf asrār al-diyāna al- nuṣayriyya*, Beirut, 1862.
Al-ʿAqīqī, Anṭūn Dāhir, *Thawra wa-fitna fī Lubnān*, Beirut, 1938.
Al-ʿĀrīf, ʿĀrīf, *Ta'rīkh Ghazza*, Jerusalem, 1943.
Al-ʿAṭṭār, Nādir, *Ta'rīkh Sūriyya fī'l-ʿuṣūr al-ḥadītha*, Damascus, 1962.
Al-ʿAwra, Ibrāhīm, *Ta'rīkh wilāyāt Sulaymān Bāshā al-ʿĀdil*, Sidon, 1936.
Al-Baʿalbakī, Mīkhā'īl Mūsā Alūf, *Ta'rīkh Baʿalbak*, Beirut, 1908.
Al-Barghuthī, ʿUmar al-Ṣāliḥ, *Ta'rīkh Filasṭīn*, Jerusalem, 1923.
Al-Bāshā, Qusṭanṭīn (ed.), *Mudhakkirāt ta'rīkhiyya*, Lebanon, n.d.
Al-Bayṭār, ʿAbd al-Razzāq, *Ḥilyat al-bashar fī ta'rīkh al-qarn al-thālith ʿashar*, 3 vols., Damascus, 1961–3.
Al-Bustānī, Sulaymān, *Al-dawla al-ʿuthmāniyya qabla al-dustūr wa-baʿdahu*, Cairo, 1908.
Al-Dibs, Yūsuf, *Ta'rīkh Sūriyya*, 8 vols., Beirut, 1893–1905.

Farīd, Muḥammad, *Ta'rīkh al-dawla al-ʿaliyya al-ʿuthmāniyya*, Egypt, 1893.
Gharāyiba, ʿAbd al-Karīm, *Sūriyya fī'l-qarn al-tāsiʿ ashar, 1840–1876*, Cairo, 1961–2.
Al-Ghazzī, Kāmil, *Nahr al-dhahab fī ta'rīkh Ḥalab*, 3 vols., Aleppo, A.H. 1342–5.
Anon., *Ḥasr al-lithām ʿan nakabāt al-Shām*, Egypt, 1890.
Al-Ḥumṣī, Qasṭakī, *Udabā' Ḥalab dha'ū al-athar fī'l-qarn al-tāsiʿ ʿashar*, Aleppo, 1925.
Al-Ḥuṣnī, Muḥammad Adīb, *Kitāb muntakhabāt al-tawārikh li-Dimashq*, Damascus, 1927.
Al-Ḥusrī, Sātiʿ, *Al-bilād al-ʿarabiyya wa'l-dawla al-ʿuthmāniyya*, Beirut, 1960.
Ibn Shāshū, ʿAbd al-Raḥmān, *Tarājim baʿḍ aʿyān Dimashq wa-udabā'ihā*, Beirut, 1886.
Jirjī, Yannī al-Ṭarābulsī, *Ta'rīkh Sūriyya*, Beirut, 1881.
Al-Jundī, Muḥammad Salīm, *Ta'rīkh Maʿarrat al-Nuʿmān*, Damascus, 1923.
Kaḥḥāla, ʿUmar Riḍā, *Muʿjam qabā'il al-ʿarab*, 3 vols., Damascus, 1949.
Khāzin, Philippe and Farīd, *Majmūʿat al-muḥarrarāt al-siyāsiyya wa'l-mufāwaḍāt al-duwaliyya ʿan Sūriyya wa-Lubnān*, 3 vols., Juniya, 1910–11.
Kurd ʿAlī, Muḥammad, *Khitat al-Shām*, 8 vols., Damascus, 1925–8.
Manṣūr, Asʿad, *Ta'rīkh al-Nāṣira*, Egypt, 1924.
Mishāqa, Mīkhā'īl, *Muntakhabāt min al-jawāb ʿalā iqtirāḥ al-aḥbāb*, Beirut, 1955.
Al-Munajjid, Ṣalāḥ al-Dīn, *Wulāt Dimashq fī'l-ʿahd al-ʿuthmānī*, Damascus, 1949.
Nawfal, ʿAbdullāh Ḥabīb, *Kitāb tarājim ʿulamā' Ṭarāblus al-fayḥā' wa-udabā'ihā*, Tripoli, 1929.
——, 'Makhṭūṭat Nawfal Nawfal al-Ṭarāblusi' (1883), *Al-Kulliyya*, xi–xiii.
Al-Nimr, Iḥsān, *Ta'rīkh Jabal Nāblus wa'l-balqā'*, Damascus, 1938.
Qāddūra, Yūsuf, *Ta'rīkh madīnat Rāmallāh*, New York, 1954.
Qarā'lī Būlus (ed.), *Futūḥāt Ibrāhīm Bāshā fī Filasṭīn wa-Lubnān wa-Sūriyya*, Ḥariṣa, 1937.
Qarā'lī Yūsuf (ed.), *Ahamm ḥawādith Ḥalab fī'l-niṣf al-awwal min al-qarn al-tāsiʿ ʿashar*, Egypt, n.d.
Al-Qasāṭilī, Nuʿmān, *Kitāb al-rawda al-ghanna fı Dimashq al-fayḥā'*, Beirut, 1879.
Al-Rāfiʿī, ʿAbd al-Raḥmān, *Aṣr Muḥammad ʿAlī*, Cairo, 1918.
Rustum, Asad, *Bashīr bayna al-sultān wa'l-ʿazīz*, Beirut, 1956–7.
——, *Al-Maḥfūẓāt al-malikiyya al-Miṣriyya*, 4 vols., Beirut, 1940–3.
Sāmī, ʿAbd al-Raḥmān, *Safar al-salām fī bilād al-Shām*, Egypt, 1896.
Sarkīs, Khalīl, *Ta'rīkh Urshalīm*, Beirut, 1874.
Al-Shaṭṭī, Jamīl, *Rawḍ al-bashar fī aʿyān Dimashq fī'l-qarn al-thālith ʿashar*, Damascus, 1946.
——, *Tarājim aʿyān Dimashq fī niṣf al-qarn al-rābiʿ ʿashar*, Damascus, 1938.

Shaykhū, Louis, *Al-Ādāb al-ʿarabiyya fī'l-qarn al-tāsiʿ ʿashar*, 2 vols. Beirut, 1924–6.
——, (ed.), *Nubdha mukhtaṣara fī ḥawādith Lubnān wa'l-Shām*, Beirut, 1927.
Al-Shidyāq, Ṭannūs, *Akhbār al-aʿyān fī Jabal Lubnān*, Beirut, 1859.
Al-Ṭabbākh, Muḥammad Rāghib, *Iʿlām al-nubalā' bi-ta'rīkh Ḥalab al-shahbā'*, 7 vols., Aleppo, 1923–6.
Taoutel, Ferdinand (ed.), *Wathā'iq ta'rikhīyya ʿan Ḥalab*, 3 vols., Aleppo, 1958–62.
Al-Ṭawīl, Muḥammad Amīn Ghālib, *Ta'rīkh al-ʿAlawiyyīn*, Latakia, 1924.
Zakī, ʿAbd al-Raḥmān, *Al-Ta'rīkh al-ḥarbī li-ʿaṣr Muḥammad ʿAlī*, Egypt, 1950.
Zaydān, Juzjī, *Asīr al-Mutmahdī*, Egypt, 1901.
Al-Zayn, ʿĀrif Aḥmad, *Ta'rīkh Saydā*, Sidon, 1913.

C. CONTEMPORARY HEBREW SOURCES, PUBLISHED AND UNPUBLISHED DOCUMENTS, MANUSCRIPTS, AND BOOKS

Abir, Mordechai, *Hammered neged ha-shilton ha-mitzri be-Eretz Israel bi-shnat 1834* (The revolt against the Egyptian rule in Palestine in 1834), M.A. thesis, The Hebrew University, Jerusalem, 1961.
Ben-Zvi Institute, Jerusalem:
Documents from the Archives of the Sephardi community in Jerusalem;
Files from Montefiore Papers;
Nahmad Collection (Aleppo);
Navon Collection (Jerusalem).
Ben-Zvi, Y. *Eretz-Israel under Ottoman Rule* (in Hebrew), Jerusalem, 5715.
Binyamin, Israel Ben-Yosef, *Sefer massaʿey Israel* (Traveller's Book), Lyck, 1859.
Dobnow, Simon, *A General History of the Jewish people* (in Hebrew), Tel-Aviv, 1952.
Grayevski, Pinhas, *Me-ginzey Yerushalayim* (Documents from Jerusalem), Jerusalem, 5690.
Heyd, Uriel, *Ḍāhir al-ʿUmar shalliṭ ha-Galil ba-me'ah ha-yod ḥet*, Jerusalem, 1942.
Hofman, Y. *Muḥammad ʿAlī in Syria* (in Hebrew), unpublished Ph.D. thesis, The Hebrew University, Jerusalem, 1963.
Ha-Karmel, (ed. S. Finn) Vilna (weekly started 1860).
Klayn, Shmuel, *Toldot ha-yeshuv ha-yehudi be-Eretz Israel* (History of Jewish settlement in Palestine), Tel-Aviv, 1950.
Kresel, G., *Korot ha-ʿitim* (including the manuscript of Menahem Mendel of Kaminitz), Jerusalem, 5710.
Levton, Izhak, *Sefer nokhaḥ ha-shulḥan* (Responser), Izmir, 5628.
Ha-Magid, (ed. E. Zilbermann) Lyck (weekly, started 1856).
Montefiore, Judith, *Yehudit* (Traveller's Book), London, 1839.
Rivlin, Yosef Y. *Sefer zikkaron* (Memory Book), Bar Ilan University, Ramat Gan, 5724.

Raysher, Moshe Menahem, *Sha'arey Yerushalayim* (Traveller's book), Lemberg, 1866.

Rozanes, Shlomo Abraham, *Divrey yemey Israel be-Togarma* (History of Jews in Turkey), 5 vols., Tel-Aviv, 5690; Sofia, 5695.

Schwartz, Yosef, *Tvu'ot ha-'aretz* (Traveller's book), Jerusalem, 5603.

Schulman, Kalman, *Sefer Ariel* (Traveller's book), Vilna, 1856.

——, *Sefer Shulamit* (Traveller's book), Vilna, 1875.

Sharon, Moshe, *Ha-bedvim be-Eretz Israel ba-me'ot ha-18 ve-ha-19* (The Bedouin in Palestine in the 18th and 19th centuries), unpublished M.A. thesis, The Hebrew University, Jerusalem, 5724.

Ya'ari, Abraham, *Iggrot Eretz Israel* (Collection of letters by Jews in Palestine), Tel-Aviv, 5703.

Ya'ari, Abraham, *Massa'ot Eretz Israel* (Accounts of Jewish Travellers in Palestine), Tel-Aviv, 1946.

——, *Massa'ot shliaḥ Tzfat* (A Jewish Traveller from Safed in 1859), Jerusalem, 5702.

Yelin, David, *Ktavim nivḥarim* (Selected works), 2 vols., Jerusalem, 5696.

——, *Zikhronot le-ven Yerushalayim* (Memoirs of a native of Jerusalem), Jerusalem, 5684.

Zion, Jerusalem (monthly, started 5686).

D. SOURCES IN EUROPEAN LANGUAGES

Unpublished Documents and Private Papers

France, Archives du Ministère des Affaires Étrangères. Turquie: Alep, vols. i–iii; Damas, vols. i–vi; Jérusalem, vols. i–vi.

Great Britain. Public Record Office, Foreign Office Archives. All volumes of dispatches from the series F.O. 78/; F.O. 195/ from the consulates in Aleppo, Beirut, Damascus, Jaffa, Jerusalem.

Israel State Archives. Collection of various files from the German Consulate in Jerusalem, 1838–1939. Correspondences Diverses de l'agent du Prusse à Ghaza, 1855–6, No. 419, A VIII. 4 (in Arabic).

Missionary Society, London. Letters, Journals and Reports. Series: CM/017 from Bowen; CM/028 from Gobat; CM/034 from Jacob; CM/041 from Klein; CM/045 from Kruze; CM/063 from Sanreczki; CM/065 from Schlien.

The Urquhart Bequest, Balliol College, Oxford.

Wood's Papers, St. Antony's College, Oxford.

Published Official Documents

Aristarchi Bey, Grégoire, *Législation Ottomane*, 7 vols., Constantinople, 1873–8.

Bucknill, John A. Strachey, and Utidjian, Haig Apisoghom S., *The Imperial Ottoman Penal Code*, London and Nicosia, 1913.

Fisher, Stanley, *Ottoman Land Laws*, London, 1919.

Galante, Abraham, *Documents officiels turcs concernant les Juifs de Turquie*, Istanbul, 1931.
Great Britain, *Parliamentary Papers, Accounts and Papers*, lx (1843).
Hurewitz, J. C., *Diplomacy in the Near and Middle East*, 2 vols., Princeton, 1956.
Hyamson, A. M., *The British Consulate in Jerusalem (in relation to the Jews of Palestine, 1838–1915)*, 2 vols., London, 1939, 1942.
Rodkey, Frederick Stanley, 'Reshid Pasha's Memorandum of August 12, 1839', *Journal of Modern History*, II, 2 (1930), pp. 251–7.
'Rural Syria in 1845' (Consul Werry's Report), *Middle East Journal*, 16, pp. 508–14.
Young, George, *Corps de droit Ottoman*, 7 vols., Oxford, 1905–6.

Accounts of Contemporary Observers and Travellers

Abkāriūs, Iskandar ibn Yaʿqūb, *The Lebanon in Turmoil* (ed. J. P. Scheltema), New Haven, 1920.
Baedeker, Karl, *Palestine and Syria, Handbook for Travellers*, Leipzig, 1876.
Barker, Edward B. B., *Syria and Egypt under the Last Five Sultans of Turkey*, 2 vols., London, 1876.
Bazili, K. M., *Siria i Palestina pod turetzkim pravitel'stvom*, St. Peterburg, 1875.
Burckhardt, John Lewis, *Travels in Syria and the Holy Land*, London, 1822.
Burton, Isabel, *The Inner Life of Syria, Palestine and the Holy Land*, London, 1875.
Burton, Richard F., and Tyrwhitt Drake, C. F., *Unexplored Syria*, London, 1872.
Churchill, C. H., *Mount Lebanon, Ten Years of Residence*, London, 1853.
Cuinet, Vital, *Syrie et Palestine*, Paris, 1896.
Curtis, G. W., *The Wanderer in Syria*, London, 1852.
(Anon.), *Damas et le Liban*, London, 1861.
Doughty, C. M., *Travels in Arabia Deserta*, London, 1926.
Edwards, Richard, *La Syrie, 1840–1862*, Paris, 1862.
Engelhardt, Ed., *La Turquie et la Tanzimat*, 2 vols., Paris, 1882–4.
Farley, J. Lewis, *Two Years in Syria*, London, 1858.
——, *The Massacres in Syria*, London, 1861.
——, *Turkey*, London, 1866.
Finn, E., 'The Fellaheen of Palestine', *The Survey of Western Palestine*, London, 1881.
——, *A Third Year in Jerusalem*, London, 1869.
Finn, James, *Byeways in Palestine*, London, 1868.
——, *Stirring Times*, 2 vols., London, 1878.
Fleischer, Prof., 'Michael Meschaka's Kultur-Statistik von Damascus' *ZDMG*, viii (1854), 346–74.
Guérin, M. V., *Déscription Geographique, Historique et Archéologique de la Palestine*, 3 vols., Paris, 1869.

Guys, Henry, *Esquisse de l'état politique et commercial de la Syrie*, Paris, 1862.

Guys, M., *Voyage en Syrie*, Paris, 1855.

Hill, S. S., *Travels in Egypt and Syria*, London, 1866.

Hunter, W. P., *Narrative of the late expedition to Syria*, 2 vols., London, 1842.

Jenner, Thomas, *That Goodly Mountain and Lebanon*, London, 1873.

Jessup, H. H., *Fifty-three Years in Syria*, 2 vols., New York, 1910.

Jochmus, A., *The Syrian War and the Decline of the Ottoman Empire, 1840–1848*, 2 vols., Berlin, 1883.

Kayat, A. Y., *A Voice from Lebanon*, London, 1847.

Lenormant, F., *Les derniers événements de Syrie*, Paris, 1860.

Lyall, Alfred, *The Life of the Marquis of Dufferin and Ava*, London, 1905.

Lyde, Samuel, *The Asian Mystery, Ansaireeh or Nusairis of Syria*, London, 1860.

Macalister, R. A. S., and Masterman, E. W. G., 'A History of Doings of the Fellahin during the first half of the Nineteenth century from Native Sources', *Palestine Exploration Fund*, 1906, pp. 33–50.

MacFarlane, Charles, *Turkey and its destiny*, 2 vols., London, 1850.

Madden, R. R., *The Turkish Empire*, 2 vols., London, 1862.

(Anon.), *The Massacres in Syria*, New York, 1860.

Margoliouth, Moses, *A Pilgrimage to The Land of my Fathers*, 2 vols., London, 1850.

Melek, Hanum, *Thirty Years in the Harem*, London, 1873. (French ed, Mme. Kibrizli Mehmet Pacha, *Trente ans dans les Harems d'orient*, Paris, 1892.)

Merril, Selah, *East of Jordan*, London, 1881.

Midhat, Ali Haydar, *The Life of Midhat Pasha*, London, 1903.

Montefiore, Moses, *Diaries* (ed. L. Loewe), 2 vols., London, 1890.

——, *An Open Letter addressed to Sir M. Montefiore*, London, 1875.

Murray, John, *A Handbook for Travellers in Syria and Palestine*, London, 1858.

Napier, Charles, *The War in Syria*, 2 vols., London, 1842.

Neale, F. A., *Eight Years in Syria, Palestine and Asia Minor*, 2 vols., London, 1851.

Newton, Charles Thomas, *Travels and Discoveries in the Levant*, 2 vols., London, 1865.

Olin, Stephen, *Travels in Egypt, Arabia, Petra and the Holy Land*, New York, 1843.

Oliphant, Laurence, *The Land of Gilead*, New York, 1880.

Palestine Exploration Fund, 1867– .

Paton, A. B., *The Modern Syrians*, London, 1844.

(Anon.), *Personal Recollections of Turkish Misrule and Corruption in Syria by a Syrian*, London, 1877.

Porter, J. L., *Five Years in Damascus*, 2 vols., London, 1855.

——, *The Giant Cities of Bashan*, London, 1867.

Poujade, Eugène, *Le Liban et La Syrie, 1845–1860*, Paris, 1867.

(Anon.), *Rambles in the Desert of Syria*, London, 1864.
Robinson, E., *Later Biblical Researches in Palestine*, London, 1856.
Rogers, E. T., *Notices of the Modern Samaritans Illustrated by Incidents in the Life of Jacob esh-Shelebi*, London, 1855.
Rogers, M. E., *Domestic Life in Palestine*, London, 1863.
Segur, Dupeyron P. de, *La Syrie et les Bédouins sous l'administration Turque*, Paris, 1855.
Spyridon, S. N. (ed.), *Annals of Palestine 1821–1841. Manuscript Monk Neophytus of Cyprus*, Jerusalem, 1938.
Thomson, W. M., *The Land and the Book*, New York, 1863.
Tristram, H. B., *The Land of Israel*, London, 1876.
——, *The Land of Moab*, London, 1874.
Ubicini, M. A., *Letters on Turkey*, 2 vols., London, 1856.
Urquhart, David, *The Lebanon*, 2 vols., London, 1860.
Velde, C. W. M. Van de, *Memoir to Accompany the Map of the Holy Lands*, Gotha, 1858.
——, *Narrative of a Journey through Syria and Palestine in 1851 and 1852*, London, 1854.
Volney, C. F., *Travels in Syria and Egypt in the years 1783, 1784 and 1785*, 2 vols., London, 1787.
Walpole, F., *The Ansayrii and the Assassins*, 3 vols., London, 1851.
White, Charles, *Three Years in Constantinople*, 2 vols., London, 1845.
Williams, George, *The Holy City*, London, 1845.
Wilson, John, *The Lands of the Bible*, 2 vols., London, 1847.
Wortabet, G. M., *Syria and the Syrians*, London, 1856.

Studies and General Works

Antonius, George, *The Arab Awakening*, London, 1938.
Bailey, Frank Edgar, *British Policy and the Turkish Reform Movement*, Cambridge, Mass., 1942.
Baron, Salo, 'The Jews and the Syrian Massacres of 1860', *Proceedings of the American Academy for Jewish Research*, iv, 1932–3, pp. 3–31.
Blunt, W. S., *The Future of Islam*, London, 1882.
Bodman, Herbert L., *Political Factions in Aleppo, 1760–1826*, North Carolina, 1963.
Davison, Roderic H., *Reform in the Ottoman Empire, 1856–1876*, Princeton, 1963.
——, 'Turkish Attitudes concerning Christian-Muslim equality in the nineteenth century', *American Historical Review*, lix, No. 4, 1953–4, pp. 844–62.
——, 'Westernized Education in Ottoman Turkey', *Middle East Journal*, 15 (1961), pp. 289–301.
Devereux, Robert, *The First Ottoman Constitutional Period*, Baltimore, 1963.
Encyclopaedia of Islam, London and Leiden, 1913–38.
—— ——, New edition, Leiden and London, 1954– .
Gibb, H. A. R., and Bowen, Harold, *Islamic Society and the West*, I, 2 vols., London, 1950, 1957.

Granott, A., *The Land System in Palestine*, London, 1952.
Great Britain, *A Handbook of Syria, including Palestine* (by the Admiralty), London, 1913(?).
——, *Syria and Palestine, Handbook* (by the Foreign Office), London, 1919.
Grunebaum, Gustave E. von, *Medieval Islam*, Chicago, 1946.
Heyd, Uriel, *Ottoman Documents on Palestine, 1552–1615*, Oxford, 1960.
——, 'The Ottoman ʿUlemā and Westernization in the time of Selim III and Mahmud II', *Studies in Islamic History and Civilization*, ed. U. Heyd, Jerusalem, 1961.
Hill, George, *A History of Cyprus, VI: The Ottoman Province*, Cambridge, 1952.
Hirshberg, H. Z., 'Ottoman Rule in Jerusalem in the Light of Firmans and shariʿa Documents', *Israel Exploration Journal*, ii (1952), pp. 237–48.
Hitti, Philip, 'The Impact of the West on Syria and Lebanon in the nineteenth century', *Cahiers d'Histoire Mondiale* (1955), ii, No. 3, pp. 608–33.
——, *Syria, A Short History*, New York, 1962.
Hopwood, Derek, *Russian Activities in Syria in the nineteenth century*, unpublished D.Phil. thesis, Oxford, 1964.
Hourani, Albert, *Arabic Thought in the Liberal Age, 1798–1939*, London, 1962.
——, 'The Changing Face of the Fertile Crescent in the Eighteenth Century', *A Vision of History*, Beirut, 1961.
——, *Syria and Lebanon*, Oxford, 1946.
Hurewitz, J. C., 'Ottoman Diplomacy and the European State System', *Middle East Journal*, 15 (1961), pp. 141–52.
Hyamson, A. M., *Palestine*, London, 1917.
Lammens, S. J. H., *La Syrie*, Beirut, 1921.
Lane-Poole, Stanley, *Turkey*, London, 1922.
Lewis, Bernard, *The Emergence of Modern Turkey*, London, 1961.
——, *The Middle East and the West*, London, 1963.
——, 'The Ottoman Archives as a Source for the History of the Arab Lands', *Journal of Royal Asian Society*, 1950, pp. 139–55.
——, 'Studies in the Ottoman Archives', *BSOAS*, xvi (1954), pp. 469–501.
Lewis, Geoffrey, *Turkey*, New York, 1955.
Lewis, Norman, 'The Frontier of Settlement in Syria 1800–1950', *International Affairs*, 31 (1955), pp. 48–60.
Longrigg, S. H., *Four Centuries of Modern Iraq*, Oxford, 1925.
Maoz, Moshe, 'Syrian Urban Politics in the Tanzimal Period between 1840 and 1861', *BSOAS*, xxix, pt. ii (1966), pp. 277–301.
Mardin, Şerif, *The Genesis of Young Ottoman Thought*, Princeton, 1962.
Miller, W., *The Ottoman Empire and its Successors*, Cambridge, 1927.
Oppenheim, M. Freiherr von, *Die Beduinen*, Leipzig, 1943.
Peake, F. G., *A History of Jordan and its Tribes*, Miami, 1958.
Petrosyan, Y. A., 'Turkish Manuscripts and Documents in the Libraries

and Archives of Bulgaria' (in Russian), *Narody Azii i Afriki*, No. 3 (1961), pp. 244–7.
Poliak, A. N., *Feudalism in Egypt, Syria, Palestine and the Lebanon, 1250–1900*, London, 1939.
Polk, William R., *The Opening of South Lebanon, 1788–1840*, Cambridge, Mass., 1963.
Rodkey, F. S., 'Ottoman concern about Western Economic penetration in the Levant 1849–1856', *Journal of Modern History*, 30; 4 (1958), pp. 348–53.
Saab, Hassan, *The Arab Federalists of the Ottoman Empire*, Djambatan, 1958.
Shamir, Shimon, 'Asʿad Pasha al-ʿAẓm and Ottoman rule in Damascus, 1743–58', *BSOAS*, xxvi (1963), pp. 1–28.
——, *The ʿAẓm wālīs of Syria, 1724–1785*, unpublished Ph.D. thesis, Princeton, 1960.
Shaw, Stanford J., 'Archival Sources for Ottoman History: The Archives of Turkey', *Journal of the American Oriental Society*, 80, i (1960), pp. 1–12.
Stavrou, Theofanis George, 'Russian Interest in the Levant, 1843–1848', *Middle East Journal*, 17 (1963), pp. 91–103.
Temperley, Harold, *England and the Near East: The Crimea*, London, 1936.
Tibawi, A. L., *British Interests in Palestine, 1800–1901*, London, 1961.
Zeine, Zeine A., *Arab-Turkish Relations and the Emergence of Arab Nationalism*, Beirut, 1958.

INDEX